SOCIAL VALUATION IN AGRICULTURAL POLICY ANALYSIS

In dedication to
my father, Ongom-Awidi, mother, Karolina Girawal
Angwec-Okoi, foster fathers, Adwong Damiano Okec
and Rev. Brother Anton CFX and elder brothers and
sisters. For them the joy of my academic achievement,
no matter how modest, is eternity.

'An' Baby Last Matthew Okai, PhD, DSC
'Apwo wu atek ateka'

Social Valuation in Agricultural Policy Analysis

Its significance for Sub-Saharan Africa

MATTHEW OKAI

Ashgate

Aldershot • Brookfield USA • Singapore • Sydney

Published by
Ashgate Publishing Ltd
Gower House
Croft Road
Aldershot
Hants GU11 3HR
England

Ashgate Publishing Company
Old Post Road
Brookfield
Vermont 05036
USA

British Library Cataloguing in Publication Data
Okai, Matthew
   Social evaluation in agricultural policy analysis : its
   significance in Sub-Saharan Africa
   1. Agriculture and state - Africa, Sub-Saharan 2. Agriculture
   - Economic aspects - Africa, Sub-Saharan - Mathematical
   models
   I. Title
   338.1'8'67

Library of Congress Catalog Card Number: 99-072333

ISBN 1 84014 885 3

Printed in Great Britain

Contents

List of Figures

List of Maps and Tables

List of Algebraic Symbols

a	the employment rate	Cg	processing costs
a	the intercept	C_h	agricultural households'
a	the mean annual incremental growth		consumption of V
	per unit of stock	Cl	cultivable land
aij	input coefficient per unit of output	Clm	land of medium to low productivity
aij	the quantity of the jth inputs used to	Cl_n	resting land of medium to high
	produce the unit of output		productivity
aw	real expected urban wage income	Clu	land of medium to high productivity
A	actual acreage under cultivation	Cmb	marketing costs from domestic
Aa	the number of activities		market to border
Aa	the rate of change in arable and	Cn	non-cultivable land
	permanent crop area	Cpw	marketing costs from port to world
A^d	the desired crop area		reference market
Ag	the rate of land being brought under	Ct	cost of conservation in time t
	cultivation	$\hat{c}$	circumflex over a variable indicates
Ag^r	the difference of the average		rate of change
	agricultural annual growth rates		
	between two periods	d	the internal rate of return
A_l	agricultural labour force	Ds	savings of agricultural households in
A_{lu}	land use types (crops, forest,		valued resources on financial
	pasture, etc.)		institutions
		Ds	stock of domestic credit extended to
b	the value of elasticity		agriculture
b	some barrier to migration	Dsr	real interest earned on savings in
bo	the intercept		financial institutions or valued
b_1, b_2	vectors of the parameters to be		resources
	investigated		
β	elasticity of the tax rate on	e	the nominal exchange rate
	agriculture	es	empirical measure of the real
Bi	net economic benefit per unit of		exchange rate
	output	et	a random error term
		E	consumers' expectation
C	consumption rate	E	exogenous variables
C	current inputs	Em	proportional change in employment
C	out-of-pocket cost in each period	Eo	official exchange rate expressed as
C_{bp}	marketing costs from the border to		the number of units of domestic
	port		currency per unit of foreign currency
C_{fm}	marketing costs from farm to	Eo	employment level of wage level Wo
	domestic market	Ep	the own-price elasticity of demand
C_{fp}	marketing costs from farm to border	Exr	the cross-price elasticity of demand

E^o_x	the average annual rate of implicit expenditure deflator minus average annual rate of inflation	La	rate of change in labour employed in agricultural production
$E_x r$	the difference of the average annual growth rate of exports between periods	Lg	the rate of change in labour force in agriculture
Ey	the income elasticity of demand	Lna	labour supplied to non-agricultural sector by farmers
$\in$	labour demand in the informal sector	Lnf	non-farm non-labour income of farmers
		Lu	livestock unit
f	the net rate of felling		
Fr	forest land	m	the psychic net return from urban amenities, prospects for promotion, additional costs in the form of rents, transportation costs, etc.
FPT	the consumer price index of the country's principal trading partners		
g	flow of variables (rate)	m	given price of land
		m	the quantity of money
Hc	household socioeconomic characteristics	m	rate of growth of market consumption
Hh	agricultural households' consumption of the non-agricultural commodities	m	net rural to urban migration
		ma	transport and other marketing costs per cent of Vm
Hlu	the number of hectares required to produce Nl_u	MPPYi	marginal physical product of the jth input in its average alternative use (Y)
Hr	the number of hours worked		
i	the index of import competing commodities	n	number of years away into the future
		n	income elasticity
ia	interest rate charged on agricultural credit	N	non-tradeables
		N	number of consumers under consideration (population)
I	government policy effect on the level of incentive-effort	N	total agricultural households' time available
In	natural logarithm		
		Na	plant nutrient accumulation
j	the index of exportable commodities	Nd	plant nutrient depletion
		Nl	non-agricultural labour force
k	the degree of minimum wage coverage	Nlu	the quantity of (kg) of herbage per head of Lu
k	that fraction of real income which people wish to have	Nol	the size of the non-agricultural labour force
K	capital	Nr	natural resource base
Kic	physical assets of land and capital	Nr	soil natural regeneration rate
Kn	natural capital	η	absolute value of the wage elasticity of demand in the formal sector
Kp	produced capital		
		ηe	the elasticity of terms of trade
L	labour		
La	total labour used in producing output	P	price or the local producer price
		P	the general price level in the economy

P	population growth rate
P^1	price in one market
P_2	price in the other market
ΔP	producer price wage
Pb	the border price of the jth input
P^b_j	accounting value at border prices of one unit of output
Pbt	the border price of tradeables
P^b_y	accounting value at border prices of the yth output
Pc	the price of a crop or price of substitute crop
Pca	the controlled price of agriculture
Pc^r	the average annual change in the real protection coefficient
Pd	the domestic price of the commodity
Pd	produced nominal price
Pdnt	domestic price of non-tradeable
Pdnt	domestic goods
Pdr	the average annual change in the real producer price of exports
Pdt*	the domestic price of tradeables including taxes or subsidies
Pe	policy environment
P^e_t	the expected price for period t
Pf	the farm gate price of a commodity
Pfa	the market price for agriculture
Pfj	domestic price of the jth input
Pfn	domestic market price for non-agriculture
Pm	price of importable commodities
Pm	domestic prices of import competing goods
Pn	the price of non-tradeables
Pn	prices of domestic goods
Pna	non-agricultural price index
P^o_t	the average annual inflation rate
Pr	real producer price
Pr	prices of related goods
Ps	prices of substitute commodities
Pt	price levels in the home country during period t
Pt	the world price of tradeables in terms of foreign currency
Pt	population growth rate
P*t	price levels in the foreign country
Pw	world price of the commodity

Pwt	the international reference price of the commodity
Px	the price of X
Pz	the price of other variable input
P*	world price in foreign currency
P*	the price of exportables
P*m	domestic prices of importables
P^*_x	domestic prices of exportables
π	the fraction of cultivable land under cultivation
πi	a fraction of land that can be cultivated taking into account the resting phase
Q	the quality and quantity of natural resources
Q	quantity produced
Q1, Q2	goods and services at the beginning of the next and subsequent years
Qa	the quantity of agricultural output
Q^d	desired output
Qm	the international price of importables
r	rate of discount (interest)
r	given price of capital
r	the coefficient of adjustment
r	the real rural wage (subsistence)
rRt	real exchange rate during period t
-rt	discount rate of future income in time t
-rn	discount rate of future income in future years
R	rainfall
R	the annual compound growth rate
R	the annual revenue which is the same in each year during the investment life
R	the range of goods and services available to consumers
Rc	rangeland carrying capacity
Re	the equilibrium or shadow exchange rate
R_1	resting land
Rlc	rental on physical assets
Rlm	resting land of medium to low productivity

Rln	resting land of medium to low productivity	Vt	the error term
Rn	the official (nominal) exchange rate	Vt	the growth rate of the volume of agricultural production in time t
S	rate of export subsidy	W	the real urban wage
S	stock of trees at time ti	W	given price of labour
S	land	Wa	nominal wage rate in agriculture
S	the quality of arable land or soil	Wf	working force participants (participation rate)
Sa	share of agriculture in total tax income	Wm	minimum wage
Se	soil erosion	$\dot{W}m$	minimum wage hike
Sf	soil formation	Wo	market clearing wage
Sn	share of non-agriculture in total tax income	Wp	working persons
		WAt	agricultural wage
		WNt	non-agricultural wage
t	time		
t^l	rate of tariff expressed as a percentage of import value	X	the rate land is being brought under cultivation
tPw	tariff payable on each unit commodity traded	X	the independent variable
		X_l	recreation taken by agricultural households
T	consumers' tastes and preferences		
T	technology	Xt	the quantity of commodity X demanded
Tfi	total fallow land		
Tl	total labour force	$\dot{X}^o_t$	the average annual rate of local currency depreciation minus average annual inflation rate
Tli	total cultivable land area of a country		
Tm	taxes on importables		
Tol	total labour force in the base year	y	growth rate of income per head
Tp	total persons or total population	y	rate at which land is being taken out of production
Tx	the rate of duties on exports (fob)	Y	the dependent variable
Tz	the average rate of taxation (tariffs) on imports (cif)	Y	the money income
		Y	total consumers' income and its distribution
u	price of non-soil inputs		
u	urban unemployment	Yn	the elasticity of real non-agricultural income
u	output level of π		
Ug	growth rate of agricultural output	Yt	the terminal value
		Yt	the elasticity of the tax rate of non-agricultural income
V	vacancy		
V	the coefficient of adjustment	Y_0	the initial observed value
V	value-added by the production process without protection		
Vc	variable costs of conservation	Z	weather conditions and other variables whose effects are not captured through the producer price variables or non-labour inputs
V_l	value-added by the production process with protection in place		
Vs	elasticity of supply		

Preface

Interest in policy analysis is to gain a better understanding of the technical, economic and social efficiency of an economy in order to improve its management.

This book, based on empirical work, experiential outlook and extensive literature review, is intended to encourage appreciation of the cardinal significance for integrating macroeconomic policy variables and environmental factors and any other relevant externalities into sectoral policy analysis as a tool for improving: i) careful choice of strategic factors in agricultural development; ii) investment allocative efficiency in agriculture and environmental protection; and iii) overall agricultural development management.

Textbooks of agricultural economics had largely been on neoclassical economy and excludes the economics of moral economy. This textbook, uniquely tailored for use by sectoral economists and policy analysts in Sub-Saharan Africa provides paradigmatic technical and socioeconomic elements and their significance for evaluating the implications of public agricultural policies on resource quality and quantity, and overall development. The book emphasises micro- and macro-coherency in the context of the internalization of internal technical (agricultural and environmental), macroeconomy, and external (international) externalities into development framework. Methodologies for the integration of these externalities are presented and adequately elaborated upon with graphical illustrations. The main concern is for: i) choosing realistic policy instruments to promote development; ii) quantifying constraints; and iii) evaluating the impacts of policy on objectives.

Acknowledgments

This work would not have been accomplished without the support of a number of institutions and individuals. In recognition of the invaluable assistance provided, I would like to acknowledge with grateful appreciation the training support received from the government of the Republic of Uganda, the Canadian International Development Agency, the United States Agency for International Development and the United Nations Food and Agriculture Organisation. I would also like to express my grateful indebtedness to many individuals, too many to mention all, but I feel most obliged to mention my mentor Professor D.G.R. Belshaw who throughout my academic and professional career, provided encouragement and professional support. I would also like to express my grateful appreciation to Professor Fergus Wilson for encouraging and supporting me in studying the development ox-cultivation in Uganda and to Professor Willem H. Boshoff for encouragement and support in carrying out work measurement and energy expenditure study. I also owe a debt of gratitude to Messrs Henry Musoke, Emmanuel Adjei and Ms Elsie, Rosemary Baeta, Gladys Augustus and Lydia Khalema for taking time to assist with typing technical papers and dissertations, and Mr Andrew Wakiro for preparing figures and illustrations. I also owe a great debt of gratitude to anonymous evaluators who made seminal and constructive suggestions regarding improvement of the manuscript. Although I received valuable comments from many FAO colleagues and many other scholars, I alone am responsible for any deficiency in the book, the content of which does not necessarily represent the views of the government of Uganda nor that of FAO.

List of Abbreviations

AEL	Agricultural Enterprises Ltd	HIV/	human immunodeficiency virus/
AIC	average incremental costs	AIDS	acquired immune deficiency
AP	average product		syndrome
ASIP	Agricultural Sector Investment		
	Programme	IBRD	International Bank for
			Reconstruction and Development
BNI	basic need index	ICOR	incremental capital output ratio
		IFAD	International Fund for Agricultural
cif	costs, insurance and freight		Development
CPI	consumer price index (NCPI =	IPI	integrated poverty index
	national CPI)	ITFP	intertemporal/interspatial total
CPR	common pool resources		factor productivity
CSE	consumer subsidy equivalent	ITK	indigenous technical knowledge
DA	domestic absorption	LDR	law of diminishing returns
DPB	domestic price bias	LEMRR	law of equimarginal rate of return
DRC	domestic resource coefficient	LIC	law of increasing costs
		LOOP	law of one price
ECA	Economic Commission for Africa		
EMB	Export Marketing Boards	MAI	mean annual incremental growth
EPC	effective protection coefficient	MAILO	on square mile basis
ESC	effective subsidy coefficient	MC	marginal costs
		MEC	marginal external costs
FAO	United Nations Food and	MOC	marginal opportunity costs
	Agriculture Organization	MP	marginal product
FE	food exports	MPC	marginal private costs
FI	food imports	MPED	Ministry of Planning and
FMA	Farmers' Marketing		Economic Development
	Administration	MRR	marginal rate of return
FMB	Food Marketing Boards	MRS	marginal rate of substitution
fob	free on board	MSY	maximum sustainable yield
FSI	food security index	MUV	manufacturer's unit value
FV	future values		
FY	foreign income	NEB	net economic benefit
		NEP	negative effective protection
GDP	gross domestic product	NEPC	net effective protection coefficient
GNP	gross national product	NER	nominal exchange rate
GPMB	Gambia Produce Marketing Board	NGO	non-governmental organization
GVAO	gross value of agricultural output	NMC	National Milling Corporation
		NNPC	net nominal protection coefficient

NPC	nominal protection coefficient\	UNCTAD	United Nations Conference on Trade and Development
NPK	nitrogen, phosphate, potassium		
		UNDP	United Nations Development Programme
OER	official exchange rate		
OFY	Operation Feed Yourself	UNESCO	United Nations Educational Scientific and Cultural Organization
PAR	private agricultural resources		
PPP	purchasing power parity	USA	United States of America
PPS	producer price shares	USAID	United States Agency for International Development
PSC	population supporting capacity		
PSE	producer subsidy equivalent	USSR	Union of Socialist Soviet Republics
PV	present values		
PVa	present values of future stream of income from the agricultural sector	UTGC	Uganda Tea Growers' Corporation
Rem	real exchange rate of importables	VAa	value-added in agriculture
RER	real exchange rate		
Rex	real exchange rate of exportables	WATR	weighted average tariff and subsidy rate
SAP	Structural Adjustment Programme	WCED	World Conference on Environmental Development
SCBA	social cost-benefit analysis		
SDR	special drawing right	WFC	World Food Conference
SER	shadow exchange rate	WHO	World Health Organization
SOC	social opportunity cost	WPI	wholesale price index
SOCL	social opportunity cost of labour		
SSA	Sub-Saharan Africa	Y	domestic income
TB	trade bias	ZEP	zero effective protection
TFC	total food consumption		
TFP	total factor productivity		
TRDB	Tanzania Rural Development Bank		

1 Framework for Social Valuation in Agricultural Policy Analysis

Scope of the Book

The intention of this work is to provide coherent and mutually supporting paradigmatic technical and socioeconomic elements which are fundamental in evaluating the impacts and consequences of agricultural policy intervention. Since adaptive response to changing ecological conditions in Sub-Saharan African (SSA) is greatly influenced by social,[1] cultural,[2] technical and economic conditions, the integrative approach to agricultural policy analysis is ideal for the Africa region. In the agrarian context, this approach facilitates diagnostic analysis of the socioeconomic, technical and agro-ecological[3] forces influencing farmers' land-use decisions and adaptive strategies. Traditionally, agricultural policy analysis relies heavily on macroeconomic parameters and does not often incorporate externalities such as internal technical and environmental factors. The key feature of this book is the integration of macroeconomy and internal technical (agricultural and environmental) externalities into agricultural policy analysis. This integrative[4] approach has become necessary because, in Sub-Saharan Africa, intervention to accelerate agricultural development has been typified by paradoxes: initiatives have often been followed by the intensification of environmental decline and rural poverty. This has arisen because policy decision-making processes were divorced from the consideration of externalities and did not anticipate unintended consequences and impacts of policy intervention on natural resources.

The indigenous technical and nontechnical knowledge[5] (cultural endowments)[6] had endogenously evolved around the use of land and land-based resources (the basic life-support resources). Each farming system (agriculture-based, animal-based, pastoralism, agro-pastoralism) had been evolved in such a way that it suited the different ecological niches. These systems were not only in harmony with the people but also in equilibrium with the environment. As the systems evolved, the old cultural practices were not abandoned but incorporated into the new ones. Following the integration of SSA into the global economy, the evolutionary development of indigenous technical knowledge (ITK) was disrupted by the superimposition of the exogenously and revolutionarily-developed science-based technologies which proved generally unsuccessful, and the resource-conserving quality of ITK had not been adequately incorporated into the externally introduced technological innovation.

The unique feature of this book is that it addresses not only the issues of the theoretical and methodological framework for agricultural policy analysis but also the pertinent imperative of the internalization of environmental externalities into the analysis. The book, therefore, goes a long way towards meeting the desire for upgrading and strengthening the analytical capacity of public sector management and filling the gap by internalizing the internal (natural resource perturbation), macroeconomy (external), and international externalities into policy analysis paradigms.

The book, with its primary geographical focus on SSA, can be used as a textbook by students of agricultural colleges, faculties of agriculture and postgraduate students of agricultural economics and policy analysis. It is also a useful companion for policy analysts, policy decision-makers and environmentalists. Most textbooks on economics or agricultural economics use examples derived from developed countries. Also, agricultural policy analysis had been divorced from macroeconomic policies. This book fills these gaps by using African examples, and demonstrates methodologies for the integration of macroeconomic policy variables into economic analyses of agricultural policies, including the internalization of environmental externalities into national policy design.

It highlights some paradigmatic elements, used here to encompass a coherent and mutually reinforcing pattern of investigation into concepts, perceptions, values, norms and interactive dynamics the synergy of which could be helpful in providing clinical evidence of farmers' adaptive response and change to changing ecological, political and socioeconomic settings and circumstances. This understanding is useful in making strategic choices of factors critical in development. It is suggested, therefore, that these elements should constitute integral components of future farm management surveys and policy analysis.

An Introduction to Paradigmatic Elements for Policy Analysis

Framework of Analysis

Essentially, agricultural policy consists of decisions that influence the levels and stability of economic determinants which govern changes in relative prices of inputs and outputs, the choice of public investment and the allocation of public funds on intellectual investment (research to improve production and processing technologies). Policies pursued create an economic environment within which enterprises and individual households operate in an economy. The variables whose levels are to be influenced are referred to as endogenous (target) variables while policy instruments used to influence endogenous factors are referred to as exogenous variables. The framework for agricultural policy analysis is premised on: i) making choice of policy instruments to promote national and sectoral objectives through government intervention in the agricultural sector; ii) quantifying constraints; and iii) estimating impacts of policies on objectives (see Figure 1). The three most common objectives are *efficiency*, concerned with the allocation of resources to effect maximum national output and income, *equity*, concerned with how the national wealth is owned, produced and distributed (the income distribution consideration), and *food and environmental security*. Typically the promotion of one objective conflicts with one or both of the others. The essence of policy analysis is to facilitate taking decisions between competing objectives. Policy decision-makers explicitly or implicitly make judgments on the value of promoting different objectives. Decision-makers then have to trade-off the value of the perceived non-efficiency benefit against the measured efficiency. Traditionally the costs and benefits are valued in social prices (*efficiency* or *shadow prices* or *accounting prices*) which lead to the most efficient allocation of scarce resources (chapter 2).

For Sub-Saharan Africa, the fourth major objective is concerned with social articulation of risks and uncertainties. The preoccupation with risk aversion can blunt technical progress. The region is in all stages of development but most people still depend on the moral economy within which individuals, within a specific cultural context (cultural homogeneity) voluntarily participate in a reciprocal sharing of the means of livelihood (income diversification and consumption stabilization) and reciprocal access to productive assets and valued resources (income stabilization). The colonial destruction of social reciprocal relations (social capital of reciprocity) subjected the moral economy to a gradual transition to modern economy. During the transition, the moral

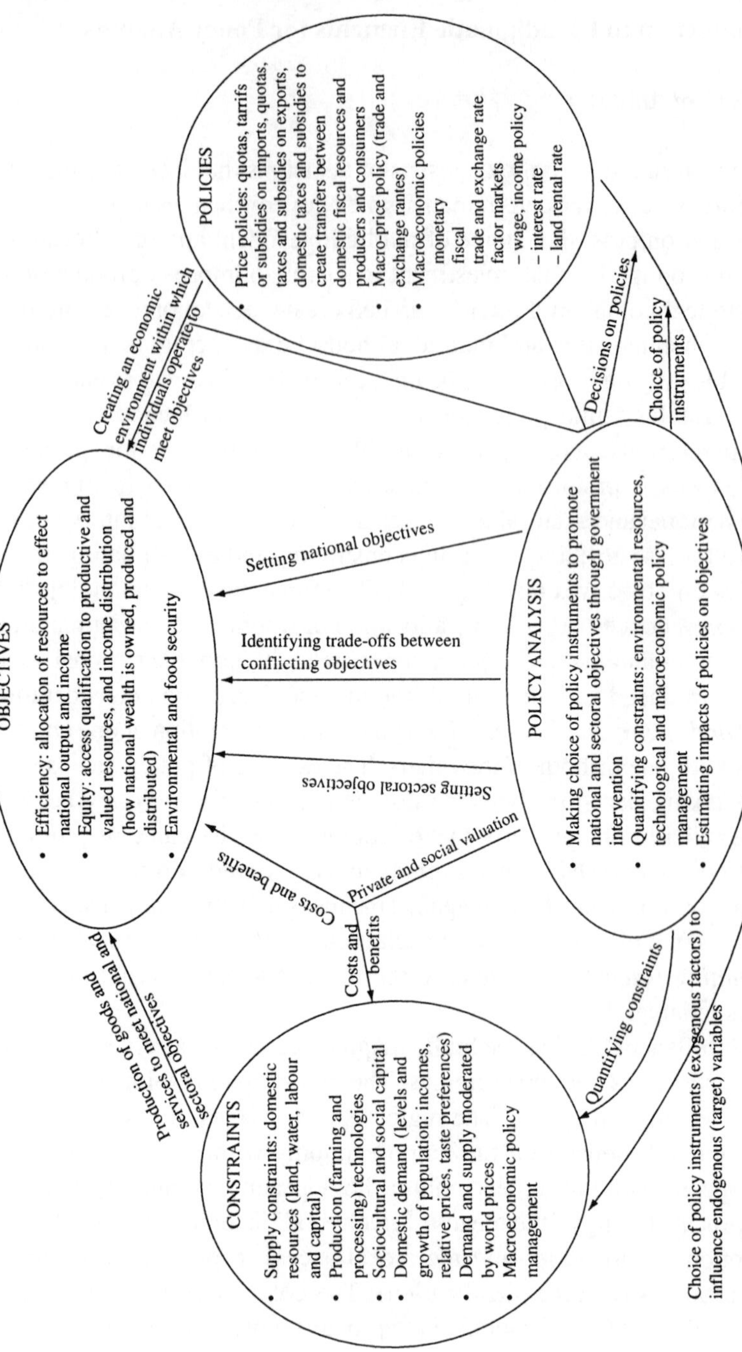

Figure 1   Framework of agricultural policy analysis

economy had been facing social dualism because of the dichotomous situation between the two economies, ultimately leading to social exclusion due to the differential wealth accumulation, the individualization of risks and the peripheralization of the disadvantaged in society. Survival is achieved through an array of diversifications. Households draw on diversified strategies and employ a variety of non-market devices and income diversifications. The main ones are activity, temporal, technical and environment diversifications. Since risk varies with environment, technology, physical endowments and social institutions to which households have recourse, strategies chosen depend on the nature of the production shocks. Households' adaptive response and change are influenced by their perceptions in terms of the capacity of an innovation in strengthening their risk-coping and risk management capacity. Social anthropology was not included in development paradigms until recently. Policy analysis in this type of social environment should include social anthropological investigation into the circumstances holding back progress.

Often the difficulty in making choices arises because of the existence of constraints in the economic system. There are principally three categories of constraints that limit the agricultural sector from realizing its full potential: *supply* constraints, due to availability and quality of domestic resources (land, water, labour and capital); *technological advances*; and the relative *costs* of all inputs (chapters 3 and 4). In the case of Sub-Saharan Africa, Farrington and Boyd (1997, pp. 371–2) observed that while in other developing regions positive change in environmental recovery is strongly driven by policy, in SSA the change depends heavily on endogenous social, cultural, internal technical and economic conditions which are not easily influenced by external interventions. Thus any development intervention should be based on a better understanding of factors (ecological, social-economic, institutional) that influence farmers' land-use decisions and the links between land use and the farmers' welfare. The value of the commodities produced is greatly determined by domestic demand constraints arising from population growth, changes in taste preferences and the relative price of agricultural commodities (chapters 2, 5 and 6).

Both the domestic supply and demand constraints are moderated by the world prices of agricultural inputs and outputs that enter the international trade. As these prices, the third constraint, determine the domestic prices of tradeable commodities, price policies either decrease, increase or stabilize prices (chapters 5 and 6). Responsiveness of producers and consumers (chapters 7 and 8) to price policy depends on the underlying supply and demand constraints which in turn condition producer and consumer behaviour. It is this behaviour that determines the supply and demand schedules.

Policy comprises the instruments of action that governments employ to effect changes. The principal development concern of any country is to promote economic growth and development, through the execution of policies, that enables the national economy to produce and deliver an economic well-being that is within its potential and capability. Thus the key features of policy intervention are to: i) encourage economic growth and stability through national monetary, fiscal, trade and foreign exchange policies; ii) encourage resource use in satisfying sector and national output growth targets through policies such as market price, price support, ceilings, subsidies, taxes and government measures affecting demand and producer supply response; and iii) achieve a socially and politically acceptable sharing of the benefits and costs of development between competing groups (i.e. basic terms of trade, consumer and producer benefits, producer income, consumption, nutrition, poverty, etc.).

For the agricultural sector, the public sector policies have considerable influence on resource allocation. These influences can be classified into three broad categories: i) public expenditure to provide infrastructure (such as roads, communication, land improvement, irrigation schemes) or services to support or regulate private consumption or production activities (research and extension services, market information, supporting services such as mechanization, research, credit facilities, agricultural education, etc.); ii) direct public sector participation in agricultural production, marketing outputs or supplying inputs with the state acting as entrepreneur; and iii) government regulation of trade, exchange rate, credit facilities, and prices of inputs and outputs. The major objective for undertaking policy impact analysis, given sectoral concern, is to focus on food and the agricultural sector in general, identifying some key issues relating to agricultural supply response, effects on food and demand, availability and nutritional effects on food demand, availability and nutritional effects of policy variables, the incidence of rural poverty and income distribution, and, given current environmental concern, the dynamic consequences of macroeconomy-environment interactions on resource quantity and quality. The essence is to recognize the importance of macro-coherency by internalizing environmental externalities into the development framework.

Of the three principal categories of policies, the first is price policy. There are two main types of price policy instruments used to alter prices of agricultural inputs and outputs. For instance, quotas, tariffs and subsidies on imports and quotas, taxes and subsidies on exports (*distorting policies*) directly decrease or increase the volume of tradeable commodities and thus alter domestic prices, some of which cause divergences between domestic and world prices (chapters 5 and 6). An overvalued exchange rate, for instance, creates an implicit tax on producers of exportable commodities because only a small amount of domestic currency is earned or paid for by imports. While those who have access to imports benefit from cheap imported commodities, exporters are effectively taxed because domestic price is lower than its efficiency level.

Domestic taxes and subsidies create transfers between domestic fiscal resources and domestic producers and consumers. Thus the second category of policy is the macroeconomic management policy. In addition, as a third category, government influences the agricultural sector through public sector investment in developing new technologies, economic and social infrastructure, services and specific agricultural projects to increase outputs. Inefficient macroeconomic policy management results in government failure.

Market failures occur whenever monopolies or monopsonies, externalities (third party impacts or external economies) or factor market imperfections arising from inadequate development of institutions fail both to provide efficient and competitive services and to prevent the market from creating an inefficient allocation of factors or products. Unless price policy is capable of offsetting some failures of a market (*efficient policies*) to operate efficiently, the policy decision drives the domestic prices away from their most efficient levels based on world prices. An efficient policy is then applied to offset the market failure. *Social (efficiency) valuation* (chapter 2) of outputs and tradeable outputs are based on world prices adjusted for locational circumstances (chapter 5). Since internal factors of production are not traded, social valuation uses *social opportunity cost* (SOC) of each factor, the amount of national income forgone for not using the factor in its next best alternative use. In the valuation it is also necessary to distinguish between *private* and *social* valuations defined as the effects of divergences. Private valuations measure the actual market cost incurred and benefits gained by individuals. They reflect the actual prices received or paid by the individuals or individual enterprises, and incorporate the underlying costs and the effects of policies and market failures that create transfers in the system.

The key feature of analysis should be the integration of macroeconomic policy variables into the framework for economic analysis of agricultural policies, including the internalization of environmental externalities into national policy design and evaluation of impacts. This is necessary because in any economy there are three distinct but interlinked levels of the economy. At the macro-level, national policies (monetary, fiscal, trade and exchange rate, price, interest rate and income) are conceived and executed. The effects of the execution of these policies are first felt at the intermediate (meso-) level, which constitutes the channel of effects of policy execution through socioeconomic and institutional infrastructure. These effects cause changes in economic determinants (relative prices), factor and product markets. At this level the principal analytical work is to study the effects of policy changes on commercial coefficients. Mathematical methodologies had been developed by econometricians to analyse both the positive and negative effects of protective regimes on the economies on which they are imposed (chapter 6).

It is at the micro-level that the impacts of macroeconomic policy execution are felt by smallholders and the individual enterprises which constitute the productive sectors of the economy. Their response (the endogenous variables) to changes in macro-policy variables (exogenous variables) determines resource use to satisfy sector and national output growth rates. Hence the array of quantitative policy analyses represents attempts to grapple with the problem of how to alleviate and quantify the net effects of protection. Thus the purpose of analysing the effects of the imposition of commercial constants is to provide a framework which makes it easier for political decision-makers to assess the desirability of any protection regime.

Objectives and Concept of Development

An economy has at its disposal potential mobilizable natural resources that can be transformed into tangible useable goods. These resources are called natural endowments at a particular moment in time. An economy may have considerable potential natural endowments for development but they cannot be said to be developing unless they are being converted into produced capital. The process of development is, therefore, concerned with the expansion of the stock of produced capital, the base of the economy, and the level of economic development is measured by the value of that stock. The conversion of the endowments from its natural stock to a flow of social utility (goods and services) involves some form of quantitative and qualitative processes. As regards agricultural production, raising the productivity of traditional farming systems from low to higher equilibrium levels requires quantitative and qualitative changes in the economy. The main quantitative changes are the increases in the amount of capital, natural resources and labour being used for the production of outputs. Qualitative changes are those which increase the efficiency of a given amount of capital and labour in producing outputs. The two types of changes are closely interrelated; for instance, increases in capital require corresponding increases in qualitative improvements towards technological and institutional development. The concept of quantitative changes, therefore, denotes economic growth, while that of qualitative changes implies improvement in the process of the diffusion of innovation. Economic development, it is expected, acquires a synergistic value because it accelerates favourable changes in attitudes and behaviours leading to more economic and social development. Intellectual investment in research, for instance, plant breeding and accretionary growth of biological investment in upgrading animal breeds produces biological yield-increasing crop varieties and animals. These technological innovations have to be accepted and adopted by the farmers to be productive.

Produced Capital

Development is generally a function of produced capital. The produced capital cannot be regarded as developing sustainably unless the conversion of natural capital into produced capital yields an aggregate of both natural and produced capital that is non-declining. Both capital stocks have values. One such value is capital that allows for both additions to future income and the maintenance of current income. In conventional economics this is called gross investment. If current additions to society's well-being are regarded as consumption, then gross income is defined as consumption plus gross investment. Net investment is defined as gross investment less that portion of capital investment necessary to maintain current levels of consumption, while net income is simply consumption plus net investment.

In resource accounting, although depreciation is defined conventionally as the difference between gross and net investment, it is necessary to make a distinction between value and physical depreciations. The physical ability of capital to generate consumable goods and services is accompanied by the decline in the quality and quantity of stock of capital. This physical depreciations also leads to the decline in the value of the capital stock, value depreciation. The relationship between income and the change in value depreciation can computationally be demonstrated as explained below. For conventional economic accounting, both natural (Kn) and produced (Kp) capital do have values because they can generate goods and services (see Figure 2) as well as disbenefits, represented by wastes such as terrestrial, aquatic and atmospheric pollution. Kn represents the value of natural capital stock at the beginning of its use, while Q_1, Q_2, Q_n represents the goods and services at the beginning of the next and the subsequent years. This is income

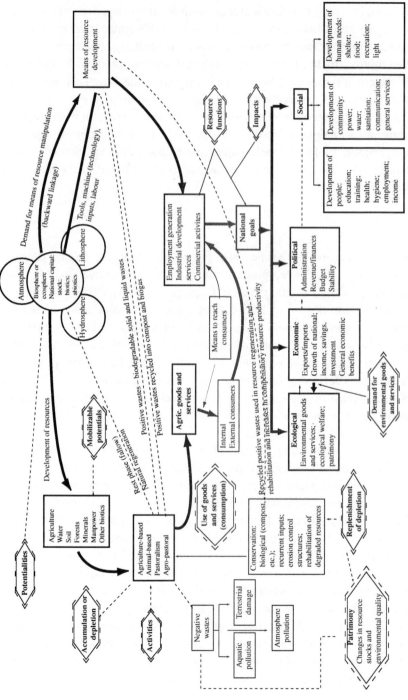

Figure 2   Linkages between human economic activities (change agents) and resource stock flow and balance

that has originated from these capitals which include the sum of current and potential future additions to society well-being.

The process of development entails expanding the stock of produced capital. The level of development is, therefore, measured by the value of produced capital stock. Since building the stock of produced capital is based on the conversion of natural capital, it implies that Kn will decline over time, and this decline cannot continue indefinitely since Kn is finite. To guarantee resource sustainability, extraction from natural resources to build produced capital should not exceed resource regeneration rate. In other words, Kn = Kp = 0.

Computationally this can be expressed as

$$Kn = Kp + Q_1 \qquad (1)$$

The equation can be rewritten as

$$Q_1 = Kn + (Kn - Kp) \qquad (2)$$

As represented in the equation, if Kp exceeds Kn, it results in the gradual depletion of Kn.

The Fundamentals of Sustainable Agricultural Development

Following the emergence of environmental stress as a major threat to mankind, the concept of sustainability with respect to resources and environmental integrity, has been used extensively by a broad spectrum of individual scholars and organizations. The word *sustain* is derived from a Latin word, *sustenere*, which means holding up or keeping elevated. An early definition of sustainability was confined within the context of biologically renewable resources such as forests and fisheries to define physical limit of sustainably exploiting resources. If a steady-state of physical equilibrium is sustained, the harvest and regeneration can be maintained indefinitely. In the case of fisheries, aquatic (or hydrospheric) resources, the annual harvest should just equal to the annual increase of fish biomass. This is defined as a biologically determined rate called *maximum sustainable yield* (MSY). This concept can also be applied to other renewable resources such as forests (an ecospheric or biospheric resource), which is referred to as *maximum sustainable cut*, and groundwater (aquifer) harvesting, which is the *maximum sustainable pumping rate*. In all cases, sustainability is primarily a physical concept by which the rate of harvest or flow of products are regulated to ensure harvest does not exceed regeneration.

Recently the concept has been enlarged to encompass: i) a purely physical concept for a single resource; ii) a physical concept for a broader system of resources (ecosystem); and iii) social-physical-economic concept which embraces economic forces and externalities such as sociosystem, which is concerned with social response to changes in the resource base, ecosystem interactions, sociosystem-ecosystem dynamic interactions, technology and weather-induced changes in productivity. Consequently, because of the various interactions, it has become necessary to broaden the concept of sustainability to include externalities (third party impact). As an illustration, what could be sustainable management of an individual resource could actually be unsustainable in the context of the entire system. Forest trees may, for instance, be harvested in a sustainable manner, but this action could create problems such as increased soil erosion and off-site dispositional sedimentation, reduced water quality and other changes in local hydrology, and the destruction of wildlife habitat resulting in loss of biodiversity. These are external costs associated with forest harvesting. Thus the consequences of the interactions among ecosystems components have both costs and trade-offs. When physical stocks of resources are used in economic activity, the resources can either be sustained at their present level, increased (enhanced) or reduced (degraded). These resources can also be transformed into another use like clearing forest (destroying) to give way to agricultural production. This involves transference costs. Thus resource exploitation acquires different forms: exploitation remaining in harmony, or resource enhanced, degraded or destroyed.

It is necessary, therefore, to investigate the conflicting objectives of the economics and ecology of sustainable agricultural development. In its ordinary sense, the primary objective of sustainable development is based on the premise that the maximum amount spent on consumption in one period should not result in a reduction of real consumption expenditure in future due to the exhaustion of natural and produced capital, or the decimation of biological capital. In other words, development based on the depletion of environmental resources can only remain sustainable so long as there exists substitutes for such natural capital, and investments in these substitutes at least compensate for the loss of the natural capital. From the ecological point of view, the main concern is to determine the minimum combination of resources that will enable the ecosystem to function in such a way that it can sustain ecological resilience. From the economic viewpoint, resource exploitation characterized by a high level of ecological resilience has not been able to satisfy the minimum condition of inter-temporal economic efficiency. Conversely, satisfying the commercial objective of agricultural production could lead to an extractive form of agriculture which cannot be compensated fully by natural regeneration rate. There is, therefore, a need to strike a balance.

Framework for Analysis of Efficiency

Social Valuation of Agricultural Sector Investment Programme

Following the popularization of development planning, especially after World War II, and the insistence of donors on well-documented projects for their financing, development programmes typically consisted of a series of bankable/ investment projects. After the attainment of political independence, the preoccupation of the international community was to accelerate economic and social development. For developing countries it was felt that the level of domestic savings necessary for investment to expand the productive base of the economy was too low. Reliance on foreign savings through borrowing was valorized and actively promoted. The mobilization of external financial resources depended on the economic viability of projects measured in terms of the economic rate of return on investment. During the 1970s, especially from 1974 to 1982, following the World Bank shift of policy in favour of rural development, there were massive public sector booms in many of the developing countries (IBRD, 1989). However, by the early 1980s, despite years of lending, economic performance, especially in the productive sectors, deteriorated significantly, a situation exacerbated by the resurgence of the balance of payment stresses, in particular following the oil crisis (IBRD, 1981, 1984).

Many reasons were advanced for this poor economic performance. A number of scholars have highlighted the incompatibility between policy instruments and the development plans. It had been observed that economic policies pursued by governments had been more important to economic performance than the magnitude of investment expenditure. A distorted policy environment thwarts incentives, and ideally economic development policy should have stimulating elements since highest investment does not necessarily translate itself into economic growth. The other limiting factor is the limited administrative capacity of government institutions to implement economic development plans effectively (IBRD, 1981). This situation is exacerbated by lack of coordination due to distorted and weak organizational structure. It was the view of most financial institutions that the concept that development could be managed provided governments with the excuse (or unfounded justification) to intervene in the management of the economy. Any intervention is usually distortionary (Killick, 1981; MacNamara, 1985).

Social cost-benefit analysis In the late 1960s there was considerable development of methods for evaluating the economic and social relevance of development projects with emphasis on applying social cost-benefit (applied welfare economics) analysis (SCBA) to investment in developing countries (Gittinger, 1982; Little and Mirrlees, 1974, 1982; Scandizzo and Bruce, 1980; Squire and Van der Tak, 1975). It was argued that the uni-dimensional measurement of the economic benefits of projects in terms of economic rate of return omitted vital consideration of social welfare, an approach that weighs a public project's costs and benefits in terms of its contribution to national (social) welfare. Based on this concept, scholars recommended a shift in emphasis on project evaluation away from a concern with precise economic rate of return towards a broader sectoral analyses and public expenditure reviews with a focus on ascertaining whether the project's social benefits exceed social costs. This determines whether it is worthwhile implementing the project. Typically, the objective of any government is to achieve and maintain economic efficiency, and this objective is attained when the economy is functioning in such a way that maximizes the value of society's consumption over time. In the neoclassical economic model, the value is measured by the society's willingness to pay for the goods and services that are consumed as outputs, or used as inputs, or both.

Traditionally, project inputs and outputs had been valued at current market prices (which include taxes, subsidies and the effects of government regulations) but these prices may not reflect the social opportunity cost of the resource, the cost in forgone benefits to society.

The use of 'shadow prices' (also called accounting prices) is intended to move the economy closer to meeting the conditions necessary to achieve improved economic efficiency, which traditionally has three elements: static, dynamic and distributional efficiency. In project social analysis all three elements are taken into account, while project economic analysis tends to focus only on static and dynamic efficiency. Static efficiency usually relates to a condition of full employment when the economy is not only using all its resources but also using them correctly by producing the 'right' combination of inputs and outputs. In this respect 'right' refers to 'relative values' measured by the society's willingness to pay for each unit of the goods and services produced. Dynamic efficiency, on the other hand, relates to the dynamic response of the economy where it (especially consumption) is growing at the 'right' rate; 'right' here refers to the society's willingness to save and invest rather than to consume. Thus dynamic efficiency is a condition when the economy is growing at the 'right' rate, and 'right' here is defined in terms of the society's choice between present and future consumption. In this case the willingness to pay relates to the price that the society would pay for each successive unit of good or service, indicated by marginal demand prices (Gittinger, 1982). Distributional efficiency relates to how the national wealth is owned, produced and distributed. It is concerned with whether a society feels that its total output (consumption) is optimally distributed.

Economic efficiency, market and government failures Economic efficiency is usually considered or analysed in the context of market conceptual framework. In neoclassical theory, freely functioning markets automatically lead to static and dynamic efficiency so long as certain conditions are met and it is referred to as 'perfect competition', characterized by a large number of buyers and sellers of undifferentiated commodities with market transactions entered into freely by both participants. However, the existence of these conditions is too idealistic in real life, because failure to attain a perfect market situation leads to market failure, which would require some form of societal intervention in order to guarantee that social welfare is maximized. Often such failures prompt government intervention designed to correct for market failure, but often such intervention is either inappropriate, insufficient, excessive or even disruptive of an otherwise efficiently functioning market. Shadow pricing, therefore, is used to correct for distortions that exist because of market and government failures (Ward, Deren and D'Silva, 1995).

A government failure occurs when the government intervenes in the economy in an unwarranted, inappropriate, or non-optimal manner. Such intervention results in 'distortions' in the financial prices faced by producers and consumers, which in turn leads to production and consumption decisions that are not economically efficient or optimal. There are varieties of government failures, but the principal economic distortions caused by these failures are: i) border distortions; and ii) domestic distortions. Border distortions include such distortions as export tax or subsidies, tariff and quota or quantitative restrictions or outright import bans. These border distortions distort the relationship between border prices (cif – cost, insurance and freight) and fob (free-on-board) prices, and domestic prices. The economic valuations process will have to adjust for distortion between border prices and domestic prices. This is necessary because the distortion affects the relative values of traded versus non-traded goods. In correcting for the distortions, 'shadow exchange rate' (SER) instead of 'official exchange rate' (OER) is used in the economic analysis – SER = (1 + WATR) x OER, where WATR equals weighted average tariff and subsidy rate. Domestic distortions affect relationships among domestic prices. A typical example is the operation of the minimum wage legislation that tends to raise the price of labour covered by the law (usually in the formal sector) relative to the cost of machinery, other inputs and labour not covered by the legislation. The latter is usually in the informal sector, including the agricultural labour force.

Traditionally, it is practically impossible for a government to remove all distortions in the economy because in the very act of eliminating one distortion another is created. Since distortions cannot all be eliminated, in practice the problem is resolved by determining the 'best ' combinations of distortions, a situation referred to as the 'broader economic problem of second best'. The 'second best shadow prices' approach takes into account inherent conflicts and trade-offs that public policy managers face while the 'first best' approach, which corrects distortions in terms of allocative efficiency only. In this approach, shadow prices are estimated in terms of equilibria that would exist after optimal correction of all distortions. 'Second best' acknowledges that not all corrections have taken or will take place.

In general, taxation in principle implies that taxes are hardly neutral in terms of their being non-distorting in the pure sense of economic efficiency. Whether taxes are imposed to raise revenue or for corrective purposes to meet income distribution objectives, they will lead to conflicts which include: i) the allocations function (static and dynamic efficiency); ii) the stabilization function (macroeconomic management); and iii) the distribution function (equity). Thus a fundamental conflict will always occur between the allocative and distribution functions of a government, especially when the government tries to provide public goods but is unable to raise revenue in a non-distorting way to pay for the goods.

Externalities The other group of market failure involves 'external economies' which occur when an economic activity affects a third person, someone other than the producer or the buyer. The result of the externalities is that some production or consumption impacts are not internalized in the financial price that is paid for the goods, some costs or benefits are not included in the financial price that is used to purchase the goods. There are four types of external economies (a third party impact): technological externality, linkage economies, information economies and pecuniary externality.

An external economy in the case of technological externality may occur in the use of insecticides and pesticides in plant protection. Some of the chemical residue may be washed into water bodies, causing loss of biotics due to aquatic pollution. In this example, the financial cost of plant protection does not reflect fully the true cost to society unless a government imposes a socially optimal pollution tax on the plant producers. This tax, in order to be optimal, should be equivalent to the net real costs borne by the water bodies (downstream). This type of external economy is known as technological externality. In shadow pricing, economic analysis should reflect these downstream externalities, including the internalization costs borne by the plant producer. In this example, if the downstream costs are not internalized in financial values of the project, economic values will exceed financial values. Put the other way, the 'internal economies' will reflect those values that accrue to the buyer or seller in the project's financial values, but exclude downstream costs (loss of biotics and employment opportunities in fishing). Linkage economies can best be explained by the principle of backward and forward linkages in the economy (intersectoral linkages). The production of livestock yield recurrent products, like milk, and also by-products. Milk production generates demand for a processing plant and packaging materials (backward linkage) and the dairy products can be used in bakery industry (forward linkage). In the same way, animal by-products like hide and skin create demand for tanneries (backward linkage), while the processed leather generates opportunities for leather industry (forward linkage) (see Figure 46).

Although not widely used in analysis, information economy is included in the external economies. A typical example is agricultural research and extension advisory services usually provided by the government. To promote a particular technology, a government engages in basic and adaptive research, and the technology transfer may be promoted through out-of-class or residential training, etc. Market information through radio and television programmes, publication, etc. is intended to provide information either to producers to assist them to take rational decision on production plans or to the traders in agricultural commodities. Although it is a public service, nevertheless it involves costs in terms of staff, equipment, etc.

As regards pecuniary externalities, production and purchase decisions usually have third-party impacts which occur through prices paid or received. In Ghana in the 1970s food crop policies favoured a few elite. Following the launching of 'Operation Feed Yourself' (OFY), a crash programme, many incentives to increase food production were introduced: loans at subsidized interest rates, subsidized inputs, central bank guarantees to commercial banks lending to agriculture, etc. The urban elite who had influence borrowed under the programme ostensibly to expand rice production. Because of rampant inflation these elite rather bought the little rice available from the peasant farmers and sold it in open markets at exorbitant prices. With these windfall gains they were able to repay their loans quickly without making any contribution to rice output (Okai, 1988).

Since rice and other cereal production did not increase, Ghana imported food commodities which were considered essential. They included maize, rice, wheat, sugar and vegetable oils. These imports were distributed either by the Ghana National Trading Corporation's own shops or by licensed wholesalers. Although retail prices were controlled, they were effectively controlled only at the corporation's shops. Under the passbook system, holders received commodities on credit for retail on commission within the informal sector. In practice the passbook holders sold in the open market where prices were much higher than the controlled prices. Sales were also controlled through the issue by sales managers of 'chits' (valued at controlled prices) to a few privileged retailers for the release of goods, but instead they renegotiated the 'chits', without even collecting the commodities, to women with access to the private marketing network. The chits could be renegotiated three or even up to five times before the commodities were collected. The Ghanaian elite soon learned the value of the 'chits', which enabled them to extract enormous rents. This gave rise to rent-seeking behaviour on a massive scale under the system of *Kalabule* (Hausa expression – *Kere Kabure*) which means 'keep it quiet'. People who had access to the system spent time in attempting to acquire the goods instead of undertaking directly productive activities. High prices contributed to secular structural inflation that reduced the purchasing power of income of all Ghanaians. Thus pecuniary externalities can have an impact on the distribution of purchasing power in society, especially rent-seeking, that cannot be controlled effectively.

Counterfactuals The other pertinent point in the agricultural sector investment programmes' (ASIP) evaluation is the analysis of every component of the programmes relative to counterfactuals in the context of what could have happened without the programmes. In the tsetse fly eradication programme in Uganda, because the infested land was idle, no national output was forgone, but beef ranching projects established on reclaimed land produced social utilities and, therefore, it produced social benefits. The project also prevented re-invasion of infested land by the fly and thus contributed to the improvement in health. Because project benefits and costs occur at different periods of time, the use of 'net present' values are relevant here in order to present the project viability in summary statistical form. The principal concern is to ascertain whether the project results in net benefit to the economy.

The other consideration is the best institutional framework for the implementation of the project and whether the project ought to be in the hands of the public or the private sector. The evaluation is expected to specify the counterfactual. In Ghana, for instance, under the OFY, the government decided to supply machinery for rice production and rice harvesting. Meanwhile the Bank of Ghana quite often delayed in issuing import licenses (issues were made if there was foreign exchange to cover imports) so that by the time the machinery arrived it was no longer either a production or harvesting season. During the following production season, the machinery required servicing before use. Again, because of difficulties with imports, the essential spare parts were not stocked or did not arrive on time. Consequently half the 1976 rice was lost because part of it was burnt and part not harvested (Okai, 1988). If the supply of machinery and servicing were profitable, it would have been better for the private sector to provide the service, since they would find it worthwhile.

In the case of tsetse fly eradication in Uganda, for instance, the public body would be a better option. As the tsetse fly infested large areas of Uganda, the private sector would not find it worth their while to undertake the eradication programme. Hence in the absence of the public sector project, the land would not have been reclaimed and brought into productive use. Thus the analyst should be concerned with comparing costs incurred and the benefits the project is expected to yield. In this respect, actual beef ranching could have been undertaken by the government on large capital intensive ranches. Although it could have been economically viable, this option's employment generation capacity might have been limited, thus it might not have been socially optimal. An alternative was for individual cattle owners to undertake the beef ranching. This option had the advantage of employing many ranchers, thus creating a much larger employment opportunity. In the evaluation the analysts should compare net present value of the public sector project over and above that of the combined individual ranchers (evaluated at the 'shadow price') to determine whether it was negative or positive. Thus, assuming that the beef ranching project is profitable, the counterfactual here is the relevant magnitude of net contribution of the beef ranching project to the national welfare either by a public project or individual ranchers.

Another consideration is to redistribute income or correct market failures.

This point can best be illustrated with the help of the smallholder tea project in Uganda. Prior to the establishment of the project, tea production was almost entirely in the private sector (positive externality). The government participated in commercial tea production and processing through a subsidiary of the then Uganda Development Corporation, the Agricultural Enterprises Ltd (AEL). Both the private sector and AEL produced a quantity of tea which did not satisfy domestic and external demand, although the country had vast areas suitable for tea production. For illustration purposes, the positive externality in the figure is represented by the marginal social benefit line, which describes how much Ugandans are willing to pay for each of the tea supplied. As presented, the amount is greater than the marginal private benefit or private demand, which is the price one is willing to pay. This amount is less than the

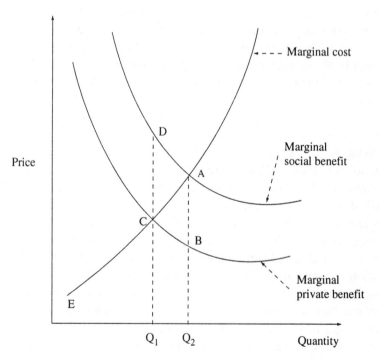

Notes 1 Marginal cost is the cost of an additional unit of output while marginal benefit is the benefit from additional unit of output. See chapter 2 for an explanation of marginal cost and benefits.
    2 UTGC = Uganda Tea Growers' Corporation.

Figure 3   UTGC (public provision) and the private sector counterfactual

marginal public benefit; alternatively the marginal social benefit is greater than the marginal private benefit (private demand). In the illustration both the marginal social and private benefit lines are assumed to represent demand curve with unit elasticity. In case of tea production, the private sector could supply up to Q_1 of tea from private estates. However the socially optimal desirable amount to be supplied is Q_2.

Following the establishment of the Uganda Tea Growers' Corporation (UTGC) the government mobilized the initiatives of smallholder tea growers to participate in tea production, leaving tea factories to be managed by the government. (Actually the management of factories was subcontracted to the private sector.) The Corporation provided tea seedlings to the tea growers at cost, but the costs of research and extension advisory services were not recovered (producers' subsidy equivalent). As the number of smallholder tea growers increased, total tea production (from the private and smallholder tea growers) greatly increased. The private sector did not expand output for a number of reasons. Tea production is a labour-intensive operation and the operation of the minimum wage legislation distorted the labour markets. The smallholder tea growers operating small tea plots and, having low overhead costs and with the availability of funds from the World Bank, were able to produce tea much more cheaply than the private sector.

Several counterfactuals should have been examined. In evaluating the tea project, correcting distortions in factor markets could have improved economic efficiency and profitability and could enable the private sector to expand output rather than the public intervention. With years of experience in organizing the outgrowers scheme, there would have been no need to establish UTGC, since the private sector could have organized the outgrowers. Thus the World Bank fund could have been used for alternative projects and thus making the Bank's fund fungible. With the tea project, the public incurred some cost in the form of subsidy. In the figure the areas under marginal cost between Q_1 and Q_2 are the total additional cost of the project, but consumers are paying only BC Q_1 Q_2; thus the additional cost is represented by the triangle ABC. It is necessary to ascertain that, at a minimum, the external benefit exceeds the cost for the government intervention in the project to be worth undertaking. In other words, tea supply should not be beyond Q_2, a point at which marginal costs exceeds marginal social benefit. Thus the relevant range for public intervention in the tea project is between Q_1 and Q_2.

The tea project example can also illustrate the objective of redistributing income. The research and advisory services (information economy) provided free to producers bears some final cost to the government, which is a cost to all tax payers. Nevertheless it is necessary to ascertain whether the value of the redistribution outweighs its final cost. As discussed earlier, taxation introduces distortionary costs into the economy. In project evaluation, these distortionary costs should be taken into account. If distortions in factor markets are removed, it could well be that the private sector would find it profitable to increase tea output. If the UTGC displaced a certain amount of private sector tea output capacity, the taxes that could have been paid by the private sector could be lost to the public sector. This loss is a cost to society. Equally relevant is that the UTGC could supply to the public at higher real cost than would the private sector. That extra real cost to the public could lead to increases in taxation to enable the government to make up for the loss.

Privatization During the heyday of the projectization of development plans, direct participation in economic activities was actively promoted. As stated earlier, administrative weaknesses in plan implementation were observed as impeding progress. Multilateral financial institutions insisted on the creation (in some cases strengthening existing ones) of institutions to manage externally financed projects. Appointment of senior staff had to be cleared by the lending institutions. Often the most experienced and competent were withdrawn from general public service to manage these projects. The UTGC, created by an act of the Ugandan parliament, is a case in point. After two decades or so it was also realized that these institutions did not perform better either and instead they overloaded budgetary resources since they relied on government subsidies to function. When the structural adjustment programme (SAP)was introduced, privatization of publicly-owned state enterprises was one of its kingpins, on the ground of fiscal discipline and prudent economic management. Meanwhile the participation of the private sector has been actively promoted. The emphasis on sector-wide reviews is to facilitate choice of strategic factors in development, decide on realistic intervention and the fungibility of external financial resources.

The internalization of environmental externalities into development framework
The principal purpose of evaluating macroeconomy-environment interactive dynamics, as stated earlier, is to investigate the conflicting objectives of the economics and ecology of sustainable agricultural development in terms of economic viability, environmental integrity and patrimony. Macroeconomic policies have the potential of encouraging unintended irrational utilization of natural resources manifested by consumption for purposes in which social costs exceed social benefits often associated with excessive rates of resource

depletion and pollution. As an example, imposing a tax on energy consumption can encourage a shift of consumption to untaxed natural fuels. In the case of the agricultural sector, for instance, the imposition of the tax on electricity consumption results in increased use of forest-based energy sources. Increased demand for wood-fuel to meet domestic energy need results in extensive destruction of forest and woodland, which can set in motion self-reinforcing processes of resource degradation, the synergy of which generates and accelerates ecological transformations. As evapo-transpiration is reduced there is not enough moisture in the atmosphere to recharge rain-bearing clouds, resulting in the rainfall variability being below the long-term normal average. This translates itself into random occurrence and/or recurrent droughts, increasing aridity and ultimately desertification (definitions provided in subsequent chapters). The elimination of agricultural input subsidies (fiscal incentives) raises input prices. As output prices lag behind input prices, the farmers often decrease their use although they are essential for sustaining soil productivity.

In order to assess the impact of land use in resource productivity, it is necessary to estimate trends in total factor productivity (TFP) obtained by deflating real value of outputs by real value of inputs. Total inputs include: i) internal resource accumulation or depletion, including expansion of the arable and permanent crop land, and the growth of agricultural labour force and productive inputs; and ii) technical production inputs. If the ratio is less than unity it implies resource depletion, and vice versa. Soil fertility in this context does not encompass only plant nutrients but also soil structure, water retentive capacity, soil organic matter content and biological activities that influence both efficiency of use and resource sustainability. From this perspective, soil fertility is essentially a capital stock and its regeneration represents the recapitalization of soil fertility. It can be eroded by consumptive (extractive) use.

Measurement of TFP is to capture any damage to the resource base. If no remedial measures are taken, the decline in soil fertility becomes a cost measured by the level and value of output forgone. This loss is the marginal opportunity cost (MOC). In order to correct this loss, it is necessary to invest in technologies which result in increases in compensatory productivity. This represents marginal (user) depletion costs (MUC).

Because of compensatory increases in productivity, as illustrated in the figure, the yield damage caused by agronomic practices (in this case a reduction in the fallow phase) that degrade the soil can be restored by adopting alternative improved cultural practices, inputs use or both. When soil quality declines from Q_{so} to Q_{sd}, yield declines from Y_o (optimal yield) to Y_{sd} which represents the total yield drop due to soil degradation in the absence of increases in compensatory productivity. The adoption of regenerative and/or rehabilitative technologies raises output from Y_{sd} to Y_{sr}, leaving a residual yield loss of Y_{sr} to Y_o. The recovery of residual yield (Y_{sr} to Y_o) depends on the economics of preventing soil degradation in the context of the consideration of option values (environmental patrimony) of resource conservation.

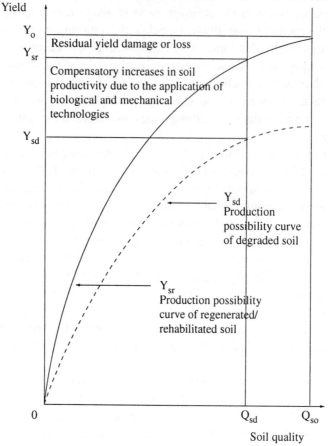

Figure 4   Compensatory increases in resource productivity of a regenerated/rehabilitated degraded soil

The use of technical production inputs like agro-chemicals is not always environmentally neutral since it can result in the pollution of aquatic and terrestrial atmosphere. Similarly, the use of water for irrigation, if not properly managed, can result in the salinization of soil due to soil-limited pollution assimilative capacity and off-site depositional pollution. These are some of the social opportunity costs of these externalities due to forgoing output which could have been raised from the degraded land. The costs of reclaiming the degraded land can be taken as the marginal external costs (MEC).

It is these environmental externalities that have to be monitored and evaluated using appropriate technical and socioeconomic criteria. From a societal perspective, the price of consuming a natural resource (including its by-products like positive wastes and the multiple functions of resources) should equal to its marginal opportunity cost. This price equals the sum of marginal private costs (MPC), marginal user (depletion) costs (MUC) and marginal external costs (MEC), i.e. MOC = MPC + MUC. Since environmental costs are often the dominant component of external costs, the MEC included in MPC usually internalize externalities such as endogenously enforced communal work, pollution taxes (if any) and formal and informal regulations. Essentially, therefore, the evaluation of environmental factors is one which recognizes that the true economic costs of incremental consumption is to be compensated by additional investment in environmental recovery and conservation. This calls for setting a price which is equal to average incremental cost (AIC) which is arrived at by computing the 'present worth' of incremental costs (discounted future unit cost) deflated by (or the ratio of) the 'present worth' (discounted unit cost of future consumption) of consumption. (Explanation of computing 'present worth' is given in subsequent chapters.) If the ratio is more than unity, it implies resource depletion and vice versa.

Prior to the recognition of environmental decline as a serious threat to the well-being of humanity, the benefits of development were measured in terms of opportunity costs of the social utility forgone by not using scarce resources in the best alternative use. Because of this preoccupation with economic efficiency, and since natural resources were regarded as the 'unpriced free gift of God', no attempts were made in tracing environmental impacts of the implementation of macroeconomic and sectoral policies. Many of these policies were often intended to address non-environmental issues. Some of the policies, although not deliberately intended to address environmental issues, nevertheless addressed environmental factors. Swamp reclamation, for instance, is usually intended to bring unused land into productive use. Eradication of the vectors of diseases, drilling water bore-holes or constructing dams and the building of physical and economic infrastructure helped to spread both human and animal population, thus avoiding the creation of pockets of population pressures on land resources. Reform of the resource tenure systems, although originally intended to increase incentive to produce for the market, nevertheless has the potential of promoting better environmental stewardship.

Certain policies pursued in the past, however, contributed to environmental decline. As a deliberate policy to promote white settler agriculture, African agricultural products were deliberately underpriced under the dual pricing system. To meet tax obligations, African farmers had to bring more land into cultivation, often without proper soil management practices. This policy distortion was not anticipated to result in inimical environmental impacts. Related to this policy distortion were the consequences for the environmental integrity of market intervention mediated through marketing parastatals, which culminated in underpricing export commodities. Again, this resulted in more land being cultivated in order to produce more in order to be able to meet statutory as well as domestic obligations. Consequently as early as the 1920s, soil erosion was recognized as being widespread in SSA. Conservation measures patterned on practices in America and Europe were inappropriate under tropical rainstorm conditions. Coupled with inappropriate exotic agronomic practices, they actually contributed substantially to soil degradation. Some institutional reforms, like the sedenterianization of the pastoral communities designed to improve rangeland productivity and management, actually in most cases resulted in rangeland degradation because officials who enforced these policies had no first hand experience with the management of the fragile ecosystems, although the pastoralists had evolved rangeland management systems that enabled pasture use to remain in equilibrium with the environment.

According to M"aler and Munasinghe (1996, pp. 149–63), the policy distortions, market failure and institutional constraints can be regarded as subsidiary imperfections. Failure to integrate these imperfections into macroeconomy framework had led and can lead to unintended environmental degradation. Essentially this concept can be equated with primary and derived causes of environmental degradation. Institution mediation of demographic pressures and farmers' intuitive resource combinations and adaptations to changing ecological conditions can be taken as primary causes, while adaptive response and adaptive change to market forces (macroeconomy externalities and external economic environment) can be taken as the derived causes of environmental decline in particular if the response and change result in extractive form of agriculture not equally matched by natural regeneration rate of resource productivity, or investment in regenerative and/or rehabilitative technologies.

Given the foregoing consideration, the contemporary concern for development intervention should shift away from a narrow sectoral approach to one which recognizes that sustainable development is not only concerned with economic efficiency but also one that protects and conserves the productive assets as a vital environmental patrimony. In this regard it is worth observing that in the past, development intervention was reactive to environmental damage because the combination of some macroeconomic and sectoral policies were never anticipated to contribute to the collapse of environmental integrity. To avoid a repetition of unintended inimical impacts of policies on environmental resources, development intervention should be pro-active by internalizing these secondary imperfections of macroeconomic policies into the environmental impact assessment. The extent of a trade-off between achieving broad macroeconomic objectives and minimizing more specific environmental damage cannot be generalized but has to be on a case-by-case basis, taking into account the locational physical, economic, and social characteristics of the specific area.

Social opportunity costs of environment Because natural resources are finite and, therefore, always scarce, there are competing demands for their use to produce desired social utilities. In order to obtain something desired with limited resources, something else must be sacrificed. The social opportunity cost of the environment, therefore, is the value of that alternative environmental use that affect society as a whole. There are a number of social opportunity costs of environment: i) environmental insecurity arising from inability to produce the desired biomass due to environmental damage; ii) labour migration due to differences in locational comparative advantage; and iii) general migration of population fleeing from environmental insecurity. The regionalization and globalization of poverty has emerged as a destabilizing feature of the contemporary social economy of many nations. The scourge of the impoverishment (both material and moral) cannot be confined to the affected country only but often extends to larger regions or is global in coverage, mediated through inequity and social tension in the country of origin, resulting in uncontrolled migration as the affected persons flee the humiliation of environmental insecurity and poverty. The host countries usually resent immigrants, often called environmental or economic refugees, because their presence leads to loss of jobs for local people, cultural conflicts and the escalation of the costs of social services. In the countries of origin, continued social unrest diverts resources from directly productive activities and social services to the containment of law and order.

The loss of biomass, if partial, is the marginal opportunity cost of environment, and investment in environmental recovery is the MEC. As regards labour, Lewis's 'unlimited labour supply' argues that labourers in rural areas in developing countries get a wage equivalent to the average product of labour that is above the marginal productivity of labour (Lewis, 1954). Thus if the creation of urban jobs results in the withdrawal of labour from the rural sector, then there will be a positive externality that will reduce social opportunity of cost of labour associated with urban employment. The concept of rural labour having zero marginal productivity has been proved to be incorrect. Because of the seasonality of agricultural production, marginal productivity varies during the entire production season (Okai, 1968). Also, labour migration upsets societal and family balances with varying degree of sexual sharing of the costs and benefits of development (Okai, 1994). It is, therefore, important to monitor and evaluate regularly the social and economic consequences of changes in environmental setting.

Logical Steps in Sector Programming

Policy analysis is usually accompanied by some form of a development plan and the preparation of an agricultural sector investment programme (ASIP). Designing a development plan consists fundamentally of making decisions on a wide range of development activities, which are then presented in a plan document. The decisions are predominantly quantitative and depend on a range of quantitative economic calculations in order to make strategic and tactical decisions. The calculations are necessary in drawing up a comprehensive plan because they provide explicit quantitative analyses of desired objectives and making aggregate projections. Any plan traditionally has ten elements, four of which deal with plan formulation and the other six, plan implementation. They include: a) *plan formulation*; i) setting development objectives; ii) undertaking diagnostic surveys and sector analyses; iii) making demand and supply projections; and iv) the quantification of objectives/target setting; b) *spelling out plan implementation procedures*; v) making choice of strategies; vi) making choice of policy and its instruments including projects; vii) undertaking intellectual investments in research and studies to obtain relevant technical, economic and social data and information; viii) organizing development or the establishment of institutional infrastructure including administration; ix) mobilizing public expenditure for financing development projects and programmes from domestic and external sources of financing;

and x) establishing a system of monitoring, reporting and control, including impact evaluations (see Figure 5).

In setting national and sectoral objectives, in most countries, political leaders usually declare the country's broad development objectives in a policy statement. These could include a desire to improve the national income, double per capita income within a specified time frame, maximize or expand exports from traditional and non-traditional export sectors, expand the industrial base and employment, encourage foreign investment, etc. The sectoral development objectives could include food self-sufficiency, agricultural production diversification, etc. Both the national and sectoral objectives are regarded as the ends and the planning process is intended to find and prescribe the means. Hence any comprehensive development plan embraces investments both in the private as well as public sectors, and outlines implementation procedures in order that the plan goals can be met.

Economic policy and planning have been used interchangeably without differentiating one from the other. Through the ages a government in power would declare its policy intention to the people. Just before the outbreak of World War II hostilities, in the former USSR and Britain in particular, economic planning and policy started to be defined as a government measure to achieve national goals or objectives, while development planning was taken as a process of mobilization of national resources through nationalization, agrarian reforms or by inducement, and channelling these resources into productive investment which would increase output substantially. Economic planning was also used in crisis management systems by adjusting the consistency of economic parameters within the national economic system. In Britain after the cessation of war hostilities, there were widespread food shortages caused by the disruption of the food supply during the war. It was felt that food distribution could not be left to market forces alone. It was, therefore, necessary to ration food. ASIP is intended to construct comprehensive quantitative models for the agricultural sub-sectors with some indications of the magnitude of the investment programme required to achieve the targets and growth rates.

Setting National Objectives

The main concern of any government is to create a conducive policy environment that will accelerate the development of the national economy in order to be able to achieve the broad national goals (Figure 5). Prior to the current concern with the environment, the principal national objectives embrace: i) economic: growth of national income, savings and investment

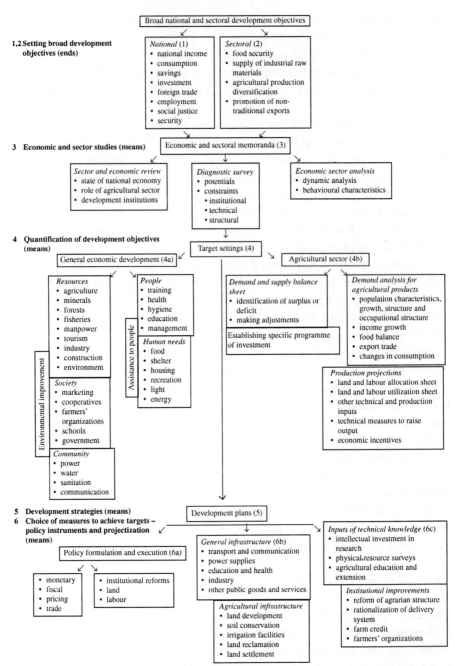

Figure 5   Schematic illustration of the logical steps in economic and sectoral planning

and general economic benefits; ii) political: concerned with national economic management and political stability; and iii) social development encompassing the development of people, community and human needs (Figures 2 and 5). Following increasing environmental determination, national objectives have been enlarged to include ecological welfare and environmental patrimony (Figure 2).

Usually at periodic intervals, economic and sector surveys should be carried out to obtain some quantitative evidence of the behavioural and structural characteristics of the economy. In a sector review, each factor, in conjunction with its linkages and interdependencies among sectors, is reviewed, using a general equilibrium (consistency framework) model which depicts the overall economic setting and the relative contribution of each sector to the overall development in the country (national output, employment, income distribution, balance of payments, etc.). This model analyses structural and behavioural relationships between macroeconomic variables (particularly imports, changes in terms of trade, etc.) and their impact on national income and consumption. The general equilibrium model also embraces sensitivity tests on the effects of alternative policies and strategies on output, rural income distribution, employment and balance of payment.

While the general equilibrium model is concerned with providing quantitative and descriptive data and information on the state of each sector within the overall setting of the economy, a diagnostic survey is used to describe the major development needs of sectors. The focus is on identifying key facilitating and restraining factors. At the micro-level, the major constraint could be labour shortages for agricultural production, poor nutritional and health conditions, institutional difficulties, ecological and technical constraints, etc. A diagnostic survey, therefore, provides qualitative, quantitative and descriptive analyses of the circumstances, policies and outcomes on the recent past and how they had been conditioned by internal and external environment. For the agricultural sector, the focus is on issues relating to agricultural output, supply response, effects of policy variables, the incidence of rural poverty and income distribution usually narrowed down to the overall impacts of macro-policy management on smallholders. This is illustrated by providing a brief description of the economy over a specified period, including the levels and changes in some basic performance indicators.

Because of sectoral relationships, there is, therefore, a need to take into account sectoral linkages. Two methods are often used. The first is the use of *multi-level planning models*, the main characteristic of which is the formal link of a *multi-sectoral, economy-wide* model with that of the rural agricultural sector. The analysis addresses itself first of all to the key macroeconomic constraints such as balance of payment, investment levels, growth of national savings, etc. The primary causes holding back the growth of these economic parameters are then searched for at different levels of aggregation. At the primary level of aggregation, the major constraint could be labour shortages, poor nutritional and health conditions, institutional difficulties, ecological constraints, etc. Some of the constraints are repeated at higher levels of aggregation, and they could be compounded by other problems, especially the problem of distortionary macroeconomic policy management. This approach, therefore, takes into account the overall macroeconomic dynamics and their impact on the rural population, especially income distribution and the quality of life.

While a *sector review* is concerned with the provision of quantitative and descriptive information on the state of the agricultural sector or sub-sectors within the overall setting of the economy, a *diagnostic survey* is concerned with the analysis of the potentials of physico-technical, institutional and structural constraints facing the sector or sub-sectors. In order to gain a better understanding of the dynamics and behavioural characteristics of the sector or sub-sectors, a *dynamic recursive sector analysis* can be undertaken. This analysis is usually carried out in order to capture the dynamics of responses to changes in policy variables such as supply and demand response, sector adaptation and transformation, factor mobility – all in response to relative changes in economic determinants. Elaboration of methodologies of dynamic analyses will be provided in subsequent chapters. The first approach, very common among academicians, is to establish a *hierarchy of linkage*, with the farm as a producing firm and a consuming household being the primary unit of observation. These farms are then grouped together into a zone on the basis of certain common criteria such as the homogeneity of ecological structure, techniques of production, size of landholding, tenurial systems, etc. This is taken as the first level of aggregation. The rural zones are consolidated to form a belt based on criteria such as climatic conditions, economic characteristics and even administrative factors. The belts are then linked to the rest of the national and/or world economy. This approach is typified by building models from the bottom to the top, and although it is based on agriculture as the primary economic activity in rural areas, it recognizes that it has to be supported by and linked with other sectors of the economy.

Closely related to this approach is the use of the *microeconomic dynamic models* built from the bottom to the top. Again the primary unit of observation is the farmer as a firm in his rural environment setting. The first step that is taken is to undertake the ordering of utility functions, the major ones being: i) satisfying subsistence consumption needs; ii) comparing cash consumption with possible future income; iii) assessing the risk-bearing capacity; and iv) estimating the maximization of net returns on investment. This is followed by the introduction of dynamic elements into the recursive programming models. These analyses, therefore, assess the farmer's response to output prices, realized sales and savings. By regression analyses, they indicate how the trend in effort-price (or effort-incentive) level has been influenced by the farmer's decision in direct response to the above elements. They are, therefore, used in supply estimation and demand response. The alternative to this is the use of system analysis involving linear programming models in a predictive capacity. Employing simulation in association with the above approaches to sector analysis, it is possible to build sub-models based on primary production, secondary and consumption activities for a number of rural agricultural enterprises which provide income to the various segments of the population in the rural setting. Changes in income and production levels, in turn, are expected to determine aggregate demand functions and labour mobility within belt, zonal or regional models. Usually these models are then linked with non-agricultural sub-models through incoming flows of consumer goods and services, and outgoing flows of raw materials.

Experience with Development Planning

The preparation of agricultural sector investment programme is essentially an improved form of sector development planning. Early development planners devoted a lot of their time on intellectual debate about whether a development plan should be growth-oriented or should emphasize equity. Some criteria for the choice of strategies were developed. The proponents of equity emphasized micro-investment on the ground that the ratio between capital and labour was claimed as being the most important sociopolitical criterion in evaluating the benefits of a development plan to society as a whole. The other criterion was the benefit of technology measured in terms of: i) incremental capital output ratio (ICOR) used to measure the efficiency of capital; and ii) the surplus-capital ratio as an indication of the capacity to generate domestic savings by using a particular process. In the latter case the surplus was computed by subtracting the wage bill from the value added.

A number of options for the choice of strategies were available in the selection of technologies which meet the country's development objectives. Although heavy capital investment has the potential of accelerating the rate of savings, it was recognized that it also has the potential disadvantage of being labour-displacing and a drain on foreign exchange. Light capital investment, while having the advantage of creating employment opportunities, was felt to have the potential to lead to a low rate of domestic savings. The choice of technology, therefore, depended on the nation's desired goal.

Approaches to development planning There were also intellectual debates about approaches to development planning, with some intellectuals favouring a macro approach while others favoured a micro approach. The proponents of a macro option contended that the macro approach should be favoured because once realistic macroeconomic policies were formulated covering pertinent key areas, farmers would make the necessary adjustments in the light of the individual capacity and resource endowments. The proponents of the micro approach felt that the macro approach alone was an inadequate vehicle for spurring motivation to increase production. The micro approach was favoured because it was felt it would improve the vigour of agricultural supply response. The other approach was based on the projectization of the development plan. It consisted of deciding on the right approach and planning for decision-making for solving specific problems, and giving direction to development. A projectization approach used operative economic criteria such as project identification and formulation, project implementation coupled with a continuous monitoring and evaluation of the economic performance of individual development projects, programmes or schemes. Most projects were identified on the strength of their potentials for earning or conserving foreign exchange or import substitution.

Although development planning went a long way in meeting the requirements of planning for action, in view of the fact that an attempt was made to outline a programme to be followed and fulfilled, nevertheless, each approach had some inherent weaknesses. The choice of technology, while commendable, could only be useful in an environment where the economy was free of distortions. So long as factor price distortions remained a persistent feature the use of factor price for choice of capital would be an unreliable guide for optimal allocation of resources. Resource allocation, it had been agreed, should take into account social opportunity cost of labour in the economy as a whole. The construction of comprehensive quantitative models based on the macro approach to planning also had some weaknesses. These models attempted to translate the overall growth rate into a set of target rates for major sectors of the economy with some indications of the magnitude of the investment programmes required to achieve the targets. However, this approach, it was realized, was highly aggregative, due to the poor quality of planning data, especially the accuracy of the input-output ratios on which the models largely depended. Experience with projections based on these models revealed that there was a wide divergence between the targets and what was actually achieved. Advances in technology improved the input-output relationships for certain products, thus over-fulfilling some targets while some other externalities caused the under-fulfilling of other targets. The micro approach was not able to produce a good plan because of inherent inaccuracy in the data series (Okai, 1974).

The projectization approach had the inherent weakness of concentrating efforts on targets that diverted attention from a wider perspective. Decisions were concentrated on narrowly-defined investment projects, with attention overly confined to analysis of economic costs and benefits. Employment-generation capacity of such projects was limited, but they diverted attention from the development and widespread use of simple technological innovation which had the potential of raising the productivity of internal resources of land and labour already committed to agriculture. It received only cursory treatment. Heavy reliance on specific projects for which economic costs and returns could be computed with comparative ease tended to exaggerate the economic return realizable from concentrating investments in a typically large operational units that adopt capital-intensive technologies. Decisions were taken on the strength of a high rate of return on investment even if the projects had low employment creation capacity.

There were three types of development plans: indicative or perspective, comprehensive and the dirigiste planning. In SSA development planning was foreign-inspired and often managed by expatriates. By and large the plans were comprehensive in scope, but indicative in their economic targets, apart from the government expenditure which was often directive. Plans provided broad strategies without detailed implementation schedules. These plans presented only detailed outlines of the national development plan, aims and objectives, but did not disaggregate projects, policies and recommendations. However these plans incorporated national policies towards technical and productive inputs, credit, manpower development, price and pricing policy, services and advisory services and lately environmental issues. Some indicative estimates of the costs of the plans were also included. Sectoral ministries were then expected to translate these policies into concrete project proposals to attract both domestic and external financial support. The sectoral ministry concerned usually reassessed in fair detail the amount of financial resources required to bring the projects or programmes into full operation, indicating the sources of funds including, where possible, funds generated from project operations, government participation share capital, and borrowings from domestic as well as external sources. To carry out these functions, sectoral planning machineries were established.

Plan implementation A major weakness was with plan implementation arising from the lack of comprehensiveness of the plan documents and budget allocation. Often, when faced with a high level of budgetary deficits, governments responded with some arbitrary cuts in expenditure. And yet the development plan was merely an expression of government intentions which had to be translated into operational content through the medium of the national budgets. National budgets were characterized by conflicts between the plan content and budget allocation. These conflicts arose in part as a consequence of the budgeting system adopted in Africa and in part as a consequence of a fall in revenue out-turn. Projects, especially externally funded ones, were based on a multi-year budget, while national budgets were prepared annually, and the release of approved funds depended on the availability of revenue. Delays in fund releases were a common feature. Also, many governments operated single-line budgeting systems (recurrent and capital expenditures) which often had no relevance to approved plan expenditure and thus impeded plan implementation.

Distortionary intervention Development planning was in the ascendency at a time when the basic thrust of development economics had been activist in character, in that it was the belief of the pioneers of development economics that development could be managed. This concept was the origin of distortionary intervention in economic development management, especially as the countries maintained levels and structure of aggregate demand and associated set of product and factor prices that were incompatible with productive capacity of the economies. In particular, the pricing policies pursued by government distorted incentive structure, and impaired competitive allocative efficiency. Consequently the productive potentials of the economies were weakened, as prices were kept artificially low, eroding domestic savings, discouraging production and leading to unnecessary subsidies, which in turn overloaded budgetary resources. The distorted policy environment exacted a heavy penalty, reflected in unsustainable structural imbalances between: consumption and savings; imports and exports; investment and domestic savings; installed physical capacity and management capacity; public expenditure and public revenues; and external debt service obligations and debt service capacity. Many projects had a low return and several could not come to full fruition. With declining domestic savings, the domestic investments were largely and increasingly financed by external borrowing (foreign savings). In many countries the intensive investment programmes contributed to foreign reserve depletion, and soon afterwards it was realized that the investment strategy adopted without an adequate complementary export programmes was itself a fairly import-intensive strategy.

Public revenue depended heavily on extracting surplus from the export sectors to finance the development activities. For many countries the agricultural commodity-export sector carried most of the burden, as it was the main source of foreign exchange as well as much of the public revenues, amassed directly through export taxes and indirectly through taxes on imports. In most countries, the agricultural pricing policies for major export crops were essentially determined with the basic aim of maximizing public revenues from export earnings. Under the then-existing tax structures, the major agricultural exports were taxed, with levies rising progressively with the world market prices, leading to a high average effective rates of taxation. Hence when the world market prices were favourable, the incentive to increase production by producers was blunted through higher export taxes as well as high profits to the marketing parastatals (Okai, 1988).

Heavy taxation on agriculture did not only retard the potential growth of agricultural output but also resulted in sizeable income transfers from agricultural to non-agricultural activities, thus aggravating the vast average income disparities between the urban and rural areas. Moreover, since the public revenues generated from the agricultural sector often exceeded the budgetary spending in agriculture, the policy was, therefore, biased against agricultural development through inadequate incentives as well as the lowest possible resource allocation for investment in the sector. In a number of countries budgetary resources were mostly spent on consumption, thus implying that the resources generated from the agricultural sector had neither been ploughed back into agriculture nor had they been allocated to development purposes in other sectors of the economy.

Restorative intervention As most development programmes had low returns, the economies developed unsustainable financial imbalances, and in order to revive the growth impulses and sustain their growth momentum, African countries had no alternative but to implement multi-annual programmes of structural adjustment. The adjustment process had been a sequential one in which: i) a stabilization phase aimed at restoring internal and external macro-economic equilibria was followed by; ii) the rehabilitation (recovery) phase aimed at regaining full economic growth; and then iii) the structural adjustment phase aimed at shifting incentives in favour of the production for exports.

Evaluation of Policy Impacts on Objectives

Once a consistent set of sectoral goals, strategies and policies is agreed upon by government, it is then followed by programme implementation. At periodic intervals, it is useful to undertake evaluations of the impacts of policy on achieving objectives. The first step is to investigate whether the translation of specific functions' objectives, including tasks of the various technical departments, were realistic. This aspect of evaluation entails undertaking: i) policy screening by testing the relevance of activities with goals, strategies and policy; ii) efficiency and sustainability of the various activities; and iii) whether the prioritization of programmes were based on some realistic measurable indicators to satisfy social wants (wants consumed by every citizen) and merit wants (wants consumed by specific group of citizens). It is, therefore, necessary to investigate whether or not programmes contributed to poverty alleviation. In this respect, different criteria and approaches can be employed: i) the technocratic approach, which focuses on directing resources to people with the greatest need; while ii) the institutional approach emphasizes strengthening the capacity of social institutions as the anti-poverty measure and government administrative capacity to deliver services. The other approaches include: i) the macro approach, focusing on the national wealth's distributional aspect; while ii) the micro approach examines the impact of the execution of macroeconomic policy instruments on supply response. The macro approach emphasizes the minimization of income distributional conflicts among the different social-economic groups as well as spatial disparities, while the micro approach lays emphasis on trends in incentive-effort and flow of social utility.

Certain activities, such as agricultural research, extension advisory services and animal health services, produce outcomes, which refer to impact. It is also necessary to measure the productivity of the programme measured by the level of outputs, which refer to products. It is also necessary to undertake economic cost/benefit analysis measured at economic prices while social cost/benefit analysis is measured using shadow (accounting) prices. Finally, it is important to measure specific agricultural supply responses, including food and environmental security.

Traditionally these more specific and detailed investigations are preceded by general trend analyses. However, the interpretation of trends can be misleading. For instance, an economy can record a high growth rate but it does not mean that every citizen has benefited. Owing to advances in technology or difference in locational resource endowments, a high growth rate can be achieved without much employment being created, or it can exacerbate spatial income disparities. It is therefore helpful to analyse the sources of growth of the economy in order to provide a meaningful interpretation. Also, the economy can be recording a high growth rate which can easily be at the cost of exhausting the resource. It is therefore imperative to adopt an integrative approach in the evaluation of policy impacts on national and sectoral objectives.

Quantitative Definitions of Sectoral Objectives

It has been common practice that most governments in developing countries, following the declaration of national development objectives, also declare sectoral objectives. In most cases these objectives focus on: i) the attainment of food security; ii) poverty alleviation; iii) the promotion of agricultural production diversification and intensification; and iv) the generation of employment within and outside the agricultural sector. Usually these are qualitative statements of objectives which require quantification in order to provide an indication of the magnitude of the problem to be tackled in order to achieve the desired goals. The quantification exercise can be a useful evaluation of the objectives if a consistent analytical framework is adopted and a brief critical survey of quantitative evidence of the vigour of performance is provided. Consequently, in order to give quantitative meaning to qualitative statements, the discussion should be illustrated with reference to the levels and changes in selected basic and ancillary indicators.

Having illustrated the trends in performance indicators, the next step is to calculate the contribution of each sub-sector to total agricultural production. In the first place the changes or variations in the value of each commodity over the previous year is calculated ($Qst - Q_{t+1}$) on an obsolete basis. The sum of the variations is totalled for each year and the grand total is used to compute the percentage share of each commodity. It is often also necessary to disaggregate sources of growth each by yield, area, capital, labour, technology, incentive (effort-price) and weather conditions. To calculate the effect of changes in area or yield on seasonal output, initially one has to compute the growth rates of total areas, yields, and production, and then calculate trends (chapter 2).

Often the primary concern of any government is the attainment of food security at household and national levels. In computing trends, the first step in the exercise is to specify a set of performance indicators linked to the issue or issues to be investigated. For the agricultural sector, since the issue focuses on food demand and nutrition, the performance indicators include dietary energy supplies (DES) per capita and consumption/expenditure by food groups, and data permitting, these would be disaggregated to geographical, socioeconomic and occupational groups. The nutritional status is very much conditioned by food supply from domestic and external sources (imports). If the domestic food supply is the primary concern of the review, then agricultural gross domestic product and the indices of food supply can be used as the indicators. Alternatively both total agricultural and food production indices can be taken as indicators. In order to interpret the trends realistically, a benchmark as a base (a base year period) for measuring and evaluating the trends should be identified, giving reasons to justify the choice.

In the interpretive analysis, initially the introductory part of the investigation should undertake a review of the major trends and developments in the field of rural and agricultural development. It should contain a clear statement for the choice of the problems to be reviewed, what is already known, a resumé of the work already carried out by previous field investigations and the objectives of the current exercise highlighting how the study is to be carried out. This means that there should by a brief literature review and evaluation of previous development efforts, including their impacts and/or outcome. Accordingly, the quantitative evaluation of the problem to be investigated should also include a review of the recent historical perspectives of the problem, usually given in a form of a narrative providing a qualitative and descriptive interpretation of the dynamics of the agricultural economy in a contextual sense, i.e. within the overall macroeconomic framework.

Quantification of Sectoral Objectives

There are several methods used in the quantification of objectives (setting targets). Following the projections of demand for food and industrial raw material supplies and the estimated total requirements for agricultural products (demand), the *first* method used is to provide some indication of the magnitude of desirable agricultural output. This is the commonest method in establishing preliminary targets on both aggregate and commodity basis. If demand cannot be met from domestic sources, the gap can either be met by additional investment in production or by imports.

Since any economy has some momentum (dynamic processes), the *second* approach of setting targets is based on a simple projection of the recent trends of output. The projection of the recent trend of supply gives the first estimation of the possible line of development of the main agricultural products including the projection of areas and yields, comparing tentative estimates of demand with the production trends. On this basis it is possible to estimate consumption requirements. This latter data on commodity supply/demand trends constitute the *third* method of establishing production targets.

As a *fourth* method, thematic groups, including sub-sectoral thematic groups as deemed appropriate, can be established to work out details of needed targets, including some indication of nutritional, social and institutional aspects of agricultural production. Where feasible, local communities (decentralized planning pattern) can also be encouraged to develop and set their own production goals within the national development broad framework. This approach could be a beneficial additional incentive for local initiative.

The *fifth* method of setting targets is based on available resources (input programming) and making estimates of additional production which can be expected from the resources' employment. In some countries teams of local officials exist and are used to consider and recommend, in quantitative terms, the types of agricultural development for different areas, including physical inputs, needed investment and other requirements to implement the programme. This is the *sixth* method of setting targets. The estimates are then aggregated to the national level to form an integral part of the national development programme.

In all the approaches of setting targets, estimates must be tested for technical feasibility, economic viability, social and political acceptability and resource-conserving qualities. The result of the tests might make it necessary to make adjustments to estimated targets. All the approaches for the quantification of sectoral objectives can be employed or the most relevant to locational circumstances can be used.

Analysis of Constraints and Potentials

Framework for Analysis of Constraints

Evolution of agriculture According to biblical stories, following our great grandfather Adam eating the 'forbidden fruit', mankind was condemned by God – 'by the sweat of thy brow shall thou liveth'. Prior to this condemnation mankind lived in perfect harmony with animals which today are wild. Following this condemnation, the harmony was replaced by aggressive relationship and man then developed instinctive vital flight responses as stratagem for survival. Notwithstanding this curse, nevertheless God still made vast amounts of pristine natural resources at the disposal of mankind, but sanctioned that resource utilization should be carried out in a sustainable way without anthropogenically destroying the basic life-support resource. In the early days life depended on gathering fruits, hunting and fishing. Because of the use of dangerous weapons for hunting, mankind evolved a sense of discipline and security among members of a society. It is felt that this was the origin of government, which evolved into different forms: feudal, semi-feudal, cultural democracy, etc., depending on the prevailing physical and social environment. These traditional institutions endogenously enforced sustainable resource utilization through benign mediation of demographic and market forces on resources.

As population grew, the fruits as well as game progressively became insufficient to meet an adequate food requirement. It was, therefore, necessary for mankind to undertake some form of agriculture. The word 'agriculture' itself is derived from a Greek word *agraire* which means 'land', and a Latin word, *cultura*, literally meaning the proper practice for managing or the law governing the rational use of land. Cultures, therefore, evolved around the use of land and other environmental resources for subsistence. Contextually it means that the evolution of the social, cultural and moral milieu of a particular community was rooted in the use and management of the basic life-support resources sustainably, without destroying them. The social equilibrium in traditional society was preserved through flexible non-exploitative resource tenure systems. Customary resource management practices were able to sustain ecological viability. This was made possible because of the resilience of traditional agriculture to withstand unstable climatic conditions, and judicious adaptations of management systems and technologies to changing ecological settings. Social production and productive relations preserved collective social security.

Through heuristic methods of resource combinations and adaptations, traditional African farming systems had evolved over many millennia into agriculture-based, animal-based and agro-pastoral based livelihoods, each of which possessed its own demographic characteristics, indigenous nontechnical and technical knowledge, social organizations and behavioural norms. Currently each culture system utilizes a dynamic mix of techniques, resource combinations and adaptations, and a complementary set of activities that spread risks inherent in traditional farming. The characteristic feature of each system is the combination of mobility, flexibility and diversity in order to maximize the productive potential of various ecological niches. The key feature and principle is to maximize production to an extent that available technologies permit satisfaction of cultural and economic needs without destroying the basic life-support resource. These systems, therefore, guarantee resource renewability and minimize livelihood system vulnerability to risks. By maintaining resource utilization in equilibrium with the environment through a range of strategies and techniques to cope with the vagaries of unstable environment, the farmers were able to lay a firm foundation for survival. As these local systems could produce products some of which had export potentials, the equilibrial production systems soon started to face some problems as they become increasingly integrated into national and international market economies which exacted economic hegemony far beyond their control. As the traditional systems lost their viability through the superimposition of paradoxically modern non-integrating exotic technologies on non-retreating traditional agriculture, the Sub-Saharan Africa region was subjected to the vagaries of systemic agrarian crisis.

The social equilibrium in traditional society was preserved through a flexible non-exploitative resource tenure system. Customary resource management practices were able to sustain ecological viability. This was made possible because of the resilience of traditional agriculture to withstand unstable climatic conditions, and judicious adaptations of management systems and technologies to changing ecological settings. Social production and productive relations preserved collective social security. Research station generated technologies, which were expected to facilitate the transition to modern agricultural economy, could not be successfully integrated into the productive fabrics of traditional farming systems. This failure was due primarily to neglecting to incorporate the indigenous knowledge and experience of local farmers into the generation of improved modern technologies which could have relevance and meaning to peasant farm conditions.

The indigenous technical knowledge (ITK), endogenously evolved, is characterized by adaptations of technologies that guaranteed sustainable use of land (*agraire*) and land-based resources. The distinctive features of the technologies are their primary concern with the activities intimately connected with security of livelihood and remaining in harmony with the people who generated them. Traditional culture (*cultura*), therefore, evolved around the sustainable use of environmental resources, thus forming a firm basis for subsistence. The social environment creates a condition referred to by social anthropologists as a rational peasant *moral economy* within which individuals, within a specific cultural context (*cultural homogeneity*) voluntarily participate in a reciprocal sharing of the means of livelihoods (consumption stabilization) and reciprocal access to productive assets and valued resources (income stabilization). Agricultural production in traditional societies contain built-in stabilizing and food security mechanisms. The voluntary participation in reciprocity networks, a form of mutual insurance or collective social security, is referred to as *social capital*. The system is, therefore, *society-centred.*

The ITK is usually unique to a given culture or society and it influences every aspect of life including acceptance of institutional and technological innovation. It is essentially a repository of information about successful ways by which people have dealt with environmental resources under their control. The ITK is not usually static but changes over time due to influences of an array of interacting elements, as illustrated in Figure 6. As the moral economy responds to these influences, it gradually transforms itself to a *modern economy*. During the transition to modern economy, the moral economy and the existing cultural homogeneity are subjected to conflicts between established cultural practices and modern ones, a situation referred to as *social dualism* because of the dichotomous situation between the two economies. The traditional societies find themselves being pulled into conflicting directions due to shifts in local traditions, economic and social relationships. In the process of resolving the conflicts, some form of *social differentiation* occurs, due to differences in the vigour of response to innovation by individuals (differential wealth accumulation). The emergence of social differentiation culminates in the gradual but steady disintegration of cultural homogeneity and democracy. As this occurs the disadvantaged in society become peripheralized, a situation called *social exclusion.* The social disaffiliation or social disqualification results in the individualization of risks following the collapse of the mechanisms for social articulation of risks which can lead to widespread rural poverty and a variety of marginalizations (economic and political) which become entrenched. This may polarize society, with a large mass of people whose common bond is their poverty emerging on the one hand, and the affluent on the other. This could lead to social and economic dislocations of the weak, ushered in by social exclusion. The horizontal integrative bonds (inter-household solidarity network) are replaced by vertical reciprocity (patron-client interpersonal relationships) either to the state or to the rural elite. As traditional agriculture loses its viability, and as the science of complexity portrays, out of the organized chaos will emerge the modern economy with emphasis on technical optima, commercialization and profitability, which are not society-centred.

The adoption of the innovation is greatly influenced by farmers' perceptions in terms of the capacity of the new idea in strengthening their risk-coping and risk-management capability (consumption and income stabilization). Adjustment to risks and uncertainties was and is still the principal preoccupation of mankind centred around the use of natural resources. Opportunity for adjustments to risks and uncertainties in the context of African agriculture is indeed very limited. However, over the years the agriculturalists and pastoralists have evolved judicious adaptations to the environment and resource combinations that minimized risks and uncertainties. Living can be equated with processes of survival; proverbially stated, 'if one cannot run at least he/she should be able to hide'. In order to survive one has to be constantly creative in developing alternative ways to successfully neutralize risks one faces in life. The principal preoccupation of mankind, therefore, is risk aversion and management. The first major task is to tame the environment and undertake efficient and productive use and management of environmental resources. The qualities and quantities of these resources such as atmospheric (climate), aquatic, terrestrial (earth) and biospheric (animals, plants and other biotics) resources, have the potential for creating the environmental basis for agricultural risks and uncertainties. Through generations of trial and error, the farmers evolved indigenous technical knowledge which was in harmony with the people who generated it and guaranteed resource renewability. The ITK is anchored on the concept of moral economy typified by the right of livelihood through mutual (voluntarily sharing on a reciprocal basis) and inter-temporal (over time) insurance.

At the time of colonization the moral economy was already well developed and deeply rooted in Sub-Saharan Africa. Although moral economy was also the norm in pre-industrial Europe, the colonialists, instead of undertaking creative diagnosis of the potential of ITK, rather trivialized it as being incapable of spurring the required level of motivation among the peasants to participate in commercial agricultural production. It was also postulated that farmers in developing countries, Africa included, had target incomes which, once reached, meant they would make no further effort to produce. It was also believed that they valued leisure greatly. Because the colonialists valorized Western culture as having the best civilizing influence and ignored the potential of ITK and farmers' preoccupation with social articulation of risks and survival, social anthropology was not one of the elements included in the development paradigm. Only social anthropologists bothered to investigate the behavioural

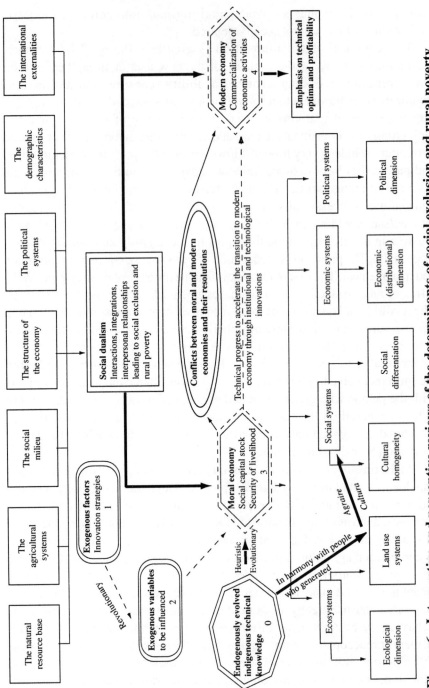

Figure 6   Interpretive and perceptive reviews of the determinants of social exclusion and rural poverty

1 Lithosphere/terrestrial resources, soil, minerals (abiotics)
2 Biosphere/ecosphere Animals, plants, micro-organisms
 • ecological or biotic environmental function
 • production function
 • biodiversity function
3 Hydrosphere/aquatic resources, e.g. fish
 • transportation
4 Atmosphere
 • climate
5 Negative wastes
 • terrestrial damage
 • aquatic pollution
 • atmospheric pollution
6 Ecosystems
 • sustainability
 • stability
 • resilience
 • development

---

1 Indigenous technical knowledge
2 Indigenous non-technical knowledge
3 Farming systems
 • agriculture-based
 • animal-based
 • pastoralism
 • multi-purpose
  – agroforestry
  – silvo-culture
  – alley cropping
4 Non-agricultural land use
 • infrastructure
 • human settlement
 • unproductive land

---

1 Social (relational) dimension:
 • social popular participation
 • social articulation of risks
  – non-exploitative resource tenure system
  – coping with risks (consumption) or
  – redistributive (horizontal solidarity)
 • risk management (income stabilization) through: risk pooling; reciprocal liens; diversification (activity, environment, temporal, technical)
2 Biological dimension
 • basic needs (housing/shelter, food)
 • health, education
 • recreation
3 Collective temporal insurance

---

1 Differential wealth accumulation
2 Inegalitarian temporal insurance
3 Vertical reciprocity: to the state or rural elite
4 Exploitative social relations
5 Individualization of risks
6 Peripheralization of the disadvantaged in society
7 Horizontal solidarity network becomes overstretched and limited diversified income structure
8 Social disqualification or social disaffiliation
9 Breakdown between society and individuals
10 Social exclusion indicators – income inequality, inegalitarian access to productive assets, resources and services
11 Social heterogeneity emerges

---

1 Ownership of national wealth, production and distribution
2 Egalitarian access to productive assets, valued resources and services
3 Ability to convert potential labour into actual labour (employment generation
4 Infrastructure
 • economic
 • commercial
 • institutional
5 Structural characteristics
6 Occupational structure

---

1 Feudal, semi-feudal and social institutions –
 • participatory, coercion,
 • representative, consultative
2 Democratic institutions rudimentary but people-centred
3 Political marginalization
 • right of political participation
 • socio-economic
  – personal security
  – equality of opportunity
 • civil
  – freedom of expression
  – freedom of association
  – rule of law
 • adversarial political relationships
4 Political instability
 • social strife
 • economic dislocation
 • migration and environmental damage
5 Regionalization and globalization of poverty

---

1 High property concentration
2 Great social inequality
3 Great income inequality
4 Production for the market
5 Capital-intensive and high productivity
6 Labour extensive
7 Dispersed institutions and services
8 Nuclear family system
9 Individual social security
10 Individual-centred

Figure 6 cont'd

characteristics of traditional society, largely from academic curiosity rather than for use in development intervention. As smallholder development proved singularly difficult, scholars, beginning the 1950s, launched farm management surveys, the scope of which was later enlarged to cover farming systems research but not investigation into the characteristic features of social economy. It is only recently that the issue has been recognized as being critical in development paradigms.

Sociosystem-ecosystem interactive dynamics Current concern with environmental deterioration has encouraged the linking of the ecological dimension with economic development and it is claimed that it is a new paradigm. This is not absolutely correct because our ancestors consistently linked ecological issues with resource utilization to guarantee resource adequate natural regeneration. Principally this was (and still is) due to the fact that increases in population pressure on increasingly scarce land resources results in the modification of the ecosystem. This change stimulates adaptive response (society action) and adaptive change (social organization) to changing ecological conditions. Through trial and error, technologies of relevance to the changing ecological settings are developed (technical change) and a set of rules, rights and obligations, including inherent environmental and social conflict resolutions, is codified into a specific culture, which Hayami and Ruttan (1971) called cultural endowments, which can be transmitted to new generations. The relationships among resource endowments, cultural endowments, technology and institutions are usually recursive in character. There is, therefore, a mutually self-reinforcing sociosystem-ecosytem combination and feedback which is maintained through a variety of mechanisms.

Some of these relationships had been expounded in co-evolutionary models. In its original concept, the co-evolutionary refers to a mutual interaction in predator-prey, host-parasite, and competitor-competitor system in which the nature of the relationship becomes more tightly defined in a struggle that could lead to extinction for one or the other (Norgaard, 1984, p. 528). In the context of agricultural development, the concept of co-evolution can be enlarged to encompass any benevolent feedback processes between two dynamic evolving systems – sociosystem and ecosystem. As man uses natural resources to satisfy his needs, these resources suffer perturbation in the form of a reduction in the quality and quantity of the stock of resources because the equilibrating mechanisms, such as nutrient recycling (natural regeneration), that have evolved get disrupted, leading to resource depletion.

In this way man's economic activities accelerate the ecosystem transformation (derived ecosystem). In response to the perturbation, and in a co-evolutionary development concept, a new sociosystem evolves to compensate for the displaced equilibrating mechanism. From a co-evolutionary perspective the feedback of technological and institutional changes on the ecosystem takes place as part of the recursive reciprocal processes. The various responses of the ecosystem to these feedbacks determine the relevance and successor failure of the new social system. These new sociosystem functions, involving labour, managerial effort, acquisition of knowledge and experience and the use of natural resources, are social costs which should be taken into account in the new interactions in order to determine net social benefits. The new interactions could include technical change (resource combinations and adaptations) and institutional changes (like resource tenure systems), including markets. Thus changes in resource endowments, technology and institutions can result in changes in cultural endowments.

In neoclassical theory, despite this fact, cultural endowments were taken as obstacles to technical change or institutional change, thus constraining economic growth. In the history of economic thought, theoretical discussion concerning economic development did not consider environmental resources as basic to economic growth. Only Malthus, in discussing the problem of population, expressed concern about the expansion of production under environmental constraints. The *laissez faire* economists advocated against state intervention in the economy in the belief that market forces would stimulate growth, and economic activities were regarded as having self-adjusting phenomena to create their own equilibrium after periodic oscillation in economic performance. These economists also favoured a piecemeal sectoral approach, since policies for individual sectors were formulated at a time such as commerce and trade during the mercantile era, and agriculture during the physiocrat period. Meanwhile Ricardo's views of the indestructible qualities of soil did help to promote the economics of resources, environment and economic growth or their linkages. It was not until the time of Keynes that economic theory was enlarged to include the concept of capital, saving, investment and consumption. Keynes also overlooked the issue of environment because he did not consider produced capital, capital generated from natural resources.

After World War II the introduction of formal economic growth models based on the rates of saving and investment and the productivity of capital literally shelved any consideration of environmental constraints to development. The use of high energy inputs in agricultural production and the adoption of high yielding crop varieties encouraged some economists to believe that the process of economic growth was making land in several Western countries less economically important (Schultz, 1951, pp. 725–40) while others concluded that changing land quality and resource availability was an insignificant *a priori* for economic growth (Kendrick, 1961, p. 393; Denison, 1962, p. 91). It was not until the mid-1960s that Boserup (1965), an anthropologist, introduced to the economic profession the thesis that agricultural development most likely occurs when population density increases sufficiently to strain a society's relationship to its environment, stimulate a new relationship and facilitate a more complex social order, a view re-echoed by Wilkinson (1973). The work of Boserup and Wilkinson, which was stimulated by environmental constraints, was the beginning of serious linking of environment with economic development.

a) *Institution mediation of demographic pressures and market forces on natural resources*

Since natural resource utilization is mediated through technology (means of manipulation-level of sophistication notwithstanding), resource renewability depends to a large extent on the magnitude, and rate of extraction, use and transformation, and the magnitude, rate and quality of feedback (depletion minus accumulation or natural regeneration). The resource utilization and management is regulated either within the informal indigenous institutions and organizations, or formal governmental machinery. One principal objective, regardless of the regulatory mechanism, is the use of resources sustainably.

It is helpful to review and analyse the relative and interacting influences of institutional arrangements, demographic pressures and market forces on land-based natural resources in order to be able to explain the situation of resource renewability. The reviews and analyses should not focus only on the larger socioeconomic variables like population and economy or micro-level cultural and institutional processes, but also should integrate both approaches in order to be able to explain forces influencing resource management and the general situation of renewable resources. Since the link between agriculture and population is mediated through indigenous (which include indigenous technical knowledge and technology) and formal institutions (such as development institutions), it is necessary to examine the nature and characteristics of local institutions essentially regarded as aggregates of specific sets of rules and cultural practices that govern resource management. These rules and practices codified in traditional norms form the basis that guides resource-user behaviour. It is, therefore, necessary to undertake micro-level examination of how communities create, adopt, respect, or break these rules regarding the management of natural resources under their control. In several instances they are broken due to hegemonic external forces. This review is essential because the result of resource utilization is an outcome of aggregate activities of resource users.

Although institutions are regarded as important in shaping the outcome of resource management, it is also necessary to identify and specify the types of practices and sets of rules which are critical in a given context within a given community. Because practices evolve over time, it is necessary to examine the contexuality from a historical perspective, with a focus on the history, social, economic and political systems from which the resource user groups emerged. In other words, practices are carried out in the social, political, economic and cultural context. This integrative approach facilitates the identification of aspects of the institutions which are crucial in resource utilization and renewability with some indication of the relative importance of different aspects. By disaggregating different aspects of the institution and the form of participation that influence user behaviour, it is possible to assess the consequences of the links between various factors that affect the status of natural resources.

Most of the demographic analyses are confined to the consequences of population pressure on soil degradation, soil erosion, loss of vegetation cover and biodiversity, growing food insecurity and general underdevelopment. Attempts should be made to explain how growing population (both human and animals) pressure contributes to environmental degradation. Finally, it is also found analytically helpful to assess the relationship between increasing marketization, and environmental degradation. As the economies of the region became integrated into larger global markets, it resulted in the commodification of land and labour creating greater market pressures on the natural resources as the population responded to economic opportunities created by the integration and then resorted to extractive form of agricultural practices with inadequate resource management practices.

b) *Micro-level analysis of land-use dimension*

The colonial administration introduced into the SSA region science-based technologies practised in advanced farming systems in developed countries at a time when they were poorly adapted to the complexities and intricacies of traditional agriculture. The consequences of these incongruent technologies had different implications for (and risks to) peasant farmers, the sustainability of the natural resource base, agricultural production and food security. Science-based technologies usually address problems of land scarcity and productivity, whereas in the case of SSA, the prevailing problems are the absence of significant capital amidst labour bottlenecks. The major household resource allocations, therefore, are centred around judicious resource combinations and adaptations to maximize output and minimize risks and uncertainties while at the same time ensuring resource renewability. In the context of the SSA region the natural resources' unique feature is characterized by open access to common pool resources (CPR) of soil, water, trees, fodder which contribute to livelihoods even though they are not privately owned. The sustainable productivity of these resources depends on the rational management of the interface between common pool resources and private agricultural resources (PAR) consisting of crops, trees and livestock. The indigenous management of the interface between CPR and PAR makes judicious and efficient use of the potentials for nutrient recycling and technical complementarities and supplementarities among resources (Figure 7).

The purpose of the micro-level analysis is to address the cardinal subject of land use in the context of the systems of land and land-based resource utilization being practised. The objective should be to investigate how variability of conditions regarding the quality of the natural resource base, household socioeconomic characteristics, policy and institutional environment faced by the farmers and how these conditions interact to determine choice of land use. Each part of the amalgam of land-use decision, it should be recognized, has implication for the other part, and therefore, land-use analysis must take into account their interactions, since conversions of land and land-based resources into different uses have different ramifications for the farmers' production function, income, food security and the sustainability of agricultural resource base. The objective is to assess the influences of: i) the natural resource endowments which have the potential of conditioning production shocks and associated income stabilization (diversification) strategies; ii) endowment dependent labour utilization such as intercropping or staggering planting essentially as a form of activity diversification to overcome labour bottleneck, and environment diversification by scattering fields of different crops to exploit spatial imbalances in resource quality; and iii) social institutions to which household has recourse (consumption stabilization and diversified income sources). The analysis can be based on the following regression equation:

$$Alu = b_0 + b_1 \, Nr + b_2 \, Hc + b_3 \, Pe + b_4 \, Ie \qquad (3)$$

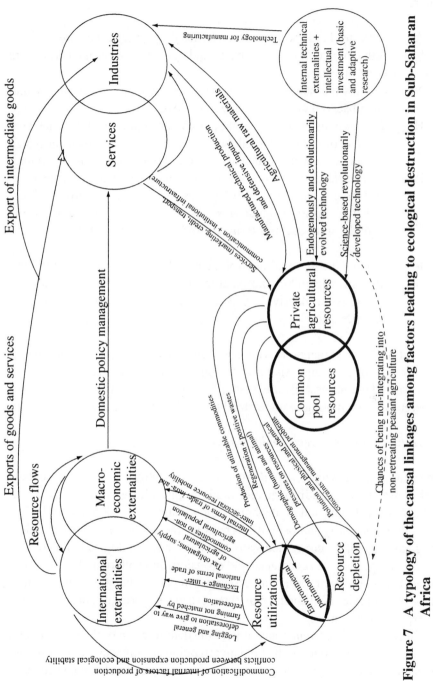

Figure 7   A typology of the causal linkages among factors leading to ecological destruction in Sub-Saharan Africa

where

Alu   indicates land use types (crops, cash crops, forest, pasture);
b_0 is the intercept; while b_1, b_2, b_3 and b_4 are vectors of the parameters to be investigated;
Nr   denotes the natural resource base represented by soil quality and any observed deterioration with use over time;
Hc   denotes household socioeconomic characteristics including the level of education, labour availability, off-farm employment, farm size and any observed trends, and any other relevant locational factors;
Pe   denotes the policy environment capturing such aspects like the broad incentive structure (relative prices of inputs and outputs, fiscal incentive, taxation, direct subsidies, internal and international terms of trade, intra-sectoral terms of trade, intersectoral terms of trade, etc.); and
Ie   denotes institutional environment including access to and quality of economic and institutional infrastructure, access to technology, access to productive assets and services, use of modern inputs, indebtedness.

Not all these explanatory variables can be used in land and land-based resources utilization analysis because some are likely to affect one type of land use and not necessarily the others. The cardinal issue is to ensure micro-coherency in attempting to understand the different land-use systems

c) *Technical and socioeconomic dimension*

The main concern with *technical progress* is to investigate the technical details and constraints of traditional and modern agriculture with emphasis on indigenous technical and nontechnical knowledge and modern technologies, and complementarity and/or conflicts between them. The analysis of technical progress is not only concerned with advances in technologies but also with their relevance, social acceptance and diffusion, and pattern and direction of speed, especially their social and economic impacts. The rate of diffusion of these technologies is influenced by three broad categories of public policies, as expressed earlier.

Because of the current concern with the deterioration of the quantity and quality of natural resources, the field investigation of technical progress should be expanded to include *ecological approaches* to studying the consequences of resource flow process – a series of dynamic interactions between the living (biotic) and the non-living (abiotic) components of the environment (see Figure 2). Following natural resources' contact with man, human activities transform part of these resources from their natural state into tangible consumable commodities, or utilizable flow resources such as soil, water, biotics and minerals. The flow of resources (social utility) has some consequences for natural resource renewability. Man is the principal catalyst in the interactions of living organisms (biological resources) with one another on the one hand, and the physical environment on the other, in a constant exchange of matter and energy, processes called the ecosystems. Human activities should, therefore, be studied not in isolation but in the context of the physical environment which consists of the lithosphere (terrestrial or earth resources), the hydrosphere (living and non-living aquatic resources) and the atmosphere (air, climate). The portion of the environment which contains life is called the biosphere. Because the biosphere interfaces with the lithosphere, atmosphere and the hydrosphere, and because it is within the biosphere that human economic activities occur, this portion of the environment is, therefore, also called the ecosphere. Because of these dynamic interactions, and to successfully neutralize any destructive consequences of macroeconomy-environment interactions, it has become necessary to shift away from a planning system which advances sectoral interest to an integrative approach that emphasizes macro-coherency in the context of internalizing environmental issues within development framework. Equally important is the micro-coherency, which addresses social factors influencing the way populations interact with the environment. The new paradigms in agricultural and rural development, therefore, are macro- and micro-coherency.

Because natural resources (renewable, flow and non-renewable) were regarded as unpriced free gift of nature, environmental issues in SSA remained peripheral to the mainstream of macroeconomic policy framework. Consequently, the implementation of development programmes did not anticipate the likely negative impacts, on the quality and quantity of natural resources, and no remedial measures were incorporated in policy framework. When natural resources were not under pressure, environmental degradation was minor. However, because of increasing population pressure on these finite resources, it has become imperative to internalize environmental externalities into development paradigms.

Social development policy analysis is concerned with the diagnosis of development constraints in terms of social factors which influence resource use and management. The major political goal, for instance, could be to achieve a socially and politically acceptable sharing of the costs and benefits of development between competing social groups (i.e. basic terms of trade, consumer and producer benefits, producer income, consumption, nutrition, poverty, income distributional conflicts, etc.). In this context the scope of the analysis is enlarged to embrace: i) an evaluation of access qualification focusing on patterns of access to productive resources, ownership of valued resources, access to services, and individual financial standing and socioeconomic status; ii) social production relations, especially resource tenure systems, labour availability and profile, sexual division of labour and labour participation rates; iii) community organizations and patterns, and forms of participation especially decision-making on issues that affect the welfare of the people; iv) assessment of perceived priority needs for economic and social development, interpersonal income distribution, and poverty profiles by sex and effective mechanisms for recognizing the role and the special needs of the disadvantaged in society; and v) cultural democracy (direct, participatory, consultative, representative, consensus, coercion, etc.).

Social development analysis has simultaneously a dual political and economic aim. In traditional societies there are indigenous institutions with multiple cultural, economic and political responsibilities. The main responsibility is to preserve family institutions for biological reproduction and inter-generational solidarity as well as agricultural production units. From the political perspective these institutions serve as media for conflict resolution and to promote horizontal inter-household harmony and a generally conducive environment for social and economic progress. From the economic perspective the institutions are responsible for ensuring rational utilization and protection of natural resources under their control, and authority to sanction any misuse of resources. They are also responsible for preserving non-exploitative social agricultural production relations such as reciprocal liens on non-produced factor (labour) and productive resources of kinsmen. All these arrangements guarantee rational resource utilization, social solidarity and security, and, above all, community survival. Under the circumstances, understanding and building the capacity of these indigenous institutions could provide a viable vehicle for a broad-based self-sustaining development.

The *economic analysis* is essentially a much more aggregate assessment of the economic viability of return on investment, analysed from the perspective of the value added by the investment, applying established economic analysis criteria. In a *socioeconomic analysis* the analyst is concerned not only with economic viability but also with how the national wealth is owned, produced and distributed. The analysis incorporates both the social and economic concerns.

In order to design appropriate development intervention, there is the need to understand the complex network of socioeconomic factors which limit the diffusion and adoption of technical and institutional innovations. These include the understanding of the local land tenure system, attitudes of farmers, their objectives, seasonal cash profiles, traditional demands for the farmers' time, and a multiplicity of other factors likely to affect the plan for the farm improvement. There are also some aspects of science and technology which involve plants, soils, animals, pests, diseases, etc. They require careful testing under local conditions before they are extended to the farmers. The other aspect concerns the growth, change and development of the rural populations, their institutions, and impacts on the environment and the performance of the agricultural sector. Many agricultural and rural development projects have failed for a number of reasons: lack of participation of project beneficiaries in rural poverty appraisal and identification and formulation of projects; lack of commitment as a consequence of this lack of participation; lack of building consensus and inadequate assessment of risks and likely impacts of the projects. It is the poor rural population who understand the nature and extent of the poverty they face. They are the ones who are better placed to know what motivates them to improve their own conditions, which will depend on their appreciation of the opportunities open to them, the perceived risks involved in taking the opportunities, and the technical, physical, institutional limitations facing them. It is, therefore, imperative to undertake creative diagnosis of constraints and potentials of the rural environment.

The farmers having reached more or less their maximum productive capacity, their acceptance of technological innovation will depend on the spread of simple improved technologies. The diffusion can be facilitated if the smallholders' values, beliefs, behavioural characteristics, natural and the institutional constraints facing them as farmers/households are understood. Some of this anthropological, sociological and economic knowledge is available from past research findings but requires updating through short-term qualitative surveys to fill the gap, and missing knowledge can be gained from concurrent research. These surveys do not only provide information on the economics of smallholder agriculture but also document what farmers do and why they do it that way. While a number of micro-level studies have been conducted in the region, they have been on an *ad hoc* basis taken largely by expatriates, in most cases for single-end purposes. In order to design strategic and tactical research programmes, it is necessary to gain a clearer understanding of the physical, social and economic environment within which the smallholder operates, and the technical and institutional constraints facing him.

Previous developments, in part, have been achieved through the enforcement of agricultural by-laws and taking advantage of the political force of the local chiefs. This approach prejudiced governments in appreciating the need for detailed appraisal of measures and inducements which motivate the farmers to adopt improved practices. The early compulsion and directions to effect change are now known to be ineffective in making the farmers perceive the merits of improved cultural practices. Improved crop varieties and animal breeds have been developed over the years but they are intended to be grown and raised under improved farming systems. The difficulties encountered in spreading the innovation stems from lack of farm management data which could have helped in appraising correctly in advance what measures should be adopted to introduce innovations successfully. Such appraisal should include aspects such as ecological, customary and economic constraints. Physical and technical aspects are fairly well documented, but these by themselves are not enough; they should be complemented by what inducements are sufficient to motivate the farmers to change to improved agricultural production methods. The pioneers of micro-level economic research argued that a major obstacle to formulating meaningful policies and programmes for assisting smallholders is the inadequate knowledge of the nature of traditional agricultural production. This knowledge can only be gained through more precise and systematic microeconomic analysis based on accurate primary micro-data. The deficiency is particularly critical in appraising the suitability of new biochemical technologies in the traditional agricultural systems which have developed over the years and are fairly stable. The pioneers believed that the generation of the technical and socioeconomic information would facilitate a better choice of strategic factors in development and investment strategies.

It is essential to examine social factors that may influence farming activities of individual smallholder. In a developing country, these social factors may be in a state of transition and, therefore, the analysis should include an examination of social and moral values of the social groups to which a farmer belongs. These values may be religious, customary or traditional in nature. The starting point is the analysis of the demographic features, which involves a study of total population of the area or country, net migration and emigration, age and sex structure, family structure, and the determination of how many persons are affected by the decisions made, etc. The analysis should be extended to include an examination of the distribution of population, density, occupational structure (to indicate any possible division of function between groups), health of the people in which sickness (morbidity) may or may not have a seasonal pattern, and the pattern of development which may determine the future development.

The analysis of labour availability and profile is critical. The analyst should examine the extent to which labour is pooled at peak labour use periods and age and sex, which may affect the division of labour. A wide decision-making process in a society may constitute a major factor which may influence or even change the pattern of agriculture and hence labour use. It should, therefore, be systematically examined. For instance, usually there are leaders in any society. Any change advocated by these leaders could facilitate acceptance of innovation or it may be regarded as being alien practice and as such may cause some antagonism from members of the society. This may happen with changes in land tenure systems, consolidation of fragmented holdings, and the right of the individual smallholder or cultivator, and that change or right may offset the development processes. It is, therefore, essential to assess factors which influence land tenure systems: the political system and situation, the natural resources, the structure of the economy, the social system, the demographic situation and the agricultural systems (Figure 6).

While examining labour problems, the analyst should also examine the size of the farms. Where land is held communally, the size of farms may be limited by labour availability. Inheritance of land or its transfer may be legal, semi-legal or even by the use of force. This is worth examining because it can affect development. Some other special environment considerations include such aspects as:

- the extent of education of the farmers compared with the rest of the population;
- the role of government in respect of general administration, tax collection, delivery services such as water supply, health facilities, etc.;
- the role of government technical departments, in particular to what extent are they complementary or supplementary to or conflicting with each other and how advice to farmers is given, such as in the form of coercion, order when enforcing agricultural bye-laws, persuasion or explanation;
- the number of technical staff in the field to effect change in respect of development; and
- an examination of the possible conflicts between groups, tribes or clans which could be an impediment to agricultural development.

In addition to social institutions, there may also be agricultural institutions to further agricultural development. Classical examples are cooperative societies, credit schemes, financial institutions (formal and informal), advisory services, farmers' clubs, agricultural and cooperative colleges, farmer training institutions. All these should be carefully examined since they influence the process of development.

A Critique of Some Social Valuation Measures

Elimination of Border Distortions

The use of shadow prices in social cost-benefit analysis has some inherent weaknesses. The heavy reliance on the use of international prices for traded goods does not take into account distortions in markets in developed countries. In many of these industrialized countries, the large presence of unemployed labour and the market wage of labour exaggerates the real scarcity of labour and does not reflect competitive equilibrium values. The existence of non-optimal income distribution of purchasing power in turn affects the structure of market prices. Other common price imperfections arise from international commodity agreements between producers and consumers. Under these agreements market management controls price movement within agreed bans, which does not necessarily reflect the real price, which could in turn distort allocation of resources. Price support given to farmers in developed countries also distorts international prices. Thus the elimination of border distortions actually distorts domestic prices. Certain policy decisions, especially the use of interest rates for macroeconomic management purposes in developed countries, omit the interest of third parties either as beneficiaries or sharers of the burden of costs. The other border distortions arise from the foreign aid conditionality, especially the requirement under tied-aid. Foreign aid is either project-tied or procurement-tied. Under these conditions the aid recipient is denied the opportunity to procure from competitive alternative markets where prices are low but forced to procure from the donor country. This results in once-and-for-all and continuing costs because of tying aid.

Elimination of Domestic Distortions

Domestic distortions are caused by many factors, especially market fragmentation and obliterated price signals. There are many causes for market fragmentation: i) the existence of surpluses in areas having locational comparative advantage and shortages in resource poor areas; ii) failure of market forces either due to poor internal distribution system and lack of market transparency or cartelization; iii) intertemporal market fragmentation due to the seasonality of agricultural production, a situation exacerbated by lack of storage facilities and delivery services; iv) differences in dietary habits among different populations that restrict intra-regional trade; and v) spatial imbalances in population. Domestic distortions also arise due to difficulty in resolving conflicting objectives between equity and efficiency pricing policy. As the principal source of fiscal resources the agricultural sector is excessively and effectively taxed resulting in resource transfer from the sector to other sectors of the economy.

Notes

1 Society is usually taken as an organized set of individuals with a given way of life, and it is taken to be an aggregate of social relations. Society emphasizes the human component, the aggregate of people and the relations between them (Ruttan, 1988, S262). Sometimes 'social system' is used to designate the specifically relational system of interaction among individuals and collectivities.

2 Culture, on the other hand emphasizes the component of accumulated resources, immaterial as well as material, which the people inherit, employ, add to and transmit. It is that complex whole which includes knowledge, belief, art, morals, law, custom and any other capabilities and habits acquired by man as a member of society.

3 Agro-ecology is a methodological framework for a better understanding of the nature of agro-ecosystems and the principles by which they function. It integrates agronomic, ecological and socioeconomic principles in evaluating the effect of technologies on farming systems and society at large, and it goes beyond a one-dimensional view of genetics, agronomy, edaphology to include ecological, social and cultural consideration. The agro-ecological approach encourages researchers/analysts to benefit from farmers' knowledge and skills. The basic technical elements of an agro-ecological strategy which can be used in environmental recovery include the following:

a) *conservation and regeneration of natural resources*:

    i) soil (erosion control, fertility and plant health);
    ii) water (harvesting, *in situ* conservation, management, irrigation);
    iii) germ plasm (plant and animal native species, land races, adapted germ plasm); and
    iv) beneficial fauna and flora (natural enemies, pollinators, multiple use vegetation).

b) *management of productive resources*:

    i) diversification covering temporal (rotation, sequences, staggering planting); spatial (polycultures, agro-forestry, crop/livestock mixed systems; genetic (multilines), regional (zonification, watershed, spatial diversification);
    ii) recycling of nutrients and organic matter: plant biomass (green manure, crop residues, nitrogen fixation), animal biomass (solid waste, manure, liquid waste); reutilization of nutrients and resources internal and external to the farm; and

iii) biotic regulation (crop protection and animal health); natural biological control (enhancement of natural control agents); artificial biological control (importation and augmentation of natural enemies, botanical insecticides, alternative veterinary drugs (UNDP, 1995).

The ecosystem encompasses the interactions of living organisms (biological resources) with one another, on the one hand, and the physical environment, on the other, in a constant exchange of matter and energy.

4   The proponents of the integrative approach advocate the integration of economic and non-economic variables in the analysis of development processes. Economic development processes tend to be analysed using almost entirely economic parameters, and the role of non-economic factors are ignored. According to Farrington and Boyd (1997) the roles of social, cultural and economic variables are critical for agricultural development.

5   Farmers' knowledge encompasses the complex nature of peasants' ethnological knowledge. Ethnology is the study and description of indigenous ethnic rural groups' knowledge systems about the natural world which includes linguistics, botany, zoology, craft skills and agriculture, which is derived from the direct interaction between human and the environment. Indigenous peoples' knowledge about soils, climates, vegetation, animals and ecosystems usually results in multidimensional productive strategies such as multiple ecosystems with multiple species.

There is also the experimental nature of traditional knowledge which is based not only on acute observation but also on experimental learning, which is very evident in the selection of seed varieties for specific environments and in testing new cultivation methods to overcome particular biological or socioeconomic constraints.

Knowledge of farming practices designed to optimize productivity include: i) spatial and temporal diversification and continuity; ii) optimal use of space and resources (combining plants with different habits, canopies, and root structures which allows better use of environmental inputs of nutrients, water and solar radiation, recycling of nutrients; and iii) control of succession and protection of crops such as mixing crops providing insurance against attacks from insects or diseases; and canopies effectively suppressing weed growth and mulching avoiding evapo-transpiration and erosive water run-off (UNDP, 1995).

6   Cultural endowments constitute part of farmers' technical and nontechnical knowledge, and are used to capture those dimensions of culture that have been transmitted from the past. Contemporary changes in resource endowments, technology, and institutions often result in changes in cultural endowments available to future generations.

2 Theoretical Basis for Social Valuation of Production Factors

Introduction

The pricing of factors of production in Africa, other than the prices of technical inputs, was the least practised. This was because the primary factor of production, land, was not yet a major constraint, or it had only an 'opportunity cost'. Labour, however, presented a major constraint to agricultural development, and was a subject for discussion and controversy over a number of years. The first argument centred around the 'target income' concept in which it was thought that once an income level has been reached, an African would make no further effort to increase output. Subsequent field investigation, however, indicated that Africans responded positively to innovations if the rewards were judged as being attractive. Apparently with this concept in mind, earlier labour policy in Eastern and Central Africa entailed the enforcement of tax laws in order to force Africans to work for wages. The other argument centred around marginal productivity concept. It was argued that as excess labour supply existed in rural areas, the marginal productivity of labour was zero. However, results of labour use surveys discounted this concept of marginal productivity of labour. Evidence from field investigation indicated that the seasonality of agricultural production caused serious labour constraints at certain periods of the year. Under these circumstances, marginal productivity of labour fluctuated throughout the year, being high at peak labour demand periods and low at slack periods (Okai, 1974).

The Concept of Structure of an Economy

The basis of the well-being of the population of any country is the quantity of goods and services produced in the country. These physical units of goods and services produced within the country are expressed or valued at market prices which reflect the willingness of the consumers and producers to pay for the goods and services they actually buy.

The primary concern of any nation is development, which includes the economy of the country and how that economy operates, and also includes the character and behaviour of the people. In other words, development is concerned with society – in particular, human welfare. Economic welfare in this respect is concerned with increased production and supply of useful commodities to meet the demand of society. The production process is based upon the use of land, tools and equipment, raw materials and human effort. In other words, production is based on an organized human effort to meet the needs of human beings and, therefore, adds to human welfare. The basic production unit is the combination of these inputs of land, tools and equipment, and human effort designed to carry out production. It is continuously seeking alternatives – the best ways to produce commodities, and the best commodities to produce in order to increase human welfare. The organized human effort is also the relation of production units within the economy such as the production and distribution of commodities taking place within markets. Increases in human welfare, therefore, depend upon the successful linking up of production units through markets. Marketing is basically a primary mechanism for coordinating production, distribution, and consumption activities.

Development planning is not only concerned with production but also with the interrelationships of production units within the economy. Production can be expected to increase as producers see opportunities for production, and these producers develop new ways of carrying out the production process. Development planning is intended to investigate and discover possible interrelationships within the economy, give *perspective* on the economy and design appropriate development intervention to accelerate increases in production. To clarify these interrelationships, it is better understood if the broad structure of the economy is presented in numerical forms. The analysis is concerned primarily with estimating in numerical terms the size and character of the overall economy. This is essential because understanding the overall dimensions of the economy enables one to see the actual or possible interrelations of sectors and the overall economy. In Table 1, a hypothetical economy is presented in a simplified form. Each figure of the different sectors is derived by multiplying the number of physical units of a commodity by its market price. The results are *values* which go to make up the total economy. The first observation that can be made about any economy is that there is a relationship between *total demand for output* and *total supply* of *inputs*. In

Table 1 the two are equal – both equal to 2,005. In this case an economy in this sense can be equated with one overall market where demand equals supply, usually taken as the size of the economy. The amount of production occurring is related to how much individuals, families and groups in the country will receive in income. Both demand for output and total supply of inputs can be grouped to give more detail about the economy. For demand there are three divisions: *intermediate, final* and *total demand*. In Table 1, under the column *total intermediate demand*, the three figures of 100, 130 and 325 are the sums of each of the respective preceding numbers in each row. For instance, the row labelled *primary* has 30, 60 and 10 adding up to 100.

Each economy traditionally is categorized into primary (represented by agriculture), secondary (consisting of industrial activities), and tertiary (the services sector both government, and private). In other words, each sector denotes various types of groupings of production. Outputs from the agricultural sector are demanded as inputs to the primary (30), secondary (60) and tertiary (10) sectors. In other words, intermediate demand means that output from one sector is to serve as inputs to another sector for further production. It is, therefore, possible to distinguish between inputs already available for production in a given period of time and inputs that have to be produced as output from within the economy. The chains of market activities are, therefore, made up, in part, of these input-output relations among sectors. In Table 1 the column *total final demand* is based on the sum of each row of the figures preceding the column *total final demand*. The primary sector consists of consumption (800) + investment (100) + exports (100) which equals to 1000 *(total final demand)*. Each of these types of final demand is based on different uses to which commodities are put by individuals, families and groups within the economy. Also, each differs from intermediate demand in that the final demand for commodities does not involve further production. Consumption is undertaken by individuals, families and groups within the economy. Consumption is undertaken by individuals like, in the case of agriculture, food crops contribute significantly to consumption within the economy. Investment contributes to commodities that are used for further production over a longer period of time. In this case investment is different from those commodities used in providing services to the country while exports are destined for use outside the country and, therefore, do not enter further production in the economy.

Referring to Table 1, each sector *total intermediate* and *total final demand* equals to *total demand for output*. Again, looking at the *value* of the total supply of commodities available in any period of time, it is essentially the

Table 1   Input-output relations and value-added for an economy in millions Maloti

Demand for output by

Supply of inputs from	Primary	Second-ary	Tertiary	Total inter-mediate demand	Con-sump-tion	Invest-ment	Govern-ment	Export	Total final demand	Total demand for output
Primary	30	60	10	100	800	100	100	1,000	1,100	
Secondary	20	80	30	130	50	200	50		300	430
Tertiary	150	75	100	325	50		100		150	475
Imports	5	30	15							
Value-added	895	185	320							
Total supply of inputs	1,100	430	475							2,005

difference between *total demand for output* and *intermediate demand*. This is because the outputs from the three producing sectors were partly absorbed into further production and only show up as part of the *total* final demand. This can be illustrated by subtracting from *total final demand for output* for each sector, the produced inputs that each sector utilized in carrying out production as follows:

Primary	1,100	-30	-20	-150	=	900
Secondary	430	-30	-80	-75	=	215
Tertiary	475	-10	-30	-100	=	335
	2,005	100	130	325		1,450

The figure 1,450 equals to the sum of *total final demand for output* by sectors (1,000 + 300 + 150). Consequently the amount of 1,450 also equals to the *value* of the total supplies of commodities available to the entire economy in a period of time. Also each sector uses imports for production. If the imports are subtracted from available supplies of commodities (900-5, 215-30, 335-15) for the respective sectors we get a value of 1,400 which equals to the sum of *value-added* for the sectors. Value-added is the value of domestic commodities available to the economy. They do not constitute part of the commodities the economy had produced since imports has been produced from abroad. This can be expressed as:

The value-added = (1,400)
Consumption + investment + government + exports - imports.
   (900)   (300)   (150)   (100) - (50)

Then the value of domestic commodities available is equal to domestic demand for output.

The value-added is referred to as gross domestic income consisting of consumption (C) + investment (I) + government (G) + exports (X) - import (M) – C+I+G+X-M is taken as gross domestic product (GDP). Domestic demand on the one hand and imported goods and services (I) on the other hand is another important aspect of the concept of structure of the economy. On the demand side, there are goods and services used within the country (domestic absorption (DA)) and those exported. The DA is further decomposed into private and public consumption and investment. The breakdown reflects the structure of domestic absorption (domestic demand) and the resource balance of the economy represented by the following equation:

$$GDP + M = C + I + X \tag{1}$$

Imports, as stated earlier, do not affect the *value* of domestic supply of commodities available, although imports are included in any economy as part of the *total final demand*. The input-output relations and the amounts and composition of gross domestic income and GDP make up what is the structure of the economy. To maintain balance of values the two sides of the equation must be equal. This is commonly not easy to maintain in a dynamic economic situation. The most frequent factor that upsets this equation is demand inflation.

These physical units of goods and services produced within the country are expressed or valued at market prices which reflect the willingness of consumers and producers to pay for the goods and services they actually buy. At the national level, the collection of goods and services valued at market prices yields the gross domestic product (GDP) at current market prices. These prices include indirect taxes (value-added, consumption, turnover taxes, etc.) which usually vary for different commodities. Many economists, therefore, prefer a more objective valuation in terms of domestic costs of production. In this case the GDP at factor costs is arrived at by subtracting from the GDP at current market prices the total value of indirect taxes imposed on different commodities.

Measurement of Values of Goods and Services

Measurement of Output Values

The first exercise introduces the concept of economic growth and the techniques for its measurement. As explained, the GDP is an indicator of the wealth of a country and the capacity of producing goods and services for the local consumption and export. The GDP growth over time is the result of two different factors; price increases (P) and quantity increases (Q), i.e. GDP = P x Q. In this expression the GDP is given at current prices with P representing the set of prices prevailing in each year and is used in measuring the GDP values. In a simple economy where two goods are produced the GDP is expressed as

$$GDP_t = (Pot \times Qot) + (Pit \times Qit) \tag{2}$$

where 'o' and 'i' indicate two different commodities and 't' is year one.

$$GDP\ t+1 = (P_{ot+1} \times Q_{ot+1}) + (P_{it+1} \times Q_{it+1}) \tag{3}$$

where t+1 is the following year.

In this case the GDP growth at current prices is measured by the change of GDP_{t+1} over GDP_{ot}. However, the main interest is to measure the growth of the welfare of the country in real terms in order to capture the actual increase in the quantities of goods and services produced. Since the GDP is the outcome of the production of a variety of different commodities, it is not possible to sum up the physical units. The procedure usually followed is to measure the GDP in constant prices which can either be at time 't' or at time 't + 1', or if it is over a long time series, the base year could be the midterm year. In the above equation the growth from GDP_t to GDP_{t+1} is measured at constant prices and it is the increase in quantities that will indicate GDP growth rate.

Traditionally the time series of GDP at current prices is provided along with the GDP implicit deflator. The GDP deflator is a price index such as the consumer price index (CPI) or the wholesale price index (WPI) or the national combined index of prices of all goods and services in the GDP. Dividing the GDP at current prices by the implicit GDP deflator and multiplying by 100 yields the GDP at constant prices. In order better to assess the evolution of GDP over time, it is usually expressed in terms of a base year. Dividing all the time series values by the base year value results in the GDP index number. The base year index number is usually 100 and all the other values are expressed in terms of relative movements from the base year. One other indicator of the overall welfare of a country is the GDP per capita. This is calculated as the ratio of GDP at current or constant prices to total population. It is used to assess the growth of per capita income overtime. The other important issue is the decomposition of GDP into its constituent industrial origin (agriculture, manufacturing, etc.).

Measurement of Growth Rates and Trends

In order to measure changes in domestic price movement and changes in terms of trade, it is necessary to decompose the GDP into its principal sectoral sources of contributions. However, measuring GDP at current prices can give an unrealistic growth rate of the economy, especially at time of high domestic inflation. To overcome this weakness, GDP values are given both in current and constant prices for the base period to measure future GDP. This yields real GDP. Estimates of GDP at current prices compared to GDP at constant prices can then be used to assess the levels of domestic price movements by computing the GDP implicit deflator, derived by deflating the current price GDP estimates at market prices (purchaser prices) by constant price GDP estimates. Traditionally, therefore, real producer price is obtained by deflating the nominal prices by the respective consumer price indices.

Once the GDP time series is expressed in constant prices, one can then compute the growth rate. In order to gain a better understanding of the meaning and significance of time data series, it is useful to compute trends as performance indicators. One of the most common methodologies for measuring trends is the calculation of annual growth rates, the percentage value that indicates how much a variable has changed on the average each year. This can be calculated in three different ways: the observed values, a linear regression and an exponential regression.

The first method, the observed values, is the simplest because it simply consists of taking the initial and the terminal values of the time series and computing the annual compound rate using the following formula:

$$Y_t = Y_0 (1+R)^t \text{ or} \tag{4}$$

$$R = {}^t Y_t / Y_0 - 1 \tag{5}$$

where

Y_o is the initial observed value;
Y_t is the terminal value;
R   is the annual compound growth rate; and
t   is time.

This method, however, has some serious drawbacks because it utilizes only the first and the terminal values of the time series, omitting the rest. If one of the two values is abnormal, the growth rate will not reflect the real trend. This problem can be overcome partially by taking an average of the first three years and the last three years, but still all the remaining years have no role in the determination of the growth rate.

The second method consists of the use of linear regression in determining the trend and then computing the growth rate. In this case all the values are used and a line is drawn among them to reflect the trend. The theoretical values of the first (the intercept) and the last value of the linear trend line are then used to derive the growth rate by applying formula (4).

Simple linear regression analysis is carried out using the following regression equation:

$$Y = a + b X \tag{6}$$

where

a   is the intercept;
b   is value of elasticity;
Y   is the dependent variable; and
X   is the independent variable

$$b = \frac{n \Sigma xY - (\Sigma x) (\Sigma Y)}{n \Sigma x^2 - (\Sigma x)^2} \text{ or } b = \frac{\Sigma xy}{\Sigma x2}$$

Where $x = X - \bar{X}$ and $y = Y - \bar{Y}$

$$a = \bar{Y} - b \bar{x} \text{ or } a = \frac{\Sigma xy - n \bar{X} \bar{Y}}{\Sigma x^2 - n \bar{x}^2} \text{ or } a = \frac{\Sigma xy}{\Sigma x^2}$$

where n is the number of observations.

$$r = \frac{n \sum XY - \sum X \sum Y}{\sqrt{[n\sum X^2 - (\sum X)^2][nY^2 - (\sum Y)^2]}}$$

Example

% growth rate of agric. output   % growth rate of agric. labour force

	Y	X
Sahelian	7.2	1.5
Coastal West	3.2	1.7
Coastal East	4.4	0.6
Equitorial	4.2	1.0
E. Central	4.2	1.1
East Africa	4.6	1.6
Σ	23.8	7.5
Mean	3.47	1.25

y	x	xy
-0.77	0.25	-0.1925
-0.77	0.45	-0.3465
0.43	-0.65	-0.2795
0.23	-0.75	-0.0575
0.23	0.15	-0.0345
0.63	0.35	0.2205
Σxy		-0.6900

$\sum x^2 = 0.895$

$\sum y^2 = 1.8734$

$b = \dfrac{0.6900}{0.895} = -0.77$

$a = +3.97 - (-0.77)\,1.25$
$= 4.9325$

∴ regression is $Y = 4.9325 - 0.77\,X$

In this example the line slopes downward (declining).

Coefficient of determination is the action which explains the variation

$$\text{i.e. } r^2 = \frac{b\,\Sigma xy}{\Sigma y^2} = -\frac{0.77 \times 0.69}{1.8734} = \frac{0.5313}{1.8734} = 0.2836$$

i.e. only 28.36 per cent of the variation in the rate of growth of agricultural production is explained by the rate growth of the agricultural labour force.

$$\text{Correlation coefficient} = \pm\sqrt{r^2} = r$$

$$\pm\sqrt{0.2836} = \pm 0.53$$

According to regression equation $r = -0.53$ which is a relatively weak negative correlation.

The other method is the use of geometric mean (gm). It is an average which is found by multiplying the number (n) of variables together and then taking the nth root of them. For instance, the geometric mean of 4 and 7 is the square root of 4 x 7. Thus GM equals:

$$\sqrt{4 \times 7} = \sqrt{28} = 5.29$$

The geometric mean of 3, 25 and 45 is:

$$\sqrt[3]{3 \times 25 \times 45} \quad = \quad \sqrt[3]{3375} = 15$$

The general formula for geometric mean is:

$$\sqrt[n]{X_1, X_2, X_3 \,\text{---}\, X_n}$$

The third method of measuring trends consists of computing the growth rate using the exponential regression. By taking the logarithm, one can linearize equation (4) as follows:

$$\text{Log } Y_t = t \;\; \text{Log } (1+R) + \text{Log } Y_o$$

This actually corresponds to the usual linear form:

$$Y = bX + A \tag{7}$$

This can be rewritten as follows:

$$\text{Curve} = Y = A\,(B)^{\,n} \tag{8}$$

Taking logarithms on both sides we get:

$$\text{Log } Y = \text{Log } A + n \text{ Log } B$$
$$\text{Log } A = a + bX$$

$$\hat{b} = \frac{\Sigma \text{ Log } Y\,(x - \bar{x})}{\Sigma\,(x - x)^{\,2}} = \frac{\dfrac{\Sigma x \Sigma \text{ Log } Y}{n}}{\Sigma x^{2} - \dfrac{(x)^{2}}{n}} \tag{9}$$

$$\hat{a} = \overline{\text{Log } Y} - b\,\bar{x} \tag{10}$$

where n is the number of observations.

This can be illustrated using data from Liberia (Table 2).

Using the above formulae

$$\hat{b} = \frac{437.748304 - \dfrac{(7 \times 61.677162)}{13}}{819 - 637} = \frac{6.008170}{182}$$

$$= 0.033012$$

or

$$\hat{B} = \text{antilog } \hat{b} = 1.078976$$

$$\hat{a} = \overline{\log Y} \quad - \quad \hat{b}\,\overline{X}$$
$$= 4.744397 - 0.033012 \times 7$$
$$= 4.744397 - 0.231084$$
$$= 4.513313$$

Table 2   Liberia: structure of exported quantities of agricultural commodities – rubber

Y	Metric tons	Log Y	X	X log Y	X 2
1961	41200	4.614897	1	4.614897	1
1962	45390	4.656962	2	9.313920	4
1963	41340	4.616370	3	13.849110	9
1964	35100	4.545307	4	18.181228	16
1965	43590	4.639386	5	23.196930	25
1966	45170	4.654850	6	27.929100	36
1967	51880	4.715000	7	33.005000	49
1968	52040	4.716337	8	37.730696	64
1969	65633	4.817122	9	43.354098	81
1970	83415	4.921244	10	49.212440	100
1971	84575	4.927242	11	54.199662	121
1972	83289	4.920588	12	59.047056	144
1973	85479	4.931859	13	64.114167	169
Totals (Σ)		61.677162	91	437.748304	819
Means ($\bar{X}$)		4.744397	7	33.672946	

A = Antilog   â = 32607
Curve = Y = A (B)^X. Y = 32607 (1.078976)^{13}.

By 1973 total exports were 81,180 tons. Computed absolute growth (81,180 - 32,607) ÷ 32,607 = 1.4896.

This is an increase from 1 to 2.4896 per cent or 148.96 per cent accumulated in 13 years resulting from an annual compound growth rate of 7.27 per cent, and the figure illustrates observed and linear trends (Figure 8).

$$\hat{B} = (1 + \frac{r}{100})$$

$$r = (\hat{B} - 1) \, 100$$
$$= (1.078976 - 1) \, 100$$
$$= 7.89 \, \%$$

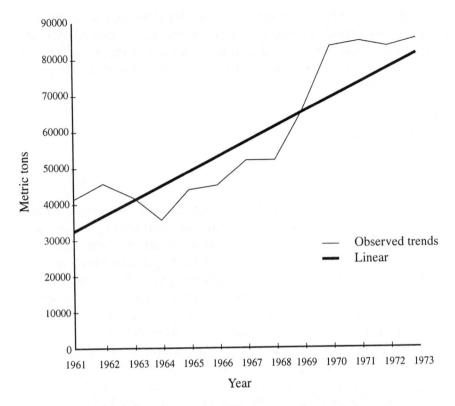

Figure 8   Liberia: structure of exported quantities of agricultural commodities – rubber

Sources of Agricultural Growth

The third step is to calculate sources of growth of total agricultural production. In the first place the changes or variations of the value of each commodity over the previous year is calculated (Qot - Qt + 1) on an absolute basis. The sum of the variations is totalled for each year and the sum is used to compute the percentage share of each commodity. Often it is also necessary to disaggregate sources of growth each by yield and area. To calculate the effect of changes in area or yield on seasonal output, initially one has to compute the growth rates of total areas, yield and production. One of the most common ways of measuring the trends is through the computation of annual growth rates (the percentage value that indicates how much a variable has changed on average each year). As with GDP, the first and simplest method consists of taking the initial (Yo) and the terminal value (Yt) of the time series and then computing the annual compound rates. To overcome the inherent weakness of this method, the other method consists of computing the growth rates by using linear regression to determine the trend and then computing the growth rate as described earlier.

Efficient Pricing

Definitional Issues

The word 'economic' is derived from a Greek word *oikonomikos*, which literally means 'good housekeeping'. An individual usually is constantly searching for and making choices of alternatives to achieve the desired goals. In growing a crop it has been demonstrated that by planting early, one gets a much higher yield than by planting late in the cropping season. The alternative would be to wait and plant later to spread out labour demand. Obviously one will get low yield, but high yield is only one of the several ends. This is to say that the high yield of a particular crop is a means and not necessarily an end itself, because the resource – in this particular example, land – has alternative uses. The use of a range of ox implements (ox ploughs, cultivators, ridges, planters, carts, etc.) can save a lot of labour, and ox cultivation can also provide better crop husbandry, increase the scope of the individual farmers by less arduous work and provide the opportunity for planning ahead and thus improving the farm productivity generally. It will reduce production cost with increased area brought under cultivation, aid the campaign for integrating livestock and crops to their mutual advantage, and train farmers in the principle of business farming, which is an essential precursor to mechanization. This example assumes the possession of the ox implements and means of animal draught by purchase. If the farmer does not have the equipment, he can decide to make the implements. In doing so the farmer sacrifices time which could have been used in other alternative ways. This is a simple illustration of making capital and the reason behind this decision or choice is because it will reduce labour costs and increase farm productivity. Whether it is the best choice to make the equipment in order to save labour and increase productivity will depend on costs in relation to savings. In this example the farmer faces a conflict between production and capital formation. If the savings made in labour costs are in excess of the costs of making the equipment, then it is advisable to make that decision, or vice versa. In other words, one cannot assume that the possession of the ox equipment is essential since labour use could be an alternative choice to achieve the desired end.

Keeping improved breeds of livestock like grade dairy cattle is aimed at getting high milk yield. The lowlands and foothills of Lesotho, for instance, cover about 30 per cent of the land area, which is also the bulk of productive arable land, but which carries some 80 per cent of the nation's population. It is in this area that dairy development is taking place. Because of high population, livestock movement is being restricted and stall feeding is becoming the principal method of raising livestock. For dairy cattle, the use of concentrates is necessary in order to get high milk yield. A quantity of the concentrate fed to the dairy cows has alternative uses; for instance, it can be fed to other animals. The main point here is that the feed input has alternative uses, and feeding it to a dairy cow is neither the only nor necessarily the best way of using the feed.

From the economic point of view, these examples serve to illustrate three technical relationships:

Factor	*Product*
Land	Output
Labour	Output
Capital	Output

Land, labour, capital and management are internal factors of production employed to produce outputs. These factors can be taken as inputs while outputs are the products. The relationship between input and output (the ratio between output to input) is regarded as technical efficiency:

$$\frac{\text{Physical output}}{\text{Physical input}} = \text{technical efficiency}$$

We also have to consider the value of output in relation to that of input, which is termed as economic efficiency.

$$\frac{\text{Value of output}}{\text{Value of input}} = \frac{\text{return}}{\text{cost}} = \text{economic efficiency}$$

Production can, therefore, be considered as an output of an individual farm or firm which is a single unit. The process of maximizing output is to achieve efficiency measured by the ratio of output to input both measured in terms of either physical or monetary values. This ratio is known as productivity, the increase of which can be realized either by increasing the numerator (output) or decreasing the denominator (input).

Land as a factor of production has alternative uses. It can be used to grow a crop or can be used for livestock production. Similarly, labour as a factor of production can be used for alternative production purposes. In other words there are alternative choices in the use of scarce resources to achieve the desired end. It is an exercise always concerned with alternatives. As can be seen in Tables 3a and b and Figure 9, in the short grass zone of northern Uganda, cotton production, the principal cash crop, was conflicting with other crops as far as labour use was concerned. Cotton and other crops are products and in this case the conflicting relationship is between products. It is, therefore, a *product/product* relationship. The making of ox implements or capital formation was to save labour, expand area being brought under cultivation and raise productivity. In this example, the relationship is between the two production factors – capital and labour. It is, therefore, a *factor/factor* relationship. The example of feeding a dairy cow with concentrate to yield milk as an output is a conflict between input and output. It is a *factor/product* relationship. These three relationships are ever asking how much to produce, how to do it and how much to put in. This type of decision carried out in small units is called *microeconomics*, whereas the aggregate decisions made by the country's farmers are called *macroeconomics*.

Management as an input is a coordinating factor which is concerned with a large number of decisions. The first set of decisions concerns what to produce or the combination of enterprises which then form a system. The second set of decisions concerns how to produce, while the third is concerned with how much to produce. These decisions are interrelated. In addition to these, decisions are usually made in time, but the future is always characterized by uncertainties. The time factor, therefore, produces uncertainties and decisions must, therefore, be made at the most opportune time. Parallel to that, a farmer has to decide when to buy and when to sell his outputs. Space factors must also be borne in mind in respect of where to sell. All these decisions and future uncertainties affect each other. All decisions are concerned with raising the productivity of traditional farming systems from low to higher equilibrium levels and require quantitative and qualitative changes in the economy.

Technical Efficiency

One factor of production In trying to understand agricultural production

Table 3a Recorded labour input in man hours (area of study – West Lango)

	Total hours	Jan.	Feb.	Mar.	Apr.	May	Jun.	Jul.	Aug.	Sep.	Oct.	Nov.	Dec.
Breaking land	85				52	33							
Second cultivation	79					42	37						
Planting	65					18	47						
Weeding and thinning	570					40	126	152	124	61	67		
Harvesting	217	83										18	116
1.65 acres cotton and beans	*1,016*	*83*			*52*	*75*	*95*	*173*	*152*	*124*	*61*	*85*	*116*
Uprooting cotton stem and sowing	71		40	31									
Clearing cotton stem	3		3										
Weeding	381				110	162	109						
Harvesting	157							131	26				
1.9 acres f. millet and sorghum and p. peas	*612*		*43*	*31*	*110*	*162*	*109*	*131*	*26*				
Breaking land	36					9	27						
Second cultivation	31						5	26					
Clearing trash	2						2						
Planting	14						2	12					
Weeding	39								32	7			
Harvesting	43										43		
0.65 acres groundnuts and cassava	*165*					*9*	*36*	*38*	*32*	*7*	*43*		
Breaking land	79						79						
Second cultivation and sowing	67							67					
Weeding	288							201	72	15			
Harvesting	42										30	7	5
1.36 acres simsim	*476*						72	268	72	15	30	7	5
5.56 acres farm	**2,269**	**83**	**43**	**31**	**162**	**246**	**319**	**610**	**282**	**146**	**134**	**92**	**121**

Table 3b Recorded labour input in man hours using some ox-ploughing and hand labour (area of study – East Lango District)

	Feb.	Mar.	Apr.	May	Jun.	Jul.	Aug.	Sep.	Oct.	Nov.	Dec.	Jan.
Millet and peas	11	106	82	49	38	39	9					
Simsim						20	30	42	16	20	22	
Groundnuts			9	8	5	26	22	17	27	32	12	
Cassava	1	2	14	14	34	12	25	29	28	24	11	4
Sweet potatoes		2	9	9	11	5	4	18	18			
Cotton and beans	84	2	45	135	152	174	151	138	110	110	169	194
	96	**110**	**152**	**215**	**238**	**282**	**242**	**230**	**199**	**204**	**214**	**198**

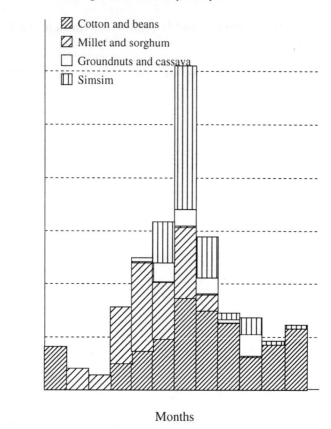

Months

Figure 9   Recorded labour inputs in man hours per month for major crops

economics, one is concerned with examining the physical relationship between units of the internal factors of production (land, labour and capital) employed and the resultant physical units of output. In producing a crop, the farmer is confronted with varying the input mix in order to maximize output. The farmer wishing to increase output is obliged to either use more labour, productive input (seed), or technical production inputs like fertilizers (the variable factors) on the same fixed supply of land or capital (the fixed factor). The best way of varying input mix is to apply the principle of the law of diminishing returns (LDR) which states that as one adds successive units of one factor of production to fixed amounts of other factors, the increments in total output initially rise and then decline. This can be illustrated by assuming a crop being grown on five hectares and labour, the variable factor as set below in Table 4.

Table 4   Non-proportional returns to labour

Labour inputs (man days) Tons	Total products	Average products	Marginal product
20	80	4.0	80
30	240	8.0	160
40	540	13.5	300
50	810	16.2	270
60	940	15.7	130
70	1,000	14.3	60
80	1,000	12.5	0
90	950	10.5	-50

Where average product = $\dfrac{\text{total product}}{\text{number of man days}}$

Marginal product being incremental output as a result of the employment of additional man days.

In the above Table 4 it is assumed that: i) labour is the only variable factor; ii) all other units of variable factors are equally efficient; and iii) there are no changes in the techniques of production. Increases in output are due entirely to the variations in the number of man days combined with other factors of production to produce output. Since labour is the only variable factor, changes in output are directly related to changes in the number of man days allocated to producing the crop. Output, therefore, is related to the productivity of labour or physical returns to labour. This is a *technical efficiency*, since the measurement has been the physical productivity of labour. In the above example as the number of man days increases from 20 to 30, the total output continues to increase. However, as the number of man days is increased from 20 to 50 the average product (AP) continues to increase from four to 16.2 tons, and as labour increases from 20 to 40 man days, marginal product (MP) increases from 80 to 270 tons and then starts to decline. These rises and falls are illustrated in Figure 10.

Up to a point when output starts to decline, the fixed factors of production are under-utilized. As marginal product starts to fall, it indicates that the proportion between the fixed and variable factors are becoming progressively less favourable. In the above example, the marginal product begins to fall after the fortieth man day is employed while the average product starts to decline when the fiftieth man day is employed, i.e. the maximum average product of labour is obtained when the fiftieth man day is employed and similarly the maximum marginal product of labour is reached after the fortieth man day is employed. It is increasing production measured by marginal product and falling productivity measured by average product which is the characteristic feature of the law of diminishing return. The employment of the eightieth man day produces no marginal product. In this case marginal productivity is regarded as being zero. These considerations are illustrated in Figure 10, which indicates total product curve depicting the relationships between employment and output where some of the factors are fixed in supply. The effects of increasing the quantity of variable factors are: i) increasing returns when total product increases at an increasing rate and the marginal product also increases; ii) constant returns when total product as well as marginal product increase at a constant rate; iii) diminishing returns when total product is increasing at a decreasing rate as well as marginal product also falling; iv) zero returns when total product is constant and marginal product is zero; and v) negative returns when total product is falling and marginal productivity is zero.

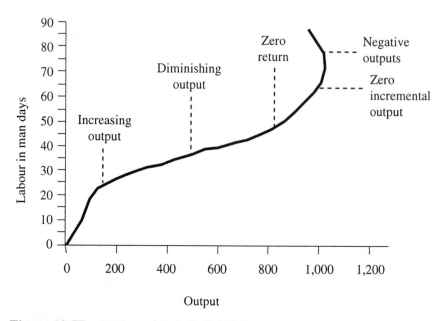

Figure 10 Illustration of technical efficiency

Law of diminishing return The law of diminishing return also applies to other factors, and the techniques of production are assumed to be constant. The marginal average productivity of capital will, at some point, start to fall as more and more of it is applied to a fixed supply of land and labour. This principle also applies to land as an increasing land area is combined with a fixed amount of labour and capital. However, technical progress can improve relationships, but experiments have demonstrated, for instance, that when increased amounts of fertilizer are applied to a given land area, the applicability of the law of diminishing returns is relevant. As will be illustrated, increments in the yields of maize in Lesotho in response to fertilizer application first increased more than proportionately, but eventually the law of diminishing return set in.

The production aspects ask how to produce an output or outputs. Let us take the case of grain production in the mountain Kingdom of Lesotho, an enclave of the Republic of South Africa, occupying some 30,358 square kilometres (or 3,035,800 hectares) of highland ranging from 1,500 metres at its lowest to 3,300 metres at its highest level above sea level.

According to the Research Division of the Lesotho Ministry of Agriculture, there was not a substantial maize production increase beginning 1981. A 10-year yield average amounted to 663.3 kg/ha, a decline from about 850 kg/ha. Meanwhile there was a substantial increase in the planting of hybrid maize which required fertilizer application. As part of farming systems research initiated in Lesotho in 1979, a project to demonstrate new maize production technologies was also introduced. The new technologies included: i) the use of optimum fertilizer rates (NPK); ii) the use of improved planter in order to obtain optimum plant population; iii) the use of hybrid maize seed as opposed to open-pollinated and farmer saved seed; and iv) the use of herbicides for weed control. The results of a survey to determine the rate of adoption of new maize production technologies produced some interesting behavioural response from participating farmers.

According to trial results, maize yields improved significantly to the use of higher rates of fertilizer application. The average yields were 1,144 kg/ha for a fertilizer rate of 150 kg/ha of 3:2:1 NPK; the yield increased to 1,695 kg/ha for the 350 kg/ha of 3:2:1 NPK fertilizer rate. However attempt to persuade farmers to apply the 350 kg/ha fertilizer was unsuccessful because the farmers preferred a lower rate of 301 kg/ha of fertilizer yielding an average maize output of 1,886 kg/ha. The farmers' behavioural response was indeed rational.

The fertilizer application rate of 100 kg/ha yielded 5.5 kg/ha of maize per kilogramme of fertilizer. At the rate of 150 kg/ha of fertilizer application the output increased to 7.6 kg of maize for each kg of fertilizer. However when the fertilizer rate was increased to 250 kg/ha, the maize output for each kilogramme of fertilizer moderately declined to 7.4 kg while at the farmers' preferred rate of fertilizer application, the maize output for each kilogramme of fertilizer declined further to 6.3 kg and for the recommended rate of 350 kg/ha of fertilizer output per unit of fertilizer declined to 4.8 kg.

Table 5   Adoption of new maize production technology on small farms in Lesotho

Input kg of fertilizer/ ha	Output average kg of maize/ha	Cost of fertilizer in Maloti	Average total cost	Value of maize in Maloti	Incremental cost of fertilizer	value of maize	Ratio of maize value to cost of fertilizer
10	313.5	20	2	141.75	–	–	–
55	525	110	2	236.25	90	94.05	1.05
100	550	200	2	247.50	90	11.25	0.13
150	1,144	300	2	514.80	100	267. 03	2.67
200	1,705	400	2	767.25	100	252.45	2.52
250	1,850	500	2	832.50	100	65.25	0.65
301	1,886	602	2	848.70	102	16.20	0.16
350	1,695	700	2	762.75	98	-85.95	-0.88
530	570	1,060	2	256.50	360	-506.25	-1.41

Source: Pomela, 1988.

The key concept to this example is the production function, a mathematical line which indicates inputs in relationship to output. Initially, as the amount of fertilizer had been increased, there was also a corresponding increase in output, which, after reaching a maximum output in proportion to the amount of fertilizer, the first increment of fertilizer was relatively low but the second increment yielded larger output than the first. After about 230 kg/ha of fertilizer application, incremental output started to fall and subsequently output began to progressively decline until further higher levels of fertilizer rate led to diminishing return because the high level of the input became toxic. This type of curve, in common, is the law of diminishing return. In other words, the diminishing return starts when the size of increment begins to decline and the cost starts to increase. This is sometime known as the law of increasing cost (Figure 11). The net benefits of adopting improved packages and attaining high yields can be calculated by computing the marginal rate of return (MRR) for each successive increase in the rate of fertilizer application.

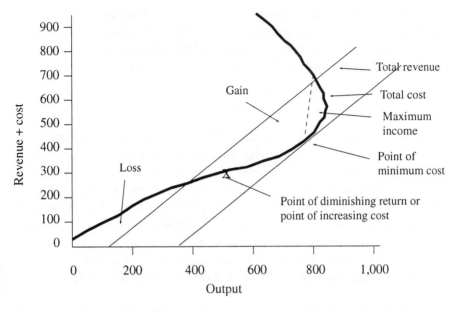

Figure 11 Adoption of new maize production technology on small farms in Lesotho

$$\text{MRR} = \frac{\text{incremental benefits}}{\text{incremental cost}} \times 100 = \frac{\text{net return } A_{t+1}}{\text{cost } A_{tx1}} - \frac{\text{net return } A_t}{\text{cost } A_t} \times 100$$

where

A_{t+1} is the cost of the new technology (fertilizer application)
A_t is the cost of old technology

The application of fertilizer increased maize yield above the level if maize was grown under traditional practices. One has to relate the above relationship in economic terms in respect of cost and revenue and also to take into account labour cost and the additional cost of fertilizer application including the overhead cost. As additional units of fertilizer (technical production inputs) were made, there was a corresponding increment in output until the law of diminishing return set in. There was also a point of minimum cost, which occurred after the point of diminishing return. As shown in Figure 11, total revenue will increase linearly, but what a farmer would like to maximize is a difference between cost and revenue, which is income.

The maximum revenue (income) occurs where the slope of revenue is parallel to a line which is tangential to the cost curve. The point at which one gets the greatest return depends on the one hand on total cost curve, which in turn depends on the slope curve of the physical production and total revenue line. If price changes, the point of maximum income will also alter.

Economic Efficiency

The application of the law of diminishing return based on the ratio of units of physical inputs to units of physical outputs which gives maximum output per unit of input is not necessarily the ratio the farmer should adopt. Usually the farmer is interested in maximizing his profit (or income) or economic efficiency. The decision of this ratio is facilitated by the choice of a combination of factors of production which depends on their prices as well as their productivity. In this case, therefore, the farmer is interested in measuring output and input in terms of revenue and costs respectively. The main concern, therefore, is to maximize the difference between costs and revenue.

Two factors of production The choice of the combination of factors of production is based on the principle that factor of production should bring in the same marginal return and where marginal product of any one factor is the same in all uses. This is the condition of efficient combination of factors of production which implies that productive resources should be used in such quantities that the ratio of marginal cost (MC) of any factor equals its marginal product (MP), i.e. equals the ratio of the marginal cost and marginal product of all the others.

$$\text{Least cost combination} = \frac{\text{price of grass}}{\text{MP of grass}} = \frac{\text{price of concentrate}}{\text{MP of concentrate}}$$

This formula is an indication of the least cost combination (lowest cost), assuming that the individual farmer buys under condition of perfect competition, and the marginal cost of each factor of production will be the same as its price. If the objective is to achieve optimum output, the marginal cost of each factor equals its marginal revenue.

In the earlier example only one factor of production was variable and the others fixed. In Lesotho, because of shortage of grazing, hay and concentrate are increasingly being used in feeding dairy cattle. In this case two factors of production (grass and concentrate) are being used. With the help of a diagram (Figure 12), the horizontal axis measures the amount of grass to be used in

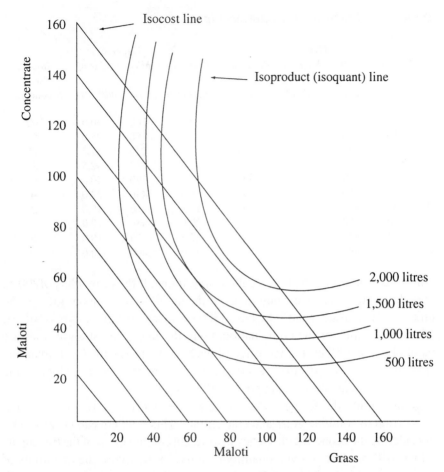

Figure 12 Least cost combination of factors of producing milk in Lesotho

feeding the dairy cattle and the vertical axis the amount of concentrate. If one item is fixed – for instance, concentrate fixed at 20 units – and grass is increased, one will find that there is an increase in milk production until a point when the law of diminishing return sets in. The same relationship will apply to concentrate if it were varied (Table 6).

If a farmer wants to produce 500 litres of milk by combining units of concentrate and units of grass and the respective costs being M4 for each unit of concentrate and M2 for each unit of grass. Assuming the farmer has M100, he can either buy 50 units of grass or 25 units of concentrate (see Figure 12), or any combination on the line between the value of 50 units of grass and 25

Table 6   Factor/factor relationship

		Grass				Concentrate		
Units of grass	Milk yield	Value of milk (M)	Marginal (MP) product	Units of concentrate	Milk yield	Value of milk (M)	Marginal (MP) product (M)
1	5	150	50	100	2.5	100	50.0	100
2	10	210	30	60	5.0	150	25.0	50
3	15	290	40	80	7.5	225	37.5	75
4	20	380	45	90	10.0	310	42.5	85
5	25	430	25	50	12.5	390	40.0	80
6	30	470	20	40	15.0	430	20.0	40
7	35	490	10	20	17.5	460	15.0	30
8	40	500	5	10	20.0	480	10.0	20
9	45	490	-5	-10	22.5	500	10.0	20
10	50	480	-5	-10	25.0	490	-10.0	-5

units of concentrate. The line is called *isocost* line. If the farmer has M200 he may decide to increase his purchases of the inputs – 100 units of grass or 50 units of concentrate – and if he has M300 the respective purchases would be 150 and 75 units or the combination along the lines. The straight lines are parallel to each other and the price of each factor is assumed to remain the same whatever the quantity used in the production process. The slope of the line represents the ratio of the price of the two factors.

The choice the farmer faces is how intensively to farm, i.e. in what proportion to combine grass and concentrate. This problem can be solved by considering the economic efficiency in different combinations of the two inputs which will produce a given quantity of milk. In the figure the quantities of milk produced are 2,000, 1,500, 1,000 and 500 litres. The slope of each combination is convex, implying that there is the law of diminishing return to each factor, as indicated in Table 6. The curve lines are called *isoproduct* (isoquant) and the slope represent the marginal rate of substitution between grass and concentrate, and the point of optimal combination of the two factors is given by the point where the isocost line, which represents the farmer's available resources, should be tangential to the isoquant.

In the above table the value of marginal product of both grass and concentrate continue to increase until the twentieth addition of the unit of grass and the tenth unit of concentrate. However, as indicated in Table 7, the unit which a loti can buy is the thirtieth unit of grass and about 12.5 unit of concentrate.

Table 7   Least cost combination

		Grass			Concentrate	
	Value of Milk (M)	*Value of MP (M)*	*Ratio of Milk to MP*	*Value of Milk (M)*	*Value of MP (M)*	*Ratio of Milk to MP*
1	75	50	1.5	100	50.0	1.5
2	105	30	3.5	75	25.0	3.0
3	145	40	3.6	112.5	37.5	3.0
4	190	45	4.2	155.0	42.5	3.6
5	215	25	8.6	195.0	40.0	4.8
6	235	20	11.7	225.0	20.0	10.7
7	245	10	24.5	230.0	15.0	15.3
8	250	5	50.0	240.0	10.0	24.0
9	245	-5	-49.0	250.0	10.0	25.0
10	240	-5	-48.0	205.0	-10.0	-20.5

As will be seen in the above table, the least cost combination

$$= \frac{30 \times m2}{40 \times .5} = \frac{15 \times m4}{40 \times .5} = 3.0$$

or

the least cost combination $= \frac{235}{20} = 11.7$ and $\frac{215}{20} = 10.7$

The differences in the second computation is due to the fact that responses of milk yield to increases inputs vary slightly. In this example, the two inputs are combined at the point of 30 units of grass and 15 units of concentrate costing M120 which is in excess of M100 available resources. It will be necessary for the farmer to increase resources through borrowing.

Many factors limiting In Uganda, as in many SSA countries, the farmers are usually exhorted by agricultural extension workers to adopt prescribed cultural practices, including the growing of improved crop varieties, the rearing of improved grade livestock breeds and adopting technology of proven superior performance to the old traditional techniques. Usually, detailed technical recommendations for individual crop and livestock of importance are available based on research results. General emphasis is placed on early and proper land preparation, timely planting, proper spacing, weeding and thinning to achieve optimum plant population, and prescribed animal husbandry practices. Official policy discourages inter-cropping and the basis of this policy stems from some observed technical optima of comparative performance between row and inter-cropped planting in terms of mean yield per unit area, mean yield per animal, productivity per labour input, tractor hours per unit area. It is claimed that if the recommended cultural packages were adopted, crop yield per unit area and output per animal would more than double output under traditional farming systems. Despite the exhortation, the crop mix has remained virtually unchanged as an essentially subsistence elements of permanent crops, cereals, pulses, root crops and a few others on which has been superimposed the cultivation of cash crops. Livestock forms a separate component of agriculture and consists mainly of unimproved local breeds of low productivity.

It is true that in order to get high yield, it is essential to plant early in order to match plant water requirements with the rainfall pattern. FAO, for instance, documented in Zambia that the early planted maize yielded 6.6 tons per hectare but output fell to 4.6 tons when planting was delayed by two weeks and to 3.4 tons when the operation was delayed by four weeks (Stocking, 1983). This, as is well known, conflicts with other crops' demand for labour. When considering product possibility curve, the line is a straight one when labour is the only factor and one product.

a)   *Labour utilization and distribution over time*

Labour use field investigations in Uganda demonstrated that the labour factor in peasant agriculture is the most important item in deciding the timing of cropping, the range of crops to be planted in holdings, which range in size depending on the level of soil fertility and tools being used. The decisions are invariably dictated by labour availability, which is closely related to the size of the family of five to six persons of whom two to three are usually children below working age. Analysis of the field investigation indicates that there is a strong correlation between the size of the family and the acreage of each holding. Acreage under food crops exceeds that of the principal cash crops. In areas where ox equipment is used, the acreages are larger than in areas where cultivation is carried out by hand. The larger acreage in ox cultivation areas is in order to compensate for the poor yield of crops due to low level of soil fertility.

The crop year commences generally with the planting of finger millet or another staple annual crops. The finger millet demands a lot of labour to weed, accounting for about 25 per cent of total labour input, except when a cultivator is used, thus reducing the demand to 3.5 per cent. Women's labour is virtually locked up in weeding and is, therefore, unavailable for other crops. Meanwhile the men undertake land preparation for the cotton, groundnuts, cassava and various other crops. In order to accommodate these other crops in the cropping calendar, it is necessary to stagger the planting of cotton and other major crops. Despite this measure, labour conflicts are not absolutely overcome. When millet is ready for harvesting, labour is also required for planting late cotton and weeding early planted cotton and other crops. At many periods of the year, therefore, a variety of crops at different stages of production compete for labour. Since family labour supplemented by hired and communal labour is limited, there is usually some temporary neglect of crops at certain stages of growth. Under these circumstances, when labour constraints cause some operations to be delayed, the farmers over the years have responded by evolving a system of agriculture which ingeniously makes use of the potential of supplementarities and complementarities from inter-planting or simultaneous production of a wide variety of crops (Okai, 1968).

All labour use surveys in Uganda confirmed that agricultural rhythm exists in which the pattern of labour use profile coincides with the rainfall distribution (see Figure 9). In areas where the rainfall pattern tends to be monomodal, there is also one peak period of labour requirement, coinciding with the rainfall peak. In a bimodal rainfall pattern, there are two peak periods of labour demand. McMaster (1965) had earlier demonstrated such a rhythm in the planting of crops.

Although these surveys were carried under Ugandan conditions, the lesson drawn from them might have limited geographical applicability. However, similar surveys carried out in other countries tend to confirm the findings. Cleave (1974) synthesized nearly 50 surveys of African farmers in the former British territories in tropical Africa. His ultimate objective was to analyse original work in order to interpret common trends and adjustments in the use of labour. He was able to establish that increase in agricultural production was achieved through bringing more land under cultivation and committing additional family labour to agriculture. Cleave did not, however, establish clearly the limit of mobilizing additional labour for the purposes of agricultural production. However, he concurred with Okai that the length of day worked 'varies with the effort involved in the task in hand and the urgency of that task'.

In all the surveys used in Cleave's study, labour was consistently treated as a limiting factor to increased agricultural production. In part this was due to the seasonality of agricultural production and in part to alternative uses of labour. Cleave confirmed that agricultural rhythm was dictated by the pattern of rainfall. Farmers react to such seasonality by adjusting crop ratios to achieve complementarity in labour use, and by changes in crops, especially favouring those which are seasonal in labour requirements and by planting over an extended period of time, etc. He also demonstrated that 'the period immediately after the start of the rains, when land preparation and planting take place, is the time of great urgency in agriculture, and harvest is also a busy period'. The single most demanding operation is usually weeding. He concurred with other studies that weeding labour may be reduced by more thorough cultivation at planting time but conversely may be aggravated by the introduction of ox ploughs without the simultaneous adoption of ox weeders.

b)   *Division of labour in farming operations*

It has quite often been stated that there is a fairly distinct labour division between sexes in a developing agriculture, with women concentrating on food crops and men on cash crops. This dictum is still apparent in many areas but is gradually breaking down (Okai, 1968). Available evidence shows that men are willing to carry out operations previously regarded as women's work once the crop can be sold for cash. However, weeding food crops is performed almost entirely by both sexes, but most of the initial cultivation remains men's work as it involves heavy digging and often the felling of trees. Competing labour demand has different implications, depending on whether the task is subject to division of labour by sex. For instance, the conflict for labour inputs between weeding millet and opening land for cotton is affected by the fact that one of the jobs is almost exclusively women's work and heavy digging is men's work; this reduces labour mobility between enterprises if a change in emphasis on the two crops is desirable. In this respect cotton and millet should perhaps be regarded as a single enterprise rather than separate ones to which differing amounts of labour can be allocated.

    Okai illustrated that men generally work a greater total number of hours on the farm than women, although differences are exaggerated by the exclusion of minor food crops, which are attended almost exclusively by women: household cares are also additional work for women. About 55–60 per cent of the total labour input is accounted for by men and the balance by women and children. More than half of men's work is concerned with cash crops, which accounts on average for about 45 per cent of combined male and female labour inputs. He further showed that farmers tend to work until a certain level of energy is expended, so that light work such as harvesting involves longer hours than heavy cultivation. The table shows that various operations are performed for fairly constant periods and heavy ones are worked for shortest times.

Table 8   Average length of 'shift' worked by day – man hours

Operation area	(1)	(2)	Progressive[1]	Farmer[2]
Initial cultivation ploughing	2.5	4	4	7
Second cultivation ploughing	3.25	4	4	7
First weeding cotton	3.5	3	4	7
Second weeding cotton	3.5	3	4	7
Harvesting	5	5	5	5
Weeding crops sown broadcast	5	5	–	–
Weeding crops sown in rows	–	–	4	7

Notes

1   Ox hours.
2   Man hours converted from ox hours by multiplying the latter by 1.75. 'Man hour' is taken as 1 and wife who guides oxen is taken as 0.75 hour.

Source: Okai, 1968.

It was also demonstrated that the adoption of improved work methods and the use of ox equipment reduce labour requirements and increase the return per unit of labour input. The combined effect of the time for opening fresh plots for supplementary crops – and the resultant low returns to labour and shortage of labour – is the principal factor in reducing the incentive to greater physical effort to grow crops in pure stand and to obtain the high yield shown achievable on research stations. This situation arises because practically no extra labour input is required for the supplementary crop other than for harvesting.

The problem that was encountered in the field labour investigation was the variabilities of quality, quantity and the nature of work being performed. Both sexes, young and old, undertook agricultural tasks and therefore one was confronted with the conversion of man, woman and child hours into standard units. In picking cotton, for example, women's performances were better than men. In other words, women were better at carrying out certain operations than were men. Figures for labour requirements, owing to the variation of ability of the worker and the intensity he/she was prepared to work and the nonspecific nature of the task, showed some wide variability. Despite these limitations, we shall use the data collected to demonstrate some problems of agricultural development caused by labour bottlenecks in peasant agriculture.

Firstly, labour inputs in hours made by women in weeding and harvesting, light operations, have to be adjusted by a conversion factor of 0.75 in order to establish real labour inputs. Secondly, having obtained the real labour input in hours for individual plots (some are over one acre while others are below), the average number of hours per acre is calculated for each crop or mixture of crops. By dividing the total real labour input by the number of hours per acre, one obtains the maximum number of acres that could be allocated to the crop or mixture of crops. For instance, during April the nominal available labour amounts to 162 hours, of which 52 hours are devoted to opening land for cotton of approximately 1.05 acres, and the balance of 110 hours (woman hours) were allocated to weeding finger millet and sorghum. The adjusted woman hours (110 x 0.75) are 82.5 hours. The total real labour inputs during the month amount to 134.5 hours. The smallholder can allocate the entire labour resource to the production of cotton. If such a decision is taken, he will be able to open

$$(134.5 \times \frac{1.05}{52}) = 2.7$$

acres for cotton production (data from Table 3).

He may also consider allocating the labour resource to the production of millet and sorghum. If he decides so, he will be able to bring

$$(134.5 \times \frac{1.9}{82.5}) = 3.1$$

acres under the cereals. The labour production possibility curve is $B_1 C_1$ (Figure 13). It should, however, be noted that the decision to limit acreage is influenced not only by labour supply but also other factors, in particular future increased demand for labour often dictated by the seasonality of agricultural production due to the rainfall pattern. At this time, therefore, it could be contended that the marginal productivity is zero because of the excess labour supply.

In May the smallholder has put in 206 hours of real labour resources into agricultural production. In the same way he may devote the whole labour resources to the growing of cotton, and he will be able to open

$(206 \times \frac{0.6}{33}) = 3.7$ acres or

$(206 \times \frac{1}{51.4}) = 4$ acres of other crops.

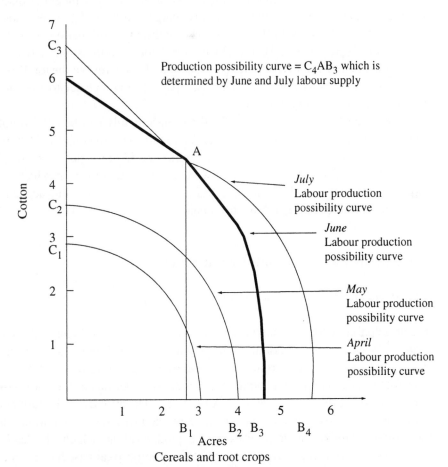

Figure 13 Several factors limiting – production possibility curve

The labour production possibility curve is represented by $B_2 C_2$. There is still excess labour. During the month of June, the total real labour resources used for farming amount to 266 hours. If the entire 266 hours were allocated to the cotton growing, the smallholder will be able to bring under cotton production 6.2 acres or 4.5 acres under other crops. The labour production possibility curve shifts to $B_3 C_3$. In July, the peak labour demand period, the smallholder commands a total of 470 hours of real labour resource for which three major crops are competing. He can either allocate the whole labour resource to look after 5.9 acres of cotton or 5.4 acres of other crops. In this case the labour production possibility curve shifts to $B_4 C_4$. If his intention is to maximize profit, he will have to apply the law of equimarginal rate of return (LEMRR). As illustrated in the figure, in June he can only bring 6.2 acres under cotton or 4.5 under other crops. In July he can only manage to bring 5.9 acres under cotton or 5.4 acres under other crops. The optimum combination is at the point where $B_3 C_3$ crosses $B_4 C_4$ which works out as follows: 4.5 acres for cotton and about 2.9 acres for other crops, a total of 7.4 acres but the total area of the smallholder was 5.56 acres. The discrepancies might be due to arbitrary use of the correction factor (Figure 13).

Alternatively, the computation for the month of July can be carried out for the three major crops (cotton, millet and sorghum, and simsim). Real labour resources allocated to simsim were 218 hours (or 153 hours per acre). If all the 470 hours of real labour resource were allocated to simsim production, some 2.2 acres would be brought under cultivation. If this is taken into account, the combined acreage could have been near the 5.56 acres.

Non-efficiency and Trade-offs Consideration

Adjustments to Risks and Uncertainties

The principal concern of agriculturalists and pastoralists in Sub-Saharan Africa, living in a harsh and uncertain environment, is survival and risk aversion. Because of an array of uncertainties, these farmers have developed a range of adjustment mechanisms. Uncertainty in this sense is defined as the choice of gaining while at the same time the risk of losing. The attitude of the farmers varies according to temperament, security-mindedness, etc. In addition, an individual farmer's reaction varies with capital position, which ultimately affects risk-bearing capacity. A farmer with a strong capital base has a better risk-bearing capacity than one with a poor capital base. The farmer can easily obtain credit from friends or conventional lending institutions because his chances of defaulting on credit repayment have been judged as being low. The other aspect concerning uncertainties is the consumption propensity of the farmers. One who spends his resources to the limit of his/her income all the time has no accumulated capital stock and, therefore, he/she is not in a position to take advantage of any windfall gain, should output and income substantially increase. Some farmers save resources and invest the reserve in productive assets so that they can improve or expand the productive base of the farm. These farmers also improve their position to withstand risk and uncertainties.

Each of these choices involves costs. In order to reduce variability, and to stabilize the farm income by reducing risks, a farmer has to incur extra cost. To stabilize or minimize risks of loss, a farmer will have to accept an income lower than his expectation. The usual approach is to discount for risks by taking into account the effect of time and opportunity cost on income. When a farmer is considering different enterprises, he/she discounts heavily on an enterprise with a greater risk. It is usually difficult to measure the costs accurately because the discount level depends on the individual temperament, capital position, etc., and traditionally it is difficult to measure temperament. (Discounting is discussed in chapter 3.) One farmer, for instance, may consider harvest as a greater risk than other operations and therefore, discounts heavily, and vice versa. Temperament, therefore, varies and similarly discounting risk is subjective and not objective. The result of discounting takes into account the level of riskiness and its effect may lead to rationing inputs. If a lot of inputs are to be made, the farmer will take it that his risks are great. He may then probably withhold, for instance, his labour and some people may pass a moral judgment that the farmer is lazy. However, it may well be that the farmer's assessment of risk is very great because peasant farming is judged to be a very risky undertaking.

Another way to withstand risk is to maintain maximum flexibility, which is essentially the ability to shift from one enterprise to another which may be profitable. Regarding machines and building, for instance, a farmer can choose a specialized one or a multipurpose machine. However, a multipurpose machine is rarely as efficient as a specialized one, and therefore, there is a sacrifice to be made. In pig production, for instance, the conversion rate of feed depends very much on the design, ventilation, etc., of the piggery unit. The building can hardly be changed to other uses. Pigs are very risky animals to produce, but all the same the farmer may decide to put up a less sophisticated and less efficient building but one which can be, over time, converted to other uses. As opposed to investment in enterprises, another form of adjustment is by increasing liquidity. This is a euphemistic way of saying 'locking up money under the bed'. In this instance the farmer does not invest the liquid resources in other form but keeps it in liquid form which is very flexible. In this example, the farmer's preference is to hold his money in cash so that he is able to switch over quickly to other enterprises. The opportunity cost of holding money in this case (what the money could have earned if it were invested elsewhere) may be high, since it could earn more elsewhere. There is, therefore, the danger of incurring a greater loss in the form of a high opportunity cost involved.

The other way of adjustment is diversification, based on the principle of not putting all one's eggs in one basket. A farmer may diversify in his farm by undertaking different enterprises, or outside his/her farm such as non-farm activities, artisanal employment. He can also diversify the one enterprise; for instance, by planting a crop at one time he runs the risk of weather, pests and/ or diseases damaging the crop. He can avoid this risk by staggering the planting of the crop over the time of the cropping season (temporal diversification). Also, by means of temporal diversification, he is able to spread out labour demand.

Another way is for the farmer to transfer his risk to a specialist risk-bearing institution such as an insurance company. If, for instance, a farmer buys a tractor on hire purchase terms, the machine may break down or be destroyed by fire or accident. The point he has to consider seriously is to minimize risk of losing the machine. He has, therefore, to insure against these risks and by doing so he incurs a definite cost. He may lose the whole tractor if not insured, but the farmer is uncertain about it. By insuring, he is safer than he would be without an insurance premium. The insurance company can stand the risk because it is able to spread risks over many farmers if the loss occurs. The insurance company can statistically predict what is likely to occur in the future. In some developed countries, even crops and livestock are insured. By getting a large number of farmers to insure, the insurance company is able to charge a reasonable insurance premium.

The other justification for incurring the cost of purchasing and insuring the machine is that it enables the farmer to adjust his/her plan to bear risk by avoiding physical uncertainty such as a drop in output if timeliness in farming operations is not achieved. The advantage of having the machine on the farm is that it overcomes this problem. A piece of work can be done within a short period of time, for instance, to achieve timeliness of operation. The farmer is, therefore, justified in having the machine because the time needed to do a piece of work is so short that the machine can perform in time. Accordingly, the extra cost in acquiring the machine is a preferred sacrifice in order to reduce the weather uncertainty. Again, the principle of plant protection against pests and diseases is an assurance, but this does not mean that the protection is always justified. In some years the insect pest attack may be negligible but the farmer will still, for instance, spray as an insurance against insect attack. Usually irrigation equipment is expensive. These extra costs are incurred to supplement the amount of rainfall. The decline in rainfall may not be adequate to justify the supplementary irrigation but the farmer, not knowing what level of rainfall amount that will be received in future, still incurs the cost of irrigation equipment to avoid physical uncertainty.

Another way a farmer can transfer risks to another person is by selling forward or making a contract. The difference between the two is essentially arbitrary. If one sells forward, he agrees to sell the quantity for a particular price but for delivery at an agreed future date. Since the price is fixed in advance, for a fixed delivery date, it is said the commodity has been sold forward. In this respect the farmer is transferring the risk of price fall onto the buyer. Although the buyer stands the risk of a price fall, usually he discounts for forward price. This is because it is usually possible that price in future might fall and the buyer, therefore, finds it essential to discount that forward price. If the forward price is 20 cents per kilogramme, the buyer may discount it to 18 cents. The seller accepts the loss of two cents since it is better than the uncertain future price. In other words, every time the seller transfers his/her risk to the buyer he/she has to pay for the transfer of that risk. Contract is selling forward and depends on a fixed date. It is usually a continuing supply of a commodity. A typical example is the selling forward of coffee or cocoa still on the tree since the crop will not be harvested until sometime later. The dealer or the farmer signs a contract to supply an agreed quantity of a commodity or goods for a definite price for a specified period of time. With contract arrangements there are advantages as well as disadvantages. The seller – in this case, the farmer – has the advantage of an assured market for a definite quantity and he can plan with that assurance in view. The disadvantage is that he can suffer from low prices in the event that the future price of the commodity rises at the time of delivery. As far as the buyer is concerned, he still stands the risk of paying a price above market price, if price falls below the contract price, but gains if the price rises at the time of delivery.

Social Articulation of Risks and Uncertainties

Opportunity for adjustments to risks and uncertainties in the context of African agriculture is indeed very limited. However, over the years the agriculturalists and pastoralists have evolved judicious adaptations to the environment and resource combinations that minimized risks and uncertainties. Living can be equated with processes of survival, proverbially stated as 'if one cannot run at least he/she should be able to hide'. In order to survive one has to be constantly creative in developing alternative ways to successfully neutralize risks one faces in life. The principal preoccupation of mankind, therefore, is risk aversion and management. The first major task is to tame the environment and undertake efficient and productive use and management of environmental resources. The qualities and quantities of these resources, such as atmospheric (climate), aquatic, terrestrial (earth), and biospheric (animals, plants and other biotics), have the potential for creating the environmental basis for agricultural risks and uncertainties. The word 'agriculture' itself, as stated earlier, is derived from a Greek word *agraire* which means 'land', and a Latin word *cultura*, literally meaning the proper practice of managing or the law governing the rational use of land. Cultures, therefore, evolved around the use of land and other environmental resources for subsistence. Contextually it means that the evolution of social, cultural and moral milieu of a particular community had been rooted in the use and management of the basic life-support resources sustainably without destroying them.

Wealth accumulation and social differentiation Valued living resources like livestock are regarded as a store of values, especially in pastoral areas, and their accumulation provides inter-temporal insurance through the flow of recurrent products. Economic prosperity undermines solidarity since it reduces individual risks. Although those who have accumulated wealth can opt out of the solidarity, usually they remain loyal members of the solidarity network. However, the interpersonal relationship can assume an exploitative form. Since the wealthy have little to gain from risk-pooling arrangements with the poor, the poor people find it beneficial to reciprocate in some other forms, like giving gifts to chiefs, widely practised in West Africa, or the provision of labour to the wealthy who need additional labour. Thus maintaining relationship with the poor is a form of labour insurance. During famine, the wealthy rural elite often have financial resources to buy food in the open market. Since the poor have no income, they have to work, for which they are rewarded by the provision of food. The rural elite, therefore, are able to improve their production capacity and income at the expense of the poor. Over time the transfers result in the concentration of wealth in the hands of a few. Fafchamps, for instance, reported that households surveyed in SSA indicated that livestock, an essential store of wealth, is distributed very unevenly across rural households. The ability of the rich to use mutual insurance systems as an instrument of exploitation (extraction of surplus) is the compensation they receive for continued participation in the system (Fafchamps, 1992, p. 161).

Wealth accumulation results in social differentiation, typified by the emergence of centre and periphery in the social economy. The privileged, usually village chiefs, teachers, religious leaders (marabouts in particular) occupy the centre, leaving the periphery to be occupied by marginalized groups like the aged, widows, etc. Those in the centre tend usually to usurp the role and participation of the poor from the decision-making processes on issues that affect their welfare. The relationship resembles the biblical story of 'he who has more will be added and he who has not, even the little he seemeth to have will be taken away from him'.

The existence of solidarity networks, although beneficial, has other implications, since it affects rural welfare, resulting in changes in the pattern of peasant behaviour with respect to food aid, changes in economic access to food, risk-bearing capacity, technology and the emergence of new institutions. When rural communities are afflicted by disasters, the solidarity network is put under extreme stress. After the shock, the life-support resource base may be greatly damaged and becomes insufficient to ensure the survival of whole communities. The strong in societies may resort to militaristic tendencies to withdraw resources from use by the weaker. Since the early 1980s, SSA has suffered from the outbreak and spread of the human immunodeficiency virus (HIV) leading to deaths. People have, therefore, been progressively liquidating their valued resources in order to raise income to care for the sick. The number of orphans in some areas has overstretched the extended family system to breaking point and the state has to take over to care for their welfare (Okai, 1997). Poor people usually run out of alienable assets much faster than the wealthy ones. The poor, therefore, are left with inalienable assets such as their own labour force, indigenous knowledge and skills. The loss of the most productive segment of the population through death also increases the dependency burden, and average labour productivity declines due to grinding morbidity (Okai, 1997).

The rural poor often also face agonizing and harrowing misery and abject grinding rural poverty arising from natural calamities. During the Ethiopian famine of 1984, the worst in living memory, mothers with starving children were reported to feed only the children who were gauged to withstand the famine and could survive. The weak ones were allowed to starve to death. This harrowing episode was due to expectation of protection the children were expected to provide to their parents at old age. These calamities result in the weakening of the vitality of mutual insurance networks.

In much of SSA the characteristic feature of survival is anchored in the moral economy of the peasants, typified by the right of the people to subsistence and the pooling of risks. Risk management in traditional societies, therefore, is embedded in the social fabric of moral economy which mirrors the biblical concept of loving one's neighbour as oneself (the love of humanity). In its literal sense, this dictum implores individuals to contribute to the survival of societies as a whole. Thus risk management is rooted in collective social security based on morally-sanctioned reciprocity, the rationale of which is for households to voluntarily share with neighbours on a reciprocal basis. Thus the system is endogenously enforced because it does not depend on any external norms or authority. The social reciprocity is essentially a form of mutual insurance which takes different forms, typically grain transfers, institutional credit, reciprocal claims on productive resources and the pooling of labour to overcome labour bottlenecks. Thus it enables households to diversify the real income sources on which they derive their livelihood. These solidarity systems evolved as a necessity, to overcome unforeseen disasters or hardships. This is an *exante* form of solidarity. The solidarity network is a social framework of interpersonal relationships in which individuals are connected to each other directly or indirectly. The primary interpersonal relationships are lineages and kinships which form the major axes of solidarity networks, although patron-client has become increasingly common.

In Sub-Saharan Africa (SSA) the age-old key features of agriculture were typified by flexibility and adaptability to changing natural and social environment since its inception some 10,000 years ago. Although the origins of African agriculture have been a subject for intellectual debate, there is now some archaeological evidence to confirm that certain forms of plant and animal domestication took place as early as the seventh and sixth millennia BC. Domesticates such as sorghum and the donkey had their origins in Africa, while sheep and goats originated from the Near East. Prior to the adoption of the actual planting or growing crops (biological factor), there was some form of pre-adaptation to agriculture by humans and pre-domestication of certain plants and animal species (Neimeijer, 1996, p. 91). Long before actual sowing or planting took place, according to Neimeijer, human activities began to interact with wild animals and plants, a co-evolution process that resulted in the increasing establishment of symbiotic relationships among biological organisms (human, plants and animals). The neolithic cultures (late Stone Age) of hunting wild animals (some later domesticated) and gathering fruits gradually incorporated more advanced tools and techniques to facilitate gathering and food preparation. As Neimeijer documented, pottery and grinding stones made it considerably easier to gather, store and process wild grains to supplement human diets (ibid.). Archaeological remains confirmed the existence of cereal-based and pastoral cultures in northern and eastern Africa, and there had also been archaeological evidence of increased use of wild grains after 8000 BC, followed by the integration of cultivation around 4000 BC into cultures. At about this time, without replacing hunting and gathering, pastoralism was adopted by the neolithic cultures (ibid., p. 92).

It was at one time popularly believed that the neolithic Africans graduated from hunter-gatherer to pastoralism and to farmer. Records of archaeological work indicate that diversification as a survival stratagem was the principal concern of the late Stone Age farmers, since specialization in non-equilibral (unstable) and harsh environment was a risky option. Accordingly, even after cultivation and livestock-keeping had been well established for several millennia, they did not replace hunting and gathering, a typical feature of neolithic Africans that persisted into the Christian era. The characteristic features of the evolution of agriculture had been complex interactive and adaptive processes of integration of, interactions and interrelationships with: physicochemical (soils, water, climate, nutrients); biological (plants, animals, pests and diseases); socioeconomic (labour, capital, markets, culture, personal preferences, social security); technological (tools, machines, practices); and managerial (indigenous knowledge and technology, decision-making, experience) factors (Blaikie, 1989). It was, therefore, complex interactions/ integrations/interrelationships influenced by environmental, economic, social and political systems that operated at a specific time period and in a given geographical setting. There was, therefore, a considerable heterogeneity in adaptations which could be distinguished into units or subsystems, differentiated according to the characteristic aspects of production interactions, with some cultures focusing on animal-based, agriculture-based, aquatic resources, various forms of pastoralisms and with some specializing in sedentary game while others focused on migratory game, agro-pastoral, etc. Typically, all of them maintained a broad resource base that permitted re-adaptations to changing potentials and constraints (Neimeijer, 1996, pp. 92–3), and the individual and collective creative choices which ultimately led to specific patterns of subsistence that changed over time in response to changing ecological settings and the social environment.

These dynamic and innovative adaptations of African farmers were primarily a rational behavioural response to changes in natural and social environment within which they operated, such as climatic perturbation, especially recurrent drought/random occurrence of drought that made fine-tuning (establishing an equilibrium system) difficult within a certain environmental or societal niche. Consequently, dynamic responses to non-equilibral (unstable) systems arising from external disturbances, flexibility and opportunistic responses formed a more important concern for survival than fine-tuning, overspecialization and optimization within the limits of specific natural and social niche. Given the broad resource base, agriculturalists as well as pastoralists shifted to preferred resources in response to internal and external changes either by adopting seasonal and/or constant mobility, or sedentary life. Some of them engaged in purely pastoral activities or farming while others adopted agro-pastoral systems. These practices and systems never remained static, since some nomadic pastoral communities have been known to settle into farming or engaged in agro-pastoral system in response to conjunctural variations such as adaptations of a subsistence-oriented farming systems to new market-oriented exchanges (Baker, undated reprint; Fumagalli, 1979; Neimeijer, 1996). The peculiar and distinctive features of prehistoric African agriculture, characterized by adaptations, re-adaptations and resource combinations, are still as relevant today as they were several millennia ago. Accordingly, the colonial superimposition of non-integrating exotic technologies on non-retreating traditional agriculture heralded the retrogression of African agriculture.

Traditional equilibrium production systems At the time of colonization of SSA countries during the nineteenth century, there was already some form of agriculture being practised and the traditional systems incorporated sophisticated resource management practices. Agriculturalists, agro-pastoralists and pastoralists evolved farming systems which were in equilibrium with the environment. In land-abundant but labour-scarce situations, the people developed farming systems which maximized return on these internal factors of production. African agriculture had been, by trial and error, a result of years of evolution from gathering fruits, extensive shifting cultivation and, currently, a move to intensive agriculture. The traditional farming systems currently consist of three complexes: a seed agricultural complex characteristic of the savannah involving the cultivation of grains and seed-bearing crops in open fields; 'vegecultural' complex peculiar to the forest region where roots and tubers predominate (Okigbo, 1988); and agriculture- and animal-based livelihood systems in semi-arid areas. In the savannah and forest regions, over the years peasants developed agricultural practices that incorporated sophisticated resource combinations and adaptations of production systems, which included shifting cultivations, mixed cropping, relay-cropping, inter-cropping, soil and forest conservation, hillside and wetland cultivations. The structure of the traditional farming systems involved different methods of soil and water management and fertility maintenance, which includes the selective clearance of forests and woodlands, a production phase and a long fallow period which allowed for the regrowth of natural vegetation and restoration of soil fertility that ensured sustainability. The long fallow cultivation systems were appropriate responses to abundant land and a limited capital situation. The characteristic feature of the practice was mobility. In order to allow soil fertility to be restored through natural vegetation and decay (recycling), people moved out of a land when yield started to decline and forage depleted.

In dryland farming, faced with the need to derive subsistence from semi-arid areas that are hazard-prone, harsh and capable of great inter-annual fluctuations in productivity, the pastoralists and agro-pastoralists have evolved an array of livelihood systems – the major ones being agriculture- and animal-based, or a mixture of both. With agriculture-based dry land farming, the most prevalent livelihood is characterized by a range of strategies and techniques enabling the farmers to cope with a high degree of rainfall variability. In these semi-arid zones, moisture maximization involves an array of diverse techniques, principally careful seasonal plantings of fast-maturing varieties of crops, scattered plantings of drought-resistant crops, careful weeding and mulching techniques and practices, the use of moist bottomlands, and the construction of bunds and dams to impound runoff. An agro-pastoralist system provides a crucial complement of animals to an uncertain agricultural situation, thereby forming an integrated agro-pastoral production system. The other agriculture-based livelihood in dryland farming is based on irrigation in the major river valleys of the arid lands.

As regards animal-based livelihood systems, the most significant feature is the emphasis on mobility. It is by movement to seasonal pastures at different locations that the pastoralists are able to balance pasture use and water through an annual cycle of movement, including escape from diseases, access to markets, etc. The other livelihood strategy is to diversify the system by rearing a herd of a mixture of animal species in order to maximize the productive potential of various ecological niches available to them, or organizing modern commercial livestock ranching having exclusive rights over range, which is in contrast to the principles of traditional animal-based exploitation regimes that emphasize mobility.

Within each livelihood system, further subdivisions can be distinguished each possessing its own demographic characteristics, technology, social organizations and behavioural features. Almost all culture groups utilize a dynamic mix or have developed complex techniques. Over time, resource combinations evolved complementary sets of activities that spread risks inherent in traditional farming environments, maximize productivity to the extent that available technologies permit and meet cultural and economic needs. These adaptations, however, face some problems, because as local systems become increasingly integrated into national and international market economies, they become exposed to forces operating beyond their territorial boundaries and control. Also, as agriculture is the principal link between people and the environment, rapid population (both human and animal) can lead to the regenerative capacity of natural resources being overwhelmed – setting in motion self-reinforcing process of ecological degradation in the absence of appropriate technological advances of relevance to farming situation.

Traditional non-exploitative social production relations It is generally believed that a cluster of people descended from one ancestor or closely related ancestors. Accordingly, because of these agnatic and affinal ties, communal claims on property rest on the notion that most resources derive from the ancestors and were created and sustained through the collective labour of past family members. Based on these perceptions, it is normally acceptable for the descendants to have a rightful claim on the fruits of their ancestors' labour, as well as the patrimony. Societal horizontal integrative bonds (inter-household mutual linkage) exist around reciprocal access to productive resources. It is this reciprocal access that is usually significant in binding the community in a network of rights and obligations. It is also these social relations (traditionally not commodified, as no payment in cash or kind is made) surrounding access to resources which often form the basis upon which other sets of relations are based. Pooling land and labour resources already invested in agricultural production ensures that these production factors are not wasted and their cost to the societies is minimized. For instance, in areas facing the vagaries of weather, low soil fertility, simple technology and slow natural fertility regeneration, agricultural output depends to a large extent on labour directly, via careful timing of agricultural operations, and indirectly, through labour allocation in resource management such as soil and water conservation, improving soil water retentive capacity through ridging and manuring. Thus, reciprocal claims on land resources allow full and relatively efficient use of land and labour resources and, therefore, avoid the need for food assistance and reduce moral hazards and social humiliation. It also ensures that latent resources are productively employed. It is the basis of how production shocks are socially articulated.

Access to productive resources is a major factor in the evolution of resource tenure system. In SSA generally the starting point regarding resource tenure is the tribe, perceived in the past in the context of the Roman legal concept of *dominium emines*, typified by communities having authority over a piece of territory without holding any formal office in a political sense (FAO, 1991). In this system, chiefs hold land in custody on behalf of the people. This has given rise to the notion of 'communal property', which is the cornerstone of the relationship between land and human existence and livelihood. Although the colonial administration referred to 'tribal economy', it is not possible to demonstrate its existence outside kinship organization. Agricultural production, therefore, is kinship based. Tribes on the other hand are regarded as autonomous self-contained units each of which comprises a variable number of clans. These clans consist of lineages and it is their heads in whom is vested the right to allocate land to their members for their use. The clan headship is derived through lineage hierarchies based on old-age seniority.

A typical village consists of kinsmen or kinswomen who, for purposes of avoiding incestuous relationship and for social reproduction, rely on wives or husbands acquired from outside the agnatic groups under a system of exogamous marriages. Each clan can be regarded as self-containing bonds in the context of their corporate nature and preoccupation with production and reproduction of material conditions for social existence. It has no relation to accumulation of value, but is concerned with optimizing use-value within a redistributive mode of social organization. The development of private property can disrupt this system and deprive some of its members of the means of livelihood. Consequently whatever means of production over which the lineage has control, such as land and valued resources, are not regarded as property but instruments of production which cannot be withdrawn by individuals without threatening the security of the group as a whole. What can be transferred to other users is not land itself but what it can produce, thus making land both inalienable and inestimable. Under this system, land is regarded as a social endowment associated with the corporate existence which is fixed in space but transcends life because of variable cycles of control over it. This allows permanency as well as flexibility of resource use, while at the same time avoiding the individualization of risks.

However, there are access qualifications. In exogamous marriages, where wives marry into the lineage but cannot belong to it, especially in patrilineal societies, wives have no rights over land and valued resources. In these societies lineage is sustained through males, and women rarely attain the status of elders and thus are denied the claim to the lineage's productive and valued resources. Hence, although women produce value for their families, they retain only latent claims over property, even those of their fathers' lineage (FAO, 1991). According to Safilios-Rothschild (1985, p. 312), sex stratification is a practice that ranks males higher than females and gives the former the dominant role of major decision-making and the control of valued items (wealth, income, credit, knowledge, technology, gainful income-generating activities, food, health, power) in society. Thus the characteristic feature of resource tenure is not one where land is communally owned, but one where land is divided into territorial entities held by recognized corporate groups in the form of lineages and exploited by the household's basic social units who comprise kin members. The system can be regarded as representing the public/jural territories and the domestic/conjugal entities respectively. Commodification of land and labour and the appropriation of value can result in the elders or clan heads losing jural authority over the means of livelihood which they owe to the whole lineage. The system, therefore, curtails processes of increasing asset inequality.

a)　*Resource tenure in arable areas*

The first major contacts between Sub-Saharan African (SSA) societies and mercantalist European nations occurred during the fifteenth century (Archarya, 1978). At this time, the overwhelming majority of Africans were engaged in subsistence farming. According to Rweyemamu (1973), prior to the advent of European contact and colonization, the vast majority of the countries in Sub-Saharan Africa consisted of small independent producers involved in pre-capitalistic modes of agriculture production, generally clustered in various sociocultural groupings typically delineated by kinship. The dominant production system was the village community, whose members consisted of peasant cultivators. Their social security was governed by their mutual relationship as members of the community who were working owners of land under their control. Membership in the community was the precondition for the appropriation of land but in their capacity as members, the individuals could consider the allotment to them as their own as long as they continued to occupy it beneficially. Security of tenure in this way was guaranteed.

This system of land tenure consisted of clusters of rights over land and its products. The traditional systems of land tenure were, therefore, almost universally characterized by: i) the rights of every individual to the productive use of land by virtue of his citizenship in a given sociocultural group; ii) the overlapping of rights over land and its products among individuals and groups; and iii) rigid prohibition against individual alienations of land over which a person had specific but never absolute right. Hence the precondition for the continued existence of the community was the maintenance of a semblance of equality among its free, self-sustaining peasants, and their individual labour as the condition for the continued existence of their property. This accounted for the absence of classes in traditional societies, as it lacked social differentiation. It also lacked wage labour as the precondition for capital accumulation, since each individual peasant was not separated from his land. The emergence of classes would have dissolved communal landed property, and hence the village community, as a productive system. Technologies for production were highly land-intensive, due mainly to people's attitudes towards land, which was that of usufruct only, and the existence at that time of unlimited supply of good land. This technique of production led to the system of shifting cultivation that made any attempts to take steps to preserve the soil fertility unnecessary.

Under the traditional society, market exchanges were peripheral in the sense that most producers did not only rely on exchange for the acquisition of the bulk of the means of production. The absence of market exchange as the dominant economic organization encouraged social control of production by kinship, religion and political organization. Primary factors of production were never traded. Land was distributed through kinship, chiefs, etc. while labour was appropriated through marriage, kinship and friendship reciprocity; for example, work parties could be called upon to do specific tasks such as land clearing, weeding or harvesting. Hence social relationships and values were the most important determinants of work organization. In this social organization that subordinated economic goals to a wider objective of societal consolidation and security, the distribution of production surpluses rested on an institutional system of socially obligatory duties of making, receiving and returning gifts. Investment effort, on the other hand, was spent on bush clearing, building, manufacturing, purchasing appropriate tools. Thus the distributive system served the purpose of social cohesion and security of subsistence to the individual. This system of village commerce, of course, had very obvious drawbacks.

The material level of life was very low, which was a result of the social organization failing to inspire innovation and technical changes that would have significantly raised the society's production frontier. Acharya further noted that the political concomitant of production was that chieftainship tended to be over people rather than land. With one or two exceptions (Ethiopia, for example), the European-style of feudalism based on land security was unknown (Archarya, 1978). This type of corporate system was highly flexible because it could accept strangers and migrants as members who could reside with the rural communities. In this case, access to land and other vital resources was not restricted to lineage but could also be grounded in loyalty and patronage relations, which were often associated with an ascriptive form of status or social identity (Berry, 1984, p. 91). In this system, lineages or social groups with surplus cultivable land could always accommodate strangers or migrants on the understanding that they would agree to enter into the local network or personal interrelationships and accept the political authority of the local chief. In this arrangement, the strangers were expected to pay regular dues, usually in the form of labour services, a share of their harvest or other types of contribution. These dues were not regarded as land rent but symbolic gifts to manifest an act of political allegiance that had to be renewed continuously. During occupancy, the users have undisputable tenurial right over the land. In some areas multiple rights over a piece of land was practised. Under such systems of land use, some persons could cultivate crops, while on the same land others could have rights over trees, or land could be used by cultivators during the cropping season and by pastoralists in the off-season or during the fallow periods.

In the context of land abundance and labour scarcity which characterized ancient African societies, the control of labour proved far more important than the control of land and constituted the real base of economic prosperity, social prestige and political power (Phillipe-Plateau, 1990). According to Robertson (1987, p. 24), it led to people-based forms of servitude that had been far more predominant in SSA than anything else resembling feudality. Under these conditions, ruling families, lineages or larger social groups often captured the peasantries or developed systems of property rights in man such as corvee or slavery. In exchange for their labour, services and monopoly on accumulated assets, the master has an obligation to meet the subsistence requirements of the slaves. According to Phillipe-Plateau (ibid., p. 77), in stratified societies rights to labour were influenced by class or caste rather than by the length of residence in the village or members' ancestry. Members of the occupational caste or slaves were required to work during the first half of the day on their master's field and they were allowed to work in the afternoon for their own subsistence on their small and comparatively infertile landholding. Similar practices were common among the Songhay-Zame in both Mali and Niger. In Rwanda, the clients of the Hutu, in payment for the right to occupy land lying fallow, had to give the village chief a specified number of hoes and beer jugs and a share of their harvest. By contract, the clients of the Tutsi rulers were installed on lands taken away from the Hutu settlers. The price paid by the clients for the right of occupation amounted to two days of labour a week on the lands of the Tutsi patron.

b) *Resource tenure in pastoral Africa*

Pastoral communities traditionally live in harsh environments marked by seasonal and inter-annual climatic instability. The pastoralists in these environments, which persistently suffer from rainfall which is erratic in amounts, timing and spatial distribution – the so-called non-equilibrium environments of arid and semi-arid areas – have evolved complex, highly variable grazing systems. The most common behavioural response to such an unstable environment is to move animals around, avoiding areas where forage is insufficient and mopping up surpluses in areas where it is abundant. For this purpose, pastoralists maintain institutions which regulate access to natural resources and the intensity of their use (Behnke, 1994). One of the ways pastoral communities adjust themselves to cope with resource insufficiencies initially is to consolidate and galvanize kinship linkages. This is the common behavioural response when the resource constraint is not so acute and, under such conditions, it is to the advantage of the pastoral communities to organize reciprocal lien on one's own property, which forms the basis for exchange or resources under the nonexclusive tenure and land use regimes. These nonexclusive tenure arrangements, which make herd mobility possible, have enabled the pastoral communities to sustain their herds in equilibrium with the unstable environment. When resources become scarce, the pastoralists' response tends to be irrational because, rather than reduce herd size to keep in balance with the environment, they resort to militaristic pursuit in order to expel weaker neighbouring clans, even erstwhile allies, who are then regarded as competitors for resources which have become inadequate to sustain competing claimants. In some areas multiple rights over a piece of land are practised.

Traditional productive relations: some examples As discussed earlier, it was quite often stated that there was a fairly distinct labour division between sexes in a developing agriculture, with women concentrating on food crops and men on cash crops. This dictum was still apparent in many areas but was gradually breaking down (Okai, 1968).

In some areas, there were organized systems of pooling labour in order to overcome labour bottlenecks at peak demand periods. In northern Uganda, for instance, three such systems existed. The largest one was the *wangtic* (communal labour organization) system by which some 20–25 male heads of households agree to pool labour, especially for carrying out major farming operations. The system had a head (*adwong wangtic*) who was responsible for assigning days when assistance is to be provided by the working party to members of the association. He was also responsible for deciding on the tasks to be performed. The party of men worked in a member's farm on a day assigned for him and at the end of the work they were rewarded by the host farmer, who served them with the local drink. Women were not eligible to be members of the association even if they were heads of households. However, women still played a critical complementary role in brewing the local beer used for rewarding members of the communal labour association. This role (brewing beer) was traditionally outside the competence of men.

Another system was a mutual arrangement (*alea*) among a party of up to six men who agreed to reciprocate assistance to each other. The tasks to be performed were mutually agreed upon by the party. This system was used largely for weeding cash crops. Women could form a separate *alea* on their own mainly for weeding and harvesting. The third system was *puro gweno* or *kongo*, which was an ad hoc system of pooling labour. A party of three men, after performing a specific task, was rewarded by serving a meal of chicken. If the number exceeded three men, beer was provided. These two systems were used usually regarded as applying to minor crops. Women again did not participate in these systems, although they played an equally critical role in the preparation of meals or the local beer.

These systems incorporated some form of informal institutional credit arrangement to members. In cases where a poor member was unable to provide the stipulated rewards for work performed by members of the association, the party would still assist. In addition to the traditional beer, he was expected to supplement it with a meal of a goat meat. This was a form of interest he had to pay. Another form of assistance, incorporated in the communal labour arrangement, was in kind. There were young men working in urban centres whose wives were sent home during harvest season to join other women in harvesting and rewarded with the provision of a small portion of the crop harvested. After the harvest season, these women would have collected sufficient food for their urban families.

Women's role in the agricultural production process varied a great deal among traditional societies. This depended on a range of facilitating and/or restraining factors which included: i) the nature of social organization (patrilineal or matrilineal); ii) cultural attitudes towards women; iii) the nature of the production organization (settled agriculture or nomadism, etc.). Women's ability to mobilize factors of production to earn income depended on social norms and prevailing practices. These relationships determined women's access to productive resources (land, labour and capital), valued resources (living animals and income) and services (marketing, credit, membership of traditional organizations, and training and extension services).

Peasant farmers traditionally have no capital assets other than simple hand tools. However, in areas where cattle rearing is a major economic activity, ox-drawn equipment is widely used for land preparation. Productive assets in these areas, such as cattle, equipment, etc., are essential to rural households since they are the primary means of earning income. Households lacking such assets are usually poor, and such a low level of asset ownership encourages males to migrate. Such migration may help men to raise some money, which is used for the purchase of cattle and equipment. Where the male does not migrate, he has the option of herding the cattle of large cattle owners, for which he is paid in kind by receiving animals in return for his labour. Women, however, do not enjoy this right of access to productive assets as they are not allowed to own land or livestock, nor are they engaged by large cattle owners, since herding cattle is traditionally a man's work. Also, as they do not migrate as much as the men, women have no savings to invest in land or the purchase of livestock. Hence the low level of asset ownership means that women are likely to remain poor.

Where a male head of a household might have migrated, women in most cases have access to land. Often, however, a woman is handicapped in crop cultivation because she may not have a team of oxen for ploughing the land. In cases where she has a team, the female lacks the physical strength to handle the ox team during ploughing. Some of these constraints might be ameliorated by male relatives extending assistance to the woman during ploughing time, but the male relatives usually plough their fields first and thus benefit from the timely planting of their crops. Hiring labour could also ameliorate this bottleneck, but at peak ploughing time the demand for male labour is so prohibitively high that it makes such help too expensive compared to its earning potential. Because of these constraints, female-headed households tend to cultivate smaller areas of land than male-headed households. In northern and eastern Uganda, male farmers who do not have ox-drawn equipment usually hire the equipment from neighbours. Although the hire service can be paid in cash, usually equipment owners prefer to be paid in kind, traditionally a goat. As women do not own livestock, they are, therefore, unable to take advantage of the hire service (Okai, 1964). Women are further disadvantaged by their role as mothers. While caring for children can be accommodated while carrying out certain agricultural activities, others, like bush-clearing, ploughing, hunting amd herding cattle are incompatible with looking after children.

Survival strategy An array of strategies is developed to mitigate the scourges of hardships. There are basically two types of managing risks, based on activity and environment diversifications. Activity diversification, for example, relates to claims households make on income-generating activities that respond differently to external shocks. A typical example is intercropping – more than one crop on the same field to diversify against specific microclimatic risks (Belshaw and Hall, 1965; Belshaw, 1980; Okai, 1968; Carter, 1997, p. 559). The success of intercropping depends to a large extent on the roots of the different crops exploring different profiles of the soil to avoid competition for plant nutrients and soil moisture. This form of diversification exploits technical complementarity and/or supplementarity among the crops. The complementary interactions among crops also help to protect the soil from erosion. There is also temporal diversification which entails staggering planting over time in the expectation that if, for instance, the early planted crops fail, the others may succeed. There are also some aspects of technical diversification. In a crop rotation, crops which require a high level of soil fertility are planted at the beginning of the rotation, followed by crops which can tolerate a low level of fertility. Towards the end of the rotation, in some practices, nitrogen-fixing leguminous crops or shrubs like pigeon peas are interplanted with other non-leguminous crops as a measure for increasing compensatory productivity.

Environment diversification involves scattering fields across microclimates and topographical niches by planting crops in different fields which respond to specific microclimatic conditions. Among pastoralists, environment diversification involves animals being scattered among relatives to herd. This is done to avoid losing all animals in the event of an outbreak of diseases. Pursuing both activity and environment diversification as a strategy for risk management depends to a large extent on the qualities and quantities of natural resources endowment. Risk minimization is, therefore, feasible if households have access to productive assets.

Pastoral communities live in harsh and unstable environments in marginal range lands typified by seasonality and variability of precipitation which accelerated towards their arid extremities. It is from such a dichotomous environment of quite extraordinary hostility that the nomads for centuries managed to derive an existence, taking advantage of short periods of plenty in different locations, which has given rise to frequent migrations in search of pasture and water. Because of these movements, some of the pastoralists have actually at times undergone drastic and swift transformation in response to changes in ecological conditions and/or new alternative productive opportunities. The Turkana separated from the Jie to become nearly pure pastoralists, while the Masai, near Arusha in northern Tanzania, settled down to become farmers. The Pokot and Kamba also settled down to a land economy with heavy reliance on both agriculture and pastoralism (Fumagalli, 1979; Baker, undated reprint, p. 725).

Living in such hostile environment, the primary concern and pattern of activities of the nomads are, therefore, for survival. They have devised a number of ways of minimizing risks and the exact stratagem selected or adopted varies from community to community, from season to season and/or a variety of combinations and sequences of events (ibid., p. 726). There is, therefore, a wide diversity in the productive base of the various pastoral communities. In some cases, the communities like the Masai of East Africa derive their livelihood almost entirely from recurrent products of their animals such as blood and milk and scorn crop agriculture (Baker, p. 723). In the Sahel of West Africa, the non-cultivating nomads, *grandes nomades*, have a diet derived from the semi-arid rangeland and cultivated land in wetter areas. The trade may be on an equal exchange of animals for grain between pastoralists and the cultivators. In other areas of West Africa, pastoralists would occasionally herd the cattle owned by the cultivators together with their animals, returning them when required by the owners bringing along useful commodities like salt in part payment for the privileges of obtaining milk from the cattle they have been herding but owned by the cultivators (Baker, p. 724). In Uganda, following the outbreak of rinderpest in 1905, the Bahima pastoralists in the southwestern part of the country, lost most of their cattle. Many of them travelled to northern and northeastern Uganda to herd the cattle belonging to agro-pastoralists of Lango and Teso in return for milk which they were permitted to sell the surplus. The Bahima were, therefore, able to reconstitute their stock through using the proceeds of the sale of milk. Schneider also reported that among the Somalis, where a small section of the society produces sufficient grain to meet almost all the needs of the pastoralists, it is traded from the grain producers to the pastoralists in return for livestock and cash. The Suk, like the Somalis, specialize in production, with those on the hill growing grain, while the pastoralists in the plains hold large herds of livestock some of which are exchanged for grains (Schneider, 1974, p. 45). Among the Turkana of northern Kenya and the Jie of East Africa, the common type of life of pastoral semi-nomadic societies is based on livestock complementing or is complemented by crop production. In the case of the Jie, the farming is the responsibility of the women, who remain on their plots with the elders and the children while the young men take the family herds in search of water and grazing (Baker, p. 721).

According to Baker, cattle amongst the pastoralists, depending on the specific society and the environment, play a significant role in meeting the subsistence needs of the communities. They are often a significant medium of exchange for food stuffs and galvanizing a network of social bonds and obligations connected ultimately with security. In terms of exchange of cattle for other commodities, usually grain, as mentioned above, many scholars of nomadism have illustrated long-standing complementarities and well-established rates of exchange. In most pastoral communities, for instance, some systems of lending exist to provide relief to afflicted families to enable them recover from the loss of their stock through drought, disease or raiding. Cattle rustling itself is a redistributive mechanism often associated with a particular time of hardship. Among the Pokot of East Africa there is an interesting arrangement for collective social security and a reduction of inequality among the nomads. One nomad with a large number of cows would give some of them to those who might have lost their animals due to natural calamities or theft. Under this arrangements the recipients are merely getting access to milk, since they do not keep calves produced (Livingstone, 1977, p. 216).

In other pastoral areas the relationship between the nomads and the cultivators is based on inequality derived from the martial superiority and militaristic pursuits of the pastoral communities, who, being mobile, could impose their rule or will on vulnerable societies who live in fear of their properties being plundered or cattle being raided. Typical examples are the relationships based on the militaristic pursuit of the great Fulani of West Africa and the more subtle authority wielded by the Tutsi over Hutu of Rwanda through the clientage system (Phillipe-Plateau, 1990). The authority of the Tutsi over the majority cultivators, the Hutu, was established over 500 years ago, initially by force of arms, and their superiority was associated with mobility. In this way, the Tutsi brought animals into areas where they were unnecessary and the pastoral autocracy gradually gained hegemony over an agricultural environment. Over time, the Hutu were willing to accept animals from the Tutsi (Baker, p. 725). In parts of West Africa and the Hejaz, the trade is based on an equal exchange of animals for grain between the pastoral communities living in a virtually nonexistent commercial infrastructure where formal retail outlets are unavailable. Accordingly, to sell one's subsistence base is to throw a pastoralist into a state of perpetual dependency. Furthermore, with extensive mobility, it would be unreasonable to expect a pastoralist to accumulate or store consumer goods which have to be carried along as they roam the rangeland. A pastoralist, therefore, finds it imperative to keep a large amount of stock from which he obtains recurrent products, and to remain within the traditional network of collective social security. Under these conditions, many scholars of nomadism have indicated that marketed offtake may be only 3 to 8 per cent, with local consumption, feasts and losses raising the figure to about 15 per cent, which is considered the ceiling for pastoral communities. The low offtake is not regarded by many scholars (Baker, Behnke, etc.) as being an indication of perverse reaction to market forces because in a situation where the environment is harsh and unstable and insecurity widespread, individual pastoralists could face extinction if they were not part of a wider network with ingenuous strategies for survival.

From the economic point of view, the pastoralists' behaviour is rational because the animals are valuable assets. The pastoralists' decisional content is dictated by expected net present values (NPV) of future stream of income accruing from the recurrent animal products. These pastoralists continually compute the NPV of these products. If sales or slaughter values of animals equal or exceed the net present values, it will be profitable to dispose of the animals.

Non-efficiency Objective Analysis

Given the importance of non-efficiency objectives, evaluation of trade-offs that arise between efficiency and non-efficiency assumes particular significance in policy analysis. Since resources are usually scarce, the pursuit of one objective will usually come about at the expense of reduced activities or outputs in other economic endeavours. However, as regards the elimination of market failures, this generalization does not hold because, in this case, policy interventions liberate resources from less efficient uses and thus increase total value of economic activities. But in most cases the attainment of objectives entails economic costs and the assessment of these trade-offs yields valuable insight regarding the desirability of promoting a particular objective.

As explained in the preceding sections, an optimizing risk-averse smallholder confronted with a subjectively risk-increasing situation manages to control the risk through a range of diversifications. One of the major commercial objectives in most countries is to increase the production of export crops. In promoting cotton production, smallholders are exhorted to adopt new improved technologies such as better and timely farm operations, including early planting in pure stand or planting in rows to obtain optimal plant population. These prescribed cultural practices are based on empirical evidence. It has been proved in Uganda that when planting is delayed by two weeks, yield of cotton declines by about 30 per cent and a further delay of two weeks results in a further decline by about 18 per cent, in total a decline of 48 per cent.

If the smallholder accepts the technological transformation, as shown in the figure, his/her output moves from the current low equilibrium A to a new frontier B (see Figure 14). However, given limited labour supply, he/she either sacrifices the growing of beans which under traditional practices are interplanted with cotton to overcome labour bottlenecks. His/her risk-decisional content will influence to what extent he/she will adopt the technological innovation. He/she may partially adopt the new technology. Staggering planting and intercropping as risk-aversion strategy may be retained. In this case the expected return will shift from B to C, thus reducing risk represented by $R_3 - R_2$. Hence on-the-farm diversification-cum-technological transformation usually forms the basis for decisions in respect of deviations from optimal planting date, which is traded in for the minimization of risks.

The trade-off between efficiency and non-efficiency objective can be illustrated by the production possibility curves. The curve ACB portrays the maximum level of production possibility for the smallholder producing beans and cotton. Producing at world prices and based on high input technology leads to a production pattern represented by point C (cotton and bean outputs are represented by OQ^c_1 and Q^b_1 respectively) and a consumption possibility frontier represented by $F_1C E_1$. By trading at world prices the smallholder can choose to consume at any point along $F_1C E_1$. In this case total income accruing to the smallholder can be measured with respect to either commodity. In terms of cotton, total income is OE_1, while that of beans is OF_1 (Figure 15).

If the government wishes to improve bean supply, it will have to increase the relative price of beans. Since the country cannot influence world prices, the production possibility curve will shift inward to A_1DB_2. Measured in terms of both crops, the potential income of the smallholder from cotton will fall to OQ^c_2 and beans to OQ^b_2. The difference in total income $(OF_1 - OF_2)$ times the world price of beans equals the efficiency cost of pursuing the non-efficiency objective.

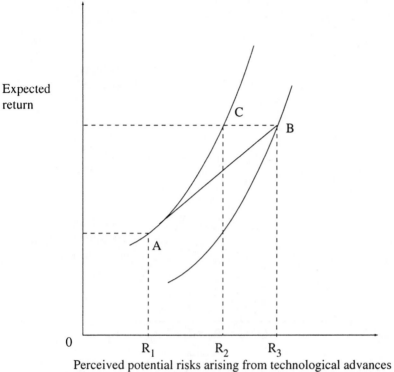

Expected return

Perceived potential risks arising from technological advances

Figure 14 On-farm diversification-cum-technological transformation

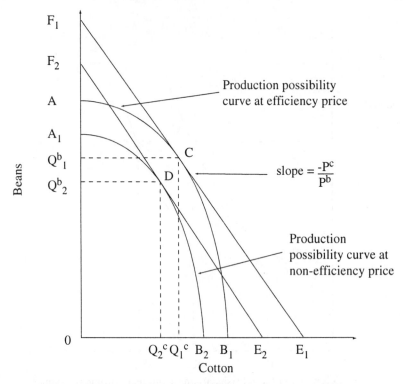

Figure 15 Non-efficiency objectives and shifts in production possibilities

3 Economics of Resource Conservation

Conservation is a technical problem which requires much research into the technical and physical situation of the natural resources. These resources can be distinguished into three types: stock of resources, which are not renewable, flow, and temporary flow resources. Typical examples of renewable resources are water (rivers, lakes, ocean) and soil, which provide streams of uses such as furnishing public utilities as electric energy, transportation, crop and animal production in a continuous fashion. Non-renewable resources are minerals, fossils, fossil oil and water, and coal which, once used, cannot be renewed. Temporary flow resources, such as forest, give a flow of services for a specified time. Many natural resources, however, are flow resources. The way the resources are used at present will affect future use. If the flow of resource is reduced, it means that the present use is in excess of natural regeneration rate.

There are about six socioeconomic determinants which affect conservation. When farmers' income falls, they will have less money and, therefore, their rate of discounting future income to present value (PV) will be high. In Uganda it was observed that following the post-World War II commodity price boom, farmers invested heavily in planting coffee and the construction of *pas palum* bunds as a soil conservation measure. This was because income increased, which ultimately encouraged the construction of conservation measures because the farmers' rate of discounting future return on investment decreased as income increased. Indefinite property right, and the associated lack of land market, discourages investment in conservation measures. Land market distortion due to institutional constraints, low investment in preserving productivity, or potential buyers having little knowledge of productivity due to lack of transparency all tend to discourage investment in land use and conservation. Conversely, improving the efficiency of land market, its productivity and value, creates incentive for land purchases. Uncertainty due to domestic instability (crime, political disturbances and other problems) discourages investment in resource utilization and conservation because the farmers use a high discount rate for fear of risks. The other source of disincentive in conservation is a high interest rate due to capital scarcity or domestic inflation. The other problem concerns institutional interest, such as land tenure system, especially common resource shared by many nations, or even in a country where the existence of common resource tenure may encourage extractive forms of utilization of the resources.

Implication of Resource Degradation for Internal Factors

One of the principal phenomena in the SSA region in general has been an increasing population pressure on fragile land, causing a breakdown of the traditional rotation systems of varying lengths of fallow periods, depending on the level of resource productivity. Decreased fallow periods without the replenishment of soil nutrients result in a decline in yield. As yield decreases, farmers are forced to increase cultivated land in order to maintain the same levels of output. Also, with declining soil quality, farmers are compelled to increase their labour in order to maintain the same output levels. As illustrated in the figure, at the initial isoquant ACB and isocost I, labour utilization is Lo and land is Ko. As cultivation expands and as the fallow system disintegrates, land quality deteriorates so that more land (K_1) is required to produce the same levels of output, and the isoquant shifts to ACD and isocost to II. At the same relative costs of land and labour, more labour (L_1) is required to maintain output level. As labour productivity is reduced by the falling land quality, the new isoquant ACE reflects this deterioration in the relative productivity of labour. The new isocost line III, therefore, results in further increases in the labour (L_2) required to maintain the same levels of output (Figure 16).

The escalation of costs in terms of land (K_2) and labour (L_2), forces farmers to adopt new technologies. As labour reserve is extended to the limit, the adoption of mechanical aids like ox-equipment reduces labour requirements to Lx, but land brought under cultivation remains at K_2 (K_x). The new isocost line IV influences isoquant shift to ACF as a result of the adoption of the new labour-saving technology. The adoption of yield-increasing technology makes it possible to reduce land under cultivation to Kt and yet maintain the same levels of output. If most farming operations are mechanized, labour requirement may increase moderately to L_t. Isoquants respectively shift to ACF and ACG and isocost lines shift to IV and V. Apart from economic and profitability consideration, farmers' conservation behaviour is also influenced by other factors such as: i) the recognition and appreciation of the gravity of environmental degradation and its consequences for livelihood; ii) perceived

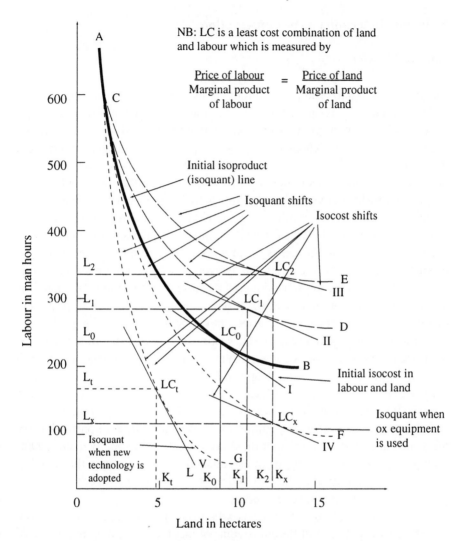

Figure 16 Isoquant shifts arising from land degradation and new technology

technical feasibility of adopting certain conservation measures; and iii) the scale of operation they entail, especially in terms of labour requirement.

Economic Determinants of Conservation

Time and Period

The time required to produce an output varies; for instance, producing annual and perennial crops is distinct in that a shorter period is needed to produce the annuals whereas it takes initially a longer time for perennials before a stream of income is received. There are usually two problems to be confronted about the expectations of the future income. The first problem concerns changes in prices at different points in the production process. At the time of planting a crop or investing in livestock, one expects to receive a certain return. There might be a bumper crop produced by many farmers. Increased supply of the crop leads to a price fall. If the price fall would lead to a loss (cost of production exceeding return), the farmer is faced with a decision either to abandon the production process or to continue. However, so long as total revenue covers those costs which are yet to be covered because of the fall in sales, then it is still profitable to continue with the production, but the change in price will offset the level of inputs of those factors which are as yet to be used. Land preparation, planting, weeding and harvesting all require time. If, for instance, the price the farmer obtains between the time of weeding and harvesting will be low, he should continue so long as harvesting cost is covered by the total revenue, because it will pay to harvest. In this example the farmer has incurred a loss, but by harvesting he minimizes his loss. The postwar commodity price boom encouraged extensive planting of cocoa and coffee, in particular. By the 1960s and 1970s the price of these commodities drastically declined but output continued increasing from established bushes, because the planting costs had been incurred in the past and the farmer was able to cover costs of picking coffee berries and cocoa pods.

The other problem with time is when trying to compare return from investments which have different streams of income over time. In the case of annual and perennial crops, an investor in annual crops has to wait for nine to 12 months to obtain a return, whereas the other investor, say in coffee, will have to wait for four years before receiving any return. The first problem to be encountered is to do with losses that might arise if the investor commits money at present in anticipation of receiving returns in future. Money at present is worth more than that in future – i.e. a bird in hand is worth two in the bush. In order to compare profitability of present investment, a process of discounting is used. The rate used in discounting the future value to arrive at present value (PV) is called the rate of interest. The interest rate is nothing more than a market price for lending and borrowing funds. Using this market interest rate, an investment is profitable if the rate of return on the investment is equal to or greater than zero, i.e. above the market rate of interest. Consider a simple example of ¢1,000 invested now at an interest of 10 per cent and ¢1,100 is expected to be repaid after one year. A loan, therefore, from the lender's point of view, is undertaken with the objective of earning a return which is usually called 'interest payment', i.e. interest is paid in addition to the amount invested. The investor (or the lender) expects to have original investment returned in addition to interest payment.

Computationally the relation between ¢1,000 and ¢1,100 is: $(1 + 0.10) \times 100 = 110$. Within the parenthesis, the '1' represents the principal (the original investment of ¢1,000) and the figure of '0.10' is the 10 per cent interest. Therefore, if an investment earns 10 per cent in one year, the 10 per cent is added to the principal, which is, in this case, ¢1,000. The sum of ¢1,000 (the original investment) and the ¢100 (the interest payment) is equal to ¢1,100. In this example we are asking what will be the current value of investment in future at 10 per cent interest rate. In this case we are compounding the present value which can be expressed by the formula:

$$\text{Future value (FV)} = \text{Present value (PV)} \times (1 + r)^n \qquad (1)$$
$$\text{or } FV = PV \times (1 + r)^n \qquad (2)$$

Conversely we can compute the present value of ¢1,100 which is expected to be received one year from now, assuming the risk of not receiving the payment in future is nonexistent. The sum of ¢1,100 received one year from now is equivalent to some amount of money now (year zero) that can be put out at interest and will grow to equal the sum of ¢1,100 after one year. If interest (or discount rate) remains at 10 per cent, the present value of ¢1,100 received one year from now can be computed as follows:

$$\text{Present value} = \frac{(\text{Future nominal value})}{(1 + 0.10)^1}$$
$$= \frac{1100}{(1 + 0.10)^1} = 1000$$
$$\text{or } PV = \frac{1}{(1 + r)^n}$$

where

1   = future nominal income (or FV);
PV = present value;
r   = rate of discount (or interest); and
n   = number of years away into the future.

The relation between the *present value* and *future nominal value* is determined by the expression $(1 + r)$ which is concerned with estimating the amount needed now in order to have it grow to equal future nominal value, and calculating the increase in the present value of the sum of money invested now at a fixed rate of interest. Each of these is concerned with time, interest rates and either looking back towards the present from the future or looking forward towards the future from the present. Any production process is carried out within a time framework, depending on the gestation and life span of the investment, which can be illustrated as follows:

	Present value (years)	**Year 1**	**Year 2**	**Year 3**
	₡ *1,000*	*1,100*	*1,210*	*1,331*
Year	*Present value*	*Future nominal value*		
0	$1,000(11,000(1+0.10)^0$	1,000.00		
1	$100(1+0.10)^1$	1,100.00		
2	$100(1+0.10)^2$	1,210.00		
3	$100(1+0.10)^3$	1,331.00		
4	$100(1+0.10)^4$	1,464.11		
5	$100(1+0.10)^5$	1,607.49		

To avoid individual computations of values, factor tables of conversion had been prepared. Each factor corresponds to the expression $(1+r)n$ which can be rewritten as

$$PV = FV \times \frac{1}{(1+r)n} \tag{3}$$

i.e. the *factor* is equivalent to $\frac{1}{(1+r)n}$.

Using the formula and the above example, the *present value* of 1 is

	Factors at		**Values at 10%**	
Year	*10%*	*20%*	*FV*	*PV*
1	0.909091	0.83333	100	90.91
2	0.826446	0.69444	200	165.29
3	0.751315	0.57870	300	225.39
4	0.683013	0.48225	150	102.45
5	0.620921	0.40181	100	69.09
	3.790786	2.99068	850	653.13

Usually there is a need to calculate the profitability of an investment on the basis of the annual rate of return on investment (i.e. how much the '*annual equivalent*') will be for the sum of the PVs. This is done in the following way. Taking the above example, when FV is discounted at a factor of 10 per cent (or 'r' per cent)

$$PV = \frac{1+1+1+1+1}{(1+0.10)^1\,(1+0.10)^2\,(1+0.10)^3\,(1+0.10)^4\,(1+0.10)^5} \qquad (4)$$

which can be also be written in the following way:

$$PV = \frac{R+R+R+R+R}{(1+0.10)^1\,(1+0.10)^2\,(1+0.10)^3\,(1+0.10)^4\,(1+0.10)^5} \qquad (5)$$

where 'R' is the annual revenue which is the same in each year during the investment life. The annual equivalent or annuity can be expressed as

$$PV = \frac{R+R+R+R+R}{(1+r)^1\,(1+r)^2\,(1+r)^3\,(1+r)^4\,(1+r)^5} \qquad (6)$$

In the above example the PV (FV discounted at 10 per cent for a period of five years), yield the following 'R' $\frac{653.13}{3.790\,786} = 172.29$.

The figure 172.29 means that if the investment yields in each year 172.29 for a period of five years, the flows of revenue will amount to 653.13. This can be reconfirmed by taking 172.29 as future nominal values which can be discounted to the present values during the five-year period.

Year	Future nominal value	Factor	Present value
1	172.29	0.909091	156.64
2	172.29	0.826446	142.39
3	172.29	0.751315	129.44
4	172.29	0.683013	117.68
5	172.29	0.620901	106.98
		3.790786	653.13

The figure 3.790786 is a factor used in calculating the annual equivalent for the sum of present values of flows of income for a period of five years at annual rate of interest of 10 per cent. Factors for calculating annual equivalents are available in a World Bank publication (Gittinger, 1973, pp. 2–101). The annual equivalents are used for computing profitability of investment and are also used in evaluating investments.

Methods for Evaluating Investments

Annual equivalent are used in computing the profitability of an investment. Three methods are usually used in evaluating the profitability of an investment: i) rate of return on investment; ii) cost-benefit analysis; and (ii) the internal rate of return. In all cases the present values are used, but slightly differently.

Rate of return on investment The rate of return on investment method uses the present value as a basis for computing the value of investment, and the annual equivalent of costs and revenues. Computationally it can be expressed as:

$$\text{Profitability} = \frac{\text{Annual equivalent of revenue - Annual equivalent of cost}}{\text{Present value of investment}}$$

In the earlier example, the annual equivalent over a five-year period was computed as 172.29. If the present value is 360.89, the annual equivalent would be 360.89 ÷ 3.79079 = 95.20. The profitability rate = $\frac{172.29 - 95.20}{850}$ x 100 = 9.07 per cent; 850 being the present value of investment. In computing the rate of return 850 on investment, costs usually include depreciation and amortizations. This means that at the end of the life of investment of, say, five years, the original money of value of the investment will be fully recovered. The rate of 9.07 per cent, therefore, refers to the return on the present value of investment over and above the 10 per cent rate of return on investment. Once depreciation and amortization are included in the annual costs and the annual equivalent for revenue, equal to or greater than the annual equivalent of costs, the investment has returned in interest payments at least as much as 10 per cent rate of interest in each year of the production period. Since the annual equivalents are based on each period, as in the interest rate of 10 per cent, any profitability rate greater than 0 means that the investment has earned more than a 10 per cent annual rate or return on investment.

If the total nominal values of costs and revenues are 480 and 1,200 respectively, which include amortization and depreciation which are not out-of-pocket costs of 180 and if this out-of-pocket cost is subtracted from revenues, we get (1,200 - 180) = 1,020, which is the total amount of money earned over the life of the investment. It is greater than the original investment of 480, and because it is greater than 480, we earn interest payments per period greater than 0.

Cost-benefit analysis Cost-benefit analysis is the second method of evaluating an investment. Again, as for return on investment, nominal costs for each year contain an amount for depreciation and amortization. If investment of 8,500 was depreciated and amortized in equal amounts each year, it equals to 1,700, which should be deducted from the nominal costs each year.

	Future nominal values			**Present values**		
Year	*Costs*	*Revenues*	*Investment*	*Costs*	*Revenues*	*Investment*
0	–	1,000	8,500	–	1,000.00	8,500
1	1,800	1,210	–	163.64	1,100.00	
2	2,000	1,460	–	165.29	1,210.00	
3	2,000	1,770	–	150.26	1,331.00	
4	2,000	2,140	–	136.62	1,464.10	
5	2,000	2,590	–	124.18	1,607.40	
	9,800	10,170	8,500	739.97	7,712.50	8,500

After deducting 1,700 from nominal costs for each year, to get the out-of-pocket costs, the table becomes

	Future nominal values			**Present values**		
Year	*Costs*	*Revenues*	*Investment*	*Costs*	*Revenues*	*Investment*
0	–	1,000	8,500	–	1,000.0	8,500
1	100	1,210	–	91	1,100.0	–
2	300	1,460	–	248	1,210.0	–
3	300	1,770	–	225	1,331.0	–
4	300	2,140	–	205	1,464.1	–
5	300	2,590	–	186	1,607.4	–
	1,300	10,170	8,500	955	7,712.5	8,500

There are four differences between the rate of return on investment and the cost-benefit analysis method. First, cost-benefit analysis excludes the estimated costs of depreciation and amortization. Second, investment is included as costs to the project. Third, the full recovery of investment is obtained by including it as a cost. Fourth, in the same way as the rate of return on investment method, cost-benefit analysis discounts all nominal costs (including investment) and all nominal revenues. At the interest rate of 10 per cent per period to discount costs, investment and revenues, the cost-benefit equals:

$$\frac{\text{Sum of discounted nominal revenues}}{\text{Sum of discounted nominal costs plus investments}} = \frac{7712.5}{955 + 8500} = 0.82$$

So long as this number equals to or is greater than 1, it means the investment has earned, over its economic lifetime, at least at 10 per cent, which is the interest rate and the rate of discount used. In the above example the result of the computation yielded 0.82 which is less than 1. In this case the investment will incur a loss.

Internal rate of return The third method of evaluating an investment is called the '*internal rate of return*' method. Using this method, what is required to be found is the rate of discount per period that actually exists in the rate of return on investment, and the cost-benefit analysis method is the use of the rate of interest discount at which loans or investments are undertaken in the economy. The internal rate of return also uses a discount rate per period based on the following formula.

$$V = \frac{R_1 - C_1}{(1+d)^1} + \frac{R_2 - C_2}{(1+d)^2} + \frac{R_3 - C_3}{(1+d)^3} + \frac{R_4 - C_4}{(1+d)^4} + \frac{R_n - C_n}{(1+d)^n} \qquad (7)$$

where

V	is the present value of investment;
R	is the revenue in each period;
C	is the out-of-pocket cost in each period (excluding depreciation and amortization);
d	is the internal rate of return; and
n	is the number of periods of the investment life.

This formula can be rearranged as follows

$$V = \frac{R_1 - C_1}{(1+d)^1} - \frac{R_2 - C_2}{(1+d)^2} - \frac{R_3 - C_3}{(1+d)^3} - \frac{R_4 - C_4}{(1+d)^4} - \frac{R_n - C_n}{(1+d)^n} \qquad (8)$$

	Future nominal values			Present values at 20% discount rate		
	Costs	*Revenues*	*Investment*	*Costs*	*Revenues*	*Investment*
0	–	1,000	8,500	-8 3	1,000	-8,500
1	1,800	1,210	–	-8 3	+1,008	
2	2,000	1,460	–	-20 8	+1,014	
3	2,000	1,770	–	-17 4	+1,024	
4	2,000	2,140	–	-14 5	+1,032	
5	2,000	2,590	–	-12 1	+1,041	
	9,800	10,170	8,500	-73 1	+6,113	-8,500

	Present values 5% discount rate			Present values at 1% discount rate		
	Costs	*Revenues*	*Investment*	*Costs*	*Revenues*	*Investment*
0		1,000	-8,500		1,000	-8,500
1	-95	1,152		-99	1,198	
2	-272	1,324		-2.94	1,431	
3	-259	1,529		-2.91	1,718	
4	-247	1,761		-2.88	2,056	
5	-235	2,029		-2.85	2,464	
	-1,108	8,795	-8,500	-12.57	9,867	-8,500

The three calculations at three different discount rates have been done for the purposes of approximating the correct internal rate of return. Costs and investments are considered negative amounts because they are payments and, therefore, reduce return on the project. Revenues, on the other hand, increase the internal rate of return (IRR). The three rates of discount of 20, 5 and 1 per cent respectively yield:

Discount rate %	Total present revenue	Total present costs	Total present investment	IRR
20	6,119	-731	-8,500	-3,112
5	8,795	-1,108	-8,500	-813
1	9,867	-1,257	-8,500	-108

The discount rate of 1 per cent per period makes these discounted values the smallest, almost equal to 0. Since the difference between present values of revenues and costs (costs + investment) should be 0 and -108 is the nearest, the rate of 1 per cent is taken as the internal rate of return of the investment. Since IRR is marginally higher than the interest rate of discount of 10 per cent, the investment is marginally profitable.

Justification for Institutional Reforms

Types of uncertainties Agricultural production is not simultaneous but takes place over time and, therefore, faces many uncertainties. Present cost or revenue are more certain than those further away in future, and the wider the range the greater is the degree of uncertainty in which future costs are incurred or revenues are received. Four main types of uncertainty can be distinguished. The first type is that of economic uncertainty regarding future costs and prices. Where costs and revenues are variable, it follows that income is likely to be more variable, and price is likely to be more variable than cost. The economic uncertainty depends on a number of factors, one of which is risk-bearing ability. A poor farmer usually has a low risk-bearing ability because of low income. A farmer with a better risk-bearing ability usually has a strong capital base, including a confident temperament. Costs and returns are affected by input costs, physical quantity of output, which is affected by type of technologies used, institutional constraints, weather, pests and diseases.

The second type of uncertainty is called technological uncertainty and takes two forms. The first relates to managerial competence, economic viability and social acceptability of new technologies. The application of new technologies is not usually neutral since it can cause significant shifts in local traditions, economic and social relationships as well as labour market conditions. Accordingly the introduction of new technologies necessitates a clear understanding, appraisal and evaluation of the economic and social costs and benefits which accrue from the their adoption. There are many questions one will have to ask in designing strategies for agricultural research that will attempt to provide answers to the existing problems. In the first instance, in adopting new cultural practices there will be a need to reorganize the traditional farming pattern, and the combination of crops and livestock enterprises which will maintain and/or increase the stability of food supply and capital investment in order to introduce the new system. The farmer may analyse, although very elementarily, the cost/benefit of such an effort, prospects for and assurance of achieving the anticipated target, and the availability of the market for the produce. He may also question the technical complementarity and supplementarity of the enterprises when the new system is adopted. As time goes on, it may also become necessary to introduce power such as ox equipment, conventional and/or single-axle tractors. He may assess his skill to operate and maintain these power sources, total usage in terms of hours and hectares to justify the owning of the power and the relative cost of doing the job by hand as compared with the powered sources.

The other technological uncertainty is the obsolescence risk. It applies when a farmer is facing a new technique but rapid advances in technologies render the machine obsolete within a short period. Prototype machines may be replaced by better types. At one time in the 1960s, single-axle tractors were rapidly improved, making the original model obsolete within a short period. In such a situation farmers may hesitate to invest money in modern machine or building.

The third type of uncertainty is ownership uncertainty. The effect of domestic instability, diseases and other scourges which could increase mortality discourage farmers from making long-term plans. This varies depending on the generations, with the older generation not taking the issue seriously, as their incentive to plan for future diminishes as they get older. This attitudinal change depends on the ability to enjoy one's labour and efforts, and assurances of property rights or access to productive assets. Farmers will have an incentive to invest because of assurances of enjoying the fruits of their labour and effort, including the right over landed property. Law and order are, therefore, important complements in investment decision-making processes. Lack of personal security will discourage investment.

The fourth type of uncertainty relates to fiscal incentive. Arbitrary taxation could adversely affect investment levels. If taxation level is arbitrarily increased as a farmer's income level rises, he might not bother to improve his farm for fear of attracting heavy taxes.

Economic Justification for the Individualization of Landed Property

Land reform is usually concerned with changing the prevailing pattern of ownership, usage and control of land. Initially it was Asia and Latin America which were the focus of attention of the proponents of land reform, because the two continents were considered to be in need of radical transformation of their agrarian structures on the ground of equity and efficiency. Africa was not on the agenda of land reform immediately after World War II because it was considered to enjoy abundant land endowments under the flexibility of communal land tenure institutions (Eicher and Baker, 1982, p. 98). However, SSA is currently in a state of transition arising from population pressure on land and the commercialization of agriculture which increased greatly in recent decades in many parts of Africa. As a result, land has acquired a scarcity value. Because of the rapid shift from land abundance to land scarcity, agrarian structures (particularly the system of land rights) typical of extensive agriculture and land-abundant economies continues to exert a strong impact on social production relations. Accordingly, the erstwhile African land tenure institutions need to be adapted to meet the emerging trend of the combined pressure of demographic growth and increased commercialization of agricultural activities. It is generally agreed that so long as a commonly-owned resource remains abundant, the absence of the individualization of landed property right does not have inimical consequences. However, as land becomes a scarce resource as a result of population growth and/or growth in demand for products of the land, communal ownership of land becomes unstable and produces harmful effects in the form of mismanagement and/or over-exploitation of the valuable life-support resource.

Accordingly, the growing population pressure and the rising demand for agricultural products, which result in an increasing (scarcity) value of land, create the need for substituting private rights for communal ownership of land. This is because customary land tenure arrangements do not provide sufficient security and incentive to encourage landholders to undertake investments on land or to adopt innovations required to shift from extensive to intensive cultivation systems, and thereby increase the value of land. Land right title will motivate the rights holder to conserve land resources. The system of private ownership also includes the right to freely sell, give or lease the resource, thus permitting resource mobility because of the development of a market in land. It will also encourage the consolidation of fragmented land, allow for cash rental payment and mortgaging thereby facilitating the expansion of commercial agriculture and the emergence of dynamic agricultural entrepreneurs who can adapt quickly to technological changes and evolving markets (Robertson, 1987, p. 147).

Reforms of Resource Tenure Systems

Intellectual debate Reforms of resource tenure systems are considered necessary to provide the necessary incentive to invest in the protection of natural resources. Behnke, recalled the arguments by economists who contend that multiple owners/users of natural resources in nonexclusive tenure systems, have a built-in incentive to compete against each other over unallocated natural benefits, resulting in over-exploitation of the common resource. There had, therefore, been concern about the misuse of the earth's natural resources, such as pasture, on which every pastoralist is entitled to graze his animals as he desires. Since there is no control over the number of animals each individual grazes, the common pasture is ultimately destroyed (Behnke, 1994, p. 15). According to Garret Harding, who first introduced the concept of the 'tragedy of the commons', individual self-interest dictates that if an additional animal is grazed on the pasture, the individual derives the total benefit from the extra livestock, whereas all the users of the pasture share the cost of over-grazing. As each individual's benefits outweigh his costs, everyone is encouraged to overuse the pasture. He, therefore, concluded that when communally held resources are over-exploited according to the individual interest, the resources will be over-exploited and destroyed by the same beneficiaries (see *Ekistics* 160, March 1969). Johnson argued also in favour of individual property right because the traditional land tenure systems lead to inefficient resource allocation since property rights are not clearly defined, costs and rewards are not internalized or do not take into account both the costs and benefits of alternative levels of resource exploitation (Johnson, 1972). He supports the concepts of the 'tragedy of the commons' because, if grazing rights are strictly communal, the individual derives economic benefits but the others bear most of the costs of range degradation. This discourages entrepreneurial individuals from investing in land improvement if the economic benefits will be consumed by all.

Recalling the neoclassical theory and hypothesis, Barrows and Roth (1990,

p. 268), convincingly argued that the individualization of land tenure (leasehold and freehold ownership) increases tenure security of the landholder, thereby reducing transactions costs, defined as the sum of all costs and risks – social, financial, quantifiable and non-quantifiable – involved in defining property rights (Behnke, 1994, p. 15). It is argued that ambiguity in property rights raises transaction costs in discovering the rightful owner, enforcing a lease or sale contract, and drives a wedge between the land's value of marginal product in the owner's use and what it would be if used by a more productive alternative user. If, based on the marginal value of land principle, a more productive user is unable to acquire land, it results in an inefficient allocation of resources. Also, high transaction costs for establishing ownership reduce the value of any fixed-place investment, while at the same time increasing the cost of investment. The existence of risks raises discount rate of future streams of net annual return on investment and, therefore, the low present value of future return discourages long-term investment in land. Uncertainty about tenure security by raising discount rate biases investment towards short-term projects. Meanwhile it had also been argued that undisputed security of tenure raises expected investment return because of the flexibility freely to convert a fixed-place asset into another form of asset to take advantage of land market price trends. It will increase demand for capital (including credit) for fixed-place investment. Because of improved creditworthiness, the cost of borrowing decreases while collateral value of assets rises. It also reduces transaction costs in land transfer, and a market in land emerges. The emergence of a land market encourages efficient utilization because land can be transferred to entrepreneurial individuals who have the ability to extract higher value of products derived from land, as productive users take a bid of land away from less productive users (Barrows and Roth, 1990, pp. 297–9).

It is, therefore, generally held that customary land tenure arrangements do not provide sufficient security and incentive to encourage landholders to undertake investments in land or to adopt innovations required to shift from extensive to intensive cultivation systems, and thereby increase the value of land. Land right title will motivate the rights holder to conserve land resources. The system of private ownership also includes the right to selling freely, giving or leasing the resource, thus permitting resource mobility because of the development of market in land. It will also encourage the consolidation of fragmented land, allow for cash rental payment and mortgaging, thereby facilitating the expansion of commercial agriculture and the emergence of a dynamic agricultural entrepreneurs who can adapt quickly to technological changes and evolving markets (Robertson, 1987, p. 147). Also, security of tenure permits pledging land as collateral for credit needed for on-farm development and operating expenses. It also removes distortion in decision-making processes. If, as argued by Feder and Noronha (1987, pp. 160–1), cattle provide a better security than land, in the absence of a title deed farmers tend to shift from crop production to rearing cattle, even though their land might perhaps be better suited to growing agricultural crops. Based on these arguments, it is the view of many scholars that a move towards individualization of landed property should be actively encouraged, since it will provide a stronger incentive to hard work and investment than customary land arrangements and traditional social organization (Phillipe-Plateau, 1990, p. 99). Under these conditions there are a variety of land reforms currently taking place.

Underlying the justification for the introduction of policies for the sedentarization of the nomadic pastoralists is that both the colonial administration and the independent African governments regarded the pastoralist way of life as conflicting and incompatible with the standard of civilized behaviour, manners and values. Other than Mauritania, Niger and Somalia, where nomads comprise the majority of the population, most African countries enshrined in their national development plans programmes to improve the standard of nomadic life, with emphasis placed on raising living conditions, improving the quality of herds and integrating nomads into national policy and economy. A further impetus for the adoption of the sedentarization policy was due to an observation that the yield of the traditionally-managed herd reaching the commercial market remained low at between 3–8 per cent of potential supply (Baldus, 1978, p. 38; Feider, 1973, p. 33). Furthermore, the animals being offered for sale were often predominantly too old, too lean or too sick. Picardi and Seifert (1977, p. 300), for instance, reported that in the Sahel during a drought year, pastoralists characteristically dump dying animals on the market in an effort to salvage something from their starving herds. This is because the pastoralists value their animals for milk production and sell older animals only after they have become useless for milk supply. Veterinary services staff continue to report high calf mortality of up to 40 per cent, very low rate of maturity – up to seven years in many cases – weight loss of up to 15 per cent *en route* to markets, and a further 15 per cent loss due to shrinkage in transit, and heavy rate of carcass condemnation in the modern abattoir (Abercrombie, 1975, p. 71).

Meanwhile, earlier notions depicted the pastoral communities of Africa as resistant to change and strictly bound to tradition and culture. Governments, faced with this intractable nomadic independence, introduced policies of the sedentarization of the nomads, often without paying due regard to or having appreciation of the pastoralist mode of life but rather laid the foundation for far-reaching changes in the economic sector, social fabric and the political organization of the nomadic communities. Accordingly, following the advent of colonization, the process of integration and encapsulation of nomadic pastoralists into centralized policies and economies was introduced and even reinforced after the attainment of political independence in the early 1960s. The basic thrust of post-independence strategy for the development of pastoral areas, apart from technological advances (immunization, water supply, disease control, etc.), has been the encouragement or enforcement of a change in the communal tenure system to landholding because it has been argued that the nonexclusive resource tenure is inappropriate, since it dissipates economic rent.

The incentive structure created by the individualization of landed property right optimizes levels of resource exploitation. Under the sedentarization programmes, groups of individual pastoralists are organized either into cooperatives, company, etc. principally for ranching and the optimization resource use while at the same time protecting and conserving the environment. Under this arrangement, nonmembers are excluded from competing for the use of originally nonexclusive resources, and derive income from it. While economic rent can be maximized by excluding nonmembers, the cost of exclusion (civil unrest, cattle raiding, bloodshed) may outweigh the benefits measured in terms of marginal cost of defending the resource exceeding the marginal rent gains (Behnke, 1994, p. 20).

Empirical evidence of expected economic benefits of tenure reforms In most SSA countries land reform, with redistribution of large farms, was of minor importance. It is in eastern and southern Africa's white settler areas that the redistributive land reform had political, social and economic objectives. During the war of liberation, the inegalitarian access to productive land resources was the major plank of the struggle. The Africans and the liberation fighters were promised a comprehensive redistribution of land after independence as a means of regaining social justice: greater equality in access to agricultural resources and income, and a higher level of employment opportunities (the equity objective). Major economic objectives were directed towards better utilization of agricultural potential and the expected consequent increases in agricultural production and farm productivity (the efficiency objectives). It was expected that the realization of these objectives would reduce political unrest and antagonistic ethnic relations (the political objective).

The individualization of landed property right is expected to raise productivity and land-carrying capacity to absorb excess population because of the adoption of improved cultural practices. Because of these arguments, a process of individual ownership secured by title deeds over land is emerging. Land administration laws are progressively being reformed to take account of this element. The laws permit entrepreneurial individuals to acquire land and have it registered to ensure security of tenure. According to Feder and Noronha (1987), there are three main types of land laws: i) countries that allow the acquisition of individual titles – a typical example is Côte d'Ivoire, which has no restrictions on the power of the titleholder, while Kenya and Malawi have more restrictions on the titleholders; ii) countries that reorganize different types of tenure; they include such countries as Senegal and Sudan where both individual title and nationalization of non-title lands are allowed, while in such countries as Botswana, Ghana, Lesotho, Liberia, Mali and Sierra Leone, Swaziland, Uganda and Zimbabwe, individuals, groups, indigenous systems and public lands are practised; and iii) countries that vest title to land in the state so that individuals have rights only of use and occupancy; these countries include Ethiopia, Mauritania, Nigeria, Tanzania, Zaire and Zambia.

Institutional reform, linked as it is to rates of structurally and socially unequal patterns of development, is unlikely to be an adequate vehicle for integrated social change, since productive resources could be usurped from one form of livelihood to another, often at the expense of the weak in society. It can increase landlessness unless the displaced people can be absorbed in employment out of agriculture. In 1987 there were an estimated 33 million landless people in SSA (IFAD, 1994). Partly, this is because the land is dwindling while new entrants into agriculture are increasing, and partly because of the individualization of landed property rights.

Fixed-place investment In Uganda, control over land in Buganda in the early years of colonization was closely associated with political power in the highly centralized and hierarchical local society. In appreciation for various traditional obligations, the *Kabaka* (king) allocated to administrators the right to control land and administer the tenants within their jurisdiction. Traditional land tenure also included individualized rights through direct grants from the *Kabaka* to a chief or a peasant. The Buganda Agreement of 1900 and the Land Law of 1908 transformed the established system by introducing essentially freehold tenure, when land was allocated on a square mile basis (MAILO). This agreement altered the relationship between political leaders and peasants, conferring permanent freehold rights to office-holders and thereby transforming them into landlords, while the peasants were transformed from peasants into subjects and freed from political obligations. Following the conclusion of the Buganda Agreement, rights were conferred on some 23,318 km^2 of freehold land to Buganda chiefs as a measure and incentive for them to promote agriculture, especially coffee and cotton production. Under the *Busuulo* and *Envujjo* Act of 1928, the peasants paid fixed absolute rents (essentially equivalent to 'unearned' income which accrued to resource owners simply because they control the stream of benefits derived from the land). Rights of tenancy, although inheritable, could not be sold nor could tenants be evicted. Despite these guarantees, a peasant felt more secure if he owned his land under the traditional system that guaranteed inheritable usufructuary rights to land (Mukwaya, 1953). The 1975 Land Reform Decree transferred the MAILO land to the state but gave leases to the previous owners, who now feel less secure under the new tenure (Barrows and Roth, 1990, p. 281). The MAILO system, which was intended to be adopted in other areas, was not enforced by the British administration. In Bunyoro the land tenure system, known locally as the *Kibanja*, obtains, in which the government issues 'certificates of occupancy' to farmers. In most parts of the country, however, individual rights over land are limited to those of the cultivation, even though they may be heritable. Today systems of land tenure are still varied and complex but most farmers hold land in an owner-like possession. Three tenurial systems can be distinguished: i) the MAILO in Buganda in the south of the country, and registered freehold held by individuals, companies or public bodies; ii) land held in freehold by the Uganda Land Commission on behalf of the government, which also includes national parks and forest reserves; and iii) public land vested in the Land Commission but administered by the District Land Committee.

According to various studies, the establishment of freehold rights on MAILO land did not induce owners to make investment in land, nor did it result in commercialized use of land, because many aspects of the land tenure laws restricted commercialization of agriculture by MAILO owners and tenants. The strong protection of tenants' rights mitigated against owners aggregating enough land to invest in machinery and capital in order to exploit economies of scale in farm operations. Also, tenants were prevented from mortgaging land to obtain credit for farm investment. Furthermore, the provision of the law that entrenched protection and security of tenants denied access to potential investors to use wealth acquired from non-farm activities to invest in land. Fixed-place investment in Uganda had been associated largely with large-scale beef ranching and dairy development. Advances in veterinary services and disease control permitted the keeping of exotic-grade cattle on large-scale ranches, each of about 3,200 acres. The basic infrastructure, comprising of access and feeder roads, earth tanks for water storage, perimeter fencing and dips, fire breaks, was constructed before the granting of 49-year lease to selected applicants for their occupation. Applicants could be individuals, cooperative societies, or companies with experience in livestock rearing and sufficient assets or cattle worth a stipulated value (at 1960 prices of Ush 60,000, approximately US $10,000). Credit facilities, technical and animal disease control services were provided at all the stages of the ranch development. Only the civil servants, rich businessmen, or the elite in society and the cooperatives were able to meet these conditions.

Emergence of land markets In Nigeria since the 1978 Land Tenure Decree, all land belongs to the state and state governors can issue a Certificate of Occupancy to farmers. Despite this decree, tenurial systems in Nigeria are not uniform, although in general access to land poses no serious problems. In the southern area, land ownership is generally vested in the various communities, with any grants or transactions being under the direct control of the head of the community in consultation with the elders. Land is allocated by the community to its constituent families or sometimes to individuals on a more or less permanent basis, according to their needs and capabilities. Granting of land by a community to one of its constituent families confers virtually permanent right of occupation so long as it is used, but normally with restrictions on rights of disposal, particularly to outsiders, to whom land is traditionally granted for the growing of annual crops. With increasing population pressure, there is a growing market in land, which, despite traditional constraints, is frequently purchased, pledged or leased, and there is a growing tendency towards individual ownership which is gaining ground. Even within the traditional system, the rights of the planter of a permanent crop to maintain and harvest it are usually well organized. In the more densely settled areas, where land might have been occupied for several generations, the family is increasingly accepted as possessing virtually 'freehold' title. Although titles are generally not recorded, family and individual rights are well known and respected within the community. Tenancy or land belonging to absentee owners of individual or family inheritance is fairly common, with the tenant paying either an agreed sum, kind or a share of the crop. In general, therefore, the land tenure system in the southern part of the country provides adequate security of tenure for agricultural development.

In the middle belt and the north, land is a communal asset and is allocated to community members according to customary usufruct. The right to cultivate usually carries the right to harvest any economic trees, though the felling of certain species protected under forestry legislation requires local government council permission and payment of a scheduled fee. Responsibility for allocation of land rights lies with the council and is administered at the local level by village chiefs and headmen. Occupancy disputes not settled at this level can be referred to a higher echelon in the council, who also can extend rights to immigrants for cultivation if sufficient land is available. Land right inheritance is primogenitory but carries with it the responsibility for the welfare of other family members who may remain and work on the farm or seek additional community land elsewhere. Land rights cannot be transferred by sale but leasing and lending are occasionally practised, while negation of the right will occur following prolonged absence, but this does not normally apply in the case of bush/fallowed land. Customary land law is well understood and accepted, and is largely problem-free when land is abundant. Under these conditions, land tenure does not constitute any major constraint to agricultural development in this zone.

There are, however, many inefficiencies and difficulties in the administration of the emerging land tenure laws. In Nigeria, for instance, the difficulties and costs of obtaining the Certificate of Occupancy are reported to be considerable and the traditional land tenure system still predominates de facto, with village elders allocating land to those who cultivate the land, a system that favours crop farmers but impedes the settlement of pastoralists. Kohen (1983) reported that occupancy certificates under the Land Use Decree of 1978 were granted according to occupation and income. Accordingly, most applicants for statutory rights of occupancy were prominent businessmen and senior civil servants. The commercialization of agricultural production also has the potential risk of marginalizing the poor rural population. For instance, in the savannah belt, valley bottom land is suitable for rice cultivation. Entrepreneurial individuals have expropriated some tracts of land in these valleys which traditionally are used by the pastoralists for grazing their animals during the dry season and also for hunting. Rice cultivation precludes seasonal grazing and hunting. Some of the chiefs in these belts, who should have protected the rights of their subjects, are giving way to lucrative cash tributes received from landowners. The benefits are retained by the chiefs and not distributed to their subjects. Shepherd, for instance, documented that in Ghana many chiefs have benefited from their control of land to acquire loans, tractors, etc., but these benefits were not redistributed to the chief's communities. As a result the chiefs have become economically quite distinct from their subjects.

This process is introducing an element of evolution from the traditional tenurial type of market economy system to a de facto semi-feudal authority exercised by the chiefs. Thus registration of land effectively provided a mechanism for the transfer of wealth to those with better social or economic positions, thereby creating tenure insecurity for less influential right holders.

The creation of economic opportunities also motivates the desire to acquire individual land titles. Lunning (1985), in a study of villages in Katsina in northern Nigeria, documented that the development of the road network and greater accessibility to markets was responsible for the greater occurrence of land sale transactions, while areas far away from the roads had a far greater incidence of customary transactions of inheritance. He concluded that four factors were responsible for the increasing demand for land: namely population growth, the introduction of cash crops, infrastructural development and distance to major roads. A similar study by Neeting (1985) in the Jos Plateau, also in Nigeria, confirmed these findings. In Uganda the MAILO land had progressively been subdivided by sale, gift or inheritance but survey, registration and issue of titles had not kept pace with the subdivision although this does not dispossess landlords or tenants of their rights over the use of land. Reasons for sale of land included raising capital for business ventures, home construction, motor vehicle purchase and payment of school fees. Non-agriculturalists also bought land to obtain the right to sit on local councils, a prelude to being eligible to political appointments: consequently ownership of land was the *sine qua non* for a political career, and was also responsible for the emergence of a class of commercial farmers, particularly dairy farmers.

The advantages of knowledge about the land laws tend to favour the elite in society. In countries where there had been substantial land reforms, the educated elite and the wealthier in society know the laws governing access to land. Haugerund's (1983) study in Kenya has confirmed that it was the civil servants and influential people like the chiefs who used their knowledge of the law to acquire land at the expense of the less knowledgeable. Feder and Noronha (1987) also reported that the advantages of knowledge of land laws favoured the urban dweller in Senegal where, under the Law of National Domain of 1964, prospective land owners were expected to establish titles and request registration within six months from the date of passage of the law. Rural people were not aware of the law and all non-deeded lands became part of the national domain.

Credit In Kenya, Barrows and Roth reported that commercial banks were reluctant to extend credit to smallholders unless title deeds were used as security, but this group of farmers was reluctant to use land as collateral. Meanwhile, because lenders had difficulty in recouping the administrative costs of small loans, the minimum size fixed by most banks exceeded the capital needs of smallholders. Consequently, preference was given to registered proprietors, those with off-farm employment, larger farmers and salaried officials. Okoth-Ogendo (1975) observed that public and private agencies were reluctant suppliers of agricultural credit to smallholders except under the most exhaustive scrutiny. Despite the fact that the institutions had wide powers of foreclosure, it was not always easy to exercise them.

Impact of the individualization of property rights Studies in Kenya, where the individualization was widespread, indicated that there was no correlation between titles and long-term investment, and that large title holders were not inclined to cultivate more of their under-utilized or uncleared land. Haugerund (1983, p. 82) reported that land consolidation and registration did not lead to agricultural development beyond the widespread incorporation of export cash crops in smallholdings. Acquisition of title deeds alone is an insufficient incentive but must be accompanied by complementary delivery of public goods and services (investment in economic, commercial, institutional and agricultural infrastructure, intellectual investment in research and manpower, and health) which have the greatest influence on output performance and incentive to invest on land improvement.

Individualization of property rights overwhelmed by social security consideration It had, as stated earlier, been expected that as population pressure on land rose, communal ownership of land would become unstable and produce harmful effects in the form of resource mismanagement and over-exploitation. It was also expected that when the gains of the internalization of externalities (transaction costs and benefits) exceeded costs due to the increase in the value of land, economic efficiency would justify substituting private ownership for communal ownership. According to Phillipe-Plateau (1996, p. 34), as pressure on land rises and it acquires a scarcity value, there is some spontaneous response by landholders to assert increasingly individualized use rights over given areas of land and a move towards increasing land sale transactions in rural societies (ibid., p. 49). Because of the expected and perceived benefits of the individualization of property rights and a reduction of community controls over land use and distribution, a number of countries in SSA have initiated programmes to replace the flexible (customary modes of land transfer through gifts, exchanges, loans, renting, pledges or possessory mortgages) indigenous land tenure arrangements with title registration. The expectations of improvement in economic efficiency and increased investment in land improvement due to the individualization of property rights have been frustrated for several reasons.

According to a study by Pinckney and Kimuyu (1994, p. 151), in Kenya most land purchases occurred in the former white settlers' farms but not in the areas reserved for Africans during the colonial period. Many owners of titled land do not consider that they can transfer their land outside the lineage or make permanent transfer without the express approval of the community. According to Phillipe-Plateau (1996, p. 49), this phenomenon is a situation of constrained land market which has been reinforced by the District Land Control Board's reluctance to grant approval for land sales that would leave families and their dependants landless destitutes. In Zimbabwe, the land tenure commission in 1994 proposed that individual peasants should have the right to buy and sell land but should be subject to approval by the Village Council (*The Economist*, 21–27 January 1995, p. 49). Other than around the irrigation schemes of West African countries such as Mali, Niger and Senegal which had long tradition of rental contracts, elsewhere in SSA land rental is indeed extremely rare in the modern sense.

Using the formal economic concepts of resource rent and transaction costs, Behnke defines 'rent' as an 'unearned' income which accrues to resource owners simply because they control the stream of benefits derived from a resource. Based on these definitions, transaction costs are not only limited to objective conditions such as the growing land scarcity's giving rise to an increase in land value, but also subjective factors such as feelings, culture, preferences, security, etc., about alternative arrangements of access to land which could either be judged as fair or risky. If the alternative tenure arrangements lack the basic attributes of access rights, the individual response is to adopt cautious strategic behaviour that distorts the working of land supply-demand mechanism. Usually, when a community access to land is threatened, especially by people regarded as strangers, it provokes a hostile response which can lead to ethnic violent conflicts. Phillipe-Plateau cited several examples: i) the 'Manifesto of the Oppressed Negro-Mauritanian', in which an extremist group belonging to the black community of Mauritania expressed its aggressive reaction to the post-1983 introduction of private land rights conferred (by adjudication) upon outside investors in the fertile area of Senegal river basin; ii) local residents also resent and oppose the appropriation of their customary lands by rich capitalists, civil servants, etc. (Phillipe-Plateau, 1996, p. 56). Robertson (1987, p. 77) also pointed out that in Ghana, as the frontier land gradually became exhausted, indigenous (Akan) ideology reasserted the inalienable rights of the native custodians of the land and the inalienable rights of individual usufruct. In the northern region of Ghana, under the practice of grants of land to 'strangers', some people migrated to the region from Togo during the fifteenth and sixteenth centuries. After fulfilling the eligibility requirements, such as good behaviour and neighbourliness, the immigrants were given tracts of land to produce food to feed themselves. When land remained plentiful, the immigrant communities and the indigenous population lived in harmony with each other. However, the emergence of inframarginal land scarcity upset this mutual relationship. The immigrants, having lived in the area for over 400 years, felt justified in being accorded full right of ownership of land, and by the late 1980s they started to make political demands for that recognition. The original land owners, sensing a threat of loss of their ancestral land, responded by reasserting their ownership right over the land. There was an outbreak of ethnic conflict in the early 1980s that was quickly controlled, but the 1994 outbreak of hostilities was much more widespread, resulting in mass displacement of both populations (personal communication during relief operations in the area).

Resistance to apparent loss of land increases transaction costs. Phillipe-Plateau (1996, p. 57), for instance, argued convincingly that tenure uncertainties lead to increases in transactions' (search, enforcement and litigation) fixed and recurrent costs of defending property rights by fencing land and related property. Lawry (1993, p. 70) also pointed out that in Lesotho farmers are usually reluctant to farm land outside their village areas because of increased supervisory costs and losses due to crop damage and theft. Landless agriculturalists, because of resentment of the loss of land, can cause considerable damage to landowners in a variety of ways, such as pilfering production inputs and deliberate mismanagement. As sharecroppers, they will under-report output. These moral hazards raise labour costs caused through high supervision and continuous tight monitoring. The high labour costs can force landowners to resort to the adoption of labour-saving technologies such as mechanization, resulting in a reduction in employment generation in rural areas. Increasing rural unemployment destabilizes social stability and raises the cost of maintaining law and order.

Formal private land rights, therefore, did not necessarily minimize transaction costs but could actually raise them in a situation of strong reaction by local communities to loss of ancestral lands, which ultimately creates land and labour market imperfection. This is because the working of market forces is distorted by social considerations which prevent land from being freely commodified. Once the land value becomes embedded in social structures of a particular community, land ownership represents far more than a mere input in an agricultural production process. In areas where job security is uncertain, as ably argued by Lawry (ibid., p. 58), land serves as both insurance against uncertain employment as well as security during old age. Land provides a fall-back position in the event of the loss of employment. Even people with secure employment outside the agricultural sector still hold land as a crucial source of livelihood, identity and in some areas the continuation of rituals to ancestors. The reluctance to part with ancestral lands is especially strong if it is felt it might be bought by strangers. In such a situation the original occupants are extremely keen to retain their land even when they reside outside the ancestral areas.

Economic viability of the individualization of property rights Although titling land ownership rights by laws grants complete control over land by title holders, the overall consideration of social security for immediate family members overrides formal land ownership arrangements. This is indeed rational social and economic behaviour in SSA, because the communities, in the absence of state social security arrangements, are called upon to carry the burden of supporting individual landless destitutes (Green, 1987, p. 7; Pinckney and Kimuyu, 1994, p. 23). Demand for land also arises for non-economic motives such as prestige and political power, as has happened in Uganda (Barrows and Roth, 1989, p. 14). The combination of all these distortions in land markets results in land sales value being far above the net present value (PV) of the future streams of agricultural income derived from the use of land. Also, because of these imperfections, titling has not been able to facilitate extensive investment in land improvement, and consequently the individualization had not contributed appreciably to increases in agricultural yields.

4   Analysis of Domestic Constraints and Resource Sustainability

Land and Land-based Resources

Land-based Resources

Following the incorporation of Africa into the world economy, the traditional systems of resource use and management came under severe pressure. The production of crops for export was superimposed on the traditional systems. While tree crops (cocoa, coffee and tea) have beneficial effects on soil conservation, the production for export of annual crops (cotton, maize, tobacco, groundnuts) exhausts soil fertility and increases its vulnerability to erosion. Where land was abundant, more could be brought under cultivation without upsetting the shifting cultivation systems. Where population density has increased to a point of exceeding the critical land population supporting capacity, land-use systems have become more intensive. However, advances in farming technology in traditional settings have not kept pace with changing conditions, and they are leading to a situation which will not permit sustainable agriculture. Hence the increasing population pressure on what was formerly the most widespread tropical farming system (shifting cultivation) can no longer be sustained. This centuries-old agricultural production technique used to be practised throughout Africa. It involves the selective clearance of forests and woodlands, the debris being burnt in controlled fires and the ashes used to fertilize fragile soils. Finely-tuned phases of cultivation, interspersed with long fallow periods to allow for the growth of natural vegetation and the restoration of soil fertility, ensured sustainability.

Increased population densities have led to a drastic reduction in fallow periods. The long fallow cultivation systems are appropriate responses to abundant land and limited capital situations. The characteristic feature of the practice was mobility: people moved out of a piece of land when crop yields started to decline and forage depleted, in order to allow soil fertility to be restored through natural vegetation growth and decay. However, with increasing population density, land-use systems are becoming more intensive, and people are increasingly compelled to remain in place and yet their farming techniques have not sufficiently evolved to permit sustainable farming. Consequently soil fertility and structure deteriorate, crop yields decline and soil erodes. This is disturbing because the continued over-exploitation of the ecosystems in the continent has the potential danger of setting in motion processes that are self-reinforcing, as each stage of ecological degradation accelerates the onset of the next. As land is cleared of vegetation, soil erosion accelerates and more rain water is lost through run-offs without seeping into the ground. With less water retained in the land for future evaporation into the atmosphere to recharge the clouds, rainfall amount declines. The declining rainfall, in turn, dries out the landscape, thereby setting in motion processes of desertification. It is these self-reinforcing processes that, in part, explain the onset of a vicious circle as the loss of vegetation cover, loss of soil, overgrazing of the rangelands and the loss of agricultural and grazing land have themselves contributed to the decline in rainfall, etc.

There is also the other factor manifested by the longer-term unfavourable developments such as accelerated encroachment of the desert. Many areas which used to support crop production such as groundnut, millet and sorghum are now deserts. This situation is being aggravated by the continuing build-up of pressure of population towards more vulnerable marginal areas and the encroachment of forest resources, thus initiating a gradual but steady degradation of the environment.

Demographic Pressure

It is generally known that SSA's area readily usable for economic activity (arable land, permanent crop land, permanent pastures, forests and woodlands) is about 17 per cent of land resource of developing countries. On average SSA countries have more than twice as much land per person as compared to other developing countries in other parts of the world (Osunsade and Gleason, 1992, p. 5). This statement can be misleading because land abundance should take into account fallow/cropping cycles and land productivity. In SSA the high population growth rate as a consequence of the combination of high fertility and the increasing life-expectancy, is correspondingly shortening fallow periods in the cropping cycle. Where land was technically abundant, more could be brought under cultivation without upsetting the fallow/cropping regimes. Over the years the annual average agricultural growth rate of 2 per cent was due to the expansion of cultivated land which increased in absolute terms by 10.3 per cent between 1960 and 1970, 8.2 per cent during 1970–80 and 3.4 per cent between 1980–89, or 0.7 per cent per annum during the period 1960–89. It was on this additional land being brought under cultivation that an increasing agricultural population had been carrying out their low productivity cultivation practices. During this period (1960–89) the average annual growth rate of labour force in agriculture was 2 per cent, just matching agricultural value-added growth rate. Total population, however, grew at an average annual growth rate of 2.7 per cent. This is an indication that labour productivity did improve well enough to raise output to match the population growth rate (FAO, various years).

Methodologies for Measuring Demographic Pressures on Natural Resources

Traditionally, measuring land abundance had been on the basis of population density per unit area of land or the number of hectares per head of population in a particular country. These methods are now regarded as being unsatisfactory because they do not take into account differences in farming systems and agro-ecological conditions such as soil productivity. For instance, of the two million square kilometres (km^2) of the total land area of SSA (excluding South Africa) over 0.7 million km (or 37 per cent) are classified as agricultural land. Since only about 20 per cent of the agricultural land was under cultivation in the 1980s, it could give an erroneous impression that land, as a basic factor of production, was not yet a major constraint. This conceals the fact that in some countries, over 50 per cent (Burundi 80 per cent, Nigeria 72 per cent, Rwanda 60 per cent, and Uganda 58 per cent) of agricultural land was under cultivation in the 1980s. In these countries the necessary fallow phase had been greatly reduced or exceeded. To obtain a better estimate for land population supporting capacity (PSC), scholars have developed methods of measuring PSC: the agro-climatic population density; farming system; and population equivalent.

Agro-climatic population density method The FAO and UNESCO recently adopted an improved method of assessing the population supporting capacity. The determination of the PSC entailed the assessment of the suitability of land for food production on the basis of the agro-climatic characteristics of the resources in relation to the requirements of the crops. The PSC was defined and measured as the number of persons that could be fed at specified calories/

protein levels from indigenous food production of the land which is suitable for producing food. It is used at various levels of farming technologies (levels of input – low, medium and high input level).

For this study the FAO/UNESCO *Soil Map of the World* describing the land resources (soil types, phase, texture and slope) was combined with data on the climate (temperature and moisture), the latter in terms of length of growing periods (i.e. the number of days when soil moisture condition permits crop growth) to produce area units (agro-ecological cells) with homogenous characteristics. Each country was, therefore, divided into a number of agro-ecological cells, and for each cell FAO estimated the maximum number of calories of food production that could be maintained at the three levels of technology. The cell figures were added up to give the total potential calories production for each country. The result of this study yielded a standardized population density, i.e. the number of people per million calories production potential. It is also called the agro-climatic population density. Based on the FAO's estimate of potential calorie for 1980, most SSA countries had already exceeded their optimum land population supporting capacity (Map 1 and Table 9).

Farming system method In estimating the PSC using the 1989 data, the humid lowlands and mixed climates zones were taken as areas where the soil productivity is regarded as being medium to high. In this area, a farming system of three year cropping followed by the planting of improved pasture for a three year rest period can be adopted. In the semi-arid area, the soil productivity was regarded as being medium to low, and a system of two years of cropping followed by a four year rest period under natural regeneration or a three year period under planted grass is practicable. On the basis of a tight rotational system adopted above and cultivated land per head of population, the land carrying capacity was arrived at by dividing available area for cultivation, due allowance being made for the land resting phase of the farming systems and one-fifth proportion of the agricultural land needed for economic and social infrastructure. Livestock was assumed to be kept on resting land.

The following formula was used to calculate the maximum carrying capacity of an area under the existing low productivity traditional farming systems:

$$\frac{\frac{4a}{10} + \frac{4b}{15}}{Y} \times 100\text{ha} = \text{carrying capacity of an area} \tag{1}$$

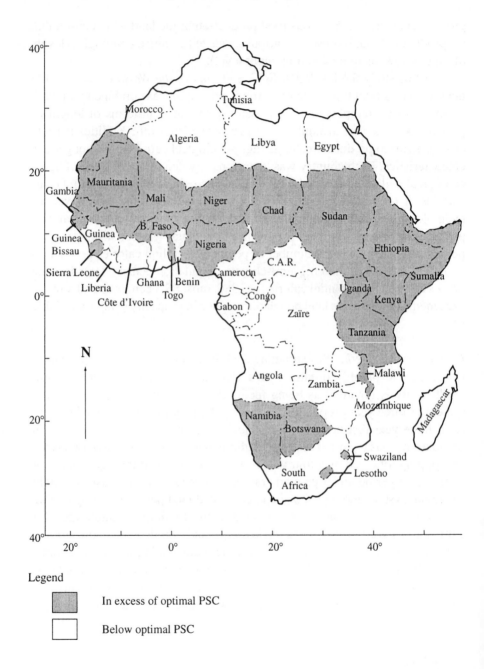

Legend

　　In excess of optimal PSC

　　Below optimal PSC

Map 1　Sub-Saharan Africa population supporting capacity 1980

Table 9 Sub-Saharan Africa land population supporting capacity

	Soil of medium to high productivity	Soil of medium to low productivity	Unsuitable land soil	Population in 1989	Estimates maximum carrying capacity
	km²			*000*	
I High density	**144,539**	**154,948**	**419,783**	**252,369**	**92,594**
a Humid lowlands	114	–	72	1,069	456
b Mixed climates	144,425	–	169,275	214,938	82,259
c Semi-arid climate	–	154,948	250,436	36,362	9,609
II Medium density	**142,383**	**41,581**	**124,851**	**92,833**	**36,096**
a Human lowlands	5,876	–	1,298	46	1,567
b Mixed climates	136,507	–	141,134	79,857	32,119
c Semi-arid climate	–	41,581	17,581	8,930	2,410
III Low density	**250,569**	–	**591,616**	**101,280**	**38,239**
a Human lowlands	49,508	–	236,829	39,143	16,503
b Mixed climates	201,061	–	354,829	62,137	21,736
SSA	537,491	196,529	591,616	446,482	166,919

Source: Computed from data available in *Country Tables: Basic Data on the Agricultural Sector*, FAO, Rome, Italy, 1989/92.

where

    a   = area of medium to high soil productivity;
    b   = area of medium to low soil productivity; and
    c   = average cultivated land per head of population.

Using this formula, the maximum population supporting capacity for SSA in 1989 was calculated. The result, presented in Table 9, indicates that even by 1960, when SSA carried a total of about 200 million people, the maximum population-carrying capacity of land had already been exceeded. On the basis of the 1989 population figure, it was clear that, based on the low productivity traditional farming technology, the PSC had been exceeded in SSA by about 2.5 times. Even if only the rural population of over 300 million was taken into account, the PSC was exceeded by about 1.75 times. Population pressure, is therefore, a real menace to the environment (Okai, 1992).

This formula can be rewritten as follows (Figure 17):

$$T_1 \geq C_1 + R_1 + F_r + C_n \tag{2}$$

where
    C_1 denotes cultivable land;
    C_n denotes non-cultivable land including land used for economic and
            social infrastructure;
    R_1 represents resting land; and
    F_r represents forest land.

$$fKc = \{Tl - [(\pi\ la\ Cln \div \pi\ lb\ Clm).(x)n + (\pi\ ja\ Rln \div \pi\ lb\ Rlm) + Fr + Cn.(y)n\ ]\} \div cph \tag{3}$$

where

    πl represents a fraction of land that can be cultivated taking into account
           the resting phase; in the above example π is 0.4 for soil of medium
           to high productivity;
    Cln represents land of medium to high productivity;
    Clm land of medium to low productivity;
    Rln is resting land of medium to high productivity;
    Rlm is resting land of medium to low productivity;
    Cph represents cultivated land per head of population;

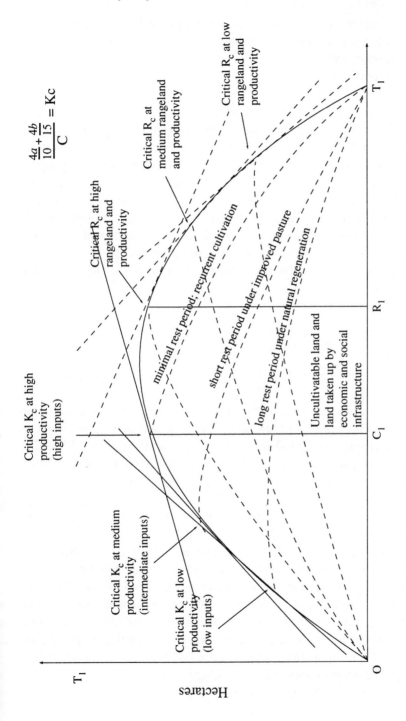

Figure 17 Land population supporting capacity

x   is the rate at which land is being brought under cultivation;
y   is the rate at which land is being taken out of production;
n   is time; and
T_1 is total land.

In analytical work it is assumed that cost and demand conditions remain constant through time for the different production activities. Under these conditions the rate of increase of land being brought under cultivation is due to the increases in population expressed as g (Cl, x). However, the rate of bringing land into production is also influenced by the effort-incentive expressed as (Cl, px) which is the unit profit of increasing production given that cost and demand conditions remain constant through time for the agricultural activities. It is also assumed that the complementary effects of keeping livestock on fallow land will be negligible and no new improved technologies are available. These conditions can be expressed notationally as

$$Kc \geq g(C_1,x) + g(C_1 + px) \tag{4}$$

where

$g(C_1, px)$ captures the profit function in the absence of externalities.

The production function can be influenced by government population policy as well as government pricing, exchange rate and trade policy, or the impact of prices determined independently outside the country in the world market. For instance, a higher fixed producer price of the products of the land obviously increases the profits as well as the marginal profit.

Technological change Land is a finite commodity but both human and animal population continues to expand until the critical land PSC has been reached or exceeded at point A. In Figure 18 the area that will be under cultivation is represented by OA li. Further increases in land being brought under cultivation to absorb more population results in a reduction of the fallow period and ultimately a decline in soil fertility. Absorbing additional population required the adoption of new improved technologies such as improved high-yielding crop variety, improved animal breeds, establishment of optimal plant population, optimal fertilizer application, weed control and the use of improved farm machinery. The adoption rate of the technology usually takes some time before it is fully adopted. In the figure, the level of population absorptive capacity will rise to point B, at intermediate input technology. The population absorbed is represented by OPii which has been achieved partly by increases in inputs AF and partly by more land being brought under cultivation Ali Aii. The population absorption possibility curve rises to the left from OAA to OBF.

As improved technologies are fully adopted, including the integration of livestock into the production systems, the PSC rises to C at high input technology level. The population absorption possibility curve rises further to OCG. At this point the production system has shifted from extensive to an

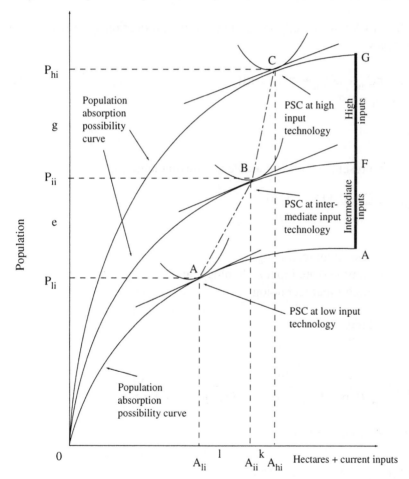

Notes: Adapted from Figure 17.

Figure 18 Land population supporting capacity at different levels of input technologies

intensive one; in other words, the adoption of recurrent cultivation practices. Equation (3) can, therefore, be rewritten as:

$$fKc = T_1 - [(F_r - (f)n + C_n - (y)n] = C_l + R_l \tag{5}$$

where

    f   is the rate of afforestation or if it is (f)-n, the rate of tree felling.

Since livestock will be fully integrated into the production system, equation (5) becomes

$$fKc = \pi C_{ln} + \pi C_{lm} + \pi R_{ln} + \pi R_{lm} \tag{6}$$
$$= c \, \pi \, C_{ln} + c \, \pi \, C_{lm}$$

where

    c   represents combined arable and resting land.

$$Cph = \frac{OAli,}{Opli} \quad \frac{OAii}{OPii} \quad \frac{OAhi}{OPhi}$$

    li   is low input technology;
    ii   is intermediate input technology; and
    hi   is high input technology.

$$Cphli = \frac{OAli}{Opli}$$

$$Cphii = \frac{OAii}{[(Op_{ii} - OP_{li}) \div (OA_{ii} - Oa_{li})]} = \frac{OAii}{OPii \times \frac{e}{1}}$$

From the figure, e is about $\frac{3}{4}$ e

$$Cphii = \frac{OAli}{OPii \times 4/3} = \frac{OAii}{1.3OPii}$$

$$Cphhi = OPhi.[(Phi-OP) \div (OAhi-OAii) = \frac{OAhi}{Phi.g/k}$$

From the figure k is just about $\frac{1}{4}$ e

$$\text{Cphhi} = \frac{\text{OAhi}}{\text{OPhi}.\ 3/k} = \frac{\text{OAhi}}{\text{OPhix}\ \frac{4}{1}} = \frac{\text{OAhi}}{4\text{OPhi}}$$

At high input technology level, the land will carry four times as many people as at low input technology level.

In SSA authorities were concerned largely with human population growth and its effects on the environment. Recently, however, it was realized that it is imperative to rely on population equivalent, a notion that takes into account the nutritional requirements of both animal and human population. The above method of calculating land carrying capacity assumes that livestock are grazed on resting land, but this condition may not necessarily hold at all the times. In the early stages, livestock may have a supplementary relationship with crop production when grazed on resting land. However, as both cropping expands and livestock number increases, the relationship becomes competitive, although under improved practices it can be complementary when livestock rearing and crop production are carried out to their mutual advantage in a mixed farming system. Mixed farming is not yet practised under traditional agriculture. It is, therefore, necessary, in assessing land population capacity, to take into account the nutritional requirements of livestock.

This relationship can be expressed as

$$R_c = \{R_l - [Lu.\ (r)n.\ N_{lu}\ ]\} \div H_{lu} \tag{7}$$

where

Rc   is rangeland carrying capacity;
Lu   represents livestock units;
Nlu   is the quantity (kg) of herbage per head of Lu; and
Hlu   is the number of hectares required to produce Nlu.

As shown in Figure 18, land population absorptive capacity depends to a large extent on land productivity and the level of inputs.

In SSA some 90 per cent of the population use fuelwood for domestic energy. According to Anderson (1987, pp. 5–13), the current annual rate of consumption exceeds the mean annual incremental growth (generally known as MAI) of local tree stocks and forest reserves. Also, the effects of land clearing contribute more to the loss of trees than does fuelwood consumption.

Once consumption exceeds the MAI, any or all of three things can happen: i) the deficit can be partly compensated by woodlots and forest plantation; ii) natural stocks can be harvested locally, which increases the gap between consumption and MAI thereby reducing stocks further; or iii) natural stocks can be harvested elsewhere, hence spreading deforestation to other areas. The growth of deficits within an area or their spread to other places escalates because consumption increases exponentially while MAI declines in proportion to the volume of stocks. These relationships are captured in a dynamic equation below. In areas where consumption begins to exceed the MAI, the rate of change in the volume of tree stocks can be expressed as:

$$dS/dt = (a - f) S\text{-}C \tag{8}$$

where

S	represents stocks of trees at time t;
C	denotes consumption rate;
a	is the MAI per unit of stock; and
f	is the net rate of felling (i.e. the removal of trees for agricultural, industrial and other activities minus the rate of planting by the forestry service and the farmers).

As population growth increases, the consumption rate can be expected to increase exponentially. However, as fuelwood becomes scarce, real costs and prices rise, and consumers begin to substitute or otherwise reduce consumption. Hence changes in consumption can be expressed as:

$$C = (A/P)^{e(pt)} \tag{9}$$

where

A	is a constant;
P	is price;
pt	is population growth rate; and
e	is exponential rate.

Price increases traditionally vary inversely with the available stocks. Thus equation (7) can be rewritten as

$$C = (Co/S_0)S^{e(pt)} \qquad (10)$$

where

C_0/S_0 is the consumption rate of stocks at t = o.

This yields

$$dS/dt = S\ [\ a-f-(C_0/S_0)^{e\ (pt)}\ ] \qquad (11)$$

In his study, Anderson (1987, p. 8) recalled that the spread of deforestation is most noticeable near urban centres. The expansion of urban centres brings about appreciable demands for fuelwood and charcoal, and accounts for much of the observed decline in tree stocks in the surrounding countryside, often for a radius of 80–160 kilometres or more.

Population equivalent For Sub-Saharan Africa, Alan pointed out that if population equivalent is taken into account, the population of Africa is estimated to be well over two billion people, with Ethiopia, Sudan and Nigeria heading the list. There are some countries with small human population while human equivalents are much larger. For instance, it has been estimated that the population of countries in climatically marginal areas like Mali, Chad and Somalia are 12 times what they are when animals are counted in terms of population equivalents. It is in these countries that severe overstocking of animals and population pressure on land occurred, resulting in general deterioration of the environment (Alan et al., 1973).

In the process of planning for the development of ranching in Uganda in the early 1960s, livestock was taken into account in calculating land carrying capacity. Initially different land categories for each district including cultivated and grazing land were taken into account. The grazing land included resting and cultivable land not under cultivation. All livestock (cattle, sheep, goats, etc.) were converted, using appropriate conversion factor, into livestock unit (LSU). The grazing requirements for each ecological zone (hectares of grazing required for each LSU) were determined on the basis of empirical evidence from research stations. On this basis, total grazing requirements were calculated and by deducting this amount from available grazing area, a grazing balance sheet was estimated. As illustrated in Tables 10 and 11, on average over 70 per cent of total land in Uganda by 1970 was available for grazing and just over 20 per cent of total land area was under cultivation. Intensity of grazing, however, varied, with certain districts like Bugisu, Bukedi and Kigezi being overgrazed while some areas still have plentiful grazing reserve (Okai, 1974).

Grazing requirements (or stocking density) can best be evaluated from both the technical and economic perspectives. In Uganda, beef ranching was actively promoted, beginning in the early 1960s. Apart from being the source of supply of beef and substituting beef import with domestic production, the other objective was to improve rangeland management. Several ranches were established, each averaging 1,250 hectares. At that time grazing requirements for a livestock unit (LSU) on an improved rangeland averaged about 2.5 hectares (Figure 19).

From the economic perspective, commercial ranchers' principal interest is to maximize economic return rather than the technical optimum (biological output). The economic profitability of alternative stocking rates can be assessed by means of economic efficiency analysis. In carrying out the analysis, physical outputs are converted into cash equivalencies. In Figure 20, the value of outputs and costs of production are shown on the vertical axis and alternative stocking rates on the horizontal axis. Output expenses increase in proportion to herd size, while variable costs like veterinary supplies are assumed to remain constant per livestock unit and, therefore, increase linearly with the addition of each animal. Since the rancher's own management input, including family labour and land, remains constant whether employed or not, it can be treated as fixed costs. Although these fixed costs are not treated as fixed expenses, they can be regarded as investment which receives rent, defined as the differential between the total variable costs and gross return to the ranch. For the commercial rancher, the economically optimal stocking density is the maximum profit the point of which, as shown in the figure, is reached at the level of output at which marginal revenue equals marginal costs. Any additional output beyond this point will increase cost.

As land becomes inframarginally scarce, farmers usually respond by retreating to intensive forms of agricultural production systems by adopting land-saving technologies such as the growing of high-yielding crop varieties and panning animals. This shift in agricultural production practices may also be associated with labour-saving technologies. As illustrated in Figure 21, at the low input technology, the initial equilibrium is defined by agricultural output isoquant OO_1, with land use being OD_1, and labour and current inputs $OPli$. This is in consonance with relative factor prices DD_1 for land, labour and minimal current inputs. As indicated in the previous Figure 18, the population absorptive capacity of land at low input level remains low at A. Increases in the use of productive (improved seeds) and technical production

Table 10   Land use in Uganda, 1970 (in km²)

	Total area	Open water	Swamp area	Total land reserve	Forest parks	National reserves	Game lands	Cultivated land	Grazing	Col. 9 as % of col. 8
	1	2	3	4	5	6	7	8	9	10
East Mengo	23,406	9,254	940	13,212	1,147	–	–	6,638	5,427	45
West Mengo	6,511	1,559	176	4,776	386	–	–	1,310	3,080	70
Masaka	20,663	9,899	972	9,792	774	–	–	2,191	6,827	76
Mubande	10,158	109	259	9,790	858	–	–	2,059	6,874	77
Bugisu	2,473	–	44	2,434	526	–	–	1,300	600	32
Busoga	17,975	8,379	678	8,918	400	–	–	5,897	2,621	31
Teso	12,831	1,209	469	11,153	135	–	–	5,703	5,315	48
Sebei	1,738	–	–	1,738	671	–	–	230	837	79
NorthKaramoja	9,975	–	–	9,975	1,480	1,259	(114)	141	7,095	90
South Karamoja	13,931	–	–	13,931	929	–	5,860	211	12,791	98
East Acholi	14,620	–	−14,620	741	–	–	900	12,979	93	
West Acholi	13,492	–	185	13,307	310	1,813	283	1,066	9,835	90
Lango	13,090	559	969	11,562	212	–	–	4,351	6,999	62
West Nile	10,927	32	155	10,740	676	–	158	3,134	6,772	68
Madi	4,745	39	259	4,447	344	–	–	539	3,564	89
Ankole	16,255	308	593	15,354	606	686	1,005	3,131	9,926	76
Buroyoro	19,632	2,774	399	16,459	1,857	2,072	1,238	1,575	9,717	86
Kigezi	5,281	215	399	16,459	1,857	2,072	1,238	1,575	9,717	86
Toro	13,553	772	491	12,290	2,046	881	1,106	1,782	6,475	78
Uganda	235,882	35,243	7,142	193,502	14,550	7,125	10,098	47,505	120,138	72
%	100.0	14.0	3.0	82.1	6.2	3.0	4.3	20.2	50.0	

Source: Okai, 1974. Compiled from reports on beef ranching in Uganda especially the fact-finding reports of Aswan and Ankole Masaka Beef Ranching Projects and atlas of Uganda, 1965.

Table 11   Grazing balance sheet of Uganda in 1970

	Total LSU	Carrying capacity ha/LSU	Grazing area required km²	Grazing[a] area available km²	Balance km²	Total land area km²	Col. 5[b] as % of col. 6
East Mango	219,249	2	4,385	5,427	1,042	13,212	8
West Mango	68,426	2	1,368	3,080	1,712	4,776	36
Masaka	104,999	2	2,100	6,827	4,727	9,792	48
Mubande	77,850	3	1,557	6,874	5,317	9,790	54
Bugisu	42,685	2	854	608	-246	2,434	–
Bukodi	108,789	2	1,276	961	-1,215	4,079	–
Busoga	159,398	2	3,188	2,621	-567	8,918	–
Teso	392,960	2	7,859	5,315	2,544	11,153	–
Sebei	30,550	2	611	837	226	1,738	13
North Karamoja	163,143	4	6,525	7,095	570	9,975	6
South Karamoja	245,586	4.5	10,328	12,791	2,763	13,931	18
East Acholi	90,859	3	2,247	12,979	10,732	14,620	73
West Acholi	61,426	2	1,227	9,835	8,608	13,307	65
Lango	270,104	2	5,402	6,999	1,597	11,562	14
West Nile	91,570	3	2,455	6,772	4,317	10,740	40
Madi	14,535	3	6,437	3,564	2,127	4,447	70
Bureyoro	44,183	2	884	9,717	8,833	16,459	53
Migezi	82,811	2	1,656	1,435	-221	4,925	–
Toro	66,276	2	1,325	6,475	5,150	12,290	42
Uganda	2,649,520		62,997	120,138	57,151	193,502	30
%			26.7	50.0	29.5	82.1	

Notes: LSU = livestock unit; a = column 9 of Table B; b = column 4 of Table B.

Source: Okai, 1974. Compiled from reports on beef ranching in Uganda, especially fact-finding reports of Aswa and Ankole/Masaka beef ranching projects and various technical reports on pasture research in Uganda.

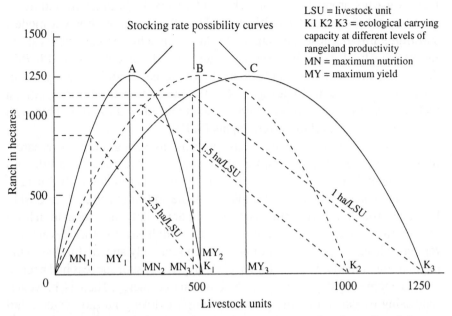

Figure 19 Stocking rates at different levels of rangeland productivity

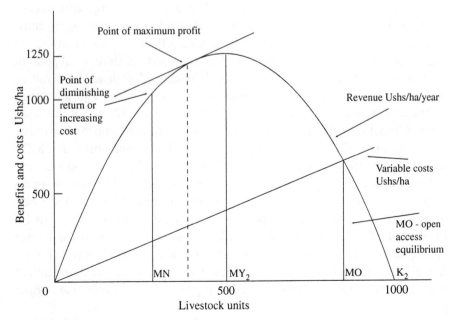

Figure 20 Stocking rate and economic return

inputs raise the production frontier, but with relatively diminishing additional land being brought under cultivation. Thus the isoquant shows a modest substitutability because the output OO_2 has been achieved partly by a slight increase in land use (OE_1) but a greater use of current inputs (Pli Pii). Technological advances due to biotechnical research and the adoption of improved technological packages raise the production frontier to isoquant OO_3 which has been achieved with a much reduced land use (OE_1) but with greatly increased level of current inputs Pii Phi.

Energy-intensive agriculture has implications for agricultural research, technology development and sustainable agricultural growth and environmental problems associated with the use of agro-chemicals. Sustainability in an economic context implies a stable and satisfactory relationship between agricultural production and consumption, implying a population level or growth rate that is supportable on a long-term basis. In other developing regions where the green revolution has been relatively successful due to the application of modern agricultural technology, the cost of success had been at an ever-increasing dependency on fossil fuel-based energy. There is, however, increasing evidence that the green revolution is losing its momentum, and there is now a growing recognition that sustaining the growth rates that were achieved in the recent past is likely to require a greater investment in biotechnology in order to reduce heavy reliance on high energy agriculture.

From the point of view of sustaining land population supporting capacity, it is true that technological progress of the kind reflected by isoquant OO_3 in Figure 21 is necessary in the long-run. This is because, if the critical point of land population carrying capacity at C is exceeded, it leads to resource degradation, thus narrowing further the resource base. The advanced technology, however, has high costs. Consider Figure 22, which has been derived from Figure 18. The demand curve Dli is associated with the possibility curve (isoquant) OO_1, and factor price DD_1. The marginal cost curve MCli defines aggregate output OT in Figure 22, and land and current inputs Og and OPli respectively in Figure 21. Owing to increasing demand for current inputs as the land base narrows, the price of inputs increases to MCii. Increased input use raises agricultural output to OU (Figure 22) and current inputs Pli Pii in Figure 21. As agricultural intensification accelerates, the MChi defines aggregate agricultural output OV and current inputs Pii Phi (Figure 21). With the shift of demand from Dli through Dii to Dhi, aggregate agricultural output may initially grow slowly but prices of inputs may rise faster than output prices.

Heavy reliance on the use of agro-chemicals to sustain land population-

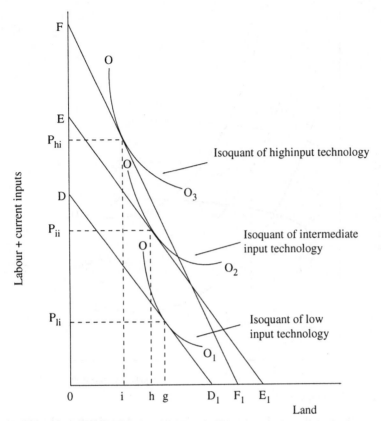

Note: Adapted from Figure 18.

Figure 21 Induced technological innovation factor use, output and land population supporting capacity

supporting capacity could result in a dilemma. Expanded use of agro-chemicals could lead to environmental damage, while their high prices require the growing of high value crops or rearing of high grade animals to make their use economically viable. If the critical level of land population-carrying capacity is exceeded, it will result in resource degradation and a further reduction in the land resource base. One area that offers the greatest promise of resolving the dilemma is advances in biological sciences for developing the necessary technologies. Advances in biotechnology can make it possible to improve biological crop insurance and biomass by: i) developing and releasing cultivars which are resistant to pests and diseases and thus reducing the need for and use of agro-chemicals; ii) improving the tolerance of certain

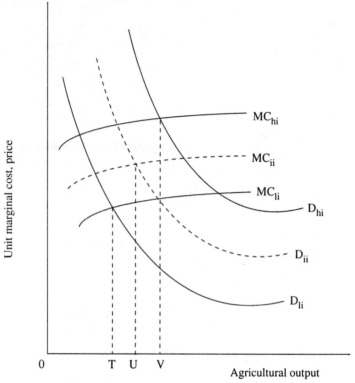

Note: Adapted from Figure 17.

Figure 22 Demand-supply of current inputs and agricultural outputs

plant species to climatic stresses like drought or cold temperatures; iii) enhancing the nitrogen-fixing capacity of plants as a substitute for chemical fertilizers; and iv) increasing the biomass or yield potential of plants. This option requires substantial investment in research in order to have an impact. New approaches to research and technology development will have to be explored. Biotechnology innovations are patentable and knowledge-intensive, but in SSA countries research is still dominated by government civil servants who often are not highly motivated to carry out research. Research is a discipline that can easily be patented and commodified so that the researchers are rewarded and, therefore, the private sector will be motivated to make major intellectual investment in biotechnology research in order to generate the technologies needed for environmental protection while at the same time ensuring a sustainable relationship between agricultural production and consumption.

Resource Sustainability

Technology Low soil fertility associated with deficiencies in nitrogen (N) and phosphorus (P) and low organic matter is a major cause of low productivity and soil degradation in SSA. One of the ways of recapitalization of soil fertility is the improvement of the soil organic matter status, and increased but prudent use of nutrient inputs. They will provide the necessary foundation for addressing the important issue of soil fertility in SSA. Improved organic management, combined with increased nitrogen and phosphorus availability, can solve the soil organic matter deficiency. If sufficient phosphorus is available, the nitrogen deficiency can partially be solved through the increased contribution of nitrogen by leguminous plant species in the agricultural production system. Although investment in the restoration of soil fertility may be heavy, the social benefits associated with the investment are significant. Such social benefits include the arrest of the cycle of shifting cultivation and the ever-increasing encroachment into marginal land, the prevention of land degradation resulting in soil erosion, making recurrent cultivation possible, the protection of waterways, coastal and estuarine zones from siltation and pollution, the protection of habitats and biodiversity, etc. Other benefits include the improvement of the natural resource base and increasing the land's green vegetation cover that will contribute to the decrease of the greenhouse effect.

Macroeconomy-agricultural resources interactive dynamics Agricultural production uses resources on the farm and not land alone. Land quality (soil productivity including plant nutrients) has a positive effect on agricultural output. However, land quality and output level do not determine the most profitable result, and one therefore has to consider a number of factors, such as non-soil inputs (Nsi) like labour, productive (seeds) and technical production inputs (agro-chemicals), water utilization and the intensity of cultivation (Ic), often greatly influenced by the level of incentive. Productivity of land, although one important factor, is only a fraction of determinants of level of output. A cropping programme has to reconcile three aspects: income (consumption) maximization (the profit aspect); a reduction of income uncertainty (the risk factor); and maintaining and increasing income over time (the conservation aspect). While these are the major aspects of a cropping programme, it is also vital to consider the technical aspects, especially soil structure and fertility level, the effect of the cropping pattern on soil water regime, effects on the control of weeds, pests and diseases, pattern of labour and machine use, factor/ product relationships (complementary, supplementary or competitive products), performance of each crop in combination with the factors in particular the physical environment, and how each crop enterprise differs with different levels of resource use.

Before deciding on a cropping programme, the farmer has to consider the economics of the production process. Firstly he/she has to consider prices and uncertainty attached to them; secondly he/she has to consider the relative costs of factors used in the production process and uncertainty attached to these costs. Once the technical aspects and the economic relationships are determined, the farmer can then decide on the cropping pattern, including the conservation aspects. The decision of the farmer, therefore, greatly influences the soil dynamics by choosing which crops to grow, animals to rear, tillage technique, cropping intensity, the nature of crop rotation, the integration of animals in the production systems, and resource conservation measures. These dynamics notationally can be expressed as

$$Nr = [(Se - Sf) + (Nd - Na)] \geq 0 \qquad (12)$$

where

Nr	denotes soil natural regeneration rate;
Se	denotes soil erosion;
Sf	indicates soil formation;
Nd	denotes plant nutrient depletion; and
Na	denotes plant nutrient accumulation.

In equation (12) Nr is greatly influenced by the intensity of cultivation (1c) and conservation measures over time (Ct). If Se exceeds Sf due to inappropriate land management practices, it leads to net loss of productive soil and land degradation. Similarly if Nd exceeds Na, it results in a decline in soil fertility.

To recover resource productivity, it is necessary to invest heavily in conservation measures. Alternatively, the farmer may decide to adopt a farming practice that sustains the soil's natural regeneration rate. Consequently, Nr is a function of conservation practices. Under traditional farming systems (shifting cultivation) soil conservation practices do not entail direct costs but their costs are felt through a decline in output level in the short run. Some soil conservation measures, however, do involve direct costs, especially non-soil inputs (Nsi). Ct is, therefore, a function of cultivation practices (lc) and Nsi. Equation (12) can then be re-expressed as

$$dNrt/dt = Nr - [(Se - Sf) + (Nd - Na)] f Ct \qquad (13)$$

where

Ct   denotes the conservation inputs in time t; and
Nrt   is the natural regeneration rate in time t;

Nrt is, therefore, a constant representing naturally occurring addition to soil. The more intensive and extractive cultivation (greater lc), the greater the soil natural resource loss, in the absence of commensurate Ct. To prevent this happening (to maintain a constant land productivity) even while practising a more intensive form of cultivation, requires greater increases in compensatory productivity (use of biological factors in soil conservation).

Agricultural output can then be expressed as a function of Q (lc, Nsi, Ct). The farmer traditionally chooses a level of cultivation intensity (lc), use of non-soil inputs (Nsi) and conservation inputs (Ct) at every instant so as to maximize the present value of the farm enterprise. This can be expressed as

$$pQ[(Lc, Nsi, Ct) - u\ Nsit - vCt]\ e^{-rt\ dt} \qquad (14)$$

where

p   denotes price of farm output;
u   is the price of non-soil inputs;
v   is the conservation inputs; and
r   is the rate of discount.

The essence of sustainable agricultural development is that the stock of natural resources remains non-declining in order to maintain maximum sustainable flow of social utility. In generating this flow one has to consider development-environment interactions. Bringing a piece of land into production when in its maximum level of productivity subjects the soil to perturbation, which can result in soil degradation unless internal externalities in the context of soil erosion are effectively harnessed and internalized. While they constitute internal technical externalities, there are also internal macroeconomy (such as monetary, fiscal, trade and exchange rate, interest rate, price and income policies) externalities that determine the technical and economic efficiency of resource utilization. There are also international externalities (for instance the hegemonic forces of international economic relations) which can prevent the domestic economy from undertaking efficient allocation of resources.

Soils, through regeneration (soil formation) can be regarded as a productive stock of resources possessing recycling qualities. Maintaining a steady flow of utility, therefore, depends on soil regeneration capacity and the associated conservation measures. As land is brought into production, it produces a flow of outputs. Meanwhile its productivity declines at a rate commensurate with the intensity of cultivation. The decline has to be replenished by means of natural regeneration complemented by conservation measures. Both outputs from the land and conservation inputs have monetary values. The relationship between resource utilization and replenishment can, therefore, be expressed in value terms as

$$VoNr = Vn\ Nrt.e^{-(y+r)} + VcCt.e^{-r} \tag{15}$$

where

VoNr is the value of Nr in time t = o;
Vn Nrt is the value of Nr in time t;
VcCt is the cost of conservation inputs in time t (the value of regeneration included);
y   is the constant rate of decline of resource productivity;
r   is the rate of discount of future income and costs.

Since conservation measures are intended to replenish decline in productivity, VcCt can be taken as y. The equation can, therefore, be rewritten as

$$VoNr = Vn\ Nrt.e^{-(VcCt^{y+r})} \tag{16}$$

$$VoNr = Vn\ Nrt \times \frac{1}{VcCt^{y+r}} \tag{17}$$

$$VoNr\ (VcCt^{y+r}) = VnNrt \tag{18}$$

$$VcCt^{y+r} = \frac{Vn\ Nrt}{Vo\ Nr} \tag{19}$$

$$\therefore y = \frac{VnNrt}{VoNr} \tag{20}$$

If y equals to 1, it means that resource renewability is being maintained; if it is more than 1 it implies increases in compensatory productivity; and if it is less than 1, it indicates resource degradation and loss of soil fertility (depletion of plant nutrients exceeding accumulation).

The government's macroeconomic policy will have great influence on resource use. High prices of outputs encourage extractive forms of agricultural production. As the farmers are motivated to produce more, they extract in excess of stored soil fertility. Conversely, if the prices of inputs are high while those of outputs are low, farmers find it not worthwhile to invest in conservation measures. Uncertainties may also oblige farmers to use high discount rates to compute the present values of future income, and may, therefore, be discouraged from investing in conservation.

With a primary focus on environmental issues, alternative farming systems ideally should explore options that can conserve environmental resources. In the past, agricultural development in SSA had always been discussed in the context of land abundance and surplus labour supply and consequently resource conservation measures were not included in agricultural development paradigms. As explained in the preceding sections, the SSA region is now facing inframarginal land scarcity and agricultural labour force has started to decline. In order to raise factor productivity and improve land population absorptive capacity, there is now a need to adopt land-saving and labour-saving technologies through the adoption of biological yield-increasing innovation and greater use of improved farm machinery.

Once such innovation is the integration of livestock into the arable agriculture in order to exploit the technical complementarity that exists between livestock and crops which can lead to increased yield per unit area, improved soil fertility, reduced soil erosion and can spread risks. Livestock solid and liquid wastes improve soil structure and aeration while at the same time recycling plant nutrients. The planting of improved pastures protects the soil from rainfall impact and thus avoids soil compaction, but instead improves water penetration into the soil and reduces soil erosion while at the same time providing herbage for the animals. Some of the plants are also complementary to each other. Leguminous crops, for example, through their nitrogen-fixation capability, improve soil fertility, which benefits the production of non-leguminous crops. Output levels can also be increased through the use of fertilizers, insecticides, herbicides, etc.

The adoption of these improved practices entails costs. One such cost is a nonmonetary one – the cost of learning a new technique of farming. In order to induce the farmer to adopt the innovation, the technique should be economically profitable to motivate the farmer to undertake the psychological change (attitudinal change). There is also the monetary costs relating, in particular, to the economy of scale. The introduction of the new technique entails increases in overhead costs. For instance, the integration of livestock into the production system involves costs in fencing, land improvement, water supply, farm buildings which constitute the initial investment. In addition there are also variable costs as the size of the farming enterprise increases. There is also the average cost of producing a unit of output. As the farmer increases output, he/she is actually spreading the overhead costs, which reach a minimum at point Y, after which variables costs outweigh the average cost curve (Figure 23). The other issue to consider is at what point the values of output will be sufficient to cover both the fixed and variable costs incurred. Values above this point mean that the enterprise has moved into profit, and values below mean losses are being incurred. This point is called break-even point. The following formula is used to obtain the breakdown point:

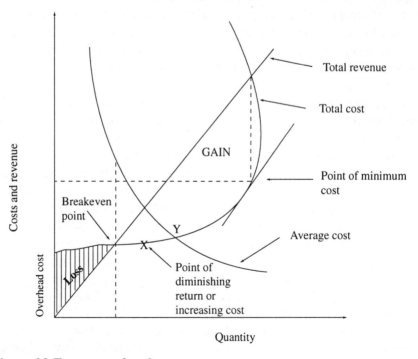

Figure 23 Economy of scale

$$\text{Number of units to break-even} = \frac{\text{fixed costs}}{\text{values-variable costs of units}}$$

Deducting the variable costs from the values of output gives us the contribution each unit value makes towards the fixed costs. The number of units produced would correspondingly reduce unit costs, due to the operation of economy of scale.

The shift to a new technique does not necessarily mean that it is economical, and the farmer has to consider relative returns on the enterprise, taking into account return to alternative techniques, time horizon and the management costs. The enterprise under the new technique must reach a minimum size in order to exploit economy of scale, and that size might be beyond the resources of the farmer or the management of the new technique might fall outside the range of his/her competence and skill. It also takes time for the effect of the new technique to manifest itself. If the farmer has a short time horizon, or there is a great deal of risk or uncertainty of security of tenure, the farmer is likely to use a high discount rate to compute future streams of income from the enterprise. One other way of calculating the profitability of the new technique is to compute the marginal rate of return (MRR).

The foregoing consideration relates to a large extent to biological yield-increasing innovation. As regards labour-saving technology, the farmer similarly has to consider costs and returns and the problem of introducing mechanical aid. The decision to buy a certain machine depends on costs and returns. Costs consist of fixed investments on the one hand and variable costs on the other. The fixed costs consist of depreciation over time, obsolescence, interest on loans, insurance, farm buildings, taxes and repairs, while variable costs consist of repairs, fuel and oil, and depreciation due to use.

The costs relating to depreciation are due to wear and tear as the machinery is used, but can also be due to obsolescence as a result of time. New models with better performance are continuously being produced following rapid advances in technology. As a result the value of the existing model declines. Obsolescence itself is not necessarily a bad thing because the fall in the price of the obsolete model can still make its use economically profitable. The other cost element relates to the acquisition of the new machine. It is common practice to raise a loan for the purchase of the machine. The loans attract variable interest charges depending on the government monetary policy. By buying the machine, the farmer is essentially locking up capital which could have been put into alternative productive use. The purchase of the machine, therefore, has opportunity cost.

It is also necessary to insure against risks of fire, accident, theft, etc. Even if the farmer opts not to insure, he/she continues to suffer from fear of loss of the machine, and this may inhibit him/her from fully mechanizing the entire farming operation. Either alternative has costs.

Housing the farm machinery in a garage is optional, but if not housed it will suffer from heavier depreciation. Building a garage is an additional fixed cost. The precise decision depends on cost of housing and the rate of depreciation of the machinery. If the depreciation rate is high, it pays to house the machinery, and if it is vice versa, say a low cost simple machine, it may not be economical to house it. Where the farmer cannot profitably obtain fuel and lubricants from a supply depot he/she may be forced to construct a supply point to stock the fuel and oil. Some farm machinery, like lorries, cars, etc., attract taxes, depending on the government fiscal policy.

Operating farm machinery, no matter how simple, requires training of operators in its use. The farmer may, due to lack of skill, have to bear the cost of training the operators. Lack of proper training could lead to inappropriate use of the machinery causing damage and a reduction in the life of the machine. The farmer may also find it necessary to provide accommodation for the farm staff, including inducements through the payment of bonuses to retain them. These are extra costs that had to be taken into account. It is also necessary to consider and estimate the life of the machine and spread the capital costs over its life, yielding annual costs. This aspect is often complicated because of obsolescence costs. An improved model may be introduced, necessitating the replacement of the obsolete machine before it reaches the end of its physical life. There is, therefore, uncertainty and risk involved. The farmer is, therefore, obliged to discount for obsolescence. Machinery will suffer heavy damages if used on land full of holes, tree stumps, rocks, etc. The farmer is, therefore, forced to incur extra cost on land development.

Due to the consideration of costs and returns, the farmer finds it obligatory to carry out partial budgeting which does not cover the whole farm operation, but specifically for the one particular farm machine.

Partial budgeting

i) extra cost   i) extra revenue
ii) revenue foregone   ii) cost saved

The use of the machine is economical if the economy of scale can be achieved due to its use over a large number of production units (e.g. hectares).

The extra revenue may be due to large hectarage, timeliness of operation resulting in higher yields, or cost saved may be due to a saving in hand labour. Labour saving does not necessarily mean monetary benefit unless the labour released can be profitably employed in alternative occupations. This brings extra revenue. If the machine is used to replace oxen used for ploughing, extra revenue may be obtained due to a saving in feeding costs, because it is a monetary cost that has been saved. Land needed for grazing oxen can also be released and put into alternative productive use which ultimately yields extra revenue. However, as land scarcity becomes acute, it may become necessary to pen the animals and practice zero grazing. Extra costs are, therefore, incurred in constructing the pens and carting the grass to the pens. The manure produced by the animals brings extra revenue due to improved soil productivity and increased output. As it conserves resources, the use of manure reduces conservation costs.

The other valid point to consider is whether it is worthwhile mechanizing farming operations. The farming system has a pattern of labour and machinery use over the year. A farmer may opt to maintain a permanent labour force and employ a small amount of casual labour. There is a risk in keeping a large labour force because some of it could be idle at slack periods. By plotting labour demand profile over the year, the farmer will be able to decide on the strength of the labour force to employ. During high peak labour demand period, the peak can be spread over by staggering planting dates (temporal diversification) and hence automatically spreading farming operations. However, the farmer will sacrifice yield due to lack of timeliness of farming operations. Alternatively, he can alter the farming patterns through changes in rotation to cope with the available labour force. In this alternative, the farmer gains by saving on machinery cost. He/she may also decide to mechanize to achieve high yield due to better timing of farming operations and gain extra revenue due to high yields.

Whatever technique is chosen, the cardinal point is that the technology being adopted should be technically feasible, economically viable, socially acceptable and have environment conserving qualities in order to be able to guarantee sustainable agricultural development. The sustainability of development can be measured by estimating the intertemporal total factor productivity, which is the next subject for explanation.

Total Factor Productivity

Sources of agricultural growth A crucial issue in agricultural development is choosing alternative systems that are relatively efficient in resource allocation and conducive to growth. The concept of total factor productivity (TFP) which measures the change in outputs to the relative change in inputs has been developed as an analytical tool in measuring trends in resource utilization. It has long been recognized that technical change, policy reform, and institutional innovation are complements required to sustain productivity growth (Binswanger and Pingali, 1988). In explaining productivity growth, however, the emphasis has been put on weather conditions and on intellectual investments that generate new technologies in whose use the farmers had to be trained in order to be able to adopt them. This objective can be realized through public sector research and development expenditures, extension services and farmer training.

While these factors are important, the conventional approach often overlooked the role of policies and investments at other stages of the agricultural system affecting farm technology adoption. These could include response to changes in relative prices of the agricultural products or factor inputs which could either stimulate the adoption or rejection of new technology and ultimately their impacts on productivity. The other factors of equal importance in promoting the realization of potential gains from research and development are non-price factors, which include transport networks, research and extension facilities, institutional infrastructure (factor, product, labour, capital and financial markets), availability of both technical production and productive inputs, and the availability of consumer goods.

Since its acceptance as an analysis tool, the TFP has been given many definitions, usually from different perspectives. Block (1994), for instance, concerned with general agricultural productivity as being a critical determinant for both the rural welfare and economic growth in SSA, defined 'productivity' as the difference between the growth rate of real product and the growth rate of real factor input. This definition is not only based on the physical relationship between inputs and outputs, but also includes the profit function or economic efficiency by incorporating price effects on input demand and output supply. By endogenizing prices, this profit function approach facilitates the measurement of policy effects on prices and in turn on productivity. In measuring TPF both real output and real input are derived as weighted averages of the rates of growth of individual factors and products. Input weights are the production elasticities as estimated in aggregate production functions.

Measuring land productivity, average labour productivity and explaining the sources of growth are carried out in a sequential way. The first step entails establishing a database consisting of farm prices, area and production time series of the main agricultural products. The Lesotho data were used to compute yield time series. The second step is to compute average land productivity. This is carried out by weighing the physical yields by constant prices, thus developing a series of economic yield to be divided by the number of hectares of crop land. This yields time series of average yield per hectare over time and computing index numbers to indicate trends in the average land productivity. Land and labour productivities can also be obtained by computing the difference between the growth rates of output and the rates of land being brought under cultivation, and growth rate of labour force in agriculture respectively. If it is greater than 1, it means that factor productivity is increasing; if it is unity it implies stagnant productivity; and if less than 1 it means productivity is declining.

Land productivity was computed by weighing the physical yields by constant prices, thus yielding a series of economic yield to be divided by hectares of cropped area. The indicator increases if the sector's performance improves. Labour productivity can be measured approximately as the ratio of real value of agricultural production to the agricultural labour force. The growth rate of this productivity measure can be taken as indicative of the growth rate of agricultural labour productivity. As illustrated in the figure, land productivity in Lesotho was declining at a rate of 1.8 per cent a year due largely to extensive land degradation (Figure 24).

Wen used a disaggregated definition: firstly he defines a partial factor productivity, called average product, as a ratio of output to a particular input. For instance, if 0 stands for output and Fi for any individual factor, the relationship can notationally be expressed as:

$$AP/_B = O/Fi \tag{21}$$

where

AP_B is the average product which measures how the output per unit output changes over time, ignoring the contribution from other factors.

Secondly therefore, the TFP can be defined as the ratio of output to the weighted sum of inputs (total factors), computationally expressed as

$$A = O/\ ai\ Fi \tag{22}$$

where

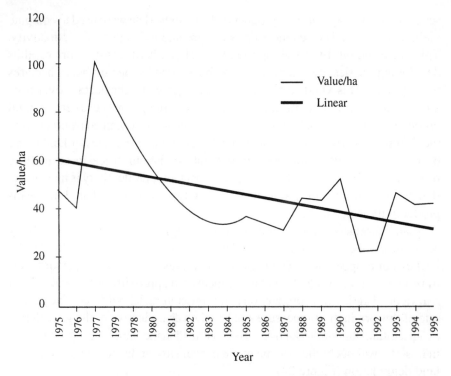

Figure 24 Lesotho: intertemporal total factor productivity – observed trends of total real value of output in Maloti

A   is the technical change (or TFP);
O   is the output;
Fi   is any factor used in the production of output; and
ai   is its weight.

Wen indicated that there are three sources of economic growth. Firstly, the traditional system of the source of growth stems from increased inputs. Development processes start from indigenous technology (Tt) whose output might be lower than improved technology (Ti) which initially is not available. Under traditional farming conditions increases in capital is reflected in the growth rising as inputs increase. The second source of growth comes from institutional innovation. Output grows as institutional constraints in resource allocation and mobility are eliminated and output increases from the traditional level to a higher equilibrium level. More output is produced with the same amount of inputs. The third source of growth is technical change (technological innovation) due to technological advances which shift the production frontier for the same amounts of inputs which produce more outputs. The rate of growth in TFP is the total factor productivity index (TFP1) which captures that part of growth rate which cannot be explained by the weighted growth of inputs and hence can only be explained by institutional innovation and technological progress. Based on this consideration, Wen defined TFP1 as follows:

$$\text{TFP} = \frac{1100 \times \text{GVAO index}}{b\,1\,(\text{L index}) + b\,2\,(\text{K index}) + b\,3\,(\text{S index}) + b\,4\,(\text{C index})} \quad (23)$$

where

b 1, b 2, b 3, and b 4 are weights; and
L   is labour,
K   is capital,
S   is land; and
C   represents current inputs.

GVAO is the gross value of agricultural output.

Ehui and Spencer pointed out that the agricultural sector utilizes a common pool of resources which affect the production environment sometimes far beyond the control of farmers. When the stock of resources is reduced the farmer faces an implicit cost in terms of forgone productivity, and conversely when the stock of resources is increased the farmer derives an implicit benefit from the system.

Relevance of technological innovation and sustainable development Prior to the global concern with environmental issues which started in the early 1970s, the preoccupation of the pioneers of development economics was with the sustainability of the economy, taken as sustained increases in per capita income and structural change in the economy. Man-made capital accumulation to expand the productive base of the economy and the associated processes of domestic savings were deemed as being essential to achieve the objective of self-sustained economic growth. Hicks (1946, p. 17), for instance, advocated that 'the purpose of income calculation in practical affairs is to give people an indication of the amount which they can consume without impoverishing themselves'. These earlier definitions of sustainability were made in the context of an open economy system with unlimited access to natural resources – the so-called 'free gifts of nature'. The principal concern of natural resource scarcities was directed towards exhaustible resources such as minerals and fossil fuels. The use of TFP should, therefore, take into account resource renewability.

The general concern with sustainable development is that the aggregate capital stock (natural and man-made) remains non-declining. This requires some form of resource combination and adaptations to changing ecological settings that neutralize the destructive effects of the synergy of the nexus between population, agriculture and the environment in order to sustain resource-productive potentials. This is the same as determining the stability of the ecosystems with respect to perturbation like resource use and the general problem of economy-environment systems dynamics. This raises four conceptual definitions: *development, sustainability, stability* and *resilience*. Conceptually, development was originally concerned with the growth of aggregate national outputs (gross domestic products). Recently, however, its definition has been enlarged to include real income per capita, health, nutrition status, educational achievement, access to resources and services, the distribution of income and basic human right – human-centred development strategies. A country usually has a stock of produced capital as well as natural resources. The process of converting the stock into produced capital in order to expand the productive base of the economy and the level of development is measured by the values of accumulated stock over time.

The natural endowments of the economy can be regarded as a potential base for development which can be converted into productive natural capital assets. To sustain development both the natural and produced capital stocks should remain non-declining to meet the criterion for *sustainable development*. In the case of agriculture, land use usually perturbs the soil, which could lead to land degradation and soil erosion (soil depletion), but this loss should be compensated for by soil formation made possible through natural recycling of organic materials. If soil depletion exceeds formation, the stock of natural resources will be depleted and the objective of sustainable agricultural development will not be realized. If resource exploitation is equally matched by natural regeneration rate, it means that the system will be ecologically stable. In traditional agriculture the *stability* is sustained through adaptations and judicious resource combinations such as shifting cultivation, which entails mobility to allow land to restore its fertility under natural conditions. In pastoral areas, faced with a harsh and non-equilibrium environment, the pastoralists sustain ecological stability by continually rearranging the spatial distribution of resource productivity (Behnke, 1994, p. 10). *Resilience*, closely related to stability, is a measure of the ecosystem's resistance to perturbation and the speed of return to original equilibrium. It is, therefore, a measure of the perturbation that can be absorbed without destroying the system. In climatically marginal areas, for instance, where vegetation is vulnerable to frequent dry conditions, adaptations of plants to the harsh environment include living parts retreating behind thorns, inside woody structures, below ground or stored in seeds that can withstand dry and hot conditions.

Conceptually, environmental insecurity is a situation when the natural environment is unable to supply in adequate quantity and quality sufficient biomass to meet the basic needs of food and nutrition, health, shelter, clothing and recreational facilities, and improve the quality of life, measured not necessarily in terms of material wealth but by the happiness index. Despite recent enlarged definitions of sustainable development, there are still nevertheless debates on the definitions of *land degradation, soil erosion, drought, aridity*, and *desertification*. From the contextual point of view the word 'environment' has been used to describe an array of conditions, situations or events: physical environment, social environment, economic environment, political environment, external environment, etc. Despite debates on definitional issues, there are, however, some concepts that help to explain environmental deterioration and insecurity which are all-embracing terminologies and which currently can be distinguished into *terrestrial, aquatic, atmospheric* and *biospheric* systems. *Environmental insecurity* denotes a reduction in the capacity of these natural resources to satisfy human needs as a result of land degradation, soil erosion, and other forms of loss of productive land due to salinity and alkalinity, water and atmospheric pollutions.

Land degradation in a broad sense is a form of land perturbation through use or land exploitation not being matched by natural regeneration rate (soil formation). Land degradation also includes net depletion of soil plant nutrients (depletion minus nutrient accumulation) resulting in land losing its potential productive capacity. *Soil erosion*, however, is the loss of productive top soil through erosive water runoff, sheet, gulley, rill, and/or wind erosions. The soil erosion, in most cases is accelerated by the loss of vegetation cover due to *deforestation* not being matched by *afforestation*. Soil erosion in turn reduces water infiltration into the soil to recharge aquifers, leading to a fall in *groundwater table*. All these forms of degradation, for convenience or simplicity, can be taken as *ecological degradation* or loss of *ecological stability*.

Ecological degradation, if not checked, acquires a synergistic quality, since it adversely affects *environmental resources*. The loss of vegetation and soil reduces the amount of *evapotranspiration* which is essential in recharging clouds to produce rains. Ecological degradation, therefore, produces adverse impacts on environmental resources, negatively affecting rainfall amounts and distribution. The decline in the rainfall results in the onset of *drought*, which is defined as a period of not more than three years during which rainfall amount is below long-term averages or normal conditions, while *aridity* is distinguished from drought as being prolonged dry conditions usually lasting over a period of time.

Resource exploitation requires some form of technology, the application of which should ensure that the accumulation of produced capital does not lead to the depletion of natural capital. Ideally, technological intervention in smallholder agriculture should be directed towards solving a particular problem or attenuating specific constraints. In this respect the choice of strategies for technology generation is carried out in the context of relative scarcity of factors of production. Where, for instance, labour tends to be the most critical factor, the labour cost will also be relatively high. In such a situation, the *direction* of advances in technology should take the *form* of labour-saving rather than land-saving technological innovation. In some cases both factors (labour and land) may be scarce, and in such a case the direction of technical change will be towards both land-saving, biological yield-increasing and labour-saving technologies.

Traditionally the *manner* by which new technologies are generated exerts considerable influence on the pattern of *diffusion* of the innovation, its ultimate environmental and societal *impacts*. The measurement of these impacts should be based on the *criterion* of sustainability of agricultural and rural development using suitable socioeconomic and environmental indicators, which should include: i) economic viability; ii) ecological and environmental sustainability; iii) social acceptability; iv) technical feasibility and risk aversion; and v) capacity to generate employment and income generating activities. The *extent* of the impact of the new technologies will depend on how they affect the production of a particular crop or the raising of a particular animal in the context of how the technological innovation alters traditional farming practices, the factor-use pattern and the characteristic features of the products they produce (quality, marketability, aggregate demand for the products, and in particular how they raise the production frontier from a low to a higher equilibrium level). Furthermore, the impact of the new technologies will depend on the *speed* of diffusion, which in turn is influenced by institutional and organizational innovation.

Accordingly, in developing new technologies one has to take into consideration which *direction* technical change should take in an economy, because the principal objective is to minimize development constraints. The application of new technologies, for instance, could change the social environment as a result of differential spatial development. It could change culture (values, beliefs and religion) and institutions (social organizations, social cohesion, tenurial systems, agrarian institutions and structures), and could provoke social mobility (internal and external migration, occupational and geographical mobility, changes in occupational structure (social differentiation, and sexual stratification, inegalitarian access to productive resources and services) and differential impacts of technology application on different socioeconomic groups and geographical regions (regional inequality in the level of development). Accordingly, if economic viability and technical feasibility are accompanied by social acceptability criteria, the new technologies will exert a profound influence on the pattern of adoption and diffusion, either widely or narrowly, across different sectors and/or geographical areas, and the consequential occupational and geographical mobility they can cause.

Technological intervention should, therefore, be preceded by: i) the specification of the *nature* and *extent* of what is to be produced, the technology used in the production process, and managerial and institutional framework influencing the generation and diffusion of innovation; ii) and the choice of use of a given technology. The technologies generated, broadly defined as available technologies, are those that are known or may be acquired with ease. They are categorized as *shelf-technologies* which embrace knowledge about the tools, machines, farm structures, etc. and the associated production process. Scholars of technologies regard them as the '*hardware*' of the production process while the managerial, knowledge, experience and skill, and the institutional infrastructure (*organiware*) to facilitate the adoption of the new technologies are regarded as the '*software*'. In the context of agricultural technologies, the '*hardware*' includes the types of tools and machines used in agricultural production and inputs, pesticides, acaricides, veterinary drugs, etc. and the spread of prescribed cultural practices.

Given the foregoing consideration, and broadly speaking, the relevance of any technological innovation should be governed by the optimum use of available resources in a given physical and socioeconomic environment, and the sensitivity and adaptability of the technologies to changing factor and produce markets to ensure the stability of economic efficiency, return on assets held by the farmers and relative cost effectiveness of different agricultural technologies, including traditional ones. The successful diffusion of the new technologies will depend on the criteria already spelt out, in particular economic profitability and viability, which depend very much on the *form* by which the technologies are diffused either as a product, a process or organizational changes, or a combination thereof. The other cardinal factor that will facilitate the adoption is the incentive structure, represented by price factors, including fiscal stimulus, and non-price factors, represented by economic and institutional infrastructure. Sustainability of agricultural production will also depend on the technologies' technical feasibility, social acceptability and environmental-conserving capacities.

There is, therefore, an urgent need for strategic and tactical technological intervention that will generate technologies that are technically feasible, economically cost-effective, socially acceptable and resource-conserving. The diffusion of such technologies has the potential benefit of raising the productivity of traditional farming systems from low to higher equilibrium levels. The principal agenda for future programmes of action should, therefore, focus primarily on developing productive, profitable and regenerative technologies which can be successfully incorporated into contemporary farming practices. This is necessary because raising resource productivity, conserving and/or rehabilitating African lands should now occupy the centre stage for future development agenda. Within the realm of this broad objective, governments should initiate and sustain a conscious implementation of innovative adaptive agricultural research programmes. The implementation of the programmes should be in a sequential fashion, initially incorporating the understanding of the complex nature of traditional agriculture, followed by the analysis of the historical and contemporary interactions between people and the environment with a view to capturing the synergical consequences of such interactive processes. With this knowledge at hand, it becomes possible or easy to design strategic and tactical technological intervention directed towards solving an array of technical, structural and institutional constraints. The newly-generated technologies should ideally be capable of mutually reinforcing positive interactions/integrations/interrelationships between natural resources (biological, physical, geographical, and ecological factors) and sociocultural and political systems. Such interactive processes should ensure that resource exploitation incorporates resource-conserving, regenerative and/or rehabilitative technologies which minimize extractive production relations and destructive agricultural practices. These interventions must be complemented by the relevant training of the farmers to build appropriate adaptations into their agricultural systems, environmental knowledge and skill.

Ehui and Spencer, concerned with measuring the sustainability and economic viability of tropical farming systems, contended that agricultural development projects should be accepted not only on the basis of the present value of output but also on whether the resulting environmental benefits compensate for environmental damage caused elsewhere. In other words, the assessment of the economic viability of projects should integrate associated environmental effects of projects so that compensatory value of benefits can be defined and evaluated. They recalled various definitions of sustainability and economic viability. The preoccupation with the definition of sustainability of development had been enlarged to include the economy-environment interactions. Karshenas, quoting the Brundtland Report (chapter 2 – 'Towards Sustainable Development'), defined sustainable development as follows:

> Development that meets the needs of the present without compromising the ability of future generations to meet their own needs .... A process of change in which exploitation of resources, the direction of investments, the reorientation of technology development, and institutional change are all in harmony and enhance both current and future potential to meet human needs and aspirations (WCED, 1987, pp. 34–6).

In consonance with the Brundtland Report definition, Pearce, Barbier and Markandya (1988, p. 6) adopted the following definition of sustainable development as:

> Constancy of the natural capital stock; more strictly, the requirement for non-negative changes in the stock of natural resources, such as soil and soil quality, ground and surface water and their quality, land biomass, water biomass, and the waste-assimilation capacity of the receiving environments.

Incorporating the concept of renewability, Young defines a sustainable land use system as one 'which achieves production combined with the conservation of the resources on which that production depends, thereby permitting the maintenance of productivity'.

Implicit in these definitions is the concept which admits that environmental problems are also associated with renewable natural resources which should be regenerated at naturally-given rates to ensure the stability of the ecosystem (Ehui and Spencer, 1994).

The definitions by Conways and Young provide a basis for measuring sustainability based on the concept of intertemporal TFP defined in terms of the productive capacity of a system over time, which should incorporate unpriced contributions from natural resources and their unpriced production flows. The intertemporal TFP, therefore, is regarded as an appropriate measure of sustainability since it addresses the issue of change in productivity of a production system between two or more periods. Unlike sustainability, economic viability is an essentially static concept referring to the efficiency with which resources are utilized in the production process at a given period. However, a new production system can be regarded as being economically more viable (or efficient) than the old or existing one if its TFP is greater at a given point in time. Similarly, by higher TFP is meant the capacity of the new system to produce more output than the existing one, after taking due account of differences in quantities of inputs and unpriced natural resources used in each system during one cropping season. Alternatively, it can also be interpreted as the capacity of the new production system to produce outputs with lower total costs than the existing system, after accounting for differences in output levels, input prices, unpriced natural resources, and other exogenous variables. Thus, to compare the economic viability of production systems, the concept of interspatial TFP defined as the productive capacity of one system over another at a given period including the unpriced contribution from natural resources to production, can be used. A system can be said to be economically more viable than another if the interspatial TFP index associated with the former, which incorporates and values spatial differences in the resource stock and flow, is higher than the interspatial TFP index associated with the latter.

In a simplified terms TFP could be represented as follows:

$$TFP1 \ Sc = 100 \times GVAO \ index \qquad\qquad (24)$$

where

TFP1 is intertemporal TFP;
TFP2 is interspatial TFP; and
Sc index is the cost of increases in compensatory productivity through the application of biological factors (manure etc.) and technical in production inputs in compensating for loss of soil productivity and environmental protection.

Resource Degradation and Environmental Patrimony: Conflictual Relationship

Transference costs of resource conservation and rehabilitation A resource in agriculture can be expanded or rehabilitated if degraded by three basic mechanisms: i) transferring resources being used in other sectors of the economy to the agricultural sector; ii) acquiring new resources from domestic capital goods producers or transforming natural resources to produced capital; or iii) acquiring capital resources from outside the economy. Conversely, the level of available resources in agriculture natural or produced capital can be reduced by transferring them to other sectors of the economy or by degrading the resources. These activities imply some transference costs which are made up of transformation, transaction, transportation and retraining costs. In the case of agriculture, resource productivity recovery from a degraded form constitutes the most important activity involving transformation and retraining costs. The transformation costs include expenses required physically to transform the resource to make it productive and suitable for new use. In this respect the degree of specificity of a given resource to any particular use determines the transformation costs of transferring it from one use to another.

Because of declining soil fertility, the current agricultural problem can be defined as the inability of the sector to maintain the relative income level of the agricultural population compared to other people in different sectors of the economy. This has come about because the low incomes are caused by persistently lower rates of return on agricultural production assets compared with return on similar factors employed in other sectors of the economy. In SSA, due both to distortions in the economy which make domestic terms of trade persistently biased against the agricultural sector and generally high costs of rural projects, income had been low and resources continue to move out of the agricultural sector.

The transfer costs incurred are made up of transportation, transaction and transformation costs. In general, the degree of the specificity of a given resource to any particular use, determines the extent of the transformation costs of transforming it from one form of use to another. Transfer costs such as training to acquire new skills, loss of social security provided by the community, conveyance costs, etc. may limit the scope to adjust to exogenous shocks such as unsuccessful integration of externally induced external development initiatives on non-retreating traditional agriculture (i.e. inability to adopt innovation). In such a case the process of adjustment in factor return tends to be slow. The transportation costs often entail emigration to new geographical areas where better economic opportunities make returns on labour, for instance, more attractive than in the old area.

In the case of investment for resource conservation or rehabilitation, the transfer costs arise as a result of a shift in demand for goods and services from the agricultural to the non-agricultural sector. This shift in demand results in the deterioration in the domestic terms of trade against the agricultural sector, resulting in differentials in the returns to assets devoted to the sector not only in the short term but also in the long run. Because of the occurrence of this shock, resources will move out of the agricultural sector to their best alternative use which will be the ones where the present value of marginal return (PVMR) is the highest. The shift of resources entails some transfer costs which sometimes necessitate migration and retraining in new enterprises. The transformation costs depend on the expected PVMR. Some individuals consider the extent of land degradation and desertification as having reached an irreversible state which cannot be restored. Consequently, these individuals may not be attracted to rehabilitate land if the cost of restoration is considered to exceed the expected benefits, and this may give the impression of land as being permanently damaged. It is, however, possible that degraded land can still be made productive again, depending on resources devoted to its rehabilitation and on allowing sufficient time for natural regeneration.

Criteria for investment decision on resource conservation and rehabilitation

Economic viability In arriving at an economic decision, a potential investor, depending on the degree of specificity and quality of a given land resource, will take into account the present value of returns to agricultural enterprises made possible by the land restoration. The returns should at least be the same at any of its uses in the economy. This is to say that the PVMR is the relevant information required for his decision. In other words, he will assess the relation between the incremental costs of acquiring a resource required for agricultural production and the present value of the expected incremental outputs as compared to the PV of incremental products in other sectors for the same level of investment. Unexpected shocks, external or internal, including deficiencies in domestic policies, that are likely adversely to affect the maximization of profits or inelastic agricultural supply responses, would immediately encourage resources to be moved to their best alternative uses. This is because the potential investor, conscious of the risk involved, would use a much higher discount rate to compute the PV of future flows of income. Computationally it can be represented by the equation

$$(PVa - PVn)^{-rt} \text{ or } (PVa - PVn)^{-rn} \tag{25}$$

where

PVa is the present value of future streams of income from the agricultural sector;

PVn is the present value of the future streams of income from non-agricultural sector;

-rt   is the discount rate of future income in time t; and

n   number of years in future.

Traditionally there exists an inverse correlation between the age of an industry because of the depreciation of capital assets such as machinery, equipment, buildings, construction, etc. and factor returns then decline. In SSA, agriculture has very low level of man-made capital assets since it relies heavily on natural resources, and only simple hand tools and labour are employed in production. For this reason depreciation is practically nonexistent. In agriculture, since land is the principal asset, its degradation can be equated with depreciation. Agriculture is the oldest source of economic growth in the region and the originator of most factors. However, because of excessive use there is now empirical evidence that factor returns in the agricultural sector are declining, principally due to irrational natural resource exploitation resulting in declining yields. The intra-sectoral transformation costs of rehabilitating land from a degraded form to a productive one or conserving land is likely to be high, while the factor return from the transformed land may not be sufficient to offset costs incurred unless it is used for the production of very high value agricultural enterprises. Alternatively, failure to rehabilitate the land would deny future generations access to productive resources (an option-value concept). If the option-value notion is taken into consideration, it becomes almost imperative to conserve land or rehabilitate degraded land rather than rendering future generations landless and destitute.

Option values of resource conservation and rehabilitation In assessing the relevance of conservation work, economists introduced the notion of option values essentially equivalent to an insurance policy – a premium one is willing to pay over and above the normal cost of an operation in order to minimize risks and uncertainty (Blaikie, 1989, p. 23). In the field of soil and water conservation, it is how much a certain amount of soil is worth to future generations measured by the value of agricultural output that is lost if costs are not incurred to conserve the resources. In the case of Lesotho, according to Nobe and Seckler (1979), the costs of soil conservation are high, given the degree of degradation, and the return to conservation of an already degraded soil is low. This argument, advanced in the 1970s, is relevant when the Basotho had opportunities to work in South Africa where it was, in the past, worthwhile to work as wage labourers rather than rely on poorly rewarded agricultural and pastoral activities. Recent political changes in South Africa will force the Basotho to return home. The option values in the face of population growth, uncertain off-farm employment and social differentiation would rise to a high level. If the analysis of the option values is expanded to include access to labour, capital and technologies (the application of chemical fertilizers, manures, the use of improved varieties of crops to compensate for yield losses of non-improved varieties due to soil loss), it could indicate that the long-term trends of return on investment in conservation would be positively beneficial. Observations elsewhere of similar conditions as in Lesotho (USAID (1981) for Rwanda and Roder (1977) for Swaziland) indicated that option values are very high due to high population pressure and dwindling non-agricultural employment opportunities.

Opportunity cost of resource degradation Because of inadequate returns on factors devoted to agricultural production and insecure resource tenure systems, investment in the conservation of natural resources has been correspondingly low. Lack of conservation and widespread ecological degradation will have grave economic and social consequences. The viability and sustainability of the macroeconomy will be threatened. On the side of the external balance, agricultural exports, which had led to the partial exhaustion of renewable natural resources without adequate renewal, will erode future export base, forcing the region to import even primary products which it used to produce. A decline in the output of primary exports due to soil fertility depletion will adversely affect employment generation and food supply, which in turn will harm macroeconomic stability as structural inflation rises and becomes secular. Instability of the macroeconomic framework destroys incentive structures because high and variable levels of inflation distort intertemporal choices concerning resource conservation, as producers and consumers, confronted with uncertainties, act as if they are facing high discount rates, thus avoiding the future, or make speculative investment in nonproductive projects such as trade with quick returns. A stable macroeconomic environment with low inflation reduces discount rates, improves allocative, productive and competitive efficiency, and, therefore, encourages investors to make longer-term view as their investment time horizon improves and becomes firm. Environmental problems, therefore, should form an integral part of macroeconomic policy.

Labour

Social Opportunity Cost of Labour

In the field of labour market, price distortion was brought about by the operation of the minimum wage legislation commonly practised in Africa. It was the declared policy of African governments to use wage policy as an important anti-inflation (cost-push effect) and income redistribution (demand-pull effect) tool. Hence the main rationale of the wage policy was to control inflationary pressure. Cost-push effects of a wage policy were usually avoided by granting only partial (commonly up to about 70 per cent) compensation for cost-of-living increases, and rural urban imbalances were reduced by promoting a more equitable income pattern within the urban and rural areas. With this goal in mind, most governments granted only the lowest wage group full compensation for cost-of-living allowance, while the middle and upper wage groups were restricted to partial compensation. Despite these good intentions, the operations of the minimum wage legislation often resulted in wages for unskilled labour being overvalued and, with trade union pressure, these groups of wage earners enjoyed a well-protected labour market. Hence average income of employees in the protected market was three to five times as high as that for smallholder income. Even allowing for differences in cost-of-living, average urban incomes were still significantly higher. This income differential was one of the principal factors responsible for encouraging rural-urban migration.

After the achievement of political independence, most independent African governments enforced a minimum wage policy to reduce income disparities. While it was possible to enforce the minimum wage legislation in the formal sector of the economy, its implementation within the informal sector proved difficult. Often the minimum wage (Wm) was set above the market clearing price. Although the minimum wage entailed a social cost to society, its impact on the labour market had not been extensively investigated in relation to disemployment, unemployment or non-participation in the labour market activities. However, scholars have developed methodologies for assessing the effects of the minimum wage policy on labour mobility. Santiago, for instance, in his study of the dynamic of minimum wage policy in economic development in Puerto Rico, assuming an absence of economy-wide minimum wage and a single market for homogenous labour, took it that a labour market clears at Wo. In the absence of workers attaching reserved price to their labour, all workers with reserved wages at or below Wo will be hired, giving rise to employment level of Eo. Workers with a reserved wage above Wo will not participate in the labour market (Santiago, 1989, pp. 1–30).

If the minimum wage (Wm) is applied and assuming a partial coverage of k (the share of total employment effectively covered by the minimum wage) the enforcement of the Wm results in disemployment effect because workers having a value of marginal productivity below Wm are laid off, and Em represents the proportional change in employment. Computationally the relationships can be expressed as:

$$\dot{W}m = Wm - Wo \tag{26}$$

where

$\dot{W}m$ is defined as the minimum wage hike; and

$$\dot{E}m = Em - Eo$$

If η represents the absolute value of the wage elasticity of demand in the formal sector, the direction and magnitude of disemployment effect is determined by the expression

$$\dot{E}m = -\eta\ \dot{W}m \text{ (sign negative because of disemployment)}.$$

which reflects the proportional effect of disemployment of the minimum wage hike. Because of the partial coverage, the $\dot{W}m$ (minimum wage hike) results in excess supply of labour in the formal sector. Since minimum wage is not binding in the informal sector, competitive wage conditions hold. Several options are available to the disemployed workers: i) continue searching for employment in the formal sector; ii) opt for informal sector employment; iii) opt for non-participation in the labour market; or iv) opt for migration.

The extent of labour mobility will depend on the vigour (elasticities) of labour demand in both the formal (η) and the informal (∈) sectors, the degree of minimum wage coverage (k), vacancy rate in the formal sector (v), elasticity of labour supply (s) and the magnitude of the Wm is the wage differential within the informal sector after the application of minimum wages then Wn = Wo - Wn. If Wn is positive it is an indication of labour mobility from the formal to informal sector and vice versa.

$$\overset{\bullet}{W}m = \frac{k(\eta - v) \times \overset{\bullet}{W}m}{kv + (1-k)\,e + s} \tag{27}$$

This general model also accounts for the possibility of withdrawal from the labour markets or new entrants into the markets because if the disemployed or retrenched workers have reserved wage level above that prevailing in the informal sector, they will opt for withdrawal from the labour force. The consequence of this is to reduce the downward pressure on wages in the informal sector, and vice versa. Thus apart from having a distributive effect on income and the standards of living, minimum wage can also influence intersectoral labour mobility.

The concept of social opportunity cost of labour (SOCL) is derived from the fact that with limited labour supply, and in order to attract it, something else must be sacrificed. In applied welfare economics (the framework within which the normative significance of economic events is evaluated), the SOCL had three aspects: demand for labour, the cost of attracting labour to a job (labour supply price) and the welfare effects that result from disturbing the old labour market.

For illustration purposes (see Figure 25), let us assume that total available labour (T) is 150,000 labourers. Initial equilibrium is determined by the intersection of the demand curve for labour at E. If it is assumed that no distorting elements exist, the equilibrium wage rate (We) is the social value of labour, and at this rate only 75,000 labourers are hired. Government may think that We is too low and may mandate an increase in the wage to Wm, which is above the free-market levels. If Wm can be enforced, producers, assuming financial resources remain the same, will use fewer amounts of labour which will result in the decline in total labour demand from Qe to Lf. If the daily We rate is 2.50 maloti and Wm is 3.50 maloti and available resources remain at 187,500 maloti (75,000 x 2.50), producers will hire only about 53,570 workers. The Wo Slt is reduced laterally by [Qe-Lf] Lf or 40 per cent.

The intersection of Wo Slf with the demand curve D Df determines the free market wage Wf at which Lf of labour is demanded. The distance Lf Qe represents the amount of the free market employment, Ugf, the higher it is the greater is the SOCL. Additional cost is also incurred in the enforcement of the minimum wage legislation. If the enforcement is ineffective, wage rate will have no relationship to Wm. If it is effective the policy will increase income of the employed workers and thus alter the pattern of income distribution and cause distributional conflicts.

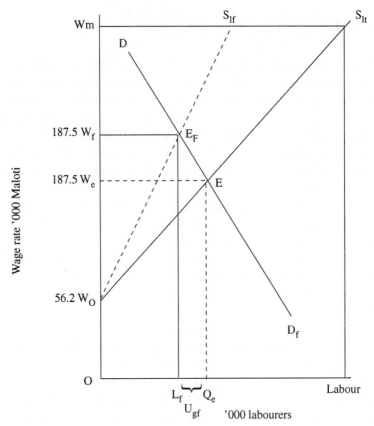

Figure 25 Social opportunity cost of labour

Labour Activity Rate in Sub-Saharan Africa

Activity rate The labour force, or the economically active population, is that segment of the population whose function is to produce the goods and services needed to satisfy the requirements of the whole. It can also be used as an alternative measure of the balance between land and labour endowments expressed as the agro-climatic labour density, defined as the number of agricultural workers per million of calories of production potential. People aged between 15 to 64 years are usually considered to be in the productive age group, while those under 15 and over 64 years are dependent on economically active population. According to the internationally recommended standards contained in the United Nations *Principles and Recommendation for the 1970 Population Census*, the labour force or economically active population, comprises all persons of either sex who furnish the supply of labour available for the production of economic goods and services, including employers, employees, self-employed persons, and those who assist without pay in family enterprises. The labour force thus consists of all persons physically able to work and, therefore, includes both employed and unemployed persons. Persons not in the labour force (the economically inactive population) are those engaged solely in activities which do not contribute directly to the production of goods and services. These persons include children not attending schools, persons of working age attending institutions of learning, persons engaged in household duties, persons who receive income from property or other investment or pension from former activities and persons who are physically or mentally unable to work or any person receiving public aid or support.

Apart from the difficulties of defining the activity rate, particularly underemployment or part-time employment, the size of the labour force depends not only on demographic factors but also on the prevailing norms of the country and the criteria used in defining employment, as explained under the section on resource mobility. Because of these factors, the economically active population as a proportion of the total population varies greatly from country to country. This proportion of the population is known as the activity rate, and observed variations are explained by the differing levels of employment of women, particularly in agriculture. For planning purposes it is necessary to consider the activity rates by sex and age, and changes likely to take place in them over a specified period. Usually males constitute about two-thirds of the total labour force in the world and females about a third. This ratio is likely to change as more and more females enter the labour force due to demographic transition. In addition, apart from the absolute numbers, there are also differences in the respective age-specific activity rate for males and females within countries and between countries. One weakness with the use of activity rate in planning is that it takes no account of differences in the intensity of work or in the number of hours worked per week or month or year. The use of activity rates in planning must be considered within their local context.

Growth of agricultural and non-agricultural labour force In many developing countries, agriculture is the main source of livelihood and forms more than 50 per cent. Those economically active in agriculture include everyone whose main economic activity is agriculture, whether as employers, own-account workers, salaried employees or unpaid family workers. In Sub-Saharan Africa just as in other developing countries, the number of those engaged in agriculture as a proportion of the total economically active population is decreasing. The reduction of the relative role of agriculture in the occupational structure of the region, is a direct corollary of expanding urbanization and

$$T t = \frac{A 1}{T 1} \times A 1 + \frac{N 1}{T 1} \times N 1 \tag{28}$$

where

T 1   denotes total labour force;
A 1   represents agricultural labour force; and
N 1   denotes non-agricultural labour force.

A critical point is reached when agricultural labour force ceases to increase and starts to decline. At this point A 1 is zero (A 1 = 0) and the above relationship becomes

$$T 1 = \frac{N 1}{T 1} \times N 1 \text{ or } \frac{T 1}{N 1} = \frac{N 1}{T 1} \tag{29}$$

In quantitative analysis, the first approximation is to assume that the rates of growth of total labour force (T 1) and of the non-agricultural labour force (N 1) remains constant. This implies two points: i) the total labour force (T 1) is increasing at a constant proportion of total population (Tp) which itself is increasing at a relatively fixed rate; ii) and employment in the non-agricultural sector are also increasing at a fixed rate. On the basis of these assumptions, it is possible to calculate the time when agricultural labour force (A 1) reaches its turning point and the size it would have reached at the time. The above formulae at least give an indication of the order of magnitude of the likely time and size of agricultural labour force involved.

On the assumption that the growth of T 1 and N 1 remains constant, a computational expression has been developed to determine the time (t) in years taken to reach the turning point of the growth of the agricultural labour force (Baldwin, 1975, pp. 124–5). The size of the total labour force (T 1) in the 'nth' year can notationally be expressed as:

$$Tnl = Tol \, (1 + T \, l)^n \tag{30}$$

where

Tol   is the size of total labour force in the base year.

Similarly non-agricultural labour force can be expressed as:

$$Nnl = Nol (1 + Nl)^n \qquad (31)$$

where

Nol   is the size of the non-agricultural population in the base year.

If Tl and Nl are constant, then combining equations (25) and (26) yields:

$$Nnl = \frac{Nol}{Tol} \times \frac{(1 + Nl)^n}{1 + Tl} \qquad (32)$$

Combining equations (27) and (24) yields:

$$\frac{Tl}{Nl} = \frac{(1 + Nl)^n}{1 + Tl} \qquad (33)$$

In natural logarythmic terms it follows that

$$t = \frac{\dfrac{\log Tl}{Nl} - \dfrac{\log Nol}{Tol}}{\log(1 + Nl) - \log(1 + Tl)} \qquad (34)$$

For illustration purposes, we shall assume that the proportion of the non-agricultural (N l) to the total labour force (T l) is 30 per cent, and the rates of growth of T l and N l are 2.5 per cent and 4.5 per cent respectively then

$$\frac{Nol}{Tol} = 0.30 \frac{(30)}{100} \text{ and growth rates Tl} = 0.025 \text{ and Nl} = 0.045$$

and

$$t = \frac{\log \dfrac{0.025}{0.045} - \log 0.30}{\log 1.045 - \log 1.025}$$

$$= \frac{-0.2553 - (-0.5229)}{0.0191 - 0.0107}$$

$$= \frac{0.2676}{0.0084}$$

$$= 32$$

The maximum size of the agricultural labour force (A l) which is attained in the year of the turning point can be computed using the following formula:

$$A l = T l - N l = Tol (1 + Tl)^t - Nol (1 + N l)^t \tag{35}$$

If the initial size of the total labour force in base year (Tol) is 100 and the non-agricultural labour force in base year (Nol) is 30, then that of the agricultural labour force is Aol - 70 in base year.

$$A t = 100 (1.025)^{32} - (1.045)^{32}$$

$$= 100 \times 2.2038 - 30 \times 4.0900$$
$$= 220.4 - 122.7 = 97.7$$
$$= 220.4 - 122.7 = 97.7$$

Expressed as a percentage of the initial size of the agricultural labour force

$$A t = \frac{97.7}{70} = 140 \text{ per cent}$$

This means that agricultural labour force will reach its maximum size after 32 years, at which time it will be 40 per cent greater than its size in the base year.

This formula can be used to estimate the length of time when agricultural labour force in SSA will reach its maximum size. According to FAO statistics, during base year 1979–81 there were a total of 142.262 million people classified as economically active (Tol) rising to 180.929 million (Tl) in 1990 yielding an annual growth rate of 2.4 per cent. During the base year there were 101.551 million people classified as agricultural labour force (Aol), rising to 120.018 million (A l) yielding an annual growth rate of 1.7 per cent. The difference between the two figures gives us a non-agricultural labour force (N l) of 40.711 million in 1979–81 rising to 60.911 million in 1990. The non-agricultural labour force was, therefore, increasing at a an annual growth rate of 4.1 per cent. Thus

$$\frac{40.711}{142.262} = 29$$

$Tl = 0.024;$ $\qquad$ $Nl = 0.041$

$$t = \frac{\log \dfrac{0.024}{0.041} - \log.29}{\log 1.041 - \log 1.024}$$

$$= \frac{-0.2326 - (-0.5376)}{0.0175 - \log 0.0103}$$

$$= \frac{-0.3050}{0.0072}$$

$$= 42 \text{ years}$$

Using the formula

$$Al. = Tl - Nl = Tol\,(1+Tl)\,t - Nol\,(1+Nl)\,t \qquad\qquad (36)$$

the maximum size of the agricultural labour force (Al) will be reached in 42 years as calculated below:

- the initial size of the total labour force in 1990, the new base year, was 180.929 million;
- the non-agricultural labour force was 60.911 million; and
- the agricultural labour force was 120.018 million.

$$Al = 180.929\,(1.024)^{42} - 66.911\,(1.041)^{42}$$
$$= 180.922 \times 2.321 - 66.911 \times 5.192$$
$$= 419.9 - 347.4 = 72.5$$
$$Al = (72.5 \div 66)100 = 110\%$$

This means that agricultural labour force will reach its maximum size after 42 years (2032) and will then be 10 per cent greater than it was in 1990.

Another characteristic feature of population is that of dependency burden. One of the comparative disadvantages of developing countries compared to developed countries is that there is a heavy dependency burden resulting from high fertility rate. Traditionally a rapid growth in the number of dependants imposes greater claims on the working population. Consequently families with a large number of dependants are likely to be less able to save, and as a result the level of investment is likely to be low. At the national level, resources are diverted from productive resources to consumption purposes.

In SSA achieving food security at the household level through labour markets, as stated earlier, is the most dominant means, although diversified income structure through artisanal work, wage employment, trade, remittances, etc. significantly contributes to minimizing food insecurity. Household labour endowment, defined as the inverse of the household's dependency ratio (inverse of the ratio of working persons to total persons) is critical in achieving food security. As the dependency ratio increases, the relative household labour endowment declines at an increasing rate. This endowment can be adversely affected by disease burden. In Africa the human immunodeficiency virus/ acquired immunodeficiency syndrome (HIV/AIDS), a pandemic without a cure, has been striking a segment of the population in their prime productive life. This means that the pandemic has a damaging impact on household income while at the same time escalating household dependency ratio and overwhelming the informal social security system which could absorb orphaned children.

The household labour force participation rate is reduced directly through the death or shifting labour resources to caring for the sick. Income is also lost as valued resources like livestock and financial assets are used to meet medical expenses. Labour diversification is restrained through the loss of diversified income possibility, or indirectly as more time is devoted to caring for the sick. Access to productive assets (land, capital) or services (credit, marketing) or unsuitable farming operations if a male head of household dies, exacerbate household income stress. Average labour supply as well as labour productivity declines due to grinding morbidity. Notationally these relationships can be expressed as:

$$\frac{\text{Household income}}{\text{Total persons}} = \frac{Wp}{Tp} \times \frac{Wf}{Wp} \times \frac{Aa}{Wp} \times \frac{Hr}{Aa} \times \frac{Y}{Hr} \tag{37}$$

where

    Wp   denotes working persons;
    Tp   represents total persons;
    Wf   denotes working force participants (participation rate);
    Aa   represents the number of activities;
    Y   is income; while
    Hr   represents the number of hours worked.

The pandemic, therefore, can have an adverse impact on labour resources at many levels: labour supply, productivity and opportunities the combination of which exacerbates household food insecurity. Given inadequate resources, demands for increases in health care expenditure divert funding from other productive sectors, and the region will have to import food or rely on food aid and emergency aid.

Capital

Capital Market

In market and emerging economies, capital markets are well developed, but in developing African countries only a few of them have stock markets. In capital markets, interest rates play a critical catalytic role in domestic resource mobilization (savings) and capital flows. Low interest rates are seen as being beneficial to economic growth because they encourage capital flows into productive investment, since return on investment is likely to be high and profitable. Curbing monetary expansion through controls on credit availability is often used as a monetary policy to control domestic inflation. Reducing aggregate demand through credit control could be counterproductive because it can reduce the expansion of economic base and economic growth. Low interest rate encourages investment as well as the adoption of new improved technology, especially by low-income borrowers such as smallholders. Conversely, high interest rate can make investment unprofitable and discourages borrowing for investment.

As illustrated in Figure 26, the demand for capital reflects marginal value product of investment, and domestic supply is provided by domestic savings. If potential investors discern adequate return on investment, they will be willing to reduce consumption levels in order to be able to save. Initial equilibrium is represented by r^s and quantity K^2. In the absence of distorting elements, r^s represents the social value of capital, and the supply curve has a positive elasticity to indicate the ability of consumers to reduce current consumption levels as the reward to increases in savings. A reduction in interest rate increases the demand for capital to K^d as more investments are profitable because the cost of capital is reduced while return remains high. If investors favour current consumption to saving, the supply of capital declines to K^c.

The lower interest rate creates an excess demand for credit until it is equal to K^d - K^c. In this case the authority has three options. It can opt for credit control, in which case investment levels and rates of return on investment

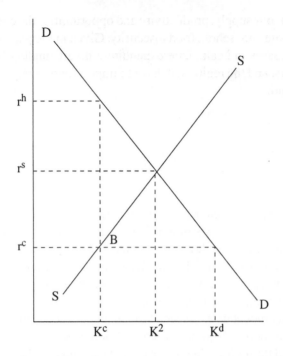

Figure 26 Consequences of interest control for capital market

return to original equilibrium levels. Increasing availability of credit for investment could either be achieved by borrowing or external aid (foreign savings), channelling tax revenues into domestic credit markets, or raising interest rates to domestic savers, which may call for some form of government subsidy. If subsidy cannot be afforded, and budget resources are too constrained to shift financial revenue into the credit programme, rationing credit becomes the only option. In this case available supplies of credit are limited to K^c. Under these conditions the private rate of return can be higher or lower than the social rate of return. In this case the demand schedule indicates that the marginal private rate of return to total investment K^c can be as high as r^h, and this rate would prevail if the operation of credit rationing mechanism allocates capital to uses that provide the highest return. Credit rationing could result in pecuniary externalities because the difference between the rate of return and the cost of borrowing represents excess profit. The potential investors could use some of the excess profit to influence easy access to credit, and the marginal private rate of return may remain as high as r^h. If the allocation procedures curb this pecuniary externalities, the private rate of return may range from r^c to r^h.

Institutional Innovation and Infrastructure

In SSA, institutions to facilitate capital flows are still very rudimentary. Some indigenous institutions incorporate some form of resource mobilization and lending or reciprocal liens on productive resources (income stabilization). Both the colonial and post-colonial administrations promoted the establishment of credit institutions. A number of countries created development banks such as Agricultural Development Bank for lending to the agricultural sector or guarantee lending to the sector by the central bank.

Agricultural credit schemes The disruption of development caused by World War II encouraged massive state intervention in African agriculture. Innovative programmes such as tractor mechanization, credit, marketing reforms and large-scale farming were introduced mainly to boost production for experts, and to control the export trade. Prior to the outbreak of the second world war, the colonial authorities pursued deliberate policies which barred Africans from receiving agricultural production credit. After the cessation of the hostilities of the second world war, however, especially beginning the early 1950s, the policy was reversed as it was believed that agricultural credit was a critical part of a package of inputs needed to boost agricultural production. The basic assumptions were that farmers needed credit, along with technical supervision, in order to adopt new technologies; that most farmers were too poor to save for investment in improved technologies; that the rural financial infrastructure was inadequate; and that the informal financial institutions were exploitative in their lending. It was, therefore, felt justified for governments to intervene. Initially credit interventions were concentrated on building institution capacity. Prior to the attainment of political independence in the early 1960s, a variety of credit institutions were created, notable ones being the establishment of the post office savings and credit banks in the British colonies. The banks provided deposit and rural agricultural credit services. The French also established specialized agricultural banks patterned on French banks. Cooperatives were formed to provide marketing services and seasonal credit. After independence, many governments established either agricultural development banks, agricultural finance corporation, or development banks for lending to the agricultural sector.

When African countries gained political independence, a number of developed countries joined the former colonial masters in providing credit. A group of Italians based in Milan (FINAFRIKA) assisted in developing saving banks and provided training courses in related topics. The Nordic countries also supported credit services, especially in East African countries, while the Swiss supported similar efforts in Rwanda and the Germans helped with developing credit institutions in several African countries. Non-governmental organizations (NGOs) from developed countries started to provide credit, beginning the late 1970s, and in some cases also provided technical training in the adoption of improved technologies and proper use and management of credit. Despite concerted efforts to reduce rural poverty, at the time of the World Food Conference (WFC) in 1974 the global food stocks were at their lowest levels, and rural poverty, especially in Africa, was intensifying. In response to this challenge, the WFC established the International Fund for Agricultural Development (IFAD), which became a significant funder of agricultural credit programmes, often targeting the rural poor.

With the financial support of the United States Agency for International Development (USAID), many African government officials (including the author) attended courses in loan docketing, agricultural finance, loan supervision patterned on the Farmers Home Administration (FMA) and the cooperative farm credit systems. Under the supervised credit scheme, it was recognized that smallholders were poor risk borrowers with little or no equity, and, therefore, were unable to obtain conventional bank credit. It was, therefore, decided that selected farmers would be chosen and developed through guidance and training in the profitable use of credit fund until they were able to become creditworthy in order to be able to receive loan from conventional lending institutions. With this notion in mind, one of the basic philosophies was to make loans available to smallholders while at the same time providing technical guidance. The idea was essentially to back up the extension staff technical advice with the provision of credit to enable the farmers to acquire improved technologies and adopt better cultural practices. In pursuit of this objective, the technical field staff initially visited the prospective credit beneficiaries, explained and discussed the basic philosophy of the supervised credit. The decision to take advantage of the credit scheme was left entirely to the farmer. If s/he was persuaded, s/he would then be listed for participation in the scheme.

Some of the fundamental requirements for participation included the following: i) the prospective borrower should be a person of legal age for the contract of the loan; ii) ability to know and honour obligation towards the loan contract; iii) physically fit and able to manage and perform agricultural operations of the type prescribed to him/her by the extension staff; iv) generally known in his/her community as a person with acceptable integrity and a person prepared to undertake an orderly repayment of loans. In addition the prospective farmer was expected to have an adequate suitable tract of land for commercial agriculture and for which he/she would ultimately obtain a title deed. The acquisition of title deed was expected to overcome the institutional problem of traditional resource tenure systems. At this time also there was an increasing number of unemployed school leavers who needed some gainful settlement in farming. However, it was recognized that they did not have mortgageable land and had no practical experience in farming. It was felt that after a year of training in practical farming, they would be successfully settled in agriculture. For successful settlement, it was realized that they should be provided with the necessary farming tools and equipment on loan. A few countries, with the support of missionaries, established farm schools for training school leavers who were expected to become commercial farmers (Okai, 1968).

Major donors, like the USA through its USAID, were particularly active in creating new credit institutions and also provided technical assistance to consolidate these institutions. Indian credit specialists played very active part in designing agricultural credit programmes in many African countries. Even the World Bank included major credit components practically in all commodities, subsectoral and integrated rural development projects, along with the provision of large amounts of funds to agricultural credit institutions for on-lending to the farmers. The Economic Development Institute of the World Bank organized agricultural credit courses aimed at strengthening the design of Bank-funded projects.

With growing emphasis on rural development, beginning the early 1970s, the World Bank, together with bilateral donors, boosted funding for agricultural credit projects as an integral part of the programme to promote rural and agricultural development with a focus on poverty alleviation. In many instances the targeted funding was accomplished by means of concessionary rediscount credit lines through selected national banks for on-lending to priority social groups, commodities, inputs or regional development efforts. All along it had been the dominant policy, based on the assumption that providing credit at low interest rates would be beneficial to the rural poor, encourage demand for credit and stimulate the use of modern technical production and productive (seeds) inputs. By the early 1980s, however, agricultural credit programmes began to face problems. As discussed in detail later on, economic decline, especially in rural areas, made it difficult for borrowers to meet their repayment obligations. Many agricultural credit institutions which had received lines of credit in foreign currency started defaulting on loan repayments because, following the devaluation of domestic currencies under the macroeconomic policy reforms, they were unable to raise sufficient local cover.

It is also worth noting that the extensive use of concessionary interest rates, and the general availability of cheap external funds, diverted financial institutions from mobilizing domestic savings. Also, using the financial intermediary schemes to transfer subsidies under the guise of concessionary interest rates and weak loan recovery, attracted rent seekers, especially rural elite, businessmen, government civil servants and political opportunists. Rent seeking was particularly severe in countries (e.g. Ghana in the 1970s) with subsidized interest rates and high domestic inflation. Consequently the integrity of the credit programmes was undermined. Although credit schemes had been more or less a failure, they had, however, been relatively successful in production programmes which integrated primary production with processing. Typical examples were the integration of sugar, tea, and tobacco production with processing. Under the scheme, the factories had their own nucleus estates and the neighbouring farmers were organized into outgrowers' schemes. The factories not only provided seedlings and ploughing services on credit to the outgrowers, but also provided technical advice free of charge. In the case of tobacco short-term loans (up to three to five years repayment) were also extended for the construction of tobacco leaf-curing barns. In all cases, loans were recovered from the proceeds of the sale of the product at the time of delivery to the factories.

Agricultural marketing Market credit interventions had undergone remarkable changes. In the early stages of colonization, internal marketing and the import/ export trade were dominated by expatriates who relied on their principal overseas partners for the provision of credit. Between and after the wars, and as a means of controlling export trade in particular, marketing parastatal organizations were created for major export commodities. These bodies used a hierarchy of agents/brokers dominated by Asians, Lebanese and expatriates. The parastatal organizations guaranteed credit, traditionally called 'crop finance', to the agents/brokers for the purposes of purchasing produce from the farmers. After the second world war, the cooperative movement was actively promoted as a vehicle for enabling the indigenous Africans to participate in the lucrative commercial activities and internal marketing by providing crop finance to cooperative unions and societies. Prior to independence, food crop marketing, which had not received much attention of the colonial authorities, was dominated by Asians, Lebanese and, to some extent, expatriates. After independence, in addition to export marketing boards (EMBs), food marketing boards (FMBs) were also established particularly to ward off food insecurity. In many countries, particularly in marginal areas where harvests fluctuate widely according to rainfall, the crop procurement by the FMBs was introduced to cushion the countries against harvest shortfall or failure in the time needed to arrange for imports or for food aid to cover deficits. It was also felt that the crop procurements would prevent inter-seasonal price oscillations.

By the late 1970s, in particular in the Sahelian countries which suffered recurrent drought, many of the FMBs faced enormous financial losses in crop procurement activities and had to rely heavily on government subsidies. As these financial burdens could not be sustained, and as a package of the World Bank and the International Monetary Fund supported structural adjustment programmes, governments were coerced to liberalize markets. However, many governments were unenthusiastic about liberalizing markets because of the uncertainty about the nature of the successor systems which would emerge. It was the view of many governments that if they ceased to have a major stockholding role, prices would become chaotic and fluctuate widely between harvest time and lean seasons, with deleterious effects on the welfare of producers, and on food-security status of rural households in particular.

Because the fluctuations were expected to be particularly wide in view of the weak state of financial systems in most African countries and the scarcity of capital with which to trade in and store agricultural produce, the United Nations Food and Agriculture Organisation (FAO), had been promoting inventory credits. Under this credit scheme, private traders and farmers would be provided with credit to carry out the buffer-stock functions by purchasing and storing produce to be released onto the market during the lean season. For this purpose, lines of credit would be made available to wholesalers, semi-wholesalers and cooperatives or associations. In brief, the scheme is expected to function on a pattern modelled on the American system. Initially it is expected that the wholesalers, cooperatives or associations would not have sufficient equity or mortgageable properties.

It had, therefore, become necessary to devise some form of security under the inventory credit scheme. Lien or mortgage (both used here interchangeably) would be taken on all the storage and equipment bought, and crops procured. This would be done by arranging for financing and security agreements which would be legally binding on the borrowers. The agreement would legally put lien on farm equipment (including storage) and crops to be procured using the loan proceeds. Whoever purchased the mortgaged properties would legally be responsible for the loan repayment. To avoid fraudulent trade, the financing and security agreement would provide details of items covered by the contract. At the time the agreement is being negotiated, the prospective borrower would indicate how he/she would sell his/her products – either by securing contracts with known buyers like schools, hospitals and other trading institutions, or by retail or auction. Where appropriate, agreement would be secured with the contracted buyers to recover the loan from the proceeds of the sales of the products and the balance would be credited to the borrower's account. In the absence of third party agreement, it is expected that the borrower would honour agreed repayment schedule.

Banks participating in the scheme are expected to use their traditional criteria of creditworthiness, measured by their knowledge of the clients, ability to maintain accounts and provide cash flow projections. In case the banks have to lend to traders who did not keep accounts, other guarantees would be explored. One such option is the pledging system, whereby the trader participating in the scheme would place his/her products in a warehouse belonging to a licensed agent as a guarantee for the loan. Loans would be provided in tranches against presentation of warehouse certificates proving that the agricultural products had been delivered and were in safe custody with the licensed agent. The products would also be released in tranches against proof that the trader had reimbursed the bank. This would be the main system by which repayment would be guaranteed. The inventory credit scheme is expected to remove government fear of liberalizing markets.

Resource Mobility

One major cause for the emergence of income differentials and resource mobility is shifts in the levels of return on resources. When changes occur (caused by unexpected exogenous shocks) such as shifts in intra- and inter-sectoral relative prices, they result in the emergence of differentials in return on resources. If the economy is in its long-run equilibrium, when resources are actually at their desired levels, and returns to any given resource are the same in every use in the economy at any moment in time, then there is no need to transfer a resource from one sector to another. Usually, in a dynamic economy, such a situation is too idealistic and impractical. With knowledge of the present and future outlook the potential investors can always allocate resources in such a way that the present value of the future returns of a resource is the same at any of its uses within an economy. The primary concern is the maximization of return on assets, and minimizing costs of transferring resources. When changes occur in relative return on assets, resources will move to their best alternative use, which will be the one where the present value of marginal return (PVMR) of any factor will be the same in both sectors. The desire for the maximization of return on resources induces transfer of assets from one sector (occupational mobility) or geographical area (geographical mobility) to another sector or place until the differential between the present value of marginal return is equal to the transfer costs of the assets.

Labour Mobility

In the case of labour, the argument being put forward is labour's response to regional labour market disequilibrium. To illustrate the adjustment process one has to consider a simple production function of labour and capital, with each factor input paid the value of its marginal product of labour (MPc) and that of capital (MP$_1$c) will be equal, i.e. each input receives the same real return in each region. In this example it is assumed that labour is relatively abundant. If MP$_1$c represents marginal products where labour is scarce and MPc equals MP$_1$c, and MPc = MP$_1$c it is an indication that factors of production receive the same real return in each region, and equilibrium is said to exist. In SSA, however, because of differences in resource quality, return on factor inputs are not the same. Consequently both labour and capital will flow to the region where they have the greatest return. As labour migrates to regions where return to labour is high (high wage), marginal product or real return on factor input will progressively fall due to increased number of workers in the high wage zone. MPc will rise with the reduction of labour in the low wage region. Capital, however, flows in the opposite direction as labour response changes factor prices.

This adjustment process continues until real regional wage differentials are explained by regional wage rigidities. In a dualistic economy, labour mobility can be expressed as:

$$M = b (w-r) \tag{38}$$

where

M	represents net rural to urban migration;
w	is the real urban wage rate;
r	is the real rural wage rate typically taken to be subsistence; and
b	is some barrier to migration due to either lack of transparency on transfer costs, social environment, etc.

This model assumes that there is free labour movement. However, distortions usually occur in the labour market, or there may be growing unemployment due to poor performance of the economy. It is usual practice that the potential migrant takes into account the probability of unemployment in urban areas, and the loss of social security provided by the rural communities. The above equation has to be modified to reflect the probability of unemployment. Harris-Tadori had developed a model that takes into account this probability.

$$M = b\,(aw - r) \tag{39}$$

where

a	$= 1 - u$;
u	is the urban unemployment rate;
a	is the employment rate; and
aw	is real expected urban wage income.

The model still views migration in a narrow sense where net migration occurs in response to income opportunities. It is an aggregate model where aggregate migration responds to regional variables, but it does not address the question of the factor that spurs the motivation to migrate. It is, therefore, better to regard migration as an investment decision. It is, therefore, necessary to rewrite the equation as

$$M = b\,(aw - r + m)$$

where

m represents the psychic net return from urban amenities, prospects for promotion, additional costs in the form of rents, personal protection from urban crime, transportation costs, etc.

Migration from agriculture will take place if the present value of the wage differentials between non-agricultural and agricultural sector within the relevant time horizon (th) or the average expected remaining productive working years is larger than migration and retraining costs (transfer costs) to be carried out by the workers, y:

$$(W N t - W A t) e^{-rt} dt > y \tag{40}$$

where

$W N_t$ is non-agricultural wage;
$W A_t$ is agricultural wage;
r   is the discount rate; and
t   is time.

Labour migration will stop when

$$(W N t - W A t) e^{-rt} = (PVMRN - PVMRA) = y$$

which, under the assumption of constant wages, leads to a steady state equilibrium yielding:

$$WN - WA = \frac{y(r)}{(1-e^{-rh})} \tag{41}$$

The new equilibrium is thus characterized by a wage gap in favour of the sector receiving the additional flow of the labour force, in this case the non-agricultural sector. The new equilibrium arises because the intersectoral flow of resources has been completed. The wage disparities (factor return disparities) and the associated labour reallocation stops when the gap equals the annualized transfer costs. In practice, the magnitude of the wage disparities rises as transfer costs escalate, and the discount rate increases but could fall as the remaining productive life of potential migrants increases.

Intra- and Intersectoral, Interspatial Income Differentials and Resource Mobility

Because of the uneven distribution of productive resources, the proletarianization of the peasantry and uneven spatial spread of economic, industrial and urban centres, there was a growing social differentiation and a diversification of agricultural production. Thus the inequality in the level of development has been responsible for rural migration within and between countries all over Africa. This is because factor proportion and productivity on individual farms varies from area to area so that labour can be attracted from labour surplus areas to those areas where total return to labour is higher (Hall, 1971). Also, because of the seasonal nature of agriculture, there is a corresponding seasonal unemployment and underemployment (Eicher et al., 1972). For instance, in the past in West Africa large numbers of farmers migrated from the savannah zone to the coastal three crop areas of the western coast, and this symbiotic relationship between the two zones alleviated seasonal unemployment in the savannah zone and helped to increase output in the coastal areas. Those farmers who remained behind engaged themselves in such activities as equipment repair, processing of agricultural products, pottery, ritual ceremonies, etc. These activities occupy only a small fraction of the farmers' time and the demand for the types of services and products produced is low (ibid.). In a situation where there is wide difference in ecological conditions, internal mobility may be beneficial in achieving the geographical specialization potential of production. Denial of any labour market to external labour force may reduce opportunities of expanding production. However, rising unemployment in individual African countries led migrants to compete with local labour force for agricultural, industrial and training jobs. To curb increasing migration from neighbouring countries, most African countries adopted policies of economic indigenization as opposed to Africanization.

Differential employment opportunities between rural and urban areas
Administering the colonies also required a core of educated local administrative officers, law and order enforcement staff. The colonial administration, with the support of religious missionaries, established and expanded education to produce the local supporting staff. As education expanded, the number of school leavers also increased rapidly. Many of these school graduates were not willing to accept jobs they regarded as inferior. Since agriculture fell within this category, many of these graduates preferred to migrate to urban centres to take advantage of a relatively stable source of cash income and social amenities. Despite progress made in economic development, unemployment and underemployment persist in rural areas. The spread of education and demographic changes introduced the element of attitudinal changes, especially towards certain types of jobs. Earlier literature defined employment by measuring marginal productivity of labour. In recent years, however, there has been renewed discussion on the question of when a person should be regarded as employed, underemployed, or unemployed. Some economists now use various criteria to define the level of employment.

It is also currently held that an adequate level of employment must be defined in terms of its capacity to provide minimum living to the population. In the wake of the indigenization of the national economies, there has been a substantial education expansion in Africa in order to meet the manpower needs of the nations. But economic growth was unable to match the output of school leavers and there is a growing number of unemployed school graduates (Caldwell et al., 1975). In the Africa region generally, the education system has tended to emphasize conventional schooling and technical education and vocation training have been overshadowed (Okai, 1974). School leavers whose education and training have geared them for white-collar jobs are now not willing to accept jobs they regard as inferior. They have also acquired some reserve price for the supply of their labour and if earnings from certain jobs fall below the price, these school graduates are not willing to accept the job. Instead they would prefer, in the absence of any attractive gainful occupation in rural areas, to migrate to urban and industrial centres in search of paid employment which quite often falls above the level of their reserve price.

Different theories were advocated for this sort of rural to urban migration. It was originally felt that the wage necessary to attract rural labour force from the subsistence to the industrial sector must be measured in terms of the marginal value of subsistence production. It was also felt that it should be measured in terms of the level of the average productivity of family labour force because all produce is shared among members of the peasant family. It was, therefore, advocated that there must be some premium paid on top of the basic wage level in order to overcome the inertia resulting from social ties (Harris et al., 1970). It has now been established that the paradox of migration from rural to urban areas in the light of open unemployment in urban areas and positive labour earnings in agriculture, is due to the fact that average wage in urban areas is two to three times the average agricultural income. Rural people, therefore, found it worth their while to migrate to urban areas even if there is only a 50 or 33 per cent probability of finding a job (MPED, 1971). However, this does not mean that there will be a fall in the rural population. Eicher et al. contended that even if rural labour force continues to migrate to urban areas, the problem of the increasing population in rural areas will continue as the result of the combination of the declining death rates with steady but rising increases in birth rates, and the slow growth rate of non-agricultural employment. Projects which could have helped to create employment opportunities are not readily forthcoming because factor price distortions, which are common in economic development strategies in the Region, encouraged the adoption of capital-intensive labour-displacing production technologies. Unskilled labour is invariably overvalued through the operation of the minimum wage legislation common in the region and trade union pressure. As a result, wages for this category of labour tend to rise, thus encouraging investment in capital-intensive techniques. Wages for skilled labour tend to be above their real value because of the relative scarcities. Wage increases have, therefore, encouraged firms to improve their labour productivity by fuller utilization of existing capacities of employed labour force, on-the-job training and increased labour efficiency arising from experience (Eicher et al., 1972).

The dualistic situation of the labour market, with the unprotected sector found predominantly in the rural areas and the protected sector secured by means of collective bargaining by organized trade unions and the operation of the minimum wage legislation, merely frustrated any attempt to retain youngsters on the land in the face of the widening disparities between rural and urban incomes. The gaps were further widened by government fiscal policy which taxed export crops, thereby depressing income in rural areas. Another labour policy weakness was the requirement that agricultural estate and plantation should pay statutory wage rates. These commercial farmers, in order to reduce their production costs, reacted by intensifying the use of capital-intensive technologies. Labour policies, therefore, acted counter to the employment generation in agriculture which was very much needed to improve the income of the rural population (Eicher et al., 1972; Okai, 1976).

5 Equity Aspects of Agricultural Pricing Policy

The Politics of Pricing Policy

The agricultural sector as a producer of food has a very high public profile and thus has become the most public in terms of policy and programme need, while at the same time the most private in terms of day-to-day decision-making on production, marketing and consumptions. In SSA it has been an established tradition that governments adopt macro and micro policies with the ultimate objective of stabilizing prices. Some of the policies do not aim at stabilizing prices *per se* but also are designed to handle the consequences of price instability for both producers and consumers. The macro policy intervention aims at the management of the internal commodity market such as the establishment and management of strategic food reserves by government parastatal bodies. The buffer stocks are built by procurement of food staples during 'hungry periods' or when a trigger price has been reached in order to dampen demand-pull price rises. The intention (although not systematically practised) is to protect the welfare of consumers by setting a ceiling above which prices are not permitted to rise. In order to be viable and sustainable, such price bands should maintain a margin between procurement price (or producer price) and the selling prices that must cover the costs of price stabilization measures.

Some of the macro policies affect both producers and consumers indirectly, such as the consequences of exchange rate realignment, the appreciation of which improves the internal terms of trade for tradeables with positive impacts on the external balance of the economy. The exchange rate adjustment can, however, smother supply response because of increases in prices of imported inputs which are not matched by prices of output that normally lag behind those of inputs. Sluggish supply responses exacerbate domestic structural inflation which in turn continues to put pressure on exchange rate, thus acquiring some sort of cyclical relationship. In such a situation the secular domestic structural inflation becomes difficult to control. Where exchange rates appreciate due to lack of regular adjustment, it acts as an indirect tax on exportable commodities, as they lose their external competitiveness but make imports cheaper and may, therefore, adversely affect the external balance. Commodity market management and the determination of realistic producer prices had always proved a daunting task.

In the past, the subject of agricultural price policy analysis was confined to the setting of producer prices, consumer (food) prices and agricultural input prices. It was closely associated with marketing efficiency studies and international trade or commercial policy relating to agricultural commodities. Post-independence in SSA demonstrated the interaction, in both directions, between sectoral price policies and the management of macroeconomic variables on the one hand, and the performance of the agricultural sector on the other. These additional areas include industrial protection policy, exchange rate policy, budgetary, monetary and general fiscal policy, and supply and distribution of consumer goods, particularly in rural areas. Consequently, the analysis of the effects of price policy decisions on the performance of the agricultural sector became a comprehensive and complex subject. The issue was complicated by the range of developmental objectives which governments chose to pursue, to which end agricultural pricing policy is frequently seen as a necessary means.

The FAO study of pricing policy in 1984 identified eight objectives: i) stabilizing prices to agricultural commodities producers; ii) encouraging food crop production to achieve self-sufficiency; iii) encouraging export commodity production for general foreign exchange earnings; iv) providing a flow of raw materials to domestic industries; v) raising rural incomes; vi) stabilizing food prices to consumers and minimizing their rate of increase in order to reduce inflationary pressure in the economy; vii) generating government revenue by taxing the surpluses of the agricultural sector; and viii) encouraging specific forms of production, organization, social and economic transformation. To this list should be added: ix) accelerating the rate of technological innovation in specific instances; x) generating additional (or protecting existing) employment; xi) accelerating development in specific regions of the country; xii) improving the impact on specific income or social groups, producers or consumers and benefiting powerful groups in society (usually an implicit objective reflected by an absence or weak presence of alternative measures) (Belshaw, 1985).

The presence of several development objectives means that: i) no single objective can be chosen for optimization. If the weights can be determined, a composite function reflecting social and political weights could be constructed;

ii) objectives may conflict even in the use of a single policy instrument, for instance, a conflict of producers' versus consumers' short-run welfare over the price of a staple foodstuff; and decision-makers would be better informed as to the consequences of the issues involved in the resolution of the conflict, a trade-off analysis of the probable consequences of different actions and/or modified or new policies which could minimize the trade-offs involved. Methods for identifying distorting elements, conflicts and analysing trade-offs were developed by economic analysts. They are discussed in chapter 6.

Because of its high public profile, price policy has been used extensively in SSA as a measure to achieve social equity. Many governments opted for an agricultural development strategy based on non-exploitative relations and market intervention was regarded as an important development instrument in shaping the orientation of development and market control; uniform producer and consumer prices were usually set nationally. An important aim of all these policies was to increase equality of consumption of basic necessities among citizens of the country. The nationally uniform producer price policy had considerable appeal to many governments in terms of administrative simplicity and interpersonal equity (social equity). The governments concerned argued that producers farther away from the main markets who, in any case, were likely to be poor rural inhabitants, should not be disadvantaged further by being paid lower prices.

Product Pricing

In Africa, governments' intervention in pricing and marketing of agricultural commodities took different forms. Producer and consumer prices were controlled for a wide variety of agricultural products, especially domestic foodstuffs, but also for some export commodities. Prices for major export crops such as cocoa, coffee, tea, cotton and tobacco were not often directly controlled but followed the international market trends. In this case, the farm gate price was arrived at by deducting insurance and freight costs to determine the cif and fob price, from which was deducted internal marketing costs. For other crops, prices were fixed on the basis of assumed average cost of production and it was a common practice in many countries that they were revised either annually or periodically to allow for changes in costs. These revisions were sometimes deliberately delayed in order to keep price increases in check and also because of administrative difficulties (FAO, 1984; Okai, 1983). In many countries, the objectives of price regulations were to protect consumers and to prevent excessive profits. This latter objective was prevalent in countries where expatriate merchants played a dominant role in commercial agriculture and domestic trade. Hence a common feature in many African countries was the indecision about the precise role of the private sector in both the provision of inputs and marketing of crops. The other objective aimed at ensuring that the producers received attractive prices for their commodities because many governments realized that farmers did react promptly to the prices offered and that relative prices between commodities played a major role in farmers' choice of crops. It was, therefore, realized that sale responses were firm indications of the approximate adequacy or inadequacy of ex-farm price.

Maximum consumer prices were decided separately and fixed in detail for a wide range of commodities. The fixing of a maximum price was an attempt to stabilize the cost of living, and any contradictions between producer and consumer price was resolved by the payment of subsidies, which took different forms – sales of commodities below import parity price, subsidizing distribution costs, etc. While many governments attempted to fix prices in a rational and timely fashion, on occasion prices generally were set and changed in a rather less orderly fashion, under the influence of sudden changes in market outlook or even non-economic considerations. Some of these deficiencies were the consequence of several factors which made it very difficult to arrive at a correct set of relative farm gate prices which could avoid misallocation of resources, losses to the economy, income inequities and sometimes unwarranted surpluses or shortages. One of these factors was the variations in the agro-ecology and climate that is common in many African countries. The other factor was the limited up-to-date knowledge regarding prevailing farming systems and production techniques for different crops and different types of farms. This knowledge could have been gained by mounting systematic micro-level economic research which could provide the needed data and information on labour inputs and returns, and on the behavioural characteristics of farmers as producers and consumers. Very limited research of this type was carried out in Africa.

Given the present limitations in farm data, the crop budget and related cost estimates prepared by the government for typical farms did not very accurately reflect actual conditions in the varied countryside. The estimated gross margins per unit of output which provided benchmarks for the farm gate price proposals were more educated guesses than actual figures and could, therefore, lead to erroneous conclusion and price recommendations. Ideally, improved budgets should have been prepared for a series of farms according to the size and eco-climate based on prevailing cultural practices, and derived from, and periodically updated through, properly designed and executed micro-level economic surveys. The result of such surveys would improve price fixing exercises and remove the elements of uncertainty and arbitrariness which could affect adversely farmers' decision-making processes.

Price Control

Controlling prices was a characteristic phenomenon in African economic management. As regards price-fixing for agricultural commodities, the major problem was the cleavage of responsibility for agricultural production and marketing policy which involved several ministries, parastatals, corporations and the private farms. The ministry responsible for promoting agricultural production was usually in charge of setting recommendation for government approval of product prices. In some cases product prices were fixed and controlled by parastatals responsible for marketing the agricultural commodities. Consumer prices were fixed and controlled in some countries by the Ministry of Finance, and in others by the ministry responsible for trade. Price fixing and controls were made difficult not only by this lack of coordination but also by the inadequacy of the information and reporting system on crop production and forecasts, as well as by inadequate market developments which inhibited the improvement of markets, leading often to poor market transparency and a low level of private investment in market infrastructure, storage and transport. Experience showed that governments were not able to administer the system effectively, since they could not guarantee to purchase all crops offered for sale at previously guaranteed prices due to inadequate storage facilities and budgetary constraints.

The characteristic feature of price control in Africa was the establishment of minimum prices, mainly for scheduled crops, and fixed prices for some cash crops. In many countries, for food crops and cattle, the price control system consisted of the establishment of an official minimum price ostensibly designed to stimulate production and protect the farmers, but many governments were unable to administer the system effectively since they would not guarantee the purchases of all crops. For instance, some countries regularly experienced cyclical output of crops, with good harvests being followed by bad ones. Although bad weather was always blamed for the poor harvest, inappropriate pricing policies, associated with rigid marketing arrangements, contributed to shortfalls in domestic supply. In years when crop production was high, marketing institutions were not able to purchase all the crops at previously guaranteed prices, often because of inadequate storage and transport facilities. This inevitably led to low prices and reduced plantings as well as failure to adopt biological yield-increasing and labour-saving innovations. Under these conditions, governments should have limited their intervention in pricing and marketing to setting minimum prices and acting as the buyers of the last resort. This could have permitted market forces more freedom in determining individual prices. The marketing parastatals could remain responsible for maintaining adequate strategic reserve stocks to counter crop failures.

In many instances the minimum prices were regarded as official and effectively become maximum prices. As minimum prices were often too low, the enforcement merely depressed prices to the farmers and in turn discouraged production. Also, in a number of African countries, parastatal bodies were required to buy and sell at minimum prices. This distorted market forces and led to financial losses for the marketing parastatals involved. Once prices were fixed, enforcement of official prices met with varying degrees of success but was invariably difficult, especially in inflationary economies where price controls quite naturally became uneven in view of the large number of controlled prices to be policed. Experience showed that the implementation of price controls differed widely between the agricultural/agro-industrial field, and the rest of the economy.

In most cases, official prices were effectively controlled only where market forces were unevenly distributed. When many smallholders, growing such crops as cotton, tea, palm oil, tobacco, etc., faced only one or a few buyers, usually a government or a processing mill, the buyers were able to enforce the minimum price or even below, because of their monopolistic position. The same also applied if there were only few producers who could make it easy for government to exercise strict control on price. This was typical with estate agriculture, especially for sugar, coffee, tea, oil palm, etc. In a few countries where cattle trade was an important economic activity, sale of cattle was either by private treaty or auction. In both cases the buyer arranged to collect cattle from the ranch or cattle market. Under a communal system of cattle raising, sale of cattle was also by treaty or auction. In the case of auctioneering, there were usually cattle market days and cattle herded into cattle market places and auctioned. Experience showed that the few buyers who usually took part were able to collude to hold down cattle prices to the sellers (Okai, 1974, 1988).

Cross-subsidization

Price distortions have adverse consequences, often resulting in one socioeconomic group subsidizing another or distorting real price signals. In practice, therefore, the objective of inter-community income equalization may not be realized because, for instance, uniform pricing is frequently adopted as a measure of minimizing costs (i.e. costs pertaining not only to production but also to distribution) in respect of geographical location demand to the position of supply. Pan-territorial pricing normally meant that inputs as well as agricultural produce were uniformly priced all over the country. The policy was justified in terms of equity; no farmer should be discriminated against just because he/she lives in a remote area. Firstly, equity was achieved just because the same price was paid for a given product. The government guaranteed price could be below the unofficial market price (i.e. demand for a given commodity could exceed supply at the official price). In such cases parallel markets have arisen, with actual prices being differentiated in accordance with the regional structure of demand and supply. Thus, if the government's intention was to attain an equitable distribution of income, pan-territorial pricing has not been a very good policy instrument to realize this objective.

The second objection to uniform pricing is that it can be immensely expensive in budgeting terms and in terms of inefficient use of resources. Let us take the production of maize in region A as being 300,000 tonnes, with most maize produced transported to region B, which produces only 10,000 tonnes. The guaranteed minimum price is uniformly set at ¢5,000 per maxi bag of 100 kg. Local assembly costs are estimated at ¢250 per tonne. Total consumption of maize in the country is 300,000 tonnes, out of which 10,000 is consumed in region B and the balance of 200,000 in region A. The transport cost to B is ¢150 per tonne. The above is summarized in Table 12.

Table 12   Production, consumption and transport costs

	Region A	Region B
Production (000 t)	300	10
Consumption (000 t)	200	100
Surplus/deficits (000 t)	100	(90)
Transport costs (¢ 000)	13,500 *	–

Note: * 90 tonnes deficit in region B is transported from region A to B at ¢150 per tonne = (90 x 150) = ¢ 13.50 million.

Because of the operation of price control, the transport cost is not passed to the consumer, and the consumers in region B are, therefore, subsidized to the extent of ¢13.5 million. This benefit does not accrue to the producers in region A. Apart from the cross-subsidization, the unemployed or employed in urban low-productive pursuits, get the wrong signals about the social desirability of their activities whereby their incentives to do things with higher priorities to society (e.g. taking up farming) are reduced.

There are other costs as well, which are hidden rather than apparent:

- cheap food policy, whether it is a result of an overvalued domestic currency or of subsidization of too low producer prices to make full use of a country's agricultural potential; and
- reinforcement of expensive tastes (maize replacing cassava, wheat replacing maize, sorghum, millet), making the country still more dependent on imports and making a necessary structural adjustment still more difficult.

Market Institutions and Distortions

Distortionary Government Market Intervention

The initial expansion of African cash crop production during the colonial period took place in a context in which private market allocations predominated. Africans participated in primary production, leaving marketing and processing in the hands of expatriate firms who controlled the distribution of consumer goods as well, through a hierarchy of private traders dominated by a group of European, Asian and Lebanese trading houses. This free market practice generated an extremely dynamic growth process in favoured regions within the reach of external markets. The big European trading houses organized cartels among themselves designed to limit competition for crops, and thereby kept down prices to growers, while at the same time making high profits. The colonial administration intervened particularly during the depression years of the 1930s to control competition and guaranteed a cost-plus pricing system even to the least efficient producers (Brett, 1973). During the war this monopolistic structure was reinforced by the creation of marketing boards with monopoly buying power and the right to set prices for both growers and intermediaries (Brett, 1986). Hence by the late colonial period, the dynamism of the early free market had been lost and a structure created which inhibited growth and social change.

Post-independence market organization and structures The dirigiste post-independent regime readily and enthusiastically inherited this system and even expanded government's participation into marketing food crops. After independence, the organization of agricultural marketing underwent varying degrees of changes in many African countries, in most cases with the ultimate objective of creating single-channel marketing systems for all important crops and also of increasing the degree of governmental control over marketing. Generally agricultural marketing was carried out by a mixture of parastatals, private merchants and processors. Some of the largest markets, particularly for major staples, were in the hands of parastatals and cooperatives, while others were handled by competitive merchants/traders who operated within the framework of legislated prices for scheduled crops. Two marketing systems could be distinguished – the formal and the informal sector. While the formal marketing system operated within the legislated prices, the other operated within a free competitive market but suffered from gross inadequacy of market infrastructure. Within the framework of the formal markets were two types of marketing boards: the Export Marketing Boards (EMBs) and the Food Marketing Boards (FMBs). The selling operations of the two types of boards differed, with the EMBs facing the overseas market while the FMBs faced the domestic market. The EMBs preferred rapid evacuation and forward selling, and this policy enabled them to keep storage and capital requirements to a minimum, thus avoiding the burden of holding and financing heavy stocks. The EMBs could effectively control prices because the market forces of the crops they handled (cocoa, coffee, oil palm, tobacco, cotton) were unevenly distributed. The producers of these crops, usually smallholders, faced only one buyer, the EMB or a processing mill. The EMB and the processing mill were able to enforce government fixed prices because of their monopolistic position. Such effective control was made possible by the creation of single-channel marketing systems and increases in the degree of government's control over marketing (Okai, 1988, p. 50).

The informal market sector The other marketing system outside the regulatory control of the governments is characterized by free entry of a large number of small traders and relatively strong competition. This marketing system is characterized by being relatively open and competitive, with flexible prices that reflect the scarcity value of the commodities, their qualities and transport cost. Very little is known about the marketing structure and the quantities of produce moving through the system. It is probably in West Africa that the system has been in existence for longest and is fairly well developed. In this area one finds a multitude of markets in the national capital, cities and towns in rural areas. The system usually consists of various categories of traders, principally assemblers, commission agents/brokers, retailers who operate at the rural as well as the urban levels. Products passing through the whole chain from producer to the final consumer in the large urban centres change hands frequently. Invariably it leads to consumer prices being much higher than producer prices because of the high margin absorbed by the long chain of intermediaries; inadequate and high cost of transportation, packing and storage problems, and high losses especially of perishable products.

This problem is exacerbated by the isolation of rural markets from consumption areas through high transportation cost, and hence the operation of this system is liable to large and sometimes violent changes in prices in response to small changes in supply and demand. The system is characterized by low turnover and the activity can be taken as being more of a social function than an economic phenomenon. However, in some West African countries, the activity is the main occupation of many women, popularly known as 'market mammies', who are capable of organizing village markets, including the provision of crop finance for the purchase of the products. Under this system the level of marketing services provided by the traders is generally low: physical marketing facilities are of low quality; grading of produce is almost nonexistent and there is no standard system of weights and measures. Even within a single market, various measures may be used. Traditionally, storage of food crops is carried out by the farmers. The majority of traders usually carry stocks for a few weeks to ensure some sort of continued supply but do not engage in speculative storage because of the inherent risks involved. The decision to sell depends on various circumstances, including outlook for future crops, subsistence needs, and the timing and extent of cash need (Okai, 1988).

Market subsidies There were three main categories of marketing subsidies: i) explicit subsidies through direct price support; ii) implicit subsidies through price controls; and iii) non-price subsidies (mainly fiscal incentives such as rebates on imports duties, subsidized interest rate, etc.). Payment of market subsidies was not a deliberate government policy but a consequence of its intervention. Price determination processes involved the balancing of the interests of consumers, mainly urban, against the provision of incentives to rural producers, and, as already stated, the conflicts between the two objectives were met by the payment of subsidies. Hence market intervention and pricing policy distorted incentive structure, impaired allocative efficiency and were inimical to agricultural development because official prices incorporated an urban bias against agriculture. The objectives were met by the payment of subsidies.

Efficiency Consideration in Agricultural Product Pricing Policy

The primary goal of an agricultural pricing policy in developing agriculture is to provide incentives to farmers by way of higher prices to stimulate agricultural production by: i) inducing producers to move closer to their production possibility frontier by efficient use of resources; ii) encouraging use of more labour and other variable production resources to achieve higher production; and iii) motivating producers to invest and adopt new technology to maximize production at least cost. Under competitive conditions, the efficient use of resources is determined by the relative profitability of various enterprises, which is ultimately the function of the relative prices of farm products and inputs. The pricing policy should try to achieve a balanced mix of crop and livestock enterprises consistent with the resource endowments, domestic consumption needs and export earning requirements of the country. A sound agricultural pricing policy would permit free movement of productive resources, manpower, and technology in order to be able to obtain the production volume and composition of output demanded at the least cost to society, and finally to obtain adequate returns to factors of production and a fair price to consumers. In brief, the resource allocation objective of the agricultural price policy is to ensure rational utilization of land, labour and other productive resources through the efficient allocation among competing enterprises.

The other objective of the agricultural price policy is to achieve a certain level of income distribution deemed desirable by the policy-makers. A price policy is often viewed as an instrument for raising the income of the agricultural sector. The terms of trade in favour of agriculture benefits the farmers by way of income transfer, which ultimately results in more equitable distribution of income. Agricultural prices also affect the income level of people engaged in other sectors, as agricultural commodities form a substantial proportion of household expenditure. The low food price policy aims at helping the large industrial and urban population with low consumer price food which, however, in turn adversely affects the farmers' income. Farmers as producers are not only interested in maximizing their farm income but also in obtaining a stable income, self-sufficiency in food, etc. Other goals of agricultural price policy include such national objectives as increase in export earnings, increase in government revenue, increase in rural saving, capital formation in agriculture, employment generation in agriculture. In brief, the principal objectives of agricultural price policy are production maximization, price stability, resource allocation and income distribution. Hence from the farmers' point of view, the 'appropriate' or 'incentive' support producer price is the price which: i) yields revenue from the sale of the product that exceeds the cost of producing that product; ii) yields a profit margin adequate to support a family and induce the producer to adopt new techniques of production to increase productivity and production; iii) yields profit that exceeds the level of profits to be earned from the production of other commodities.

Several alternative methodologies can be used in determining appropriate producer and consumer price levels. Whichever method is used will depend on the objective of the agricultural price policy. Important factors that have to be taken into account in price determination include: i) cost of production and prices of inputs; ii) demand and supply relationships; iii) prices of competing crop and livestock products; iv) market prices of consumer goods and the effect on the cost of living; v) parity ratio between prices received and prices paid by farmers which determines the terms of trade between agriculture and non-agriculture sectors; and vi) the international market price. However, many governments in SSA in the past adopted packages of price and other policies that actually reduced agricultural production incentives and literally encouraged a flow of resources out of the agricultural sector.

Product/Product Relationship (Inter-crop Parity)

The principle of marginal rate of substitution also applies to output relationships. There are four product/product relationships, and the precise relationship depends on the type of crop or animal enterprise and the type of production in relationship to available productive resources. The first case is when the production of commodities with each other competing for the same productive resources. For instance, land may be the fixed productive resource for the production of maize and groundnut. As the farmer increases the area devoted to maize production, he has to sacrifice that used for groundnut. This is a *competitive relationship* and land is the scarce resource. If land is not limiting, labour may be the limiting factor, and there will not be competition over land. Over some scale of enterprise, one enterprise may be using a factor which is not used by others. Poultry, for instance, can be kept together without competing with other enterprises, i.e. factors that may not earn in any way. This is a *supplementary relationship* which, however, holds over a certain scale. If a farmer continues to increase the amount of poultry, the birds will start to compete for food, which becomes a scarce commodity. As the scale increases, the relationship moves out of being supplementary to a competitive one. In the case of animal production, the increase in the size of the herd will improve soil fertility through animal manure which in turn improves pasture and crops. In this case the integration of animal and crop production is said to be to their mutual advantage, i.e. the two products have a *complementary relationship*. However, with further increases over a certain scale, the two products start to compete for land and labour, thus moving into a competitive relationship. The other product/product relationship is a *joint product* relationship, where the decision to produce one product leads to the production of the other. The raising of dairy cattle for milk supply automatically leads to the production of calves; a similar argument applies to the production of mutton.

In order to arrive at the most economically efficient product relationship, it is necessary to compute relative prices or inter-crop parity, which is essentially an assessment of economic efficiency for the agricultural economy as a whole (Figure 27). When cotton production competes with that of maize the competitive relationship is represented by the production possibility curve. As the farmer increases the production of cotton (Y_1) he has to accept a decline in the output of maize (Y_2), and the decline of Y_2 takes an increasing unit, which boils down to the law of diminishing return. On the other hand, as the farmer reduces the size of Y_1, Y_2 moves in the opposite direction of the law of diminishing return and there is a decline in the law of diminishing return. In economic analysis this relationship uses the principle of marginal rate of substitution (MRS) which can be expressed as

$$\text{MRS} = \frac{\text{Marginal cost of labour}}{\text{Marginal product of maize}} = \frac{\text{Marginal labour cost}}{\text{Marginal product of cotton}} \quad (1)$$

Essentially this means that there is competition for the use of productive resources. The farmer has, therefore, to ration out his/her scarce resources between or among competing enterprises. How far he can pursue one enterprise or a combination of enterprises depends on the principle of the law of equimarginal return (LEMR), which states that profit will be maximized where the last unit of a factor of production can earn a higher return than in any other use. In other words, the opportunity cost of marginal input equals marginal output. This is illustrated in Table 13. Assuming that labour is hired at ush 3, it pays if marginal cost equals marginal revenue. Assume that available resources limits employment of labour to 60 man days. If the farmer adopts a policy of maximizing cotton production, he/she can use a greater proportion of labour on cotton and the other on other crops such as maize.

In Table 13, the farmer can allocate up to 35 to 40 man days to cotton when the marginal return to labour for both crops is about equal, and the balance of man days will then be allocated to maize. The law of equimarginal

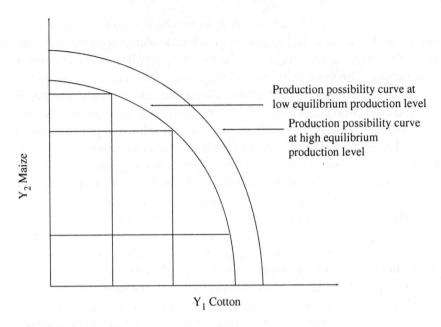

Figure 27 Product/product relationship

Table 13   Factor/product relationship

		Cotton					Maize		
Labour/acre (man days)	Total cost	Total revenue	Marginal revenue	Marginal cost	Labour/acre (man days)	Total cost	Total revenue	Marginal revenue	Marginal cost
			UShs					UShs	
10	30	100	100	30	10	30	50	50	30
20	60	350	250	30	20	60	130	80	30
30	90	400	50	30	30	90	190	60	30
35	105	430	30	15	25	120	–	60	30
40	120	460	30	15	40	150	220	30	30
50	150	490	30	30	50	180	240	20	30
60	180	510	20	30	60	210	250	10	30

$$\text{MRS} = \frac{15}{30} = 0.2 \text{ for cotton}$$

$$\text{MRS} = \frac{30}{60} = 0.2 \text{ for maize}$$

return is, therefore, in use in relative pricing or inter-crop parity pricing. When the fortieth man day is allocated to cotton production the MRS equals 0.2 and MRS of twenty-fifth man day allocated to maize also equals to 0.2. As output increases, initially income (profit) will be increasing because for each additional unit produced, the increase in marginal revenue (MR) is greater than the increase in marginal cost (MC). As output is expanded, total profit will be decreasing because for each additional unit produced, the increase in total revenue is less than the increase in cost. This occurs where MR crosses MC curve, a point where MR = MC (Figure 28).

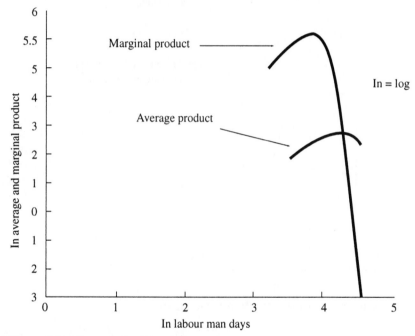

Figure 28 Average and marginal productivity

This analysis of economic efficiency also applies to a complementary product relationship (Figure 29). As a farmer introduces cattle, he/she initially gets an increase in the crop output because of the compensatory increase in soil fertility due to cattle droppings, which increase plant nutrients (recycling), improve water penetration into the soil and reduce soil erosion. Further increases in cattle numbers continue until the law of diminishing return comes into effect. The effect of manure offsets the decline in maize and one gets an increase in maize output. As the population of cattle increases, it becomes difficult to get sufficient manure to offset the decline in maize output, until the point is reached where further increases in cattle population just equals a loss. After this point the relationship between cattle and maize enters into a competitive relationship. It will pay to continue increasing the number of cattle until a point is reached which gives the highest profit (the difference between revenue and cost, i.e. profit or income). The line that indicates this point is tangential to the product possibility curve. If price changes, the revenue also changes. If the price of cattle falls, it will be necessary to grow more maize.

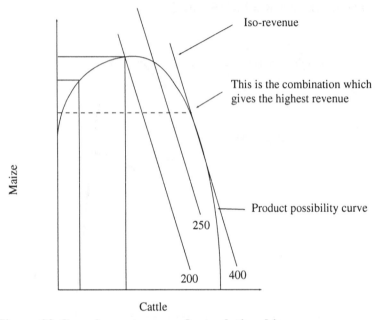

Figure 29 Complementary product relationship

In some instances, extreme product relationship may exist, especially where one of the products has no value. An example is fallow land which can be used for grazing. In cases of excess availability of grazing, its value may be zero. The iso-revenue line is horizontal. In this case a point is reached where the complementary relationship ceases. Even with a slight slope of iso-revenue line, a farmer will need a large area of fallow in order to compensate for the loss (Figures 30 and 31). As regards supplementary relationship, land could be idle for a year. In Africa land is used after harvest for grazing, or poultry are allowed to roam, picking grains which might be left over. In Africa labour is a critical scarce factor of production. Usually intercropping is practised to maximize labour return or to circumvent labour shortages for

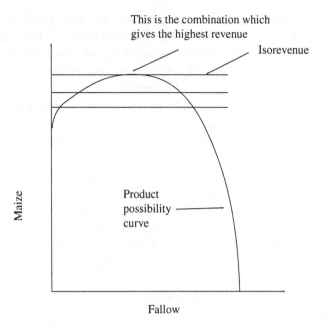

Figure 30 Supplementary product relationship

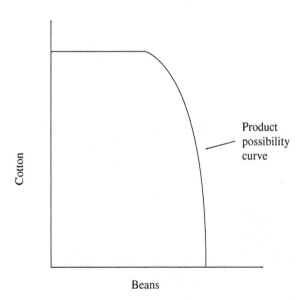

Figure 31 Supplementary relationship

agricultural production. Land is usually opened for cotton production. After planting cotton in rows, beans are planted between the rows. The only labour required is for planting beans and harvesting them, because most labour input is for cotton. Cotton also benefits from improved soil fertility since beans are nitrogen-fixing leguminous plants. The combined output of cotton and beans raises returns to labour. However, the plant populations of both crops maintain a supplementary relationship until such point when further increases in the bean population pushes the relationship to a competitive one as they start to compete for land and labour.

The last relationship is a joint product relationship. In Lesotho both sheep and goats are kept for their wool, mohair and meat. As the number of animals increases, the quantity of wool, mohair and meat increases. To maintain the uniformity of fibre of wool and mohair, only merino sheep and Angola breeds of goats are allowed to be raised. In this respect the only flexibility is the use of different breeds which can produce different types of wool. A breed may be a good producer of wool but not necessarily of mutton. One would, therefore, look for a breed of sheep which is good both in producing wool and mutton (Figure 32).

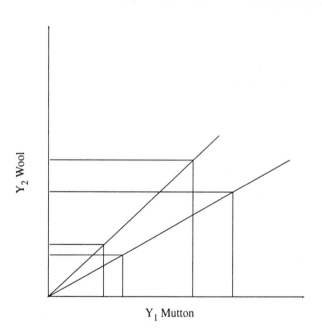

Figure 32 Joint product relationship

The intention of the inter-crop parity approach is to sustain an existing relationship between prices of various crops or set a new relationship to induce the desired changes in the commodity composition of output. To maintain the desired crop mix, the parity price ratios of various crops and relative profitability are worked out and compared and adjusted to derive relative incentive prices which are sufficient to induce changes in the commodity composition in line with the national consumption and export requirements. The parity ratios are worked out either on market price basis (inter-crop price parity) or income basis (on inter-crop income parity). Time data series are used for constructing indices and parity ratios, and in the absence of time data series, the market prices for a given year are used for working out the parity and price adjustment. This approach also has some limitations in that it does not take into consideration other important price determining factors such as terms of trade, international prices, etc., or the use of market prices, due to imperfections in market structure, which limits the validity of employing this method in setting prices.

Essentially, the computation of relative price or inter-crop parity is parallel to the assessment of economic efficiency for the agricultural sector as a whole. The ideal is that the producer should maximize his monetary profit and this can be achieved where the last unit of money spent on any one factor of production (land, labour, capital) brings in the same marginal return, and where marginal product of any factor is the same in all uses. This is the condition of efficient combination of factors of production in such a way that productive resources are used in such quantities that the ratio of the marginal cost and marginal product of all others are equal.

Where there are no time data series, parity ratios are calculated on the basis of a given year's prices received and paid by farmers, compared with the previous year parity ratios for price adjustment. This approach is useful in that prices determined are capable of sustaining the purchasing power of farmers' produce in terms of production inputs and consumer goods. It also ensures that increases in producer prices are not offset by changes in input and consumer goods. The principal advantage is that the terms of trade between agriculture and the non-agricultural sector do not move against farmers to distort incentives. In Kenya, for instance, pricing policy in the past was directed towards achieving: i) the goal of national self-sufficiency in staple food grains; ii) the maintenance of producers' real income; iii) measuring producer prices against estimated changes in the cost of production. As shown in Table 14, the objective of maintaining producers' income could not be achieved because of the escalation of production costs while output prices lagged behind.

Table 14   Kenya: price and terms of trade indices for agriculture, 1980–84 (1982 = 100)

	1980	1981	1982	1983	1984*
Prices received	83.6	86.9	100.0	117.0	140.1
Total crops	89.4	92.8	100.0	138.2	144.1
Domestic export	81.1	84.3	100.0	107.9	138.3
Livestock and products	74.6	85.3	100.0	97.8	115.1
Weighted average					
of above	82.5	87.3	100.0	115.9	135.7
General index of					
agricultural output prices	83.7	90.8	100.0	108.6	118.6
Prices paid:					
purchased input	94.2	97.4	100.0	103.5	106.0
Index of purchased consumer goods:					
Rural area	69.9	82.7	100.0	113.8	134.0
Indices of prices paid	77.2	87.1	100.0	110.7	125.6
Agricultural sector					
terms of trade	108.4	104.2	100.0	98.1	94.4

Notes

1   This is the output price index used in calculating the terms of trade.
2   * Provisional.

Source: Government of Kenya,1985, Table 8.8.

Unit Cost of Production

To ascertain that the objective of sustaining the purchasing power of income is realized requires some objectives, consisting of the internal factors of production and services and appropriate pricing of output. One method is the use of unit costs of production in price analysis and the other is crop income equalization. The intention of this method is that the producer price should cover the full average costs, including an imputed return on capital and management. To obtain better cost estimates, costing should include variable costs (seeds, fertilizers, chemicals, hired labour, etc.) and fixed costs (including depreciation and maintenance of machinery, equipment, wage cost of labour, interest on loan, transport and marketing costs, etc.). This method is intended to provide appropriate or incentive support to producer price that exceeds the cost of production and could provide sufficient inducements to the farmer to adopt innovation. For this reason the cost-price relationship is crucial if the approach is to achieve its objective.

To arrive at realistic cost estimate for the country, various computational methods are involved. The first decision is to adopt an appropriate concept of costing, whether average cost, marginal cost or bulk-line cost. The second decision regards the level of aggregation of cost, whether at district, regional or national level or on agro-ecological basis. Because of difficulty in determining marginal cost, most analysts prefer the use of average cost, although this approach also has a weakness in that the bulk of the farmers might have costs exceeding the average. To overcome this difficulty inherent in the average cost approach, 'bulk-line' costings approaches are regularly used, in which a percentile of costs to cover the cost of 75–80 per cent of producers, area, or outputs, are selected. This approach has, however, been criticized on the grounds of inefficient use of resources, the high cost of data collection and the need for careful aggregation of data to reflect inter-farm and inter-regional heterogeneity of agro-ecological conditions. Another problem of this approach is the valuation of costs, as certain inputs like family labour have only opportunity cost. The other weakness of this approach is its inability to take into account prices of competing crops (equimarginal return principle), terms of trade between agriculture and non-agricultural sectors and international prices. To overcome some of these weaknesses, the 'synthetic budget' approach has been used. This method is similar to the cost of production approach except that it is more flexible because yields and other assumptions can be varied, and because it does not involve extensive farm surveys since budgetary data for representative farms are used.

Crop Income Equalization

The 'income equalization' approach, also known as the 'gross margin' approach, equates estimated net returns to producers across alternative enterprises in order to develop a balanced crop mix required by the country to achieve set targets of production. The value-added or gross margin is computed after deduction of the direct cost of production (seeds, fertilizers, chemicals, maintenance cost of machinery and plants, etc.) from the sale proceeds of crops. Since the gross margin is the return on internal factors of production used for growing a particular crop, it provides a common measure or indicator for examining the resource efficiency and comparative advantage of growing different crops. The data required for this method are similar to the cost of production approach, and the objective is similar to crop parity or relative profitability approaches, with emphasis being placed on maintaining parity in costs, prices and incomes of different crops. It is, therefore, a useful method of reducing inequalities in regional development and promoting equitable income distribution among producers of different crops. Any advantageous or disadvantageous position of any crop is removed by the adoption of parity income among different crops. The approach, however, has some limitations in that it does not take into account such factors as terms of trade, effect on cost of living, international market prices, etc.

Terms of Trade Approach (Parity Price Factor)

One other way of circumventing the weaknesses of the cost of production approach is based on the inter-sectoral terms of trade, which are determined by the ratio between the prices paid by the farmers for their farming and domestic requirements and prices received by the farmers for their products. Parity ratios (for input/output; farm products/consumer goods; total exports/ imports) are adopted as the main factors for fixing administered prices. In order to be able to determine these ratios, time data series are required for: i) products/commodities exchanged between the two sectors; ii) relative share of each product/community in the total consumption of products sold and commodities purchased by the agricultural sector; iii) prices at which the products/commodities are exchanged; and iv) volume of products sold and commodities purchased.

Although this approach has much to commend it, it nevertheless suffers from some limitations, especially unreliability of time data series, price indicators and the construction of indices which could underestimate or overestimate the rise in prices of non-agricultural goods and inflate or underestimate the rise in agricultural commodities. The usefulness of this approach very much depends on the coverage or comprehensiveness of the pattern of trade, reliability of weights used for constructing the price indices and availability of retail prices instead of wholesale prices. The use of the market price reduces the validity of this approach in a situation where market prices due to distortions in the economy or imperfections in the market structure fail to provide the correct signals. Its other weakness is that it does not take into consideration international market prices.

International Price Approach

To take account of the international price, the international price approach uses world equivalent prices as the 'true' economic or shadow price for valuing farm products, adopting fob price for exports and cif price for imports for calculating equivalent prices. By adjusting for internal marketing costs, farm gate prices are derived. This method, although commendable, also suffers from some limitations. Undoubtedly it is useful in providing a guide for resource allocation on the basis of comparative advantage principles and provides a relatively objective measure of the value of the commodity. This method, therefore, can be used to measure the trends in the purchasing power of export earnings. This method is intended to overcome the problem of border distortions.

It is, however, doubtful whether it is the best way of reflecting the world demand and supply situation for valuing agricultural products, given the various distortions in the world market. World market management for major commodities under international commodity agreements often distorts the world market situation. The other source of weakness of this method relates to distortions in exchange rates in which overvalued currencies undervalues farmers' produce and exports and favours imports, and vice versa, thereby distorting price incentives. Apart from these limitations, the method also does not take into consideration other important price determining factors such as cost of production, terms of trade effects on cost of living, prices of competing enterprises, etc.

Analysis of Marketing Costs and Margins

Marketing entails some transactions costs which depends on the different types and phases of the exchange process. In the first instance the exchange process requires transparency such as searching for participants, types, quantities and qualities of products to be marketed and sharing information (market transparency). If a large number of individuals are involved, the second transaction costs involve bargaining to determine the terms of trade and coordinating marketing activities. After obtaining a bargain, the third transaction costs involve monitoring and enforcing the agreement to ensure that the stipulated rights and obligations are respected by the contracting parties. These transaction costs covering searching, bargaining and agreement, policing and enforcement costs have to be coordinated under a set of rules which control behavioural responses to changes in the marketing environment. These sets of rules represent the institutional structure. Markets and their supporting organizations represent a body of rules and regulations which reduce uncertainty, and thus reduce transaction costs and allow exchange to take place in an orderly fashion. The institutional rules and regulations governing production and exchange link producers and consumers into a network. In the informal market this institutional infrastructure is lacking. The market is, therefore, an institution with the help of which the equilibrium price is attained. If demand happens to be higher than supply then the price will rise. If demand is lower than supply, the price falls. In other words, the main function of the market is to find that price that equals supply and demand (see Figure 33). The equilibrium price occurs at the intersection of demand and supply curves. As regards prices, the first and foremost function is the transmission of information to producers and consumers. When the price of a commodity is rising, it is a signal to consumers that the product is scarce in relation to production. At the same time it is a signal to producers that profitability from producing the commodity is increasing. The second function of prices is that they give incentives. Rising prices motivate producers to increase production. The third function of price is to redistribute income.

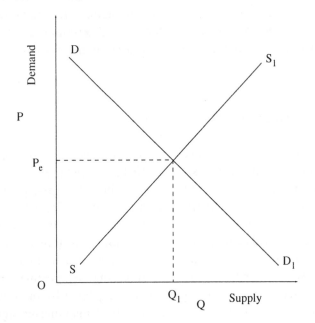

Figure 33 Demand and supply relations

Conceptual Framework

Despite the existence of several marketing organizations, the estimation of marketing, processing and transport costs and margins for major agricultural commodities, an important area in price policy analysis, has hitherto received scant attention compared to that given to the analysis of trends in produce prices, price instability and bias towards world market prices. And yet the performance of the agricultural marketing system is an important determinant of the relative income of farmers and the cost of food to urban consumers. Accurate estimates of marketing costs relative to commodity prices and trends in various components of marketing costs (transportation, processing, etc.) are basic requirements for a sound analysis of relationships between domestic producer prices at the farm gate with either cif import prices or fob export prices for food grains or export commodities. These comparisons require correction to account for domestic marketing, processing and transport costs. Which of these to include depends on whether or not the commodity in question is an import-competing or export commodity and whether or not the commodity is traded in processed or unprocessed form. In other words, the estimation of marketing costs should result in correct and consistent estimation of farm-to-retail marketing and processing margins as well as the estimation of nominal protection coefficients (NPCs) for import-competing and export crops.

Under competitive conditions, studies of market equilibrium are based on the analysis of supply and demand relationship. In studying supply response, the analyst is concerned with identifying factors related to the structure of the market within a particular economic and social setting which explain output behaviour and the price at which a given quantity is exchanged. As explained in chapter 2, the product can either be used as inputs (intermediate product markets) or can be sold directly to the consumers (final product markets). Just as supply is a function of many variables, demand also is influenced by many factors such as price, income, tastes, preferences, population growth, substitutes commodities, etc. The relationship between supply and demand forms the basis of market equilibrium analysis. In a competitive situation equilibrium occurs when a balance between supply and demand is reached, and when a price is established at which the quantities offered for sale equal the quantities demanded by consumers (Figure 34). Notationally this can be expressed as

$$Qd_t = Q_{st} \tag{2}$$

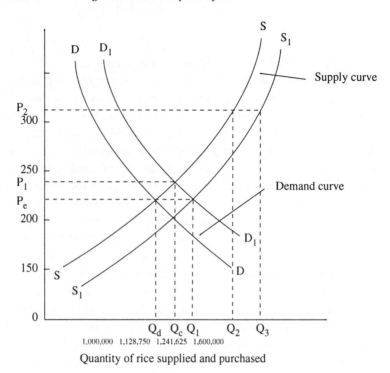

Figure 34 Demand and supply relationship

where

Qd_t represents quantities demanded at time t; and
Q_{st} represents quantities supplied at time t.

In a competitive market, at P_1 price, which is above the equilibrium price Pe, there is excess demand represented by OQ_c - OQ_d. Usually a government would like to put a ceiling on price as part of its deliberate anti-inflation policy and P_1 could be taken as the price ceiling. As shown in Figure 34, the quantity that will be demanded will be OQ_c but the quantity supplied is PO Q_d, leaving a shortfall of OQ_c - OQ_d. Because of shortage of supply, some consumers will be willing to pay a higher price than P_1. Competition among consumers will cause the price of the commodity to rise. In response to the price increase, producers react by increasing the supply until equilibrium price is re-established at quantity Q_c. Conversely if prices were set above P_c, say at P_2, as a deliberate policy to stimulate increased production, there will be excess supply OQ_3 - OQ_c. Competition between sellers will drive the price downwards until the equilibrium price and quantity demanded are re-established. It is, therefore, the interaction between consumers and producers in the market place which determines the market price and quantity exchanged.

The market is, therefore, just a medium within which transfer of ownership, creating time, place and form of utilities, takes place. The product is only part of the consumer demand but the assembly, transportation, processing, handling, distribution and other services between the farm and the consumer are important additional costs. The analysis can best be considered within the marketing conceptual framework which governs the spatial, endogenous and exogenous relationships. The spatial dimension could correspond to the rural and urban areas where marketing activities occur. These activities are viewed in terms of their interrelationships, involving economic, social, geographical and technical variables. These parameters and variables defining the interrelationships, form an endogenous system, while: i) market linkages with other rural market systems; ii) market linkages with urban and industrial areas; iii) international market linkages; and iv) government policies and programmes form the exogenous factors. In this conceptual framework, one can conceive a supply-demand curve at each point in the marketing channel where a product (or a factor) changes ownership with each new owner adding values to the product (factor). The difference between the price of the commodity as a product and as an input is known as the marketing margin which, in a competitive market, is determined by the interplay of supply and demand. The marketing margin between the farm and the consumer is the aggregation of intermediary demand functions.

Market Integration and Fragmentation

In perfect conditions the marketing margin would equal the cost of providing the services; seasonal price would equal the cost of storage; price difference from one place to another would represent transport cost. Often it is generalized that a small marketing margin is an indication of marketing efficiency and large margins are blamed on the exploitative activities of middlemen. This view can be erroneous because large margins do not necessarily imply inefficiency but rather are an indication of the number of marketing functions that have to be performed by middlemen. Because of the large margins, it is frequently felt that they may contribute to the low producer prices. This can be true if consumer prices are set at such low levels that they do not cover both production and marketing costs of the final products. This can happen in countries where the consumer price method is used to determine the producer price by working back from the price which the consumer may reasonably be expected to bear, taking into account supply and demand factors and cost of processing and selling. The expected consumer market prices can be estimated on the basis of time series data projection, and in the absence of these data it can be worked out on the basis of demand and supply situation in the country for the product or products. This methodology of producer price determination has been used in many developing countries. The method, however, has limitations since it does not take into account important price determining factors such as the terms of trade, prices of other competing crops, cost of production, world market situation, etc.

Spatial price differentials Using the consumer price approach in determining producer price is intended to keep urban food prices deliberately low, usually at the expense of the rural poor. Falling relative real food prices have obviously beneficial implications for domestic inflation rate and can be attributed to many factors, such as favourable climatic conditions, and not necessarily to price incentive. However, the maintenance of lower producer prices for food crops relative to competing tradeables usually constrains growth in food production.

Some of the misinterpretation of marketing margins could be resolved by testing for the stability of price spread between markets, and undertaking analysis of seasonal price behaviour, which could help to throw light onto the overall commodity market structure. Despite their usefulness, few marketing studies have empirically tested for market integration or fragmentation or analysed seasonal price behaviour of agricultural commodities. The existence of a stable price differential between two markets in which prices differ by no more than the cost of commodity arbitrage is an indication of a relatively competitive marketing, and any localized scarcity in one market is quickly eliminated by unaided response by traders to price differentials induced by such scarcity. This is because prices of a commodity do not behave independently but differ by no more that the cost of commodity arbitrage.

Intertemporal price differentials To isolate the seasonal price pattern of the commodities, the 12 month moving average prices can be used. It is a measure of the seasonal variation in the monthly prices around the trend line (or mean). It rests on the assumption that observed monthly price is responding to four forces: a long-term trend; a cyclical response; a seasonal factor; and random events. The random events could arise due to a number of factors, such as exploitative practices by middlemen or over/under estimation of post-harvest demand, all of which can cause the expected difference between seasonal high and seasonal low prices (storage cost) to vary from year to year and differ from actual price change. The random effects are finally eliminated by averaging the ratios (the appropriate monthly prices are divided by the corresponding centred trend figures to obtain seasonal ratios and random effects) over several years to give pure seasonal variation ratios.

Market integration The test for market integration assumes a homogenous commodity quality and the empirical analysis is based on the degree to which prices of the same commodity between markets are proportional or exhibit a stable price differential. The relationship can be established using simple bivariate regression between time series of prices for the commodity in different markets. It can notationally be written as:

$$P_1 = a + b P_2 \tag{3}$$

where

P_1 denotes price in one market;
P_2 denotes price in the other market;
a   represents the intercept; and
b   represents the coefficient.

If the coefficient is positive it denotes a strong correlation or market integration; while the intercept represent arbitrage cost. The estimation of the seasonal price behaviour of the commodity provides a further insight into the structure of the market. Because of the seasonality of agricultural production, crops are harvested at a particular time and the entire harvest must suffice for an whole year. Accordingly, a substantive part of the harvests have to be stored for use until the next harvest. Prices are, therefore, lowest at harvest time but gradually rise in line with storage costs until the next harvest. The sequence of monthly prices within each of the years is expected to be the same, reflecting the costs of storage which are expected to be covered by the differences between seasonal high and seasonal low.

Analysis of Costs and Margins

In dealing with a particular commodity, the analyst is usually confronted with two or more marketing channels, each performing the same function. For instance, there may be a cooperative, private or public marketing system, each of which purchases directly from farmers and delivers to processing facilities. Where estimated costs of each of these systems are available, they should be analysed separately. It should also be noted that there are many possible frameworks for the analysis of marketing performance. One approach is to start with a fixed quantity of a product at the consumer level and trade this back to the producer, determining what is required at various intermediate stages in terms of raw product to produce one kilogramme of the final product. This has always proved difficult, and so many analysts use an alternative approach, which starts with a fixed quantity of the farm product and works forward, tracing how much of the final consumer product is produced from a kilogramme of the farm product. This approach fits exactly with the calculation of the nominal protection coefficient.

Basic marketing data The tables used for basic marketing data fall into three sets: the first is used for tabulating basic marketing data and is the basis for the other two; the second is used for analysing total gross marketing margins; and the third lays out steps for the calculation of nominal protection coefficient. The examples given are intended to clarify some aspects of the use of the tables. The formats have been developed by FAO.

a) *Marketing margins: domestically traded commodity*

In the major paddy rice growing region of the country under consideration (Ghana), the domestic marketing channel is as follows: usually a farmer sells to an assembly trader in the rural market. The assembly trader, in turn, sells to a miller (if the product requires processing) who processes it into a product. This is then sold to a wholesaler who, in turn, sells to a retailer who finally sells to a final consumer. The domestic price structure could be as follows: the farmer receives cedis ($\cancel{c}$) 150 per kg for his paddy, but incurs cedis $\cancel{c}$20 per kg costs in transporting it to the market. The local trader transports the paddy to the mill at a cost of $\cancel{c}$50 per kg purchased. His handling costs are $\cancel{c}$20/kg, his return (profit) is $\cancel{c}$2.5/kg purchased. The miller produces 700g of rice and 300g of by-product (mainly bran) for each kg of paddy purchased. The by-product sells at $\cancel{c}$50/kg and the rice at $\cancel{c}$450/kg. His costs (all in $\cancel{c}$/kg of paddy) are as follows: packing materials ($\cancel{c}$6); hired labour ($\cancel{c}$15), amortization of capital ($\cancel{c}$15); fuel ($\cancel{c}$10) transport to wholesaler ($\cancel{c}$13), and other costs ($\cancel{c}$7); all totalling $\cancel{c}$65/kg of paddy and his profit is $\cancel{c}$5/kg of paddy processed.

The wholesaler sells his rice to a retailer for ₡500/kg. His transport and handling costs (including profits) amount to ₡15/kg and ₡25/kg of rice purchased respectively. The retailer sells to the consumer at ₡600/kg. He incurs losses of 5 per cent of the amount bought from the wholesaler, and handling costs (including returns to labour and capital) to ₡60/kg sold to the consumer. The following sections show the transformation of the domestic price structure as set out in Table 15.

Farmer's stage – Stage I. Column 1 is for information in terms of one kg of product in the form it enters that stage (i.e. paddy rice). Raw data are therefore, entered in this column. The farmer's selling price ₡150/kg is entered in row I.4, column 1 (for ease of reference this is usually written as I.4.1, i.e. stage I, line 4, column 1 or I.4.2, i.e. stage I, line 4, column 2, etc.). Transport costs amounting to ₡20/kg is entered in I.2.1. As there are no handling costs, the farm gate price is ₡130/kg (₡150–20). Column 2 records percentage weight change/loss during this stage. This is necessary to adjust prices and costs, normally given in ₡/kg of the product as it appears at that point in the marketing system, for changes in weight (usually losses). As costs should be expressed in terms of the commodity as it enters the marketing stage, this figure is entered opposite the selling price. At this stage there is no change in weight and so a conversion factor of 1.00 is entered in I.4.2. Column 3 shows the cumulative effect of weight/physical loss throughout the marketing system, to allow costs and prices to be expressed in terms of the original commodity at the farm gate. At this stage (the first) prices and costs are in this form already, and so 1.00 can be entered throughout column 3. Column 4 equals column 1 multiplied by column 3, i.e. prices and costs adjusted for the cumulative conversion factor. At this stage, this is the same as column 1. In general, column 4 contains the same data as column 1 except that whereas in column 1 the data are in a raw form and could be for different forms of the commodity, in column 4 the data are expressed in terms of units of the commodity as it leaves the farm. There are no by-products as yet and so column 5 is left blank.

Primary marketing stage – Stage II. Transport costs are entered in II.1.1 and the traders' profits and handling costs are amalgamated and inserted in II.2.1. There is no tax/subsidy and so II.2.3 is zero. Total costs and purchase prices are added together and inserted in II 4.1. If there were taxes or subsidies, these would be included in this total. The selling price is inserted in II.5.1. Because of the physical losses, the selling price is in different units from the costs, and therefore II.5.1 and II.4.1 should not be compared. There is a 3 per cent physical loss at this stage (i.e. for every kg entering only .97 kg leave). Therefore, the selling price has to be converted and is entered in II.5.2 (i.e.

1.00 - .03 = 0.97). At the beginning of stage II, the product is still as it was at the farm gate. Therefore, the cumulative conversion factor is still 1.00 until II.5.3 when it becomes 0.97 (1.00 x .97 = 0.97). The cumulative conversion factor for a stage is always obtained by *multiplying* the cumulative conversion factor for the previous stage by the conversion factor for the current stage. Column 4 is column 1 multiplied by column 3. If these are the only legitimate costs (including normal profit) charged for during this stage, II.4.4 should equal II.5.4. When this is not the case, it implies either that there are losses (when II.4.4 is greater than II.5.4), or excess profits (when II.5.4 is greater than II.4.4). The balancing item, which is filled in column 4 only, is, at this stage, zero (i.e. II.5.4 - II.4.4 = 0). There are no by-products.

Processing – Stage III. From the miller's cost figures, the analyst can derive figures for transport cost (III.1.1) of the cedis 13, handling (III.2.1) costs of ¢12 (packaging materials + other costs) and processing costs of ¢40 (hired labour, capital amortization, fuel). The miller's profits (¢15/kg) are added onto processing costs, as this is his major function. This gives gross processing costs of ¢55/kg. There are 300g of by-product sold at ¢50 per kg i.e. a value of ¢15/kg paddy processed. This accrues to the miller. This can be subtracted from the gross processing costs to give a figure for processing costs net of by-product (III.4.1). In this case we get a value of ¢40. This is largely because figures are often only available in this form, with no separate figures given for the by-product value. III.6.1 is calculated in a similar fashion to the previous stage (¢250 + ¢13 + ¢12 + ¢40) and the selling price inserted in III.7.1. In column 2, the conversion factor from paddy, (the input to the marketing process) to rice (the output) is inserted opposite the selling price (III.7.2). In column 3, the cumulative conversion factor at the end of the last stage is inserted, to enable the calculation of costs in terms of farm gate paddy, until the row for the selling price is reached, when III.7.2, the conversion factor for the stage, is multiplied to take account of the paddy/rice transformation. This gives (0.70 x 0.97) = 0.679 inserted in III.7.3. Column 4 is column 1 multiplied by column 3, with the exception of III.3A.4 and III.3B.4, the gross processing costs and the by-product value, which are implicitly included in the processing costs (net). Since III.6.4 equals III.7.4, the balancing item is zero. In column 5, the value of the by-product multiplied by the appropriate conversion factor (0.97) is inserted for use in future tables.

Wholesale – Stage IV. This is calculated as for previous stages, with profits being included in the handling costs obtained from the raw data. The cumulative factor from III.7.3 is carried forward to adjust costs in rows IV.1–4. The 2 per cent physical loss is accounted for by the conversion factor of

Table 15   Marketing costs and margins of domestically traded commodity

	Country	Commodity (1)	(2)	Year (3)	(4)	Currency (5)
Stages		Prices and costs associated with 1 kg produce at each stage	Conversion factor for each stage	Cumulative conversion factor	Prices and costs associated with 1 kg of original product	Total value of by-product is value of by-product included in profits
I	*Farmer's stage*					
1	Average price received by farmer at farm gate – 1 = 4 - 2 - 3	130.00		1.00	130.00	
2	Transport costs incurred by farmer from farm gate to selling point	20.00		1.00	20.00	
3	Handling costs incurred by farmer from farm gate to selling point	–		1.00	–	
4	Farmer selling price to primary trader	150.00	1.00	1.00	150.00	
II	*Primary marketing stage*					
1	Transport costs incurred by primary traders	50.00		1.00	50.00	
2	Handling costs incurred by primary traders	42.50		1.00	42.50	
3	Explicit tax/subsidy incurred by primary traders	–		1.00	–	
4	Total costs (II.1 + II.2 + II.3 + purchase price I.4)	242.50		1.00	242.50	
5	Selling price to processors/wholesalers	250.00	0.97	0.97	242.50	
6	Balancing item				–	
III	*Processing stage (if applicable)*					
1	Transport costs incurred by processor	13.00		0.97		
2	Handling costs incurred by processor	12.00		0.97		
3a	Processing costs (gross)	55.00		0.97		
3b	Value of by-products	15.00		0.97		
4	Processing costs (net of by-product value)	40.00		0.97		
5	Explicit tax/susbidy	–		0.97		
6	Total costs (III.1 + III.2 + III.4 + III.5 + purchase price II.5)					
7	Selling price to next stage	450.00	0.70	0.679	305.55	
8	Balancing item					
IV	*Wholesale stage*					
1	Transport costs incurred by wholesaler	15.00		0.679	10.20	
2	Handling costs incurred by wholesaler	25.00		0.679	17.00	
3	Explicit tax/subsidy	–		0.679	–	
4	Total costs (IV.1 + IV.2 + IV.3 + purchase price III.7)	490.00		0.679	332.50	
5	Selling price to retailer	500.00	0.98	0.665	332.50	
6	Balancing item				(10.2)	
V	*Retail stage*					
1	Transport costs incurred by retailer	–		0.665		
2	Handling costs incurred by retailer	63.20		0.665	42.00	
3	Explicit tax/subsidy	–		0.665	–	
4	Total costs (V.1 + V.2 + V.3 + purchase price IV.5)	563.20		0.665	374.50	
5	Selling price to final consumer	600.00		0.632	379.20	
6	Balancing item				4.70	

0.98 which, adjusted by the previous factor (0.679), gives the cumulative conversion factor (0.665) for the selling price. When column 4 is calculated (col. 3 x col. 1), it can be seen that IV.5.4 - IV.4.4 is negative (-0.02) showing a slight loss on the part of the wholesaler.

Retail – Stage V. Again this is filled in as above. The only implication is that handling costs are given in terms of kilogrammes of rice sold. As the analyst needs costs in terms of rice bought from the previous stage, the figure must be adjusted for the 5 per cent loss. Therefore, instead of ¢60/kg, 63.20/kg (i.e. ¢60/ x 0.95) is used. The figures show that the dealer makes a small excess profit.

b) *Marketing margins: export traded commodity*

The same commodity, paddy, is taken, but for a surplus year when, as well as being traded domestically, it is also exported. Paddy follows the same marketing chain as domestically-traded rice until it leaves the miller, who sells surplus rice to a government import/export agency at ¢20/kg. The government agency incurs transport costs of ¢20/kg of rice purchased, and handling and port charges of ¢30/kg up to the for point. Physical losses of 2 per cent occur. The for price is cedis 32/kg. Table 16 is exactly the same as Table 15 until stage IV. In this case, there is no wholesaler between the miller and the exporter, and so stage IV is left blank. Stage V is filled in the general manner described for Table 15. There are two points to note: firstly as stage IV is blank, the relevant purchase price for V.4.1 is III.7.1 not 5.1. In general where stages are missing, adjustments may have to be made according to the logic of the marketing system. Secondly, the balancing item is heavily negative, an indication that the government is implicitly subsidizing the exports of surplus rice quite substantially, even though no explicit subsidy is being given.

c) *Marketing margins: import traded commodity*

In a deficit year, the government agency imports rice at ¢350/kg cif. It incurs handling costs of ¢30/kg and transport costs from port to wholesaler of ¢20/kg. There are physical losses of 5 per cent and the rice is sold to the wholesaler at the same price as domestically produced rice, i.e. ¢150/kg. Thereafter, imported rice follows the same channel as domestically produced rice. Figures are filled in for column 1 in the same manner as before, but care must be taken with the cumulative conversion factor. Rice is being imported, but our calculations are in terms of farm gate product, i.e. paddy. The conversion

Table 16   Marketing costs and margins of export traded commodity

		Country	Commodity		Year	Currency	
			(1)	(2)	(3)	(4)	(5)
	Stages		Prices and costs associated with 1 kg produce at each stage	Conversion factor for each stage	Cumulative conversion factor	Prices and costs associated with 1 kg of original product	Total value of by-product is value of by-product included in profits
I	*Farmer's stage*						
1	Average price received by farmer at farm gate – 1 = 4 - 2 - 3		130.00		1.0	130.00	
2	Transport costs incurred by farmer from farm gate to selling point		20.00		1.00	20.00	
3	Handling costs incurred by farmer from farm gate to selling point		–		1.00	–	
4	Farmer selling price to primary trader		150.00	1.00	1.00	150.00	
II	*Primary marketing stage*						
1	Transport costs incurred by primary traders		50.00		1.00	50.00	
2	Handling costs incurred by primary traders		42.50		1.00	42.50	
3	Explicit tax/subsidy incurred by primary traders		–		1.00	–	
4	Total costs (II.1 + II.2 + II.3 + purchase price I.4)		242.50		1.00	242.50	
5	Selling price to processors/wholesalers		250.00	0.97	0.97	242.50	
6	Balancing item					–	
III	*Processing stage (if applicable)*						
1	Transport costs incurred by processor		13.00		0.97	12.60	
2	Handling costs incurred by processor		12.00		0.97	11.60	
3a	Processing costs (gross)		55.00		0.97	–	
3b	Value of by-products		15.00		0.97		
4	Processing costs (net of by-product value)		40.00		0.97	38.30	
5	Explicit tax/susbidy		–		0.97	–	
6	Total costs (III.1 + III.2 + III.4 + III.5 + purchase price II.5)					305.55	
7	Selling price to next stage		450.00	0.70	0.679	305.55	
8	Balancing item						
IV	*Wholesale stage*						
1	Transport costs incurred by wholesaler		–		–	–	
2	Handling costs incurred by wholesaler		–		–	–	
3	Explicit tax/subsidy		–		–	–	
4	Total costs (IV.1 + IV.2 + IV.3 + purchase price III.7)		–		–	–	
5	Selling price to retailer						
6	Balancing item						
V	*Retail stage*						
1	Transport costs incurred by exporter up to the FOB point		20.00		0.679	13.58	
2	Handling costs incurred by exporter up to the FOB point		30.00		0.679	20.37	
3	Explicit tax/subsidy		–		0.679	–	
4	Total costs (V.1 + V.2 + V.3 + purchase price IV.5)		500.00		0.679	339.50	
5	FOB price		320.00	0.98		212.80	
6	Balancing item					126.70	

factor from processing (0.70) is, therefore, used as the starting point of the table, to convert everything to paddy equivalents. From then on, calculations proceed as before. Stages II and III are blank; stages IV and V are similar to those of Table 15 with the exception of the conversion factors which will differ slightly because of different loss rates.

Analysis of gross marketing margins The purpose of this set of tables (16, 17 and 18) is to give data which can be used in a comparative sense, either between countries or across time, to show the relative importance, differences and trends at individual stages, or components of the marketing margin.

a) Domestically traded commodity – Table 18

The data for this table are taken exclusively from columns 4 and 5 of Table 15. The first column of Table 18a is filled out by adding together, for each stage, all the marketing costs and charges (this does not equal the total costs row because it does not include the purchase price of the commodity) plus any by-product value associated with that stage, plus the balancing item (if the balancing is negative then its absolute value should be subtracted). The total gross margin is the sum of all of the individual stage margins, and should be equal to the selling price to the consumer (as shown in column 4) plus the total value of by-products (as shown in column 5) minus the farm gate price (I.1.4). Columns 2 and 3 of Table 18a are simply column 1 expressed firstly as a percentage of the farm gate price, and secondly as a percentage of the total gross margin. The second part of Table 18a (columns 4–6) is calculated in a similar manner with the following exceptions: taxes, subsidies and the balancing item are not included in the marketing costs; and the gross margin equals the selling price to the consumer (V.5.4) plus the total value of by-products minus the total value of taxes, subsidies and the balancing item for all stages minus the farm gate price. Table 18b is calculated by adding up the entries under the appropriate headings for all stages in the marketing system. The total gross margins should be the same for Tables 18a and b.

b) Export traded commodity – Table 19

The data for this is taken from Table 16. The main points to note from this example are the absence of one of the marketing stages (therefore, a blank row against whole price and margins) and negative processor – fob margin as a result of heavy subsidization. The second part of the table (excluding taxes/

Table 17 Marketing costs and margins of imported traded commodity

	Country	Commodity		Year		Currency
		(1)	(2)	(3)	(4)	(5)
Stages		Prices and costs associated with 1 kg produce at each stage	Conversion factor for each stage	Cumulative conversion factor	Prices and costs associated with 1 kg of original product	Total value of by-product is value of by-product included in profits
I	*Import stage*					
1	CIF price	350.00		0.70	245.00	
2	Transport costs incurred by importer	30.00		0.70	21.00	
3	Transport costs from port to next stage	20.00		0.70	14.00	
4	Explicit tax/subsidy	–		0.70	–	
5	Total costs (I.2 + I.3 + I.4 + purchase price I.1)	400.00		0.70	280.00	
6	Importer selling price next stage	450.00	0.95	0.665	299.25	
7	Balancing item				19.25	
II	*Wholesale stage (if applicable)*					
1	Transport costs incurred by wholesaler					
2	Handling costs incurred by wholesaler					
3	Explicit tax/subsidy					
4	Total costs (II.1 + II.2 + II.3 + purchase price I.4)					
5	Wholesale selling price					
6	Balancing item					
III	*Processing stage (if applicable)*					
1	Transport costs incurred by wholesaler					
2	Handling costs incurred by wholesaler					
3a	Processing costs (gross)					
3b	Value of by-products					
4	Processing costs (net)					
5	Explicit tax/susbidy					
6	Total costs (III.1 + III.2 + III.3 + III.5 + purchase price II.5)					
7	Selling price to next stage					
8	Balancing item					
IV	*Wholesale stage*					
1	Transport costs incurred by wholesaler	150.00		0.665	9.98	
2	Handling costs incurred by wholesaler	250.00		0.665	16.62	
3	Explicit tax/subsidy	–		0.665	–	
4	Total costs (IV.1 + IV.2 + IV.3 + purchase price III.7)	490.00		0.665	325.85	
5	Selling price to retailer	500.00	0.98	0.653	326.00	
6	Balancing item					
V	*Retail stage*					
1	Transport costs incurred by retailer					
2	Handling costs incurred by retailer	63.20		0.652	–	
3	Explicit tax/subsidy	–		0.652	41.21	
4	Total costs (V.1 + V.2 + V.3 + purchase price IV.5)	563.20		0.652	367.21	
5	Selling price to final consumer	600.00	0.95	0.619	371.40	
6	Balancing item				4.19	

Table 18   Marketing margins on domestically traded commodity

Country: Commodity: Year:

a   Composition of total margin by marketing stage

	Including taxes/subsidies and balancing item			Excluding taxes/subsidies and balancing item		
	Marketing charges C	As % of farm gate price	As % of total gross margin	Marketing charges C	As % of farm gate price	As % of total gross margin
Farm stage	20.00	15.38	7.58	20.00	15.38	7.72
Primary trader stage	92.50	71.15	35.08	92.50	71.15	35.69
Processor stage	77.55	59.65	29.41	77.55	59.65	29.92
Wholesaler stage	27.00	20.73	10.22	27.15	20.88	10.47
Retailer stage	46.70	35.92	17.71	42.00	32.31	16.20
Total gross margin	263.70	202.85	100.00	259.20	199.38	100.00
Farm gate price	130.00	100.00		130.00	100.00	

b   Composition of total margin marketing component

	Including taxes/subsidies and balancing item			Excluding taxes/subsidies and balancing item	
	Marketing charges C	As % of farm gate price	As % of total gross margin	Marketing charges C	As % of total gross margin
Transport	92.80	71.38	35.19	92.80	35.80
Handling	113.10	87.00	42.89	113.10	43.63
Processing (net)	38.80	29.85	14.71	38.80	14.97
By-product value	14.50	11.15	5.50	14.50	5.60
Taxes/subsidies					
Balancing item	4.50	3.46	1.71		
Total gross margin	263.70	202.85	100.00	259.20	100.00
Farm gate price	130.00	100.00		130.00	

subsidies and the balancing item) gives a much better idea of the marketing costs.

c) *Imported commodities – Table 20*

The data for this are taken from Table 17 and the same procedure is followed as for the other tables in the second set.

Table 19   Marketing margins on exported traded commodity

Country: Commodity: Year:

a   *Composition of total margin by marketing stage*

	Including taxes/subsidies and balancing item			Excluding taxes/subsidies and balancing item		
	Marketing charges C	As % of farm gate price	As % of total gross margin	Marketing charges C	As % of farm gate price	As % of total gross margin
Farm stage	20.00	15.38	20.55	20.00	8.93	7.72
Primary trader stage	92.50	71.15	95.07	92.50	71.15	41.29
Processor stage	77.55	59.65	79.70	77.55	59.65	32.62
Wholesaler stage						
FOB price	93.00	(71.35)	(95.32)	33.95	26.12	15.16
Total gross margin	97.30	74.85	100.00	224.00	172.31	100.00
Farm gate price	130.00	100.00		130.00	100.00	

b   *Composition of total margin marketing component*

	Including taxes/subsidies and balancing item			Excluding taxes/subsidies and balancing item	
	Marketing charges C	As % of farm gate price	As % of total gross margin	Marketing charges C	As % of total gross margin
Transport	96.18	73.98	114.50	96.18	40.48
Handling	74.47	57.28	104.82	74.47	37.06
Processing (net)	38.80	29.85	46.19	38.80	16.33
By-product value	14.50	11.15	17.26	14.50	6.10
Taxes/subsidies					
Balancing item	(126.70)	(97.46)	(182.83)		
Total gross margin	97.30	202.85	100.00	224.00	100.00
Farm gate price	130.00	100.00		130.00	

Calculation of Nominal Protection Coefficient

One of the important uses to which marketing cost data can be put, in the area of price policy, is to help achieve a more accurate estimation of nominal protection coefficients. In a competitive world, farmers would receive the equivalent of world prices for their commodities, allowing for appropriate marketing costs to and from the port. The nominal protection coefficient (NPC)

Table 20   Marketing margins on imported commodity

Country: Commodity: Year:

a   *Composition of total margin by marketing stage*

	Including taxes/subsidies and balancing item			Excluding taxes/subsidies and balancing item		
	Marketing charges C	As % of farm gate price	As % of total gross margin	Marketing charges C	As % of farm gate price	As % of total gross margin
Importer stage	542.50	22.14	42.92	35.00	14.29	34.04
Processor stage (if applicable)						
Wholesaler stage (if applicable)	26.75	10.92	21.16	26.60	10.86	25.87
Retailer stage	45.40	18.53	35.92	41.21	16.82	40.08
Total gross margin	126.40	51.59	100.00	102.81	41.96	100.00
Farm gate price	240.50	100.00		240.50	100.00	

b   *Composition of total margin marketing component*

	Including taxes/subsidies and balancing item			Excluding taxes/subsidies and balancing item		
	Marketing charges C	As % of farm gate price	As % of total gross margin	Marketing charges C	As % of total gross margin
Transport	23.98	9.79	18.98	23.98	23.32
Handling	78.83	32.18	62.37	78.83	76.68
Processing (net)					
By-product value					
Taxes/subsidies					
Balancing item	23.59	9.78	18.67		
Total gross margin	126.40	51.59	100.00	102.01	100.00
CIF price	245.00	100.00		245.00	

is a way of measuring the extent to which this is the case. Often, the farm gate price is measured directly against the world (or more accurately, border) price without making adjustments for marketing costs – hereafter called the crude NPC. As the following example will show, the *adjusted* (for marketing costs) NPC can be very different. An adjusted NPC of 1 indicates that the farmer is receiving the border equivalent price, and of less than 1 that he is getting less than the border equivalent price, and vice versa. These are based on the same data as reported in Table 21a and b. The details of the method for calculating NPCs varies according to whether domestic production is competing with imports or is being exported, and whether the commodity is traded in processed or unprocessed form. There are four sections to the table, one for each possibility.

In the example, the analyst is dealing with a country which is marginally self-sufficient in rice, but sometimes imports and exports. The commodity is traded in processed form. Two NPCs are calculated (the appropriate sections of the table are A and C). Where a commodity is clearly imported, or exported, only one section of the table is necessary but the difference in NPC for import-competing and export conditions for the same commodity can be startling, so it is useful to calculate both where a country is marginally self-sufficient in the commodity, as it eliminates one of the dilemmas in pricing policy. Part A of the table shows the import-competing NPC. For a processed commodity, imports compete with domestic production directly at the wholesale level in most countries, and the table has been devised on this assumption. Thus, the costs of moving the imported commodity from cif port to the wholesaler have to be added to the cif price to get the cost to the wholesaler. Then the various costs of moving paddy from the farmer through the processor to the wholesaler have to be *subtracted* to get the farm gate equivalent of the border price. Note that taxes/subsidies and the balancing item are not included in this calculation. This is because they are not true costs, in the economic sense, and are, in fact, the main reason the farmer may not receive the farm gate equivalent of the border price. Net processing costs are used in this calculation, because this implicitly adds in the value of the by-product to the price of the imported rice.

The table gives the source, in terms of the first set of tables, where the information should be found. Where there are stages in the tables which do not exist in the actual marketing system one is analysing, care will have to be taken to follow through the logic of the exercise. At the bottom of the table, both the crude and the adjusted NPC are calculated, as discussed above. In this example, the crude NPC would indicate that the farmer is getting less than his due, whereas the adjusted NPC shows a considerable degree of protection.

Section C shows the calculation for rice as an export crop. For an export crop, the point of comparison is with the fob price at the port. Therefore, all marketing costs are subtracted from the fob price. Other than this, the section is similar to section A. The example given here gives a slightly unusual case, where costs to get to the port are almost as much as the fob price. This results in a very small farm gate equivalent of border price and a very high adjusted

Table 21a   Nominal protection coefficient

Country: Commodity: Year: Currency:

A   Commodity imported in processed form   **Source: Tables**

	CIF price		245.00	19, I.1.4
C =	CIF price (adjusted for quality difference)	245.00		
	+ unloading/port handling costs	+21.00	= 266.00	19, I.2.4
	+ transport from port to wholesaler/importer	+14.00	= 280.00	19, I.3.4
	- transport from processor to wholesaler	-26.00	= 267.40	17, III.1.4
	- handling costs at processing stage	-11.60	= 255.80	17, III.2.4
	- processing costs (net)	-38.80	= 217.00	17, III.4.4
	- transport from local trader to processor	-50.00	= 167.00	17, II.1.4
	- handling costs at local trader stage	-45.00	= 124.50	17, II.2.4
	- transport from farm to local trader	-20.00	= 104.50	17, I.2.4
	- handling costs of farmer (ex-farm)	0	104.50	17, I.3.4
E =	farm gate equivalent of border price		104.50	
F =	actual farm gate price		130.00	17, I.1.4

Crude NPC = F/C = 130.00/245.00 = 0.53
Adjusted NPC F/E = 130.00/124.50 = 1.24

B   Commodity imported in unprocessed form

CIF price

Source: Tables

(C)	CIF price (adjusted for quality difference)	19, I.1.4
	+ unloading/port handling costs	19, I.2.4
	+ transport from port to processor/wholesaler	19, I.3.4
	- transport from local trader to processor	17, II.1.4
	- handling costs at local trader stage	17, II.2.4
	- transport from farmer to local trader	17, I.2.4
	- handling costs of farmer (ex-farm)	17, I.3.4
(E)	Farm gate equivalent of border price	
(F)	Actual farmer price	17.I.1.4

Crude NPC = F/C =
Adjusted NPC = F/E =

Table 21b Nominal protection coefficient

Country: Commodity: Year: Currency:

C   Commodity imported in processed form   Source: Tables

C =	FOB price		212.80	18.V.5.4
	- loading/port handling costs	-20.37	192.43	18.V.2.4
	- transport from processor to port	-(13.58-12.60)	166.25	18, V.1.4 + III.1.4
	- handling costs at processing stage	-11.60	154.65	17,III.2.4
	- processing costs (net)	-38.80	115.55	17, III.4.4
	- transport from local trader to processor	-50.00	65.85	17, II.1.4
	- handling costs at local trader stage	-42.50	23.35	17, II.2.4
	- transport from farm to local trader	-20.00	3.35	17, I.2.4
	- handling costs of farmer (ex-farm)			17, I.3.4
E =	farm gate equivalent of border price		104.50	
F =	actual farm gate price		130.00	17.I.1.4

Crude NPC = F/C = 130.00/
Adjusted NPC F/E = 130.00/

D   Commodity exported in unprocessed form   Source: Tables

C	FOB price	19, V.5.4
	- loading/port handling costs	19, V.2.4
	- transport from wholesaler/trader to port	19, V.i.4 + IV.1.4
	- transport from local trader to wholesaler	17, II.1.4
	- handling costs at local trader stage	17, II.2.4
	- transport from farmer to local trader	17, I.2.4
	- handling costs of farmer (ex-farm)	17, I.3.4
E	Farm gate equivalent of border price	
F	Actual farmer price	17.I.1.4

Crude NPC = F/C =
Adjusted NPC = F/E =

NPC, implying substantial subsidization of the rice exports. Where rice is traded in an unprocessed form, sections B and D would be filled in. The major difference here is that since an unprocessed domestic commodity is competing with an unprocessed commodity on the world market, domestic processing costs are irrelevant. For example, imported wheat and domestically produced wheat 'meet' at the mill door, prior to processing.

It is extremely important to trace out the marketing channels used for imported commodities and work out at what point this first coincides with the channel used for domestic product. This is the point at which the link between the domestically produced and imported commodity has to be made. Marketing costs of the imported commodity should be added onto this point and then the total reduced by the marketing costs of the domestically produced product to that same point in order to get an accurate estimate of the farm gate equivalent of the border price. If data do not exist back to the level of the farm gate, but only to a buying station, one has to calculate the NPC on that basis, but go as far back to the farm gate as possible.

6 Effects of Trade and Exchange Rate Policies on Incentive Structure

Conceptual Framework

The principal objective of influencing the endogenous variables is to stimulate increases in output in order to satisfy demand. Endogenous variables (the dependent variables) respond to exogenous variables such as policies and non-policy factors. A persistent imbalance between absorption (aggregate domestic demand) and aggregate supply is reflected in the deterioration of the external balance of payment position, an acceleration in domestic inflation and slower rate of economic growth. To regain the external balance, it is necessary to bring an orderly adjustment between absorption and aggregate supply either by reducing aggregate domestic demand, or by increasing domestic output, or both. On the supply side, this objective can be achieved through measures that increase the incentive or ability of the domestic productive sector to supply real goods and services at a given level of aggregate nominal domestic demand. Such policies are categorized into: i) those designed to increase current output by improving the efficiency with which the internal factors of production (land, labour, capital) are utilized and allocated to competing uses. They include measures which reduce distortions that drive a wedge between prices and marginal costs arising principally from price controls, imperfect competition, taxes, subsidies, and trade restrictions; ii) the other measures concern long-run growth of the productive base of the economy by stimulating domestic saving and investment; intellectual investment, technological innovation and human capital development, creating an environment conducive to the inflow of foreign direct investment or increased development assistance. The two policies' measures are closely interrelated because policies that increase current output also lead to a larger flow of domestic saving and a higher rate of growth of capacity output.

Supply-oriented policies to improve the allocation of given productive

261

resources include measures that restrict resource mobility. There are two such aspects: i) the financial system, public sector enterprises, producer pricing and agricultural marketing, and labour markets including other measures such as the exchange and trade systems, taxes and public expenditures. The financial system plays a cardinal role in mobilizing savings and channelling them to the most efficient investment. Distortionary interventions in the financial system, which include control on deposit and lending rates (low, negative or positive), could lead to credit rationing resulting in the increase in the cost of financial intermediation, the growth of unofficial credit market and resource allocation problem, and subsidized interest rate which overburdens government budgetary resources and distorts allocation of financial resources; ii) the use of credit limits for individual banks to control monetary aggregates.

Public enterprises suffer from a range of problems resulting in a wide-ranging subsidization because of inadequate pricing policies, overstaffing and poor investment policies. Implicit subsidies usually arise from preferential treatment of these public entities in the allocation of credit, foreign exchange, and noncompetitive procurement and marketing policies. Poor financial performance has direct implication for government finance, credit and monetary aggregates and the balance of payment principally because of their large and growing deficits contributing to rising inflationary pressure, a crowding-out of the private sector and a deterioration of the balance of payment, and a direct bearing on economic growth. Often, underpricing of inputs produced by the public enterprises for the domestic private sector raises arbitrarily the profitability of certain sectors and, therefore, gives a false signal as to the areas of the economy that should receive emphasis in the overall development strategy.

Self-sustained economic growth depends on consumption and investment, and the nature and quality of capital stock being added. This requires policies that favour investments and savings to expand the productive base of the economy which can be achieved by increasing the rate of investment and improving its quality. Increasing investment can be improved or constrained by the availability or shortage of savings. This objective can be realized through policies such as the elimination of distortions in the financial markets targeted at mobilizing domestic private capital formation to enlarge the rate of output capacity. The stability of the macroeconomic policies are also needed to create an atmosphere of confidence in the future economy and its management in order to avoid capital flight, etc.

Improvement in the quality of investment as the change in gross domestic product (GDP) to investment is influenced by real interest rates that reflect real rates of return on investments, relative costs and prices that represent real underlying scarcities, including exchange, which that reflects the true cost of foreign exchange, intellectual investment, and investment in infrastructure such as land development for agricultural production, resource conservation to protect the natural resource base, improvement in transport infrastructure to improve internal distributive system. As regards private savings and improving their investment allocation, this depends on the elimination of distortions in financial markets, removal of tax disincentives and maintaining macroeconomic stability. Substituting income for consumption taxes may encourage savings, although its general applicability remains debatable on account of social equity implications.

The structure of the labour market and the price obtained in the market, the real wage, are crucial in determining the allocation of internal factors of production and maintaining international competitiveness. Distortions in the labour markets and prices arise from: i) wage-setting policy such as the minimum wage that has the effect of reducing real wage flexibility; ii) segmented labour markets caused often by not being subjected to financial discipline which leads to distortions and rigidity in the markets; iii) and the public sector as a residual employer resulting in an increase in the wage bill and leading to over-employment of labour compared to non-labour inputs. This is likely to have adverse implications far beyond the rate of increase in productivity and is likely to hurt both growth and labour intensity, which in turn impedes growth in employment.

Intervention in agricultural pricing and marketing was a common practice which took various forms, such as state control of domestic and international marketing, regulation of producer and consumer prices, and taxation of exports and imports. Usually, the interventions were targeted at achieving a wide range of economic and social objectives, such as stabilizing producer prices or income, influencing the distribution of income between socioeconomic groups, raising tax revenue and strengthening food security status. These interventions usually result in severe distortions in the level and structure of domestic producer and consumer prices, with negative impacts on output and production efficiency.

Determinants of Exchange Rates

Exchange Rate Determination

The exchange rate is one of the key variables in the management of the economy. Many methods are employed in the determination of exchange rate but the simplest one, easy to understand, despite its admitted weaknesses, is the purchasing power parity (PPP). The PPP theory, based on the concept of the law of one price (LOOP), is derived essentially from a monetary approach to balance of payments adjustment. To the extent, for example, that monetary expansion generated a more rapid rate of inflation than existed in the rest of the world in one country, and exchange rate remained fixed, the prices of non-tradeables would rise more rapidly than the prices of tradeables, causing consumers to shift towards the consumption of tradeables (imports) and producers to move towards the direction of producing more non-tradeables. The current account would move into deficit under these circumstances. In the absence of government price or trade policy, and assuming no structural changes, equilibrium in the long run would be achieved through some combination of a movement in the exchange rate and in the absolute level of prices in the country compared with its major trading partners that would offset the original price changes caused by monetary expansion and inflation.

Nominal exchange rate The simplest definition of an exchange rate is the nominal exchange rate, which is the domestic currency price of a unit of foreign currency. If Ghana, for instance, is trading with the United States, it means the number of cedis (the Ghanian currency) needed to buy one US dollar. Alternatively the exchange rate can be expressed in terms of how many US dollars can buy one Ghanian cedi (₵). Thus

$$\text{the nominal exchange rate} = \frac{₵}{\$} = \frac{₵2.75}{1} = ₵2.75$$

or

$$\frac{\$}{₵} = \frac{1}{2.75} = 0.36$$

This domestic exchange rate defined in terms of a single foreign currency is termed a bilateral exchange rate (i.e. the rate at which two currencies are exchanged for each other). This is known as the absolute version of exchange rate. In this example, if the amount of cedis required to buy one US dollar increases from ₵2.75 to ₵30, as it did in January 1982, the cedi is taken as being depreciated because more of it is required to buy one US dollar. In terms of nominal exchange rate, higher values signify a depreciation. Meanwhile the US dollar is taken as having appreciated because only 0.03 US dollars are required to buy a cedi.

Hence, if it is taken that a nominal exchange rate is the price of a unit of foreign currency in domestic currency, an increase in its exchange rate is a depreciation of the domestic currency, which will be reflected in the rise of domestic prices. A decrease in the nominal exchange rate is an appreciation of the domestic currency. The nominal exchange rate may be either officially and/or unofficially determined. If an exchange market is not officially sanctioned it is regarded as a parallel market. If there are trade restrictions and strict enforcement of currency regulations, local people where the domestic currency is depreciating will lose confidence in the currency. Pressures will build up which ultimately will lead to a parallel market pricing for either the good or foreign currency. For instance, in the 1970s, when the cedi was overvalued, cocoa producers smuggled their products to neighbouring Togo and Côte d'Ivoire, where the currency (the CFA) was not overvalued. A parallel market or a parallel foreign exchange system is one in which transactions in foreign currency take place at more than one exchange rate, one of the prevailing rates being legal or illegal, freely floating, market-determined rate (the parallel exchange rate). This usually entails some parallel premium, which is the percentage by which the parallel exchange rate exceeds the official exchange rate.

There are two major exchange rate systems in which the government, to limit the short-term effects of depreciation of the exchange rate on domestic prices, assigns an important share of current account transactions to a commercial exchange rate (official rate) and all legal transactions, including capital account transactions, to officially floating financial exchange rate. The commercial rate is usually pegged or managed. By pegging to a basket of currencies as an alternative approach to exchange rate policy determination, a country is able to avoid large swings in respect to several trading partners' currencies, and is thus able to stabilize its nominal effective exchange rate and avoid price instability resulting from exchange rate changes.

In Sub-Saharan Africa, the decision either to produce for the domestic and/or the export markets and to consume domestic or imported products, as well as the decision to save and invest, has been influenced by the real exchange rate. Policies for exchange rate management in most countries in Sub-Saharan Africa, except the CFA zone, where currency values are related to the French franc, can be grouped into three periods: inactive rate (1965–73); active rate but pegged (1974–79); and active adustable rate since 1980.

Often, to counteract the adverse effects of external shocks, Sub-Saharan African countries reacted by cutting down imports to ease pressure on the balance of payments. This was achieved through licensing, quantitative restrictions, including outright bans on certain commodities, heavy import duties, etc., and foreign exchange rationing as a means of regulating the inflow of trade. These measures, although intended to solve the balance of payments difficulties, often exacerbated the very problem the countries had intended to solve. By restricting imports and availability of foreign exchange, strong competitive parallel markets usually developed in foreign currency. Since most central banks were not able to meet all demand for foreign exchange, or borrow to defend the official exchange rate, those whose demand would not be met were prepared to offer prices above the official exchange rates. The rapid erosion of the value of domestic currency by the high domestic inflation, and the currency subsequent over-evaluation, undermined the confidence of the local currency holders. The combination of the collapse of the value of domestic currency and cheaper imports than the domestic substitute, encouraged the emergence of strong parallel markets whose transactions were carried out by privileged customers (foreigners, diplomats, exporters/importers and nationals living abroad). Expatriate nationals repatriated their earnings not through official channels but through the parallel markets. Within the countries themselves, those who had access to foreign exchange were encouraged to sell in the parallel markets. The windfall gains made in the transactions provided additional incentive to purchase foreign exchange from that market. Other means of acquiring foreign exchange included underpricing the value of imports or participating in cross-border unrecorded trade (smuggling). Diverting foreign exchange from official channels, including other unofficial transactions, actually exacerbated the foreign reserve situation of many countries, especially the non-CFA countries. As the tax base was also eroded by tax evasion, these parallel market transactions, therefore, contributed to a reduction in revenue generation but increased expenditures – thus undermining the financial viability of public finance.

Meanwhile at the regional level, since the late 1950s, the African governments demonstrated sustained interest in efforts to expand African trade as evidenced by the conclusion of several multilateral trade agreements, the establishment of a number of sub-regional preferential trade agreements and the creation of sub-regional payments and clearing arrangements in central, eastern, southern and western Africa. To provide some sense of direction to the economic development of their countries, independent African governments relied heavily on the use of legislative and regulatory means to control growth in international and intra-African trade transactions. The first set of these measures comprised the use of high tariffs such as import and export duties, and other domestic taxes (excise and consumption taxes) which had equivalent effects as tariffs. These taxes increased the costs of production and the effect of restraining growth of imports and exports. They also generated inflation. These price distortions were frequently reflected in an overvalued exchange rate in the absence of periodic domestic price adjustments and low or even negative interest rates, a situation that discouraged domestic savings, distorted investment decisions and made export uncompetitive. Consequently, exchange rate and price distortions, in turn, encouraged smuggling and unrecorded trade transactions. In the same way, the imposition of high export duties inhibited domestic production for exports.

Economic management in Africa also included stringent trade and exchange control practices such as restrictions on payment for imports, invisible and capital transfers, etc. These measures were enforced through quantitative import and export limitations through licensing, advance import deposits, and keeping the domestic currency inconvertible. This resulted in unrecorded taxes. Hence, the emergence of restrictive trade practices, undervaluation of exports and disharmonized exchange rates and interest rates, resulted in a situation that did not promote inter-regional and intra-African trade and dampened efforts to produce for exports.

Lack of harmonization of economic policy will continue to discourage trade because, for instance, in a country with an overvalued domestic currency, imports from countries with undervalued domestic exchange rates were cheaper than they ought to be. On the other hand, in countries with an under-valued exchange rate regime, importers lost when they traded with countries with overvalued exchange rates. Consequently the effects of exchange rate misalignment discouraged legal trade among countries. It encouraged the emergence of parallel markets which in turn introduced other complications: i) unrecorded trade resulting in tax evasion (revenue from custom and export duties); and ii) transfer of wealth (transfer of foreign exchange) from one country to another. In terms of export commodities, the transfer of wealth could be measured as the difference between the domestic producer price in the country receiving the smuggled commodities and the price ruling on the world market multiplied by the quantity of the smuggled goods.

Real exchange rate The real exchange rate (RER), as opposed to the nominal exchange rate (NER), attempts to measure the rate at which goods and services are exchanged between the domestic economy and the outside world. This is computed by adjusting the nominal exchange rate to the differentials in prices at home and abroad. Let us assume that a decline in the number of units of a commodity that has resulted in domestic price increases was more gradual in the United States than in Ghana. In Ghana the units declined from 10,000 to 8,750 and then to 7,875 units, the increase in the price level averaged 12 per cent during the first decline and to 15 per cent during second fall. In the USA the respective declines were from 10,000 to 9,165 and then to 9,105 units of the commodity, or 8 and 10 per cent rise in prices respectively. If Ghana insists on exchanging its currency at ₵2.75 to the US dollar, it means that the Ghanian currency will be above its true value by 3 per cent. This means that the Ghanian cedi is overvalued by

$$\frac{(₵2.75 \times 3)}{100} = ₵0.0825 \; (₵2.75 + \frac{2.75 \times 3}{100}) = ₵2.8325$$

meanwhile the US dollar will also be overvalued by 2 per cent or

$$(\$1 + \frac{1 \times 2}{100}) = \$1.02$$

In this instance, if no adjustment is made in the exchange rate, the US dollar vis-à-vis the Ghanian cedi will be undervalued. The new exchange rate should be ₵2.8325 to $1.02, i.e.

$$\$1 = \frac{2.8325}{1.02} = ₵2.78$$

$$\text{or } ₵1 = \frac{1.02}{2.8325} = \$0.36$$

This means that to maintain purchasing power parity of the Ghanian cedi with the US dollar, the Ghanian currency must be adjusted by the ratio of price differentials.

$$(\frac{3}{12} \div \frac{2}{10}) \frac{2.78}{1.02} + 2.78 = (0.25 \div 0.20) \, 2.7255 + 2.78$$

$$= 1.25 \times 2.696 + 2.78 = 3.4068 + 2.78 = 6.1875$$

In this case it can be seen that the nominal exchange rate is different from ₵2.78 to the dollar. Adjusting the exchange rate by the price differentials based on the ratio of price increase to the price level the previous year, yields this new exchange rate of ₡6.1875 to the dollar. However, if the adjustment was based on the ratio of the price increase to the new price level, the exchange rate would be

$$\frac{\overline{3}}{15/2} \times \frac{2.75}{1.02} + 2.75 = ₡6.06 \text{ to the dollar}$$

In Ghana, when the cedi was devalued from ₡2.75 to the dollar to approximately ₡30 to the dollar, different rates of the extent of depreciation were given – some stating that it was 900 per cent while others thought the cedi was depreciated by 91 per cent. The exchange rate of a currency is given by the change in the exchange rate in the numerator (in this case the cedi) to the exchange rate of the foreign currency in this case the US dollar (the denominator). Depending on what exchange rate is used in the denominator (the old or the new), the resulting ratio would be radically different:

$$Eo = 2.75 \qquad En = 30, \qquad \text{thus } rE = En - Eo = 27.75$$

$$rE = \frac{27.25}{2.75} \times 100 = ₡991 \text{ or } rE = \frac{27.25}{30} \times 100 = 91$$

where

    Eo   is old exchange rate;
    En   new exchange rate; and
    rE   the adjusted exchange rate.

Based on the above definition, the correct r E was 91 per cent. In our example the cedi has depreciated by 54 per cent against the US dollar Eo = ₡2.78, En = 6.06.
    Thus r E = 6.06 - 2.78 = ₡3.28

$$r E = \frac{3.28}{6.06} \times 100 = 54 \text{ per cent}$$

This suggests that there is a relationship between price levels and exchange rate, or at least between changes in price levels and the exchange rate. Accordingly, the relative version of the purchasing power parity concept is a percentage change in exchange rate which will be equal to the ratio of differences between the percentage changes in the two price levels. The real exchange rate can thus be determined using this formula:

$$r Rt + 1 = \frac{\dfrac{Pt + 1}{P}}{\dfrac{P^*t + 1}{P^*t}} \tag{1}$$

where

r Rt   denotes real exchange rate during period, t; and
r Rt + 1 denotes the real exchange rate during the following period (t + 1).

Similarly

Pt and Pt + 1 represent price levels in the home country during period t
    and t + 1 respectively; and
P*t and P*t + 1 representing price levels in the foreign country.

Thus this formula has been employed in determining the appropriate level of the exchange rate. The index of this rate, normally called the real exchange rate index, is computed and then adjusted for movements in prices or costs at home relative to those abroad. An increase in a country's real exchange rate index over its level in a base period is made when the external position is considered adequate to provide an indication that external competitiveness has deteriorated. Competitiveness can be restored to its exchange rate by adjusting for a change in the level of domestic prices or costs relative to those abroad, or some combination of the two. A real appreciation (or depreciation) means an increase (decrease) in the purchasing power of the domestic currency in foreign markets (or in domestic traded goods markets relative to domestic non-traded goods markets).

Real effective exchange rate Increased exchange rate flexibility since the mid-1970s led to the construction of exchange indices designed to measure the average change of a country's exchange rate against a number of other currencies during a specified period. The concept of an average relationship between a currency and a set of other currencies is referred to as the effective exchange rate (EER), which is essentially the average of bilateral exchange rates. Correspondingly movements in the effective exchange rates index indicate either an appreciation or depreciation of the domestic currency vis-à-vis the set of other currencies.

The effective exchange rate is a nominal index since it is calculated as an average of nominal bilateral exchange rates. In order for an effective exchange rate index to be useful in measuring a country's external competitiveness, it is necessary to compute the real effective exchange rate (REER). In this case, the nominal index of real exchange rate must be adjusted for price movements in prices or costs at home relative to those abroad. The nominal index adjusted for relative price movements is referred to as the real effective index. Alternatively, the real effective index may be considered as an index of relative prices (i.e. domestic prices relative to an average of the price of a group of countries) adjusted for nominal exchange rate movements. In this case the definition is equivalent to an index of relative prices expressed in a common currency. Therefore, assuming that the exchange rate is stated as the price of a unit of domestic currency in terms of foreign currency, an increase in a country's real effective exchange rate index, or in its effective price index adjusted for nominal exchange rate movements, is an indication that external competitiveness had deteriorated. Conversely, a decrease in a country's real effective exchange rate (a real depreciation of the currency), or a decrease in its effective price index, is an indication that competitiveness has improved. Currencies which have shown real effective appreciation over levels in the base periods when external position is considered adequate are said to have become overvalued and vice versa. The computation of exchange rate, therefore, is used as the indicator of competitiveness and the one most commonly used is the real effective exchange rate index. Competitiveness can be restored to its base period level through a change in the nominal exchange rate, a change in the level of domestic prices or costs relative to those abroad, or some combination of the two. Real effective exchange rate indices can be constructed with various patterns of partner country weights and with various indicators of costs or prices (IBRD, 1993).

The two-index approach is used to approximate empirically the theoretical concept of the real exchange rate:

$$e_s = r \frac{P}{P*} \tag{2}$$

where

e_s denotes the empirical measure of the real exchange rate;
r is the nominal exchange rate; and
P and P* refer to a domestic price index and foreign price index respectively.

The purchasing power parity, therefore, provides the simplest way of estimating the equilibrium exchange rate. According to the theory of purchasing power parity, the exchange rate change between two currencies over any time period is determined by the change in the two currencies relative to price level. This is notationally expressed as follows:

$$e_s = r.\frac{P}{P*} \tag{3}$$

$$e^{\tilde{}}_s = -_r (^{\tilde{}}P - ^{\tilde{}}P*) \tag{4}$$

where

$e^{\tilde{}}$ $r^{\tilde{}}$ $p^{\tilde{}}$ $p*^{\tilde{}}$ are the percentage changes in the variables.

In our earlier examples if the relative change in price levels in Ghana falls by a ratio of 0.166 and the US price change remains at 0.166 per cent then

$$e_s = r. (0.166-0.166) - 0$$

In this case, therefore, the real exchange rate is in equilibrium.

The purchasing power parity approach, though simple to compute, has been criticized for a number of weaknesses. One such weakness is the choice of the historical base year during which the exchange rate was in equilibrium. Another weakness is to measure P and P*. Often domestic and foreign aggregate prices such as the consumer price index (CPI), the wholesale price index (WPI), wage index, and the gross domestic product deflator, are used as proxies. These aggregate indices are not consistent with strict purchasing power parity principles because the same goods do not enter each country's market basket with the same weights. Also these price indices include both tradeables and non-tradeables. The alternative interpretation considered better than the above, rests on the distinction between tradeables and non-tradeables. In this context the real exchange rate is defined as the domestic relative price of tradeable to non-tradeable goods. Thus, assuming no price distorting elements such as taxes and subsidies, the real exchange rate can be presented as:

$$\text{Real exchange rate (RER)} = \frac{e\,Pt}{Pn} \tag{5}$$

where

e   is the nominal exchange rate;
Pt   is the world price of tradeables in terms of foreign currency; and
Pn   is the price of non-tradeables.

Tradeables consist of exportable and importable goods and services whose price behaviour is determined by the world market, subject to trade policies (tariffs and subsidies), nominal exchange rates and the international transport costs. Exportables comprise actual exports as well as substitutes for exports that are sold domestically while importables include imports as well as goods produced and sold domestically that are close substitutes of imports, i.e. import-competing goods. Non-tradeables consist of all those goods and services whose prices are domestically determined by changes in domestic supply and demand. This category consists mainly of services (see Table 22 for Ghana example). The interpretation of RER assumes that the two countries are price takers in world markets facing perfectly elastic demand and supply schedules for their exports and imports. Accordingly the nominal price of tradeables is exogenously determined by foreign prices, commercial policy and exchange rate policy.

The reason for expressing RER in this way is because, in the context of a dependent open economy model, the trade and current accounts will depend on the domestic relative price of tradeables to non-tradeables since in this type of model, the current account is equal to the excess of supply of tradeable goods (e Pt/Pn) is positive while the corresponding demand elasticity is negative, then the current account will improve because the higher relative price of tradeables increase supply and reduce demand for these goods. The modern interpretation of the real exchange rate is a measure of profitability (competitiveness) of the tradeable goods sector in the domestic economy. An increase in the real exchange rate, *ceteris paribus*, is an indication of improvement of competitiveness of the domestic tradeable good sector and vice versa. In Ghana, as shown in the table, under the country's economic recovery programme, which began in 1983, the main focus of government policy was to revive the cocoa industry through higher producer prices. The cocoa real exchange rate greatly increased. To be a good measure of the real exchange rate, price indices should be based on weighted averages of traded and non-traded goods. Since cocoa's share of tradeables is only 20 per cent, its RER has to be adjusted accordingly (IBRD, 1993).

Table 22   Ghana: trends in domestic price bias

| | Inter-crop parity Internal (Terms of trade) | | | | Relative real exchange rates | | | | |
| | | | | | Agricultural | | Cocoa | | |
	Pnat/Pa	Pnat/Pc	Pt/Pc	Pa/Pc	Pf/Pc	Pa/Pnat	RER	RER x (Pa/Pnat)	RER x (co.Pnat)
1981	1.08	1.08	1.11	0.99	0.96	0.92	29	26	27
1982	0.96	1.00	1.00	1.05	1.05	1.04	37	38	30
1983	0.86	0.92	0.93	1.07	1.08	1.16	86	107	59
1984	1.29	1.15	1.14	0.89	0.87	0.77	123	101	71
1985	1.65	1.30	1.27	0.79	0.74	0.61	134	82	118
1986	1.65	1.30	1.28	0.79	0.73	0.61	140	85	152
1987	1.71	1.33	1.31	0.78	0.72	0.58	371	217	487
1988	1.68	1.33	1.30	0.79	0.73	0.59	442	266	561
1989	1.67	1.31	1.30	0.79	0.73	0.60	–	–	–
1990	1.51	1.51	1.51	0.79	0.73	0.66	–	–	–
Av. growth %	7.1	2.9	2.6	-3.6	-4.7	-6.5	14.7	13.3	15.8

Notes

1 Consumer price indices weighted averages.
2 Tradeable Pt excludes food but includes beverages and tobacco, clothing and footwear, furniture and furnishings and durable goods (miscellaneous).
3 Non-tradeable Pnt/non-food Pnt includes all items except clothing and footwear, furniture and furnishings and durable goods.
4 Agricultural Pa includes food, beverages and tobacco.
5 Non-agricultural Pna includes all times except food, beverages and tobacco.
6 Non-agricultural non-tradeable Pnant includes all items except food, beverages and tobacco, clothing and footwear, furniture and furnishings and durables.
7 Non-agricultural tradeables Pnat includes clothing and footwear, furniture and durables.
8 a/b ratio of maize price indices to fertilizer price indices and a/c to SA fertilizer price indices Cois nominal cocoa food prices.

Elasticity, approach to determining exchange rate The purchasing parity is one of the many ways for determining currency exchange rate. Elasticity analysis is also used for assessing the degree of responsiveness of the elements of the balance of payments to the exchange rate. By influencing domestic relative prices, an exchange rate adjustment exerts real effects on import demand and export supply. The elasticity of demand for tradeable goods, which partly determines the import-demand and export-supply responses, will depend largely on the income effects of the devaluation because the elasticity of substitution between tradeables and non-tradeable goods depends on these effects. In addition, the elasticities of import demand and export supply will depend on the supply response in the tradeable goods. The discussion of this topic is outside the scope of this book.

Effects of Exchange Rate Misalignment

Net effect (indirect) of exchange distortion on relative prices Exchange rate distortion can have an impact on incentives especially prices. In many Sub-

Table 23   Togo: effect of exchange rate on relative prices

	Official exchange rate[1]	Real exchange rate[2]	Exchange rate adjustment	Actual farm gate[3] prices			Adjusted farm gate prices
					SorghumSorghum		
	Eo	*Ex*	*Ex/Eo*	*Maize*	*Millet*	*Millet*	*Millet*
1975	214.32	197.66	.92	32	35	29.44	32.20
1976	238.98	220.47	.92	49	44	45.08	40.48
1977	245.67	209.22	.85	64	77	54.40	90.59
1978	225.64	204.64	.91	39	37	35.49	33.67
1979	212.72	197.24	.93	33	30	30.69	27.90
1980	211.30	236.60	1.12	40	40	44.80	44.80
1981	271.73	292.38	1.07	96	84	102.72	89.88
1982	328.62	307.92	.94	100	97	94.00	91.18
1983	381.07	385.37	1.01	104	111	105.04	112.11
1984	436.96	385.84	.88	75	89	66.00	78.32
1985	449.26	453.65	1.01	48	64	48.48	64.64

Note: The actual farm gate prices are adjusted by the ratio of real exchange rate to the official (nominal) exchange rate.

Sources: 1) *International Financial Statistics Yearbook*, 1989; 2) computed consumer price index against the index of manufacturing unit value (MUV); 3) *Sub-Saharan Africa Economic and Financial Data*, UNDP/World Bank, 1989.

Saharan African countries the domestic currency became increasingly overvalued in the 1970s and the early 1980s, with only some year-to-year variations of trade. This is illustrated in Table 23.

An increase in the adjusted farm gate prices above nominal prices indicates that the currency is overvalued and the difference between the adjusted and nominal price can be taken as a tax on the producer. If the adjusted farm gate price is below the nominal price, the producer is taken as receiving a subsidy due to distortion in the exchange rate.

Table 24   Cost of alternative maize production technologies

	Domestic costs in cedis ¢	Foreign exchange costs in US$
Smallholder	15,000	500
Mechanized	7,500	1,000

Cost of alternative maize production technologies

US$1 = ¢2.75

	Domestic costs ¢	Foreign exchange costs $	Total cost ¢
Smallholder	15,000	1,375[1]	16,375
Mechanized	7,500	2,750[2]	10,250

1   500 x 2.75 = 1,375;
2   10,000 x 2.75 = 27,500

Costs of alternative maize production technologies

US$1 = ¢35

	Domestic costs ¢	Foreign exchange costs ¢	Total costs ¢
Smallholder	15,000	17,500	32,500
Mechanized	7,500	35,000	42,500

Choice of technologies A distorted foreign exchange may also transmit erroneous information as to the choice of technology. Let us consider the production of maize, which can be produced by a variety of technologies including home-grown seeds, technical production inputs, improved seeds, mechanization, etc. Let us present these estimates in a tabular form.

Comparing the tables we find that mechanized farming is more cost-effective (had least cost) if the current price of the dollar was ₡2.75, while smallholder farming is the most cost-effective technology if the exchange rate was ₡35 to the dollar. Hence, if the domestic currency is overvalued the government could support mechanized farming and vice versa.

Effects on value-added To assess the net effect of direct and indirect price intervention on farmers it is also necessary to examine not only the effect of intervention on the prices received for their produce but also on the prices paid for their inputs. In other words, it is necessary to estimate effective rates of protection or rates of protection in value added. The concept is explained in detail in the subsequent section.

In Zambia, the government was at one time subsidizing fertilizer on a national scale. Table 25 presents estimates of the average rates of subsidy (implicit rather than budgetary) from 1971 to 1984. These are implicit rates of subsidy calculated as the difference between the landed cost of fertilizer and the price actually paid by the farmer. The first column presents the subsidy rate when the cost of imported fertilizer is converted to local currency at the official exchange rate. In the third column, the subsidy is based on conversion at the equilibrium exchange rate. As can be seen from the table, the comparison between the two implicit subsidy rates is astonishing. At the official rate of exchange, the subsidy averaged about 60 per cent per metric ton, whereas at the equilibrium exchange rate it averaged about 725 per cent. Therefore, farmers who used fertilizer benefited enormously. Such a policy has a serious implication for income distribution because the beneficiaries were commercial farmers.

Changes in the real exchange rate affects the competition between tradeable and non-tradeable commodities in the agricultural sector. Within the agricultural sector, a macroeconomic-induced appreciation in the real exchange rate will reduce the production of exportables and import substitutes, and expand the production of non-tradeables, consisting largely of food crops and livestock or vice versa. A sustained period of excess domestic absorption, and its impact on the real exchange rate, results in the deterioration of the terms of trade between the agricultural and other sectors. Taking Tanzania's experience as an example, there was a much higher price increase of the national consumer price index, which consisted largely of tradeables, but less for non-tradeable crops, as illustrated in Table 26.

A longer-term structural impact on the agricultural sector resulted in the deterioration in the net barter terms of trade for the agricultural sector. This

Table 25   Implicit fertilizer subsidy

	Subsidy calculated using official exchange rate		Subsidy calculated using equilibrium exchange rate	
	Price per 50kg (Kw)	*as % of producer price*	*Price per 50kg bag (Kw)*	*as % of producer price*
1971	1.50	11.5	4.75	36.5
1972	-0.25	-1.5	4.50	26.9
1973	5.00	25.3	9.25	46.8
1974	18.00	93.5	33.25	172.7
1975	54.75	280.8	106.50	546.2
1976	28.50	87.7	86.50	266.2
1977	16.75	53.2	67.25	213.5
1978	23.75	67.6	102.50	248.5
1979	12.00	20.7	114.50	197.4
1980	43.75	94.6	224.75	485.9
1981	46.75	81.3	376.50	654.8
1982	16.00	21.5	342.75	461.6
1983	-12.00	-10.1	288.00	243.6
1984	22.25	17.0	295.25	225.8
Average 1971–84	19.77	59.5	146.88	273.3

Source: Jansen, D., Trade, *Exchange Rate and Agricultural Pricing Policies*, The World Bank, 1988.

discourages investment in the agricultural sector as investable resources, labour and capital are withdrawn and reinvested in other sectors of the economy. When agriculture is discriminated against, its production either stagnates or even declines. Farmers see their incomes in real terms decline. This is reflected in the income terms of trade defined as the ratio between producer's income derived from agricultural commodities and prices paid by them for certain goods (Table 27).

Both the net barter terms of trade and the income terms of trade provide an overall indicator of the relative price effects on the agricultural sector as a whole. Disaggregation to commodities, regions or groups of producers is required for useful and meaningful conclusions to be drawn about differential impact within the agricultural sector. It will also be helpful to calculate the terms of trade effect on producer prices. This can be done by deflating producer

Table 26   Tanzania: net barter terms of trade index for the agricultural sector (1970 = 100)

	Agricultural price index all crops	Modified NCPI*	Net barter terms of trade
	Pa	Pn	Pa/Pn
1970	100.0	100.0	100.0
1971	96.4	105.1	91.7
1972	100.5	113.7	88.3
1973	104.2	127.3	81.5
1974	108.1	162.3	66.6
1975	124.1	207.4	59.8
1976	208.7	233.8	89.3
1977	277.0	248.4	111.5
1978	239.8	279.8	86.5
1979	239.0	313.5	76.3
1980	261.7	408.2	64.1

Note: * The modification of the National Consumer Price Index (NCPI) involves omission of rents, personal care and hygiene, recreation and entertainments, all of which are non-tradeables.

Source: Ellis, F. 'Agricultural Price Policy in Tanzania', *World Development*, World Bank, Washington, 1982.

nominal (official) price (Pd) by the ratio of agricultural price (P_a) index to non-agricultural price (Pna) index. Consequently, the adjusted producer price is Pd = (Pa/Pna x Pd).

In Kenya in the past, the government used to set guaranteed minimum prices (in effect maximum prices) for the principal export and staple food crops. As can be seen in Table 28, the producer prices of these crops actually declined in the 1980s relative to the prices for non-agricultural products.

Export Boom

The export boom which occurred in Nigeria was translated into a substantial shift in the structure of the economy following the discovery of fuel oil. The oil boom appreciated the real exchange. This appreciation occurred because of the spending effect of the additional income earned, which raised the demand for both tradeables and non-tradeables and increased the prices of the latter.

Table 27   Tanzania: income terms of trade for the agricultural sector, 1970–80 (1970 = 100)

	Gross producer incomes $Q_a \times P_a$	Cost of living P_n	Income terms of trade $Q_a \times P_a / P_n$
1970	100.0	100.0	100.0
1971			
1972	105.8	110.9	95.4
1973	114.9	124.1	92.6
1974	106.0	158.3	67.0
1975	124.8	202.2	61.7
1976	176.5	228.0	77.4
1977	244.1	242.2	100.9
1978	231.7	272.8	84.5
1979			
1980	234.4	351.9	66.6

Note: Base year is an average of 1970 and 1971 and final year is an average of 1979 and 1980. The calendar years shown correspond to the crop seasons, of which they are the second years.

Source: Ellis, 1982, Appendix, Table A3.

Table 28   Crop producer prices relative to prices of non-agricultural products

	Terms of trade adjustment* $1980 = 100$ Pa/Pna	Official producer price Kshs/Kg						Adjusted official producer price Kshs/Kg $Pa/Pns \times Pd$
		Coffee	Tea	Maize	Coffee	Tea	Maize	
1980	1.0	22.6	17.7	1.0	22.6	17.7	1.0	
1981	0.9	27.8	19.4	1.1	25.9	18.1	1.0	
1982	0.8	34.9	21.8	1.5	29.3	18.3	1.3	
1983	0.8	38.4	51.8	1.8	30.8	41.3	1.4	
1984	0.7	39.7	33.7	1.9	27.3	24.9	1.4	
1985	0.7	46.6	33.7	2.1	29.3	23.1	1.4	

Note: * Index of GDP deflator of the manufacturing sector (excluding agriculture) is used to represent non-agricultural products Pna)

Source: Computed from *World Tables, World Bank and African Financial and Economic Indicators*, UNDP/World Bank.

The structure of exports underwent dramatic changes, with the country moving from a diversified and a reasonably-balanced agriculture-led export to one of overwhelming domination by oil exports, which increased its share of exports to over 90 per cent, with the agricultural share dropping to less than 3 per cent by the 1970s. The rapid increase in the oil revenue was translated into significant development gains in many sectors of the economy, particularly infrastructure and social sectors. Consequently, major sectoral imbalances developed in the economy, resulting in substantial shifts in the structure of the economy, with agriculture's share of total domestic output falling from about 60 per cent in the 1960s to about 30 per cent and its share of exports falling from about 70 per cent in the 1960s to less than 3 per cent. The service sector (non-tradeable sector), on the other hand, increased its share of total output to about 35 per cent and of employment from 10 to 20 per cent.

All the shifts in the structure of the economy that had taken place reflected the inter-sectoral movement of resources as a result of the impact of the oil boom. Increased income and increased federal spending on non-tradeables stimulated excess internal demand for these items, resulting ultimately in a rise in their prices relative to prices of tradeables. The increased demand for consumer items has been translated into increased domestic inflation, and the high incidence of inflation in the Nigerian economy in turn resulted in the appreciation of the domestic exchange rate, as indicated in Table 29.

The real exchange rate was calculated by adjusting for inflation differential between Nigeria and the basket of currencies of Nigeria's major trading partners. The stimulation of excess internal demand for non-tradeables resulted in the rise of their prices relative to tradeables, and the real exchange rate for non-tradeables appreciated, as shown in the Table 30.

There was also some evidence of resource movement out of the agricultural sector (both tradeables and non-tradeables). The increased spending on non-tradeables led to a wage increase, which in turn induced labour to shift from agriculture to the booming sectors, most of them located in urban and industrial centres. Since the relative prices of trade agricultural goods fell during the oil boom, domestic factors of production also shifted substantially out of the agricultural sector into non-traded goods. The shift had adverse consequences for the agricultural sector and environmental renewal. The combination of the inter-sectoral shift of resources and the rural-urban exodus resulted in the draining from the rural areas of the manpower needed for agricultural production, environmental recovery and a resulting decline in output, and the loss of self-sufficiency in food supply. On the supply side, there was a significant resource movement effect as economic incentives drew invest-

Table 29   Nigeria: real exchange rate

Year	Nigeria consumer price index	Basket of currencies weighted average WP[2]	Official exchange rate[1] N/$	Purchasing power parity[3] exchange rate relative to:		
				trading partners WPI, N/$	industrial countries CPI N/$	MUV II[4]
1970	100.0	100.0	.71	.69	.69	.69
1971	115.8	105.9	.71	.75	.77	.75
1972	118.8	111.4	.66	.75	.76	.72
1973	125.7	124.3	.66	.71	.72	.63
1974	141.6	154.1	.63	.64	.66	.59
1975	189.1	166.4	.62	.79	.83	.71
1976	230.7	179.4	.63	.89	.95	.87
1977	280.2	194.9	.64	.99	1.08	.96
1978	341.6	202.6	.64	1.16	1.25	1.02
1979	381.2	221.6	.60	1.18	1.26	.98
1980	418.8	242.5	.55	1.18	1.22	.98
1981	506.9	263.5	.62	1.44	1.49	1.37
1982	545.5	282.3	.67	1.45	1.52	1.52
1983	672.3	290.3	.72	1.74	1.81	1.97
1984	938.6	302.4	.77	2.33	2.43	2.81
1985	990.1	310.8	.89	2.39	2.53	2.81
1986	1043.6	310.6	1.75	2.62	2.76	2.58
1987	1149.5	311.4	4.02	2.88	3.01	5.36
1988	1589.1	318.9	4.54	3.89	4.04	6.71

Notes: 1 Local currency rate to the dollar.
2 Import-weighted wholesale price indices of Nigeria major trading partners.
3 The average of exchange rates for 1970, 1971 and 1972 was taken as the purchasing power parity base, and the rate of the nominal exchange rate that would keep the real exchange rate (RER) constant over a given period (year).
4 Index of unit values of exports of manufactures from industrial countries.

Source: Computed from data available in the *International Financial Statistics Yearbook*, IMF, 1989.

ments, manpower and talents out of the lagging agricultural sector and the declining environmental resources into the petroleum sector and non-tradeables especially import-induced services sector. According to Watts and Bassett, the individuals who were most likely to invest in agriculture (traders, bureaucrats, civil servants, etc.) tended to be attracted either to state patronage (lucrative government contracts, imports and to mercantile operation) or to high-value agrarian pursuits, particularly poultry production, where returns

Table 30   Nigeria: sectoral real exchange rate

	Real exchange rate N/$[1]	Sectoral consumer price indices		Terms of trade	Agric. tradeables real exchange rate	
		Agricultural tradeables[2]	Non-agricultural non-tradeables[3]			
	a	b	c	b/c	a (b/c)	N/$
1975	.79	100	100	1.00	.79	
1976	.89	143	141	1.01	.90	
1977	.99	183	141	1.30	1.28	
1978	1.16	186	161	1.15	1.34	
1979	1.18	203	188	1.08	1.27	
1980	1.18	229	231	.99	1.17	
1981	1.44	265	265	1.00	1.44	
1982	1.45	278	283	.98	1.42	
1983	1.74	318	364	.87	1.52	
1984	2.33	436	531	.82	1.90	
1985	2.39	549	586	.94	2.24	
1986	2.62	673	733	.92	2.41	
1987	2.88	768	854	.90	2.59	
1988	3.89	830	915	.91	3.53	

Notes: 1 Source: table 6, Okai, 1991.
2 Includes exported foods and beverages.
3 Includes clothing, household goods, other purchases and services.

on investments were attractive. The construction boom generated a high demand for labour. Thus the urban construction boom and the associated growth of the informal sector (roadside vehicle repairs, domestic servants, tailoring) siphoned labour from the rural economy which exacerbated the problem of seasonal labour shortage. The development in the non-agricultural sector provided off-farm employment opportunities and encouraged massive off-farm migration of the active labour force out of agriculture, which in turn raised rural labour wages, as shown in the table. Paradoxically, there was also arise in demand for labour in the rural agricultural sector, but because of the seasonality of agricultural production, wages were also seasonal and were, therefore, unable to offer attractive alternative employment.

Labour shortages in rural areas inflated rural wage levels in real term by roughly twice the minimum wage rate. In conjunction with a more general price escalation of all farm inputs but relatively lower real producer prices, rising rural wage levels was responsible for reduced profit margin in agriculture. In another study it was indicated that the index of the real rural wage rate rose from 100 in 1970 to 232 in 1982 before beginning to decline (Okai ,1991). As shown in Table 31, it is clear that the real rural wage declined relatively less than the minimum and government wages, while the real agricultural wage remained consistently above the minimum wage.

Table 31　Minimum and rural wages in Nigeria: Naira/year

	Nominal			Real		
	Minimum wage	*Agricultural wage*	*Government wage*	*Minimum [b] wage*	*Agricultural [a] wage*	*Government [b] wage*
1975	720	913	3,264	720	913	3,264
1976	720	1,058	3,264	585	860	2,654
1977	720	1,203	3,264	503	841	2,283
1978	720	1,348	3,264	431	817	1,954
1979	846	1,638	3,564	455	885	1,916
1980	846	1,701	3,564	413	838	1,738
1981	1,500	1,764	3,564	605	720	1,437
1982	1,500	1,890	3,924	562	716	1,470
1983	1,500	1,890	3,924	457	578	1,196
1984	1,500	2,048	3,924	328	449	857
1985	1,500	2,205	3,924	310	457	769

Notes:　a　Nominal wages deflated by the rural consumer price index (CPI).
　　　　　b　Nominal wages deflated by composite CPI.

Sources:　*Annual Abstracts of Statistics*, various years; Federal Office of Statistics, Lagos, Nigeria.

Quantitative Effects of Exchange Movements

The main concern in empirical work is to trace how economic determinants influence the real economies. A common approach in recent years in empirical analysis is the use of the independent-economy model of the orthodox model based on the Meade-Salter-Swan model. Initially it is assumed that the economy is in a comparatively static equilibrium status. The purpose, therefore, is analytically to trace the dynamic response of the economy to various policy variables or exogenous shocks. The advantage of the analysis is the revelation of how different policy instruments influence real economies. In the dependent economy the core of analysis is the distinction between tradeable and non-tradeable goods and services. Non-tradeables are goods and services whose prices are determined by the domestic supply and demand factors. This depends on the nature of the goods involved, such as public services, housing and construction, or owing to prohibitively high transport costs the goods cannot be traded. Tradeable goods and services on the other hand, are those that cross frontiers, and in theory their prices are determined by world market conditions, and hence for small open economies, prices of tradeable goods and services are exogenously given. However, it should be noted that a commodity can switch categories often in response to the type of policy changes under investigation. Goods may not be traded because of commercial policies such as quantitative restrictions like quotas, or outright import bans, and prohibitively high transport costs. The other problem is classification which may arise due to geographical proximity which makes it possible for a commodity to be exported or imported because a reduction in transport costs make it possible for trade to occur. In the empirical analysis, it is important to identify which such changes occur.

Using a three-sector model several assumptions precede actual analysis:

- a country is regarded as a price taker in world markets;
- two tradeable commodities are produced, an exportable (X) and an importable (M). Their prices (Px and Pm respectively) are determined by world market conditions, and nominal exchange rate fixed; a non-tradeable (N) is also produced, with its price being Pdnt;
- Pdnt is determined by domestic supply and demand factors, the latter being partly dependent on monetary and fiscal policy. Other things being equal, an expansionary monetary and fiscal policy will raise Pdnt;
- product and factor (labour and capital) markets are perfectly competitive so that the economy is in equilibrium on its production frontier; and
- capital is sector-specific in the short-run, so that only labour reallocation can change the output index in the economy. In the long run, however, both capital and labour may be reallocated between sectors (IBRD, 1990).

In empirical analysis the terms of trade (Px/Pm) taken as being fixed, exportables and importables are combined into tradeables and can be used in analysing the effects of policies such as currency devaluation designed to change the real exchange rate.

The Tradeable/Non-tradeable Real Exchange Rate

In a small open economy (dependent economy) the rate of exchange between tradeables and non-tradeables is defined as the commodity exchange rate of tradeables (t) to non-tradeables (nt). Using the dollar to the cedi ($¢) conversion (how many US dollars can be obtained for one cedi):

$$RER = \frac{\$¢ \, Pbt}{¢1/Pdnt} \tag{6}$$

where

    Pbt   is the border price of tradeables; and
    Pdnt is the domestic price of non-tradeables.

Alternatively one can use the domestic currency price of a unit of a foreign exchange conversion.

$$RER = \frac{\$¢ \, Pdnt}{Pbt} \tag{7}$$

where

    $¢ Pbt expresses the quantity of tradeables that can be purchased at any nominal exchange rate; whereas
    Pdnt are non-tradeables that can be purchased for one unit of the domestic currency.

If the real exchange depreciates, it can be due to a rise in the border price of tradeables (one needs more domestic currency to purchase tradeables) and/ or a fall in domestic price (cost of producing) non-tradeables. In other words, a depreciation means that fewer tradeables are exchanged for a given amount of non-tradeables. In the second convention, an appreciation of the real exchange rate reflects a rise in the domestic price (cost of producing) of non-tradeables relative to tradeables and/or an appreciation of the nominal dollar to the cedi rate. Domestic producers of tradeable goods can match the cost increases by paying higher wages to attract and retain the labour force from moving to the non-tradeable good sector. This is done at the risk of losing international competitiveness. In order to sustain competitiveness, producers of tradeables have to keep wages or profit low. From the foregoing it is clear that the tradeable-non tradeable exchange rate has important implication for resource allocation. The computation of the real exchange rate can be simplified by using the ratio between the two to calculate nominal exchange rate (NER).

$$NER = \frac{Pdnt}{Pdt^*} \qquad (8)$$

where

Pdt* is the domestic price of tradeables including taxes (or subsidies).

Policies to improve incentives to the producers of tradeables require that the ratio be kept low by maintaining low costs of production in non-tradeable good sector, reducing trade taxes and increasing trade subsidies. Reducing trade taxes and increasing trade subsidies have the effect of increasing the producers' share for any given domestic price of tradeables.

Usually the Pdnt/Pdt cannot be observed directly in a market but has to be computed by comparing a price index for groups of commodities which represent non-tradeables with one which represents tradeables. When the real exchange rate is rising it represents an incentive to producers to expand the production of non-tradeables. This could be due to an increase in their prices. When the real exchange rate is falling it induces an increase in tradeables and import substitute production. This could be due to the stimulative effects of exchange rate depreciation. If a government pursues a fixed nominal exchange rate policy, then the influence of domestic absorption on the real exchange rate will occur mainly through its impact on the price of non-tradeable goods. The relationship between absorption, the real exchange rate and the foreign or nominal exchange rate is best explained by the Australian model or the Salter-Swan model as represented in Figure 35. The model attempts to explain macroeconomic influence on tradeable and non-tradeable prices. The production possibilities curve X AEW depicts a country's capacity for producing tradeable and non-tradeable goods. When there is no excess domestic absorption, the production possibility curve and absorption possibility curve coincide, and production and consumption are at point A where the consumer indifference curve is tangent to the transformation curve. The price line Po, which is at a tangent to the production possibility curve, represents equilibrium real exchange of Pdnt/Pdt.

If the government increases expenditure substantially beyond its revenue earning capacity, it puts additional income into the hands of consumers. Consumers will spend this additional income on either non-tradeable or tradeable goods, including imports. The prices of non-tradeables are determined by domestic forces of supply and demand, while those of tradeables are determined in the world market. Increased demand for non-tradeable

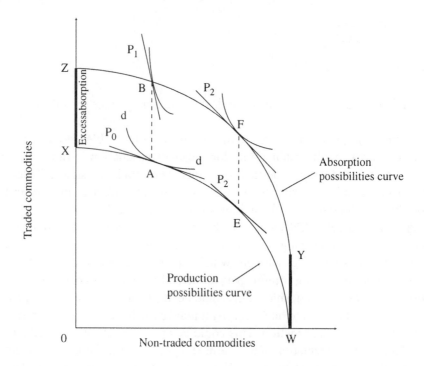

Figure 35 Macroeconomic impact on agricultural prices

Source: *Economic Analysis of Agricultural Policies: A Basic Training Manual with Special Reference to Price Analysis*, Training Materials for Agricultural Planning 30, FAO, 1991.

goods will result in excess absorption, represented by an upward shift of the absorption possibility curve ZBFYW beyond the production possibility curve XAEW. This represents the potential absorption accommodated by the production possibility curve plus additional absorption made possible by foreign reserves, foreign loans and grants. This means the budget deficit has been sustained mainly by depleting the country's foreign exchange reserves, by foreign borrowing, etc., with deleterious effects on trade balance and diversion of domestic financial resources from productive activities to debt servicing. While the absorption possibility curve shifts upward, that of the production possibility curve remains unchanged.

The excess demand results in an increase in imports and trade deficit, and part of excess demand is directed towards non-tradeables. Initially, therefore, there is an increase in demand for both tradeables and non-tradeables. However, as the price of non-tradeables remains unchanged, its output also remains unchanged. Since increases in demand for non-tradeables cannot be satisfied, the excess demand leads to an increase in their prices, represented by P_1 at point B, ultimately leading to a rise in the real exchange rate. As the production of non-tradeables increases in response to price rises and profitability relative to tradeables, and as output of non-tradeables increases, their prices start to fall until a new equilibrium is re-established at consumption point F and the real exchange rate at P_2, a point where consumer preferences, prices and the production of non-tradeables goods are consistent. The new consumption corresponds with the production combination at point E on the transformation curve. It is clear that excess absorption of tradeables represented by EF still persists because production of tradeables does not match demand. The imbalance can be sustained only if there are sufficient foreign reserves or foreign saving to finance the excess imports. To restore balance, adjustment in macroeconomic policy is required. A common approach has often been to devalue the nominal exchange. This will increase the domestic price of tradeables relative to non-tradeables, a depreciation of the real exchange rate.

For a devaluation to be effective, the value of the domestic currency has to depreciate in real terms. In this respect the increase in the relative price and tradeable commodities, due to devaluation, can easily be eroded by the subsequent rise in the price of non-tradeables. This is caused by a number of factors. Increases in domestic prices due to devaluation are usually reflected in government expenditures on goods and services which rise in proportion to their import content and the size of devaluation. An erosion of purchasing power of income caused by domestic inflation consequent upon devaluation leads to a pressure for wage justice. An increase in the domestic currency equivalent of the debt service will divert fiscal resources from investment in productive sectors of the domestic economy. To a certain extent, the higher fiscal costs can be offset by an increase in revenue receipts from taxes on international trade (export and import trade).

Taxes on international trade traditionally have been one of the major sources of fiscal resources. Trade policies are, therefore, directed towards imports and exports. The former could include changes in import tariffs while the latter reflects changes in export duties and subsidies. As domestic import prices decline as a result of tariff reductions, import demand will increase. A deficit in trade account emerges, which requires a higher real exchange to restore external balance. If an import tariff is imposed, the domestic price of the protected products tends to rise relative to non-tradeables and other unprotected tradeables. Import barriers, therefore, tend to appreciate the real exchange, which in turn encourages imports and discourages exports. Trade liberalization (generalized reduction in tariffs and quantitative control) increases the level of the real exchange. Export promotion policies make exports more attractive by lowering the real exchange rate so that export supplies increase.

Monetary Expansion

Monetary expansion is usually taken as the main source of domestic inflation. Usually, as more domestic output enters the market economy, the quantity of money which the public wish to hold increases because more money is required for transactions. Consequently holding of money balances (transactions demand) depends on the level of economic activities which is usually approximately the level of GDP of a country. Computationally it is expressed by the equation:

$$m = kY \tag{9}$$

where

m   is the quantity of money;
Y   is the money income;
k   is the coefficient that brings the two side of the equation in balance. It is the fraction of money income which the public wish to hold in the form of money; and
Y = PO or price level multiplied by output.

Accordingly the above equation can be written as follows:

$$m = k\,PO \tag{10}$$

the k being defined as that fraction of real income which people wish to have.

Money is also used as a store of value. The demand for money for this purpose depends on how well money keeps its purchasing power. If, for instance, the rate of interest paid on bank deposits is in excess of inflation rate, there will be an incentive for the public to hold money balances with the banking system. Expectation of high inflation reduces the likely purchasing power of money and its attractiveness as a store of value. Usually a judgmental approach is employed to assess the demand for money on the basis of the expected movement of the ratio of money supply to nominal GDP.

Alternatively one may focus on the velocity of money, which is defined as the ratio of income to demand deposits plus currency held outside the banking system. Sometimes empirical estimation of the demand for money is based on a statistical relationship with GDP, inflation, interest rates, and other relevant variables based on historical data. Where there have been substantial structural changes in the economy, past relationship may prove of limited value in predicting future development.

A discussion of the instruments used in monetary control is outside the scope of this book, whose primary focus is on excessive growth in the money supply and its effect on rates of spending on domestic and foreign goods. Since domestic supply lags behind demand in the short run, it could result in substantial demand-pull inflationary pressure in the economy. If the domestic spending is directed towards foreign goods (or assets), it leads to balance of payment stresses. Also, in a broader sense, financial policy can also play a key role in efficient resource use in the economy by mobilizing and employing financial resources such as the role of financial intermediation (money or credit) in influencing savings and investments, as indicated earlier.

The main interest in curbing monetary growth is to maintain financial and price stability, and to avoid inflationary pressure. However, it has been demonstrated that monetary expansion is not the only source of domestic inflation. There are two schools of thought about the sources of inflation, with some scholars associating inflation with indiscipline in monetary expansion, while others feel that the structural characteristics of the economy could be the principal source of inflation.

The structuralist approach actually originated in Latin America when, in the 1960s, it was realized that the concepts of unemployment, the natural rate of unemployment and full employment, were totally inapplicable to developing economies. It was also observed that measures for demand management such as currency devaluation, budgetary austerity, etc. did not attack the root causes of inflation in developing countries and the adoption of such measures provoked responses which did not control inflation. Under the auspices of the Economic Commission for Latin America (ECLA) both theorists and policy-makers developed a structural concept of the sources of inflation. In the light of the endemic bottlenecks and the rigidities in supply that exist in developing countries, rather than explain inflation in terms of aggregate supply and demand function, the structuralists championed the concept of the fragmentation between supplies and demands in and between different sectors of the economy as the root causes of inflation. In this respect, inflation is viewed in the context of the structural composition of the economy as being the basic underlying causes of inflation, exerting all-pervading pressure on economic growth of an underdeveloped social and economic structure, a process or series of processes that make it difficult to avoid inflation. In this context it is the view of the structuralists that the problem of inflation had to be approached from a much broader front than that suggested by the mainstream macroeconomists.

Short-term stabilization policies, especially if adopted independently of structural changes, would merely have the effect of reducing economic growth and preventing the achievement of the long-run structural changes which are essential in the eventual containment of inflation. However, the monetarists' view concerning inflation arising from government-induced price and exchange distortion (for instance price controls of foodstuffs, overvalued exchange rates, high tariff barriers, and direct import controls) which generate inflation, cannot be jettisoned altogether. Sustaining macroeconomic stability through prudent policy management could eliminate many of the bottlenecks which exist due to greater participation of the private sector in the economy. Thus the monetarist model of inflation, which contends that if the increase in aggregate demand is kept equal to the real growth in output plus the expected increase in prices, inflation will continue at the equilibrium expected rate, is still valid. It is argued that the balance of payments disequilibrium is the result, not of any fundamental structural imbalances within the economy, but rather of the consequences of pursuing a policy of money supply at a rate that is incompatible with the maintenance of existing exchange rate. Balance of payments pressures could be ameliorated either through a reduction in the rate of domestic credit expansion or the abandonment of a fixed exchange rate.

The basic premise, as far as agricultural supply bottleneck is concerned, is that, following rapid population growth and urbanization, food supply, in the absence of improved technological advances, has not been able to match demand, causing inflationary price rises. As the domestic terms of trade remain against agriculture, few resources are spent on improving the quality of land or technology, thus causing production to lag behind demand and the sector remains unresponsive to favourable economic signals. Consequently, severe strains are placed on the existing agricultural structure, with severe consequences for relative prices. The basic structuralist's paradigm, therefore, is that the existence of excess demand in both the agricultural and the foreign trade sectors, and the price and wage flows into non-food, non-traded goods sectors, the relative price increases felt in the former will spill-over into the latter sectors, with the result that the general rate of inflation will be raised throughout the economy (Struthers, 1988, pp. 178, 187, 200). The only way to prevent relative prices from increasing is to curtail increases in excess demand for both agricultural and traded goods. This cannot simply be achieved through restrictive monetary and fiscal policies but only through extensive structural change in such a way that could improve supply response. This basically combines the agricultural supply bottleneck with the model of labour resources flowing out of the agricultural sector.

The second bottleneck is of the export-instability index, which has to be viewed in the context of an exacerbating effect on the agricultural supply bottleneck. The excess demand for agricultural products could be satisfied by food imports. This could lead to the curtailment of imports of essential intermediate goods and spare parts in order to maintain balance of payments equilibrium. Shortage of intermediate goods and spare parts needed for domestic production is likely to lead to price increases of non-agricultural sectors, further exacerbating domestic terms of trade against agriculture and also resulting in under-utilization of installed capacity. With the price of tradeables under fixed exchange rate being linked with the world price, only the price of non-tradeables will rise. Demand for non-tradeables, therefore, falls while their production will be encouraged. Conversely, if the price of tradeables rises, demand will be discouraged while production is encouraged. There will be an imbalance, with a balance of trade deficit in respect of tradeables and excess production of non-tradeables. The reverse applies for the tradeable goods sector – resulting in excess production of tradeables and eliminating balance of trade deficit.

Trade Policies

Trade, exchange rate and price policies influence the structure of relative prices facing different sectors of the economy, and this determines the allocation of resources within and among sectors. It is through the real exchange rate that trade policies affect the agricultural sector. Changes in the real exchange rate affect not only trade flows and the balance of payments, but also the structure and level of production and consumption, employment and the allocation of resources in an economy. While the nominal exchange rate is typically used as a policy instrument, the real exchange rate is an endogenous variable that responds to both exogenous and policy-induced shocks. To restore balance of payment equilibrium, many governments rely on various expenditure-switching policies, including devaluation of the nominal exchange rate *ceteris paribus*. Devaluation raises the domestic currency price of imports and reduces the foreign currency price of exports. Thus by changing the relative prices of domestic and foreign goods, devaluing attempts to switch the pattern of expenditure in favour of goods and services of the devaluing country. The presumption is that by altering the relative price of importables relative to exportables, devaluation will expand the tradeables goods sector and reduces domestic absorption.

However, the devaluation has only a transitory impact on real exchange since in the long term it will be eroded by domestic wage claims and price rises by the full level of devaluation. This does not help in achieving an international competitive advantage usually associated with devaluation. Unless it is accompanied by restraining increases in domestic factor cost caused by devaluation, the real exchange returns to its original level. Apart from the price effects on imports and exports, the supply response to these price changes are important. Usually the supply response lags behind the price increases as in Ghana due to devaluation of the cedi. The profitability of the use of agro-chemicals declined substantially (see Table 32) because the rise in price of cereals lagged behind those of the imported inputs. The slow adjustment of trade volumes to the price changes induced by devaluation may worsen the terms of trade resulting in trade balance worsening before getting better. If exports are involved in foreign currency, the initial effect of a devaluation is to cause a deterioration in the trade balance as the value of exports in foreign currency declines. In the meantime, the foreign currency value of imports remain unchanged.

Table 32   Ghana: relative profitability of fertilizer use

Consumer price indices

	Maize	15–15–15 fertilizer	Sulphate of ammonia	Relative profitability %	
	a	*b*	*c*	*a/b*	*a/c*
1980	100	100	100	100.0	100.0
1981	187	208	200	89.9	93.5
1982	193	208	200	92.8	96.5
1983	933	374	387	248.8	241.0
1984	567	2,458	2,933	23.1	19.3
1985	494	2,458	2,933	20.1	16.8
1986	798	4,023	4,667	19.8	17.1
1987	1,350	6,833	9,203	19.8	14.7
1988	1652	13,333	15,333	12.4	10.8

Average annual growth rate (%) of profitability	−13.7	−14.1

The absorption approach to devaluation states that the balance of payment position improves if devaluation raises domestic output or reduces domestic absorption. Domestic absorption which equals domestic expenditure, requires switching expenditure in such a way that expenditures fall relative to real income. By raising domestic price level, devaluation reduces real level of financial assets held by the public (real income). This results in a decline in consumption, while saving is expected to increase. Meanwhile higher domestic prices result in increases in nominal demand for money, leading to a rise in nominal interest rates and a fall in expenditure. For devaluation to be effective, there should also be a shift of expenditure from foreign to domestic goods. Higher domestic output will reflect itself in increases in real income, resulting in an improvement in the current account.

Real exchange can change when either the nominal exchange alters or the relative price of tradeables in respect of non-tradeable changes. Consequently factors which affect the nominal exchange rate and the relative price of tradeables are the determinants of the real exchange. They include monetary and fiscal policies, terms of trade changes, commercial policies, changes in real interest rates, etc. Policy analysts have developed methodologies for estimating the incidence of trade, exchange rate and other price policies on relative agricultural prices, as discussed in subsequent sections.

Terms of Trade Shocks

The deterioration in the terms of trade reduces real income and depends on whether the deterioration is due to an import or an export price shock. The deterioration in the purchasing power of exports in SSA in the past was adversely affected by the continuing decline in the international prices, as illustrated by the Tanzania experience (see Table 33).

The performance of exports was very much influenced by the demand of the export commodities. Changes in the international terms of trade, defined as the indices of the value of commodity exports deflated by import unit value indices, resulted in a decline in the purchasing power of exports earnings. In SSA in general, the index of real prices (i.e. commodity export prices deflated by manufactured import prices) for non-oil commodities peaked in 1977 and by the early 1980s it was half the level (see Figures 36 and 37).

Policy analysts have developed methodologies for estimating the incidence of exchange rate, trade and price policies on relative prices. Trade, exchange rate, and other price policy variables enter the models through the assumption that excess demand for importables, excess supply of exportables and excess

Table 33   International trade indices, 1973–80: Tanzania
(1973 = 100[a])

	Volume		Prices/unit values		International net barter terms of trade (P_x/P_m)	Purchasing power of export earnings[b] $(P_x Q_x/P_m)$
	Exports (Q_x)	Imports (Q_m)	Exports (P_x)	Imports (P_m)		
1973	100	100	100	100	100	100
1974	74	101	153	156	99	73
1975	79	96	135	169	81	64
1976	85	84	163	165	99	84
1977	68	87	227	181	126	86
1978	66	118	206	204	101	67
1979	69	97	223	237	95	66
1980	64	99	253	285	89	57

Av. annual rate of growth

1973–80	-6.2	–	14.2	16.1	-1.7	-7.3

Notes: a Base year period of 1976–78 has been converted to a base year of 1973.
          b In terms of current US dollars.

Source: *Economic Memorandum on Tanzania*, IBRD, 1981, p.54, Table 3.3.

demand for domestic goods depends only on relative prices ($P_m/P_{dn}t$, P_x/P_{dnt}) and real income (Y):

where

P_m denotes importables;
P_x represents exportables; and
P_{dnt} represents domestic goods.

A distortion, say an import tariff, raises the domestic price to consumers of importables relative to exportables and domestic goods, and makes export and import substitute goods relatively less profitable to producers. This induces consumers to shift their demand from imported goods to exportables and domestic goods. It also induces the transfer of resources away from the production of exportables and domestic goods but leads to increased domestic production of import substitutes. These processes create a reduction in the supply of domestic goods and an increase in demand. This in turn places pressure on the price of non-tradeables until prices increase to the point at which a new equilibrium is achieved in the domestic goods market. The final

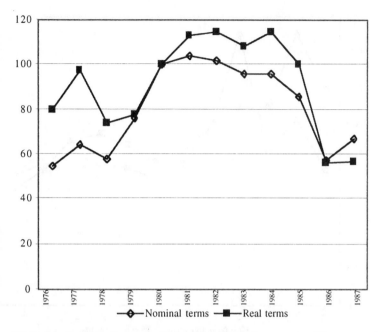

Figure 36 Price indices for Sub-Saharan Africa's commodity exports, including oil, 1976–87 (1980 = 100)

Note: In the figure, petroleum is included in the index. The real indices are the nominal indices deflated by the United Nation's index of the dollar prices of the manufactured exports of industrial countries

Source: *Financing Africa's Recovery*, op. cit.

equilibrium position is such that the import tariff has increased the price of domestic goods, but this increase is partially offset because the nominal price of non-tradeables has also risen somewhat. An export tax on exportables will reduce price to the producer of export goods. This will reduce incentive to produce. Alternatively an export subsidy (fiscal incentive) can be granted to export goods producers. This will increase the domestic price of exportables relative to importables and non-tradeables. It also induces increased production of exportables as resources are shifted from importables and domestic goods toward exportables. In the non-tradeable goods sector, these processes create a contraction in supply and an increase in demand placing upward pressure on the price of domestic goods until a new supply and demand equilibrium is reached.

These relationships can be formalized through two main approaches. One approach is based on a direct comparison between relative prices of importables

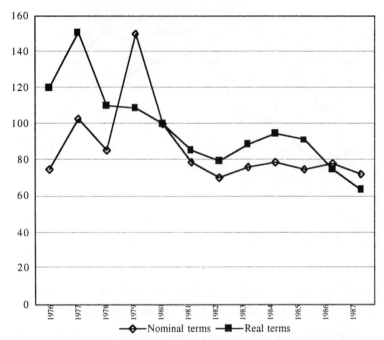

**Figure 37 Price indices for Sub-Saharan Africa's non-oil commodity
exports, 1976–87 (1980 = 100)**

Note: The nominal index in the fiugre is based on the dollar prices of 16 major commodities
(exlcuding petroleum), weighted by the share of the region's exports.

Source: *Financing Africa's Recovery*, op. cit.

and exportables. In this approach a particular tradeable sector is promoted
relative to the others if the price ratio is greater than unity. If the price ratio is
less than unity, then the sector will be taxed relative to others. If the price
ratio of exportables relative to importables is less than one, the production of
imported goods will be encouraged relative to exportables. If the real exchange
for importables (P_m/P_n) relative to that for exportables (P_x/P_n) is greater than
unity then importables are favoured. The ratio of exportable and importable
exchange rates is used as a measure of trade bias. Analyses using this approach
measure the consequences of trade policies on agricultural incentives by
comparing the effects on relative prices of direct interventions with the effects
of overall indirect (exchange rates) intervention. Notationally it can be
expressed as follows:

$$\frac{Px}{Pn} = \frac{(1 - tx)}{Pn} eP*x = (Rex) P* x \qquad (11)$$

$$\frac{Pm}{Pn} = \frac{(1+tm)}{Pn} eP*y = (REm)P*m \qquad (12)$$

where

Pm and Px are the domestic prices of importables and exportables;
P*m and P*x are their corresponding border prices;
tm and tx are import tariff and the implicit export tax rates;
Pn is the price of domestic goods;
e is the nominal exchange rate; and
Rex and Rem are the real exchange rates for exportables and importables respectively.

Dividing the first equation by the second, the trade bias (TB) is obtained.

$$TB = \frac{Px/P*x}{Pm/P*m} = \frac{(1 - tx)}{1+tin} = \frac{REx}{REm} \qquad (13)$$

If TB is greater than one, the trade bias favours exportables, and if it is less than one it implies that the TB is against exportables and in favour of importables. If it is unity it implies no trade bias, an indication that neither export promotion nor substitution is being encouraged by commercial and exchange rate policies.

Terms of trade shock can also bring in other complications, such as resource mobility between sectors. In SSA, exports consist largely of agricultural raw materials, the production of which is labour-intensive. It is, therefore, necessary to trace terms of trade shock on the factor markets. As the purchasing power of export earnings plummets, governments are tempted to control imports, thereby destabilizing relative prices. As prices of importables increase, resources flow out of the labour-intensive exportables sector to the importables. If government is forced to curb imports of intermediate goods because of shortage of foreign exchange, the production of both tradeables and non-tradeables will decline. The decline will depend on how the scarce import quotas are rationed among competing sectors, and on the possibilities of substituting domestically-produced inputs for imports in the production process. As import control tightens, capacity utilization and output fall. This will be reflected in unemployment as a result of the contraction of capacity utilization. Faced with growing unemployment in the formal sector, employment in the informal sector increases. However as aggregate real income declines, average income in the informal sector also falls. Accordingly, in addition to the contraction of goods due to imports curbs, aggregate domestic supply will also fall through the reduction in domestic output of both tradeables and non-tradeables.

In an attempt to restore internal and external equilibria, governments are forced to adopt vigorous trade policies. In Ghana, for instance, under the country's economic recovery programme which began in 1983, the main focus of government policy was to revive the cocoa production and exports through higher producer prices. Thus producer pricing policy served to block a rapid decline in the real price of cocoa and to change the inter-crop price structure in favour of cocoa (Table 34).

Table 34   Relative prices of agricultural crops, 1977–88 (1977 = 100)

	Consumer price index (combined)	Consumer price index (food)	Real food price index	Nominal cocoa price index	Real cocoa price index	Terms of trade c/a
	a	b	b/a	c	c/a	b/a
	i	ii	$iii = ii \div i$	iv	$v = iv \div i$	$vi = v \div iii$
1977	100	100	100	100	100	100
1978	173	159	92	200	115	125
1979	267	258	97	300	112	115
1980	401	393	98	300	75	78
1981	869	829	95	900	103	108
1982	1,062	1,125	105	900	85	81
1983	2,357	2,755	117	1,500	64	55
1984	3,304	3,059	93	2,251	68	73
1985	3,647	2,718	75	4,246	116	155
1986	4,523	3,269	72	6,414	142	197
1987	6,591	4,775	72	11,253	171	238
1988	8,581	6,283	73	14,066	164	225

Source: Computed.

Thus, using the national food index as a proxy, food prices remained fairly high but constant between 1978 to 1984 but then declined significantly. This decline has been very pronounced relative to cocoa, as illustrated in the above table. For food producers, the domestic terms of trade fell by about 50 per cent between 1982 and 1988. The changes in the domestic terms of trade in favour of export crops, especially due to price increases relative to non-tradeable agricultural commodities which consisted largely of food crops, raised the real exchange rate in favour of cocoa (Table 22).

Importers'/Exporters' Real Exchange Rates

Traditionally an importer rarely pays the world price for importing a particular commodity, and for any given nominal exchange rate the real exchange rates faced by exporters and importers are totally different. Generally, import taxes are levied on imports and export duties imposed on exports. Using the dollar to the cedi exchange rate convention, the exchange rate faced by importers can be notationally expressed as

$$\frac{\text{Real exchange rate}}{\text{RERz}} = \frac{E \cancel{c} \$/Pw\ (1+tz)}{\cancel{c}1/Pd} = \frac{E\$\cancel{c}\ (Pd)}{Pw\ (1+tz)} \qquad (14)$$

where

    tz   is the average rate of taxation (tariffs) on imports (CIF);
    RERz is the importers' exchange rate;
    Pw   is world price of the commodity; and
    Pd   is the domestic price of the commodity.

An increase in the import tax implies a depreciation in the real exchange rate faced by importers (i.e. RERz declines). In this case, for any amount of domestic currency, an importer acquires fewer imported goods. Conversely, a decrease in the input tax rate implies that a greater quantity of imported goods can be acquired.

    The real exchange rate faced by exporters can similarly be expressed as:

$$RERx = \frac{E\cancel{c}\$/Pn\ (1+tx)}{\cancel{c}1/Pd} = \frac{E\$\cancel{c}\ (Pd)}{Pw\ (1+tx)} \qquad (15)$$

where

    tx   is the rate of duties on exports (FOB); and
    RERx is real exchange rate for exports.

An increase in export tax rate implies an appreciation of the real exchange rate faced by exporters since the RERx increases. This implies that the competitive position of exporters is being eroded in the international markets.

Choice of Instruments for Policy Reform

Most SSA countries in the 1970s developed unsustainable financial imbalances in their economies and were compelled to implement macroeconomic policy reforms. In general it was a sequential process in which: i) a stabilization phase aimed at restoring internal and external macroeconomic equilibria was followed by; ii) a rehabilitation (or recovery) phase aimed at regaining full economic growth capacity; and then iii) a structural adjustment programme by the elimination of overvalued exchange rate reduction in industrial protection, and fiscal austerity. They involved a combination of demand-reducing policies to bring aggregate demand in line with aggregate supply and supply-increasing policies aimed at shifting incentives towards the production for exports. The purpose of the dynamic analysis at this level is to test whether the objective of macroeconomic stability is being met.

In the design of structural adjustment programmes, policies were grouped according to where their primary impact could be felt: i) domestic absorption (demand management policies); ii) current and potential output (structural policies); iii) the composition of absorption and production of tradeable and non-tradeable goods (exchange rate policies); and iv) capital flows (external financing policies) (Khan and Knight, 1985, pp. 13–7). Prudent demand management achieved through fiscal austerity was a prerequisite in adjustment policy aimed at regaining price and financial stability. The main instruments used for containing aggregate demand were restraint of monetary expansion and realistic tax policy. The major policy objectives aimed at strengthening the budgetary position through measures designed to increase revenues and restrain expenditures. This was achieved through programmes which encouraged substantial reductions in overall budget deficit and a corresponding decline in a government recourse to bank borrowing in order to curtail monetary expansion. Containing growth of liquidity and domestic credit was expected to moderate inflationary pressure. Exchange rate adjustment was used to hold down demand to manageable levels because a devaluation of the domestic currency increased the level of foreign prices measured in local currency, and therefore, prices of tradeable goods increased relative to non-traded goods in the domestic economy. On the demand side, therefore, the effect of devaluation on domestic absorption was expected to be negative by reducing private sector real wealth and expenditure owing to the impact on the overall price level on the real value of private sector financial assets, real wages and other factor incomes whose nominal values could not rise proportionately with the devaluation. From the point of view of current absorption, therefore, devaluation had a contractionary effect.

Structural policies to stimulate supply generally aimed at improving the efficiency of resource allocation and increasing the level or rate of growth of capacity output in the economy. Improving resource allocation relied heavily on the removal of distortions in the economy, the main sources of which were monopolies, public sector pricing policies, government price control, taxes and subsidies, tariffs and quota which resulted in the failure to set domestic prices at their international opportunity cost. Protective measures, and inefficiency derived from distortions associated with agricultural pricing policies, often caused prices of agricultural commodities to deviate in competitive markets. Such policies had a strong impact on the level of resource allocation to the agricultural sector as they acted as taxes on output and exports.

As regards increasing capacity output, policies which fostered the expansion of savings focused particularly on increasing the return on savings usually influenced by the interest rate. It was argued that if financial savings were interest sensitive, adjusting interest rates to realistic levels was expected to stimulate flows of both domestic and foreign savings. The increase in savings was expected to increase investment, and hence capacity growth. With appropriate exchange rates, positive real interest would influence capital inflows by creating a climate of confidence in the economy, and a resulting increase in foreign savings through capital inflows or remittances, which were expected to have a strong effect on the capital account of the balance of payments. Maintaining positive real interest rate policy was expected to: i) discourage investment in projects which could not yield adequate rate of return over the long run; ii) increase the supply of foreign savings; iii) eliminate distortions imposed by interest rate ceilings; iv) increase the flow of savings-investment process. Exchange rate policies, apart from restraining demand, on the supply side the effects of devaluation was expected to be stimulative because of the domestic price increases of domestic products it would provide to producers and exporters. It was expected that it would boost output, in that the prices of domestic factors of production would rise less than proportionately to the domestic currency price of final product.

Methodologies for Measuring the Effects of Market Intervention

In general the effects of policies that affect agricultural prices can be ascertained using one of several standard measures of market distortions which traditionally attempt to account for the divergence between domestic prices

(Pd) and world prices (Pw). All these measures are based on the principle of using comparable world prices or border prices as the social evolution of commodities or inputs that are traded internationally, since these world prices determine domestic prices in the absence of government policies. The principal sources of policy distortions are those affecting prices of outputs and inputs, factor costs and the exchange rate. A divergence between domestic prices and their border price equivalent will indicate the distorting effect of government policies of one of these types.

The measures used assumes that all differences between (Pd) and (Pw) not explicitly accounted for are due to policy distortions. The advantage of this approach is that it captures not only the obvious effects of official price policies but also the difficulty of measuring effects of policies such as quantitative restrictions on trade, or indirect effects transmitted through cross-elasticities of demand and supply of agricultural commodities that are substitutes or complements. The principal drawback of these methods is that any errors or discrepancies in taking account of explained differences in (Pd) and (Pw) (conversion, processing and transport costs, losses, quality premia, etc.) will be dumped together with policy effects. Despite these ambiguities, these measures provide the first approximation for measuring policy changes. This is done by computing commercial coefficients.

Commercial policy is the application of that body of economic theory which seeks to explain the effects of protective measures such as tariffs and subsidies on the performance of an economy. At first sight, the application of a protective measure will cause the price of imports to rise in the domestic market and thus make it easier for the domestic industry to operate profitably. If this were the only effect of the protective measure, it would be a very useful weapon in encouraging the development of a domestic industry in the face of well established competition from overseas which may be obtaining the benefits of economies of scale which are not, at first, available to the domestic industry. There are, however, other effects of protective measures which make the benefits they bestow less certain.

Sometimes a protective regime extends protection not only to consumer goods but also to raw materials. If the domestic price of raw materials is so raised by protection, the net effect may be to raise costs for domestic producers and make them less competitive in international markets. It can also happen that a protective regime can choke off a sufficient quantity of imports to result in an improvement in the balance of payments and a resulting upward pressure on the exchange rate. This will cause the exports of the country in question to become more expensive and imports to become cheaper. The aim of the protective regime may, therefore, be frustrated as competitive gains are eliminated. Furthermore, a protective regime may encourage one industry (producing exports or import substitutes) and in so doing may pull resources away from a domestic industry producing for consumption in the home market. The net effect may be to produce adverse symptoms within the economy rather than improvements.

In response to the widely-observed situation in developing countries of the deterioration in the domestic terms of trade facing the agricultural sector, and the proliferation of forms of intervention in response to failures of past policies, both the World Bank and the FAO initiated a series of methodological studies, as well as country-specific advisory studies in the area of agricultural pricing policy (FAO, 1984; Jaeger, 1988). The set of recently-developed analytical procedures for assessing the effects on agricultural production and consumption of government pricing policy (partial equilibrium measures of price efficiency) and economic growth was used, although some additional understanding of distributional consequences can also be secured.

The main thrusts of this methodological work have been threefold. Firstly, informal partial equilibrium measures of the incentive effects of price, taxation and protection policies have been developed on the basis of those schema for social cost-benefit analysis (SCBA) at the project level developed by Little and Mirlees (1974) and Squire and Van der Tak (1975). Secondly, these have been modified and extended to include the impact on the agricultural sector of macroeconomic policies which are not specifically concerned with agriculture as such especially the effects of deficit budgets and overvalued exchange rates. These methods have focused particularly on the efficiency implications of policies. Some work has also been done, thirdly, on aggregative measures identifying the distributional consequences of policies, especially between producers, consumers and government in the area of food policy. These measures have been derived from the application of the theory of consumer surplus. Considerably less work has been done in this and other 'equity' objective areas as compared with the efficiency objective.

The section that follows seeks to outline some of the mathematical constants that economists have developed to study both the positive and the negative effects of protective regimes on the economies on which they are imposed. They represent attempts to grapple with the problem of how to calculate the net effect of protection and to quantify it. The purpose of formulating these constants is to provide a framework which makes it easier for political decision-makers to assess the desirability of any protective regime.

It must be stated that, whilst the theoretical development of these constants has progressed to a stage of considerable sophistication, there remain substantial problems of application. These problems are caused by the difficulty of collecting data that must be input into the constants to bring them to life; in some instances this is simply because the data, though available, have not been collected; in other cases, the data are exceedingly hard to isolate and may be virtually uncollectable. The difficulty in actually calculating the commercial policy coefficients for many countries does not entirely degrade their usefulness. In that they draw attention to the various effects of protection, they are likely to lend to a more enlightened approach to its imposition.

Measures of Policy Distortions

The principal measures for evaluating policy distortions include:

- the producer price share (PPS);
- the nominal protection coefficient (NPC);
- the net nominal protection coefficient (NNPC);
- the effective protection coefficient (EPC);
- the net effective protection coefficient (NEPC);
- the producer subsidy equivalent (PSE);
- the consumer subsidy equivalent (CSE);
- the domestic resource cost (DRC); and
- the net economic benefit (NEB).

Each measure is defined mathematically in the section that follows.

Producer price share (PPS) This first measure is a simple ratio of producer price to the international price converted at the official exchange rate. This measure is the most widely used, probably because of its simplicity. Marketing costs of moving from one market to the other are ignored commonly on the presumption that they are small. Many studies inappropriately refer to this as the nominal protection coefficient (NPC). The producer price share (PPS) is distinct from the NPC in that no account is taken of the marketing and processing costs associated with moving from the farm to the border along the marketing channel by which the two prices are linked (Jaeger and Humphrey, 1988).

$$PPS = \frac{Pf}{P_w \cdot R_n} \qquad (16)$$

where

    Pf   = the farm gate price of the commodity;
    Pw   = the world reference price of the commodity; and
    Rn   = the official (nominal) exchange rate.

The causes of periodic rises and falls in the share of the value of the crop going to the farmer cannot be ascertained from the PPS above since the PPS is a function of domestic producer price, a rise in the international price or an adjustment of the exchange rate.

In order to decompose the change in a given year into its component parts a different equation can be derived which is separable into effects of each of the three variables: producer price, border price and exchange rate.

$$PPSt = Pdt/Rt\ Pwt \tag{17}$$

where

    PPSt = producer price share for a given commodity in period t;
    Pdt   = official producer price for a given commodity;
    Rn   = official exchange rate (nominal); and
    Pwt   = international reference price for the commodity.

The total derivative for the above is

$$dPPS = dPd/(RtPw) - Pd\ dR/(Pw\ R^2n) - Pd\ dPw/(Rn\ Pw2) \tag{18}$$

$$DPPS = \frac{dPd}{Rt\ Pw} - \frac{PddR}{Pw\ R^2_n} - \frac{Pd\ dPw}{Rn\ P^2_w} \tag{19}$$

Using this formula, the result of the analysis of major export crops (Kenya coffee, Kenya tea, Malawi tobacco, Malawi cotton, Nigeria cocoa and Nigeria cotton) is presented in Table 35.

The result of the decomposition indicates that, in general, changes in producer prices were in most years insufficient to offset the negative effect of changes in the international prices and exchange rate. This is because in years when the net effect was negative, the rises in producer prices did not receive the full extent of the rise in international prices nor the effect of currency devaluation.

Table 35   **The decomposition of annual changes in the ratio of official producer prices to international prices of principal export crops**

Year	Official producer	International price effect	Exchange rate effect	Net effect
1971	-.042	-.239	-.030	-.311
1972	+.027	-.251	+.065	-.159
1973	-.092	-.281	+.245	-.128
1974	+.023	-.385	+.112	-.250
1975	+.613	-.367	-.204	+.109
1976	-.101	-.367	-.204	-.672
1977	+.044	-.222	+.004	-.174
1978	+.140	-.185	+.020	-.025
1979	+.102	-.185	+.084	+.001
1980	+.108	-.130	-.029	-.051
1981	+.103	-.238	-.119	-.254
1982	+.008	-.181	-.033	-.206
1983	-.079	-.252	-.022	-.195
1984	-.039	-.237	-.139	-.415
1985	+.002	-.309	+.037	-.370

If all prices were freely determined in open markets and if effective rates of taxation were the same for all commodities, the value added in agriculture (VAa) as a ratio to GDP (Y) would have been much higher than is currently the case. But for many years the agricultural sector vis-à-vis non-agricultural sectors (industry and services) has been faced with negative effective protection. This has arisen because of the adverse public policy-induced controlled real price for agriculture that has been kept less than should have been realized under open-markets-cum-equal taxation, i.e.

$$\frac{Pca - Pfa}{P} \tag{20}$$

where

Pca = the controlled price of agriculture;
Pfa = the free market price for agriculture; and
P   = the general price level in the economy.

The purpose of the subsequent section is to indicate, describe and assess members of a set of recently-developed analytical procedures for assessing the effects on agricultural production and consumption of government pricing policy on allocative efficiency, and economic growth, although some additional understanding of distributional consequences is also secured.

The nominal protection coefficient (NPC) The NPC of a commodity is defined as the percentage excess of the domestic price over the world market price resulting from the application of a protective measure. It is expressed in percentage term, and it is called the nominal rate of protection. In a situation where the only protective measure in use is a tariff, and assuming that this is not so severe to completely choke off all trade, then the nominal rate of protection will, therefore, be the difference between the domestic price so calculated and the world price, expressed as a percentage of the world market price.

Let Pw = world market price;

t = rate of tariff expressed as a percentage of import value;

then tPw = tariff payable on each unit of commodity traded.

Let Pd = domestic price;

Pwt = world market price + tariff payable.

If the nominal protection is the percentage excess of domestic market price over world price, then the nominal protection coefficient (NPC) can be calculated as follows:

$$NPC = \frac{Pwt - Pw}{Pw} \tag{21}$$

$$= \frac{(Pw + tPw) - Pw}{Pw}$$

$$= t.$$

In this simple case it follows that the nominal rate of protection is equal to the *ad valorem* rate of tariff. The nominal rate of protection can also be computed for a regime that has export subsidies in place. In this case, let s = rate of export subsidy

$$NPC = \frac{Pws - Pw}{Pw} \tag{22}$$

$$= \frac{(Pw + Pws) - Pw}{Pw}$$

$$= s$$

In the same way nominal rates of protection can also be computed for a regime in which there are export taxes. These can be regarded as negative subsidies because they reduce domestic prices and therefore give negative nominal protection.

Let t' = export tax expressed as a percentage of export value, then

$$NPC = \frac{Pwt' - Pw}{Pw} \tag{23}$$

$$= \frac{(Pw + t'Pw) - Pw}{Pw}$$

$$= t'$$

The nominal rate of protection obviously affects prices in the market for goods and services, and will, therefore, affect the decision taken by consumers. However, tariffs can also be applied to producer goods – the imported raw materials that are used in a manufacturing process; for instance, and if this occurs, then the nominal rate of protection will not reflect the impact of the protective measure on the producers. We shall revert to this subject when considering effective protection coefficient.

Marketing studies have indicated that neglecting marketing costs can produce misleading results. Choosing the appropriate point along the marketing channel at which comparison is made is equally important. Accordingly, NPC should compare producer price and international price net of transport and processing costs required to bring the commodity from both sources to a single point along the actual marketing channel and in the same form. It is appropriate for exported commodities to be compared at the border, and for commodities that compete for imports to be compared at the principal domestic marketing centre. Taking this into account (see chapter 5) the NPC $= \dfrac{(Pf + Cfb + Cs) / Rn}{Pw - Cbp - Cpw}$ (24)

where

Pf = farm gate price;
Cbp = marketing costs from border to port;
Cfb = marketing costs from farm to border;
Cpw = marketing cost, port to world reference market;
Cs = processing cost,

and for commodities that compete with imports NPC is computed,

NPC (imported commodity) $= \dfrac{(Pf + Cfm + Cs)/Rn}{Pw + Cmb + Cbp + Cpw}$ (25)

where

Cfm = marketing costs from farm to domestic market;
Cmb = marketing costs from domestic market to border;
Cbp = marketing costs from border to port;
Cpw = marketing cost from port to world reference market; and
Cs = processing cost.

Net nominal protection coefficient (NNPC) Since exchange rate policy has an important effect on the competitiveness of agricultural production, it is essential to assess whether these policies impose an implicit tax or subsidy on domestic production. The net NPC is analogous to the nominal protection coefficient, but a shadow or estimated equilibrium exchange rate is used to convert prices to comparable units. Estimating the degree of over- or undervaluation has been explained. The use of the calculated shadow or equilibrium exchange rate will give some indication of the impact of exchange rates on incentives, and are an improvement over simply relying on official exchange rates for these comparisons which, in some cases, would give very misleading results on the degree of taxation (or subsidy) of agriculture. The NNPC is computed as follows (i.e. using equation 21), the border price equivalents are in foreign currency multiplied by equilibrium exchange rate.

NNPC $= \dfrac{(Pf + Cfb + Cs) / Re}{Pw - Cbp - Cpw}$ (26)

where

Re = the equilibrium or shadow exchange rate.

An overvalued exchange rate will penalize producers of exports by reducing the domestic currency value of their products and will reward importers by making imports cheaper than they ought to be.

$$\text{NNPC (for imported commodities)} = \frac{(Pf + Cfm + Cs)/Re}{Pw + Cmb + Cbp + Cpw} \qquad (27)$$

The introduction of equilibrium exchange rate is to assess the effect of indirect price intervention on relative prices. The most important of these is the trade policy – namely the maintenance of an overvalued exchange rate. Usually the producer prices are adjusted by the ratio of the equilibrium to the official exchange rate – thus providing an indication of what they would have been in the absence of trade restrictions and the maintenance of an over- or undervalued exchange rate.

The measures presented so far address the extent of price distortions on agricultural output. In many countries, however, government policy effects on inputs prices are equally important – especially in the case of fertilizer subsidies. To take account of policy distortions for both inputs and outputs, and to assess the net effect, one uses effective protection coefficient. It is equivalent to the ratio of value added expressed in domestic market prices to value added in border prices, and can be interpreted as a measure of the net effect of policies on value added.

Effective protection coefficient (EPC) The business of many firms is to import raw materials to combine these with other domestic inputs (e.g. labour) to add value in the production process and to sell the product on world market. If there is a tariff imposed on all imports, this will extend protection to sales of the product at home, as competing foreign goods will be priced more highly as a result of the tariff. However, the tariff will also have the effect of increasing the cost of production in that it raises the price of the imported raw materials used in the production process. Obviously, if the import content of the product is high, then the tariff will offset some of the value added by the production process.

The effective rate of protection expresses the margin of protection on value added in the production process (rather than on the product price as in the case of nominal protection). It is defined as the percentage excess of domestic value added which results from the imposition of a tariff or any other protective measure on the product and its inputs over world market valued added

V_1 = value-added by the production process with protection in place; and

V = value-added by the production process without protection.

By definition, the effective protection coefficient is the excess of domestic value-added over world market value-added.

$$EPC = \frac{V_1 - V}{V} \tag{28}$$

Consider a country which is without any tariff protection and which produces machines which sell at a world price of US$2,000; the remaining US$8,000 represents the costs of other imported inputs. If a 10 per cent tariff is imposed on all imported machines, this has the effect of raising the domestic price to US$11,000. Thus the reward of the production process is now US$3,000, which is US$1,000, or 50 per cent more than would be possible with no tariff. We can see that in this example, whilst the nominal rate of protection is 10 per cent, the effective rate of production is 50 per cent.

Suppose in the above example the production process added US$1,000 (instead of US$2,000) and the remaining US$9,000 of the world market price represented the import costs. The 10 per cent tariff now causes the domestic price to rise to US$11,000, which doubles the rewards payable to production process (from US$1,000 to US$2,000). The effective rate of protection is therefore 100 per cent.

It can be seen that the smaller the value added by the domestic process, the greater the level of effective protection or a given rate of nominal protection. This relationship is described by the equation:

$$EPC = \frac{NPC}{1-a} \tag{29}$$

where

a = the proportion of importable inputs (here assumed to carry no tariffs).

1-a, therefore, represents the proportion of the inputs that have a domestic origin.

This example demonstrates the calculation of EPC when a tariff is imposed on a finished product and it assumes that no tariff payable on the imported materials. Such is not often the case and it is possible to build into the calculation of EPC the effect of nominal tariffs on raw material imports.

A duty on imported inputs is equivalent to a tax on the process using these inputs and this tax reduces the effective rate of protection that the process would have enjoyed from a tariff on its outputs alone. We can illustrate this point by reference to the previous example, where there was a 10 per cent tariff on the firm output and where the value added by the process was 20 per cent. This situation resulted in an EPC of 0.5 or 50 per cent. Assume now that there is a 5 per cent nominal tariff imposed on the import of all raw materials. This raises the input price from US$8,000 to US$8,400. With the 10 per cent duty payable on the finished product the machine will cost US$11,000 in the home market and the domestic value-added is US$2,600.

$$\mathrm{EPC} = \frac{V1 - V}{V} \tag{30}$$

$$= \frac{2600 - 2000}{2000}$$

$$= 0.3 \text{ (or 30 per cent)}$$

It is possible for the effective rate of protection to be negative if the tariff structure is such as to discourage the domestic production process. This will occur when the duty on imported raw materials is so great as to reduce the value added by the process even when the duty on finished product is taken into account.

Consider a country whose farmers produce rice for sale on the world markets. Assume that the country imposes a 10 per cent duty on the fertilizer used for rice production. If the fertilizer accounts for 60 per cent of the price of rice then, when the tariff is imposed, the value added by the rice farmers decreases from 40 per cent to 34 per cent. Before the imposition of the tariff, rice selling for US$1,000 on the world market required US$60 of fertilizer, yielding a reward to the farmers of US40. If the tariff results in the fertilizer costs rising by 10 per cent to US$60, then only US$34 remains to the farmers. Mathematically this can be computed as follows:

$$EPC = \frac{V1 - V}{V} \tag{31}$$

$$= \frac{40 - 34}{40}$$

$$= .15 \ (15\%)$$

In general it can be seen that the EPC will be higher than, equal to, or lower than the rate of tariff on the product depending on whether this tariff exceeds, equals, or falls short of the average rate of tariff on the material inputs.

Again, as with NPC, it will be misleading to look at EPC only on the basis of tariffs; marketing and processing costs must also be taken into account, because value added is normally defined as the value of the output at any point in the production, and distribution process in any given period, less the value of the purchased inputs in the same period less depreciation. Hence

$$EPC = \frac{(Pf - aij \times Pfj) + Cfb + Cs)/Rn}{(Pwm - aij \times Pw) - Cbp - Cpw} \tag{32}$$

where

aij = the quantity of the jth inputs used to produce the unit of output;
Pfj = the domestic price of the jth input; and
Pb = the border price of the jth input.

For commodities which compete with imports domestically

$$EPC \ (for \ imported \ commodities) = \frac{[(Pf-aijxPfj)+Cfm-Cs]/Rn}{[(Pw-aijxPwj)-Cms-Cpw} \tag{33}$$

where

Cfm = marketing costs from farm to domestic market;
Cmb = marketing costs from domestic market to border;
Cbp = marketing costs from border to port;
Cpw = marketing costs from port; and
Cs = processing costs and margin.

$$Net \ EPC = \frac{[(Pf - aij \times Pfj) + Cfb + Cs]/Re}{[(Pw - aij \times Pwj) - Cbp - Cpw]} \tag{34}$$

where

Re = the equilibrium or shadow rate.

Effective subsidy coefficient (ESC) Effective subsidy coefficient measures the degree of protection extended to the value-added by a production process on export subsidy, i.e. export subsidies can provide protection to domestic production processes as well as tariffs. In other words, the ESC is the effective protection coefficient (EPC) adjusted for subsidies. For instance, this measure covers the common practice whereby marketing boards deduct from the producer prices the net cost of domestically-produced farm inputs which are provided to producers at subsidized prices. The ESCs will be larger than the EPCs for products which utilize such inputs.

Net nominal and net effective protection are, therefore, useful in price analysis. If a domestic industry is protected by a tariff or export subsidy, it can operate with a value-added that is higher than under free trade. This will encourage the movement of factors of production into the protected industry, and the implication is that resources will be removed from some other non-protected industry. The shift in resources introduces complicated changes in relative prices that have to be taken into account in price analysis.

Protection also has the effect of improving the balance of payments situation in that it discourages the domestic consumption of imported goods and encourages the production of import substitutes. In this way it is possible to maintain a balance of payments equilibrium at a lower rate of exchange than would be possible under a free trade regime. The greater the scope of protection, the greater will be the foreign exchange effect. However, the more industries that are protected, the less will be the reallocative effect due to the tariffs within the economy. If only one industry is protected then it will enjoy considerable advantage over others, and factors of production will be pulled in its direction. If all industries are protected then the reallocative effect will be negligible, as no single industry is particularly favoured.

An example may help to illustrate this point. Consider a country producing textiles whose world market price is US$1 per unit, and the cost of whose imported materials is US$0.6. This yields a world market value added of US$0.4. Assume also that the going exchange rate is ¢1.00 to the dollar so that the value added in the domestic market is ¢40. If there is a 20 per cent tariff on imports of the finished product and a 10 per cent tariff on the imported inputs, then the domestic price rises from ¢100 to ¢120, and the cost of the input rises from ¢60 to ¢66. Domestic value added is now ¢54. Under these circumstances, where only one industry is protected, it is unlikely that the exchange rate will be much affected because the import savings due to only one industry will be small in comparison to the total import bill. However, if all industries are protected, this will alter the exchange rate. Assume, for instance, that under free trade the exchange rate is ₡10 to the dollar but general protection reduces the exchange rate to ₡100 to the dollar. If there is a specific tariff on textiles of 20 per cent, then the domestic price will rise to ₡120. This can be compared to the domestic price under free trade (where the higher rate of exchange rate holds) of ₡110, demonstrating that the specific tariff has the effect of raising domestic prices by 9 per cent. We say that net nominal protection coefficient is 9 per cent. Note that this is considerably less than might be expected from simple observation of the tariff on textiles if one took no account of the foreign exchange effect of the general tariff on other manufactures.

Hence net nominal protection is the measure of nominal protection that takes into account the foreign exchange effect of general protection. It can be defined as the percentage excess of the domestic price (measured at the actual rate of exchange) under the world market price (measured at the free trade rate of exchange) resulting in the application of a specific protection measure. Net effective protection also takes into account the foreign exchange effect of a general tariff but is concerned with the necessary adjustments to the calculation of value-added rather that the domestic price.

In the example above, we have seen that if only the textile industry is protected then the value-added by the production process is ₡54. This can be compared to the free trade value added of ₡ 40 to calculate the rate of effective protection.

i.e. $EPC = \dfrac{V1 - V}{V}$ (35)

$= \dfrac{54 - 40}{40}$

$= .35 \ (35\%)$

However, if the 20 per cent tariff on textiles is operating as part of a regime of general protection which has the effect of improving the exchange rate from ₡110 to ₡100 to the dollar, then the free trade value added becomes ₡44. This is because the world market value-added is US$0.4, which at the rate of exchange induced by general protection (₡110 = $1) is worth ₡44.

The calculation of effective protection that takes into account exchange rate changes (net effective protection) is now

$$NEP = \frac{54 - 44}{44}$$

$$= .227 \ (22.7\%)$$

Note that this is less than the 35 per cent EPC, which results from the establishment of a 20 per cent tariff on textiles in the absence of a general tariff regime and the resulting improvement in the exchange rate.

We have seen that general protection overvalues the price of the currency as compared to the price that would hold in a free trade situation and we have also seen that effective rates of protection which take no account of this in their calculation will overstate the degree of protection extended to a particular industry by any specific protective measure. Similarly, where tariffs exist in exported materials of an exporting industry, EPC so calculated will understate the damage that protective measures do to the industry. We can also see that the degree of protection applied and the exchange rate are independent and various combinations can be produced which will result in a balance of payments equilibrium. EPC is calculated assuming a static rate of exchange and, if this is altered, so too will be the EPC. Net effective protection, on the other hand, takes into account the overvaluation of the exchange rate as compared to a hypothetical free trade situation. If there is considerable factor mobility, the degree of exchange rate overvaluation will be quite small. This is because, as tariff is imposed, the movement of factors from export to import competing industries is very efficient and any loss in export earnings can be made up by savings in the import bill. There is, therefore, no tendency for the exchange rate to change and EPC calculations would therefore need no adjustment to allow for exchange rate overvaluation. Such is not the case. Often reallocations between export and import competing industries result in changing costs of production and a resulting loss of competitiveness.

Consumer and producer subsidy equivalent The producer subsidy equivalent is the percentage of the total revenue received by a producer as a result of a protective measure. Thus if a producer of food stuffs could market his output for US$0.5 million under free trade, but with protection he can obtain US$1 million, then the producer subsidy equivalent is US$0.5 (50 per cent). The consumer subsidy equivalent measures the implicit tax rate on the consumer that results from the imposition of the tariff regime. Thus if the consumer paid US$1 per unit of a commodity under free trade, but with protection the prices rise to US$1.50, then the consumer subsidy equivalent is 0.5 (50 per cent).

While the NPC, EPC, NNPC and ESC relate primarily to the incentive effects in resource allocation, the producer subsidy equivalent (PSE) and consumer subsidy equivalent (CSE) are indicators of both incentives and the broad allocation of incomes between producers and consumers of specific commodities. As stated above, the PSE comprises of the producer subsidy less the indirect taxes expressed as a percentage of the market value ('price' x quantity per annum) of each commodity. 'Price' must include any direct payments to producers over and above market value. CSE on the other hand, comprises the subsidy given to consumers of a particular commodity; thus, indirect taxes paid on it, expressed as a percentage of the total value consumed domestically (volume of consumption x retail price).

Domestic resource cost and international trade (DRC) The sale of an export will have the effect of generating foreign exchange. However, production of exportables obviously involves an opportunity cost in terms of the resources the economy must deploy to produce it and which could be used instead to produce another good – perhaps one which could be consumed at home. The domestic resource cost measures the real opportunity cost in terms of domestic resources of producing a real marginal unit of foreign exchange. This could best be explained by the theory of comparative advantage, which says that if the relative costs of producing two commodities differ in two countries, then both countries would gain from trade, i.e. each country specializes in the production of that commodity in which it has relative cost advantage. Consider Côte d'Ivoire and Ghana, both countries able to grow beans and maize. It is further assumed that there are equal numbers of farm units in each country, with each farm producing one commodity.

Production per farm in tonnes

	Maize	*Beans*
Côte d'Ivoire	4	2
Ghana	2	1.2

The average farm in Côte d'Ivoire either produces four tonnes of maize or two tonnes of beans, and not both quantities at the same time. Assume further that in Côte d'Ivoire, half of the 10,000 farms produce maize and the remainder beans, while in Ghana 70 per cent of the 10,000 farms produce maize and the rest beans. Côte d'Ivoire will produce 20,000 tonnes of maize (5,000 x 4) and 10,000 tonnes of beans (5,000 x 2) while Ghana produces 14,000 tonnes of maize (7,000 x 2) and 3,600 tonnes of beans (3,000 x 1.2), as summarized below.

Production of maize and beans (tonnes)

	Maize	*Beans*
Côte d'Ivoire	20,000	10,000
Ghana	14,000	3,600

In this example, Côte d' Ivoire has absolute cost advantage in producing beans over Ghana because it can produce two tonnes of beans while Ghana produces 1.2 tonnes per farm. If the objective is to maximize the production of both, the absolute cost advantage may not be relevant. If Ghana decides to produce beans only, and 9,000 farms in Côte d'Ivoire produce maize and 1,000 produce beans, the outcome will be as follows:

Production of maize and beans (tonnes)

	Maize	*Beans*
Côte d'Ivoire	36,000	2,000
Ghana	0	12,000

If Côte d'Ivoire barters 16,000 tonnes of maize for 8,200 tonnes of beans, the people in both countries will be better off than before because, while consumption of maize in Côte d'Ivoire will be unchanged, that of beans will increase to 10,200 tonnes, and the consumption of both maize and beans in Ghana will increase to 16,000 tonnes and 3,800 tonnes respectively. Let these quantities be represented by Qm for maize and Qb for beans respectively.

When farmers in Côte d'Ivoire raise their production of maize by four tonnes, they have to reduce their production of beans by two tonnes. Thus the cost of maize can be expressed in terms of beans (Qb/Qm), i.e. the opportunity cost of one tonne of maize is equal to half a tonne of beans because on average, half a tonne of beans is given up when an extra tonne of maize is produced in Côte d'Ivoire = 2/4 = 0.5 tonnes of beans, while opportunity cost of one tonne of beans (Qm/Qb) = 4/2 = 2 tonnes of maize. In Ghana the opportunity cost of one tonne of maize (Qb/Qm) = 1.2/2 = 0.6 tonnes while the opportunity cost of one tonne of beans (Qm/Qb) = 2/1.2 = 1.67 tonnes of maize. Thus the opportunity cost of producing maize is lowest in Côte d'Ivoire while that of producing beans is lowest in Ghana. This implies that total production can be increased if each country specializes in the production of that commodity which it produces with the lowest opportunity cost.

These examples confirm that, as long as opportunity costs differ among nations, all trading countries benefit by specializing in the production and export of that commodity in which a country has a relative or comparative advantage. Differences in opportunity costs arise due to differences in the level of technological advances, in the proportion of potentially mobile factors (between sectors see chapter 3) or in the availability of specific non-mobile factors such as land and natural resources. The above example can be illustrated graphically, as in Figure 38, taking the case of Côte d'Ivoire as the small home country and Ghana representing the rest of the world. Côte d'Ivoire is regarded as being small in the sense that it may buy or sell all it wants at world prices. In the figure, HH^1 represents the production possibility curve and it is linear because a constant return to factors is assumed and its slope is - Qb/Qm. TT represents isoincome expressed in terms of tonnage of commodities produced part of which can be traded along TT. Côte d'Ivoire can decide to sell the whole 36,000 tonnes of maize represented by T^{1}T^1. The country will be better off producing 36,000 but bartering 16,000 tonnes, with 8,200 tonnes of beans from Ghana. The trading is along TT.

One difficulty with this two goods model is that it implies complete specialization, which seldom occurs. As was discussed in chapter 2, empirical evidence of the production function starts with increasing incremental output for additional factor input, but at some scale the production process begins to experience diminishing marginal return to incremental factor inputs. The production possibility curve is, therefore, convex, as shown in Figure 39, with HH^1 representing the curve and complete specialization cannot, therefore, be expected. The maximum income is determined where the isoincome line touches the production possibility curve at A and the terms of trade line TT. Essentially, as explained in chapter 2, the optimal combination of the two commodities is given by the point where the isoincome line is tangential to TT. As the terms of trade rise in favour of maize, farmers will reallocate some resources from beans to the production of maize in order to take advantage of the higher world prices. The gains from trade can be divided into two parts: production and consumption gains.

Beginning at point A, the autarchy point, and assuming open trade, the

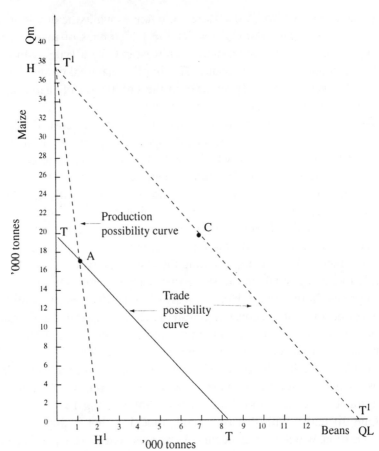

Figure 38 Comparative advantage and specialization

rise in the international terms of trade raises the optimal combination of the production of the two crops to point C. Since Côte d'Ivoire trades along TT, maize production will increase from S_1 to D_1. If the country has to sustain autarchy, it will export $S_1 - D_1$ and imports beans $S_2 - D_2$. As the terms of trade improve further in favour of maize to T_1T_1, the movement from A to B represents the consumption gains from trade that follows from allowing the Ivorians to buy beans at cheaper international prices. The movement from B to C represents gains that accrue as a result of the country specializing in the production of maize in which it has comparative advantage. If there are further improvements in the international terms of trade, the country production will increase to D_1 of which $D^1_1 - S^1_1$ will be exported, thus allowing Côte d'Ivoire to import $S^1_2 - D^1_2$ tonnes of beans. Thus the country will gain, represented

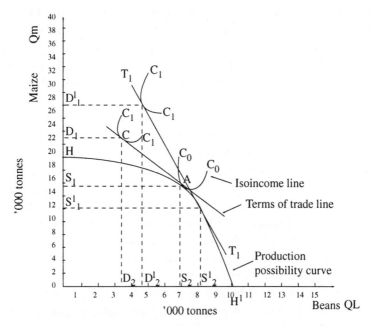

Figure 39 The impact of changes in international terms of trade on exports and imports

by $C_1D^1_2$, and Côte d'Ivoire will be able to expand exports and increase imports of beans. These will be gains to the country because of the export at higher relative prices but importing at lower relative prices. The international terms of trade can, however, be altered by the imposition of tariffs, or increased supply of the commodity could lower its world price. As the international terms of trade for maize deteriorate, farmers will transfer resources to the production of alternative crops.

The DRC concept, based on comparative advantage principle, was developed as a measure of the degree of protection that could be extended by the use of tariffs and export subsidies. This was necessary as for many developing countries, measures of EPC are not accurately reflecting the degree of protection produced by a given tariff regime and, therefore, they misstate the domestic reallocative effect of the protection.

In many countries there are market imperfection such as subsidies on the use of capital and minimum wage legislation, so that factor prices fail to describe the true opportunity cost of producing an export. If factor costs are inappropriate, value added calculations (and, therefore, calculation of EPC) cannot properly be made. Moreover, the net direction of the resource pull will be influenced not just by the tariff regime but also by the factor market imperfections. This can be seen by considering an industry in which the labour market is made imperfect by militant trade unions who hold the price of labour above the world going rate. This would cause the price of the product to rise in such a way as to reduce the effect of an export subsidy (if such were in place).

It was also observed in many economies that there were few firms producing any single commodity, and this permitted the exploitation of monopoly power in protected domestic markets. If protection resulted in increased monopoly profit rather than a reallocation of resources within the economy in favour of exporting industries, it was clearly a bad thing. Furthermore, monopoly power allowed prices to be higher in the protected domestic market. Measures of EPC which depend on the calculation of value added were likely to be misleading, because opportunity costs are not easily measured. Applied economics, therefore, has to find proxies which are close enough to be the ideal of measurements. One such proxy is the DRC calculated by adjusting estimates of the cost of inputs of factors of production (capital and labour) to reflect shadow prices rather than market prices. Shadow prices are estimated to reflect the true social opportunity cost of the factors and take into account whatever subsidies or restraints on their existence.

$$DRC = \cfrac{\text{The economic value in domestic currency at accounting prices of domestic resources used in the production of a unit of commodity}}{\left(\begin{array}{c}\text{economic unit value} \\ \text{in foreign currency of} \\ \text{the commodity}\end{array}\right) - \left(\begin{array}{c}\text{economic value in foreign} \\ \text{currency of the imported} \\ \text{resources consumed in the} \\ \text{production of the commodity}\end{array}\right)}$$

Mathematically it can be expressed as follows:

$$DRC_i = \frac{S_j V_{ji}}{IVA} \tag{36}$$

where

S_j = the shadow price of the jth domestic factor of production;
V_{ji} = is the amount of the jth factor used per unit of output of i; and
IVA = the international value-added by the ith activity.

The shadow price of the factor is multiplied by the amount used, given a measure of the total factor cost of producing i. This may be regarded as the value-added measured in resource terms. It can be seen that DRC is a measure of the total value added as a fraction of international value added. This may be contrasted to EPC which is exceeded by value added as the percentage of international value-added. Domestic resource costs are used along with EPCs in estimating the height of a protective barrier in developing countries. Usually, EPC gives a better indication of the reallocative incentive (efficiency) created by the regime, while DRC provides a better measure of the cost of the regime.

Domestic price bias If there is a free market in a commodity, its price can easily be established by reference to world markets. On the other hand, if there is a protective regime in operation, domestic prices may be substantially different. Price bias compares prices under the two systems. It measures the degree to which incentives are provided by the protective regime to exporting and import competing industries as opposed to the situation that would prevail under free trade. In a world in which there are only two commodities, price bias is the ratio of the domestic price of import competing to exportable goods to the international relative price of importables relative to exportables. Mathematically, domestic price bias (DPB) is expressed as:

$$DPB = \frac{Pm/Qm}{Px/Qx} \qquad (37)$$

where

Pm = domestic price of import competing goods;
Qm = international price of importables;
Px = domestic prices of exportables; and
Qx = international price of exportables.

In the trade regime in which there are more than two products and where there are varying levels of protection extended to different industries, individual industries rates of production must be aggregated before a regime can be discovered. In this case DPB can be expressed:

$$DPB = \frac{Wi\,\dfrac{(Pmi)}{(Qmi)}}{Wj\,\dfrac{(Pxi)}{(Qxj)}} \qquad (38)$$

where

W   = weighting;
P   = domestic price;
Q   = international price;
i   = index of import competing commodities; and
j   = index of exportable commodities.

A difficulty arises in measuring the correct weighting that would be given to each of the prices in question. For trade regimes which prohibit the import of goods that are produced locally, it seems clear that weighting different commodity prices by the values of the import would fail to measure the true extent of the bias. The DPB has been developed by the FAO, alongside the net nominal protection coefficient, to estimate how far the domestic price policies, including the exchange rate, have affected, over a given period of time, the incentive pattern for import-competing and export commodities. Notionally, based on FAO work, the DPB reflects for a set of commodities the ratio of (a) the index of national terms of trade to (b) the international terms of trade.

An alternative (and more data demanding) method of calculation is given by the following equation:

$$DPB_t = \frac{NNPC_t - NNPC_b}{NNPC_b} \times 100 \qquad (39)$$

where

DPB_t = domestic price bias for period t;
$NNPC_t$ = net nominal protection coefficient for period t; and
$NNPC_b$ = net nominal protection coefficient for base period.

The measure is one of change in the domestic price bias over the period in question; the absolute level would depend on the degree of bias at the base period. A negative change (see Table 36) could either mean that a bias in favour of that commodity had been reduced or that an adverse bias was being accentuated.

Net economic benefit Economic decisions often have to be taken where there is no adequate market test for the pricing of some of the major inputs. For example, building a road will produce costs such as the cost of raw materials

Table 36   Kenya: income terms of trade index for the agricultural sector, 1970–82 (1972 = 100)

	Official marketed production Qa	Net barter terms of trade P1/P2	Income term of trade Qa P1/P2
1970	85	100	85
1971	86	92	79
1972	100	100	100
1973	108	96	104
1974	107	91	97
1975	107	88	94
1976	117	121	142
1977	131	152	198
1978	126	124	157
1979	123	113	139
1980	133	106	141
1981	140	98	136
1982	141	88	124
Average annual rate of growth	3.5	-1.3	2.2

Source: Belshaw, 1985.

and labour which can easily be estimated with reference to market prices and some, such as the cost of additional pollution and congestion which cannot be ignored. Similarly the outputs of such a project may well be difficult to quantify in money terms – for instance, the benefit which accrues to users of the road in terms of the journey time saved. This difficulty has led to the development of an extensive literature in the area of cost-benefit analysis. The underlying principle of this work is that in evaluating the social profitability of a project, the real total opportunity costs of production should be compared with real social benefits outweighing the social costs, then the project should be undertaken; if on the other hand, the net marginal benefit is negative (i.e. the costs outweigh the benefits), then it should be shelved.

In theory, cost-benefit analysis can be applied to any economic problem such as changes in the rate of exchange or in the tariff regime. These measures will have wide repercussions for the economy but these can be divided into the effects on production and consumption of final goods and the effects on material inputs. This will cause export prices to fall on world markets and, assuming that demand is responsive to changes in price, then sales will increase and extra revenue will be earned abroad. One of the benefits of the exchange depreciation is, therefore, the sum of all the extra foreign revenues earned by exporting firms as a consequence of the devaluation. It is possible that some exporting industries will face a market which is unlikely to lead to an increase in sales of extra foreign revenue being earned. In fact export earnings may decrease because the reduction in price consequent on the depreciation is not offset by extra export volumes. For these industries, depreciation is a bad thing and the sum of their loss in export earnings will represent an economic cost.

In a similar way it is possible to assess the impact of the exchange depreciation on input prices and volumes. Most obvious is the extra cost to the economy of the increase in the price of material imports. This could lead to the development of domestic sources of supply with the extra employment and investment that this would entail (a benefit): it certainly will result in higher costs for the industries that are dependent on importable raw materials.

Net economic benefit measures the difference between the total economic costs and the total economic benefits. It may be regarded as a measure of how worthwhile a project is. By comparing the NEB for two or more rival projects, decisions can be made between alternatives – the project with the highest NEB being selected in preference to the others. Generally NEB is used to decide whether some specific projects should go ahead rather than assessing the desirability of a macroeconomic change, such as a change in the exchange rate. The NEB of a project can be defined as the sum of all benefits minus costs on the input side, and all benefits minus costs on the output side. Suppose we have commodity groups (branches of production) in the economy which use primary factors. Suppose also that the accounting (shadow) price for the ith commodity is Pi and for the s the primary factor is Vs. Now consider any suggested project for the jth commodity. Any such project can be represented by a set of (n+m) coefficients uij (i = 1, 2...) for commodities and Sss (S = 1, 2...n) for primary factors, say, in terms of inputs or outputs of the m commodities and n factors respectively. If a positive coefficient is used to represent an output and a negative coefficient is used to represent an input of the factor or commodity in question, then the NEB can be expressed as B where

$$B_j = \sum_{i=1}^{n} a_{ij}P_i + \sum_{s=1}^{m} S\,s_{j}V_s \qquad (40)$$

This expression is general enough to allow for costs and benefits that occur over time. We simply feed into the formula the cost of capital (say) in the first period and in the second and so on.

Net economic benefit is another way of looking at comparative advantage in terms of economic efficiency, involving the appraisal of the existing use of resources. It is used in order to answer the question whether, in the agricultural sector as a whole or in a broad sub-sector of it, total benefits exceed total costs (including capital consumption allowances generally called capital depreciation), or the resources could be put to more profitable use elsewhere.

$$Bi = P^b_i - \sum_{j=1}^{k} (aij \times P^b_j) - \sum_{j=k+1}^{1} (aij \times MPPY \times P^b_y) \qquad (41)$$

where

Bi = net economic benefit per unit of output;
P^b_j = accounting value at border prices of one unit of output;
aij = input coefficient per unit of output;
$MPPYi$ = marginal physical product of the j th input in its average alternative use (Y);
P^b_y = accounting value at border prices of y th output (average alternative use); and
$j=1...k$ = inputs of directly traded goods plus the traded elements of non-traded goods, after decomposition; $j=k+1..j$ =inputs of primary non-traded factors ... includes those obtained as a result of the decomposition of non-traded goods.

Source: Scandizzo and Bruce, 1980, p. 21.

The assumption made is that the present pattern of the sector or sub-sector reflects the development of a large number of project investment decisions, i.e. that 'full development' net project benefits have been attained. This ignores the possibility that major efficiency gains could be achieved, for example, through institutional or administrative reforms, or an improved pricing policy framework. Nevertheless, successive estimates of the sectoral and sub-sectoral NEB may be useful as one means of monitoring progress in improving the design and implementation of agricultural development strategy, if the required data for a major exercise can be provided.

Significance of Commercial Constants in Policy Analysis

The application of commercial constants is useful in clarifying the locus or loci of distortions in the economy and the allocative efficiency. They are, therefore, used in assessing the efficiency of macroeconomic policy management. While such measures as NPC, EPC, NNPC, DPB, ESC, PSE and CSE relate to incentive effects and allocation of incomes, the DRC and NEB provide indicators of competitive or comparative advantages.

7   Demand Analysis

Framework of Demand Analysis

Demand analysis is traditionally embedded in the theory of consumer behaviour. Various consumption hypotheses and their underlying proportions have been the focus of empirical investigations and synthesis of observed consumption behaviour. Some of the early contributors to demand analysis included King (1696), who computed a demand schedule for maize and developed King's law based on the inverse relationship between price and the quantity demanded. In 1844 Dupuit identified utility with demand and provided an explanation of the relationship between marginal utility, total utility and price. Utility was and is still defined as the satisfaction which is derived from the consumption of some goods or services. As a person buys more of the good or services, the total utility derived from it increases. The additional utility derived from the last unit purchased is defined as marginal utility of the commodity. Generally marginal utility diminishes as consumption increases. Utility cannot be measured as it is subjective.

Another area of demand theory which originated from the budget studies was pioneered by Ernest Engel (1887), a German economist. His analyses considered demand of a commodity as a function of income only. He demonstrated that demand of a commodity is a relationship between quantities of an item per unit of time that a consumer will take at various levels of income, while holding prices and other factors constant. Engel's empirical analyses led to the establishment of the following Engel's law: i) food is the most important item in the household budget; ii) the proportion of total expenditures allocated to food decreases as income rises; iii) the proportion of total expenditure devoted to clothing and housing is approximately constant, while the share of luxury items increases as income rises.

Currently the demand theory in the neoclassical approach is based on the concept of the marginal utility of the goods consumed by consumers who are willing to buy a good until its price is below the utility they receive from its consumption. Changes in relative prices will affect the consumption structure assuming that utility received for each good remains constant. There are

331

different compositions of the basket of goods to which the consumer is indifferent, the maximum possible consumption is determined by the total available income. An increase in disposable income raises the overall consumption as well as (probably) the structure of consumption. The elasticity concept measures changes in the consumption of a good when income increases (income elasticity), when price of goods changes (price elasticity) and the price of other goods changes (cross-price elasticity) (Asuming-Brempong, 1992).

Consumer Demand

Traditionally a market is the measure of the number of commodities sold at various prices in a given period of time. A market, therefore, measures a flow of commodities. In order to be able to estimate the present and future flow of commodities and their prices, it is necessary to determine the main probable changes in prices over a given period of time. The demand of a commodity is defined as the various quantities of it which consumers are willing to purchase per unit time, all other things remaining *ceteris paribus*. Since demand is a flow concept, it must, therefore, be expressed per unit time, and the above definition is basically the 'law of demand' which states that the market demand of a commodity is inversely related to its price. Since demand has a multivariate relationship (determined by many factors simultaneously) some economists consider the definition as misleading, since it considers price as the sole determinant of demand. However, it is still acceptable (on account of its simplicity) as the starting point of basic demand analysis.

Rice, other than the countries in West Africa, was not a staple in the diet of Africans. However, the expansion of the urban population raised demand for the commodity. It is usually necessary to analyse trends in consumption as illustrated in the hypothetical figures (40, 41). The horizontal axis is the time in years, while the vertical axis is the tonnage of rice demanded. The projected dotted line is one possible way in which the market in future will behave. The analysis is usually concerned with explaining whether the projection represents a realistic amount of rice that will be consumed in future, represented by years 5 and 6 that lie in the future. The numbers -3, -2, -1, -0 beside lack coordinates for each combination of a year and the quantity of rice consumed each representing a year. The year 0 is the present time.

In demand analysis it is recognized that the demand for a commodity is determined by the interaction of many factors apart from its price. The most

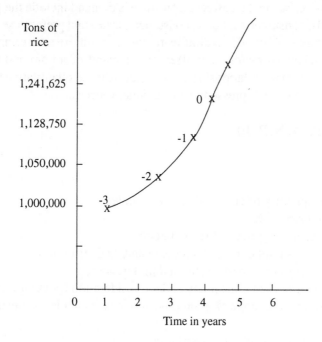

Figure 40 Trends in consumption of rice

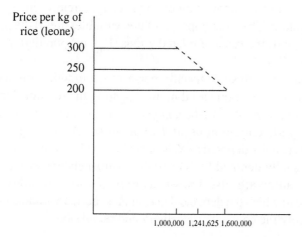

Volume of market purchases in a given period of time

Figure 41 General market behaviour in response to price changes

important of these factors that affect a consumer's demand include the prices of related goods, consumer's income, consumer's tastes and preferences, total population, range of goods available to the consumer, and consumer expectations. When all factors that affect the demand of a commodity are taken together, a demand relationship can be established in quantitative terms. This relationship can be expressed in a functional form as:

$$X_t = f (P_x, P_n, Y, N, R, E)$$

where

X_t	is the quantity of commodity X demanded;
P_x	is the price of X;
P_n	represents the prices of related goods;
Y	represents total consumers income and its distribution;
T	represents consumers' tastes and preferences;
N	is the number of consumers under consideration (population);
R	represents the range of goods and services available to consumers; and
E	represents consumers' expectations.

The demand analysis centres around the estimation of the above relationships using various functional forms depending on the specific circumstances and issues under investigation. The most important three variables are: i) the price of the commodity (P_x); ii) the price of related goods (P_n); iii) population (N) and consumer income (Y).

Quantitative demand analysis is usually performed through correlation analysis and regression, a technique used in investigating the relationship or association between two variables. In the analysis there are usually two types of variables employed: endogenous and exogenous. An endogenous (dependent) variable, usually denoted as Y, is one whose values are explained by the exogenous (usually denoted by X) variables (independent variables). The exogenous variables are also known as explanatory variables. To investigate the degree to which the demand determinants influence endogenous variables one can apply the concept of elasticity and regression.

Concept of Elasticity

Any individual who purchases a commodity gives an indication that he desires the goods. Groups in a population can be observed purchasing commodities they desire. Apart from the desire to purchase, they must also have income or money to pay for the commodity. Income per head is, therefore, likely to bear some relationship to the volume of market purchases. In general, rising income per caput is associated with increasing market purchases. A comprehensive approach to food commodity projection should be based on an integrated approach in demand for agricultural products and particularly foodstuffs. The demand for these goods is highly sensitive to social and economic changes, and variables such as population growth and income per caput play an overwhelming role in explaining growth rate of demand. Consequently the other factor influencing the level of consumption is the increase in population. The effect in the population growth is to cause the consumption of commodities to rise. Income per head and population growth rates, therefore, are two important determinants of consumption. Usually one has to relate income per head to the quality of commodities likely to be purchased in a market. This relation can be expressed in a number of ways which should be helpful in predicting future trends.

Income elasticity demand It is, therefore, necessary to know the percentage changes in the amount of rice purchased and the percentage changes of income per head in a period of time, the initial amount purchased and the initial income per head in a period of time. The increase in income per head can be estimated on the basis of GDP and population growth forecasts. These estimates are generally available from national accounts statistics. Per caput growth rate is the difference between GDP growth rate and population growth rate. The impact on the consumption expenditure for the commodity is then measured, i.e. the percentage change in consumption resulting from each 1 per cent increase in income. This is done by multiplying the income elasticity coefficient by changes in income. This effect is then added to the population effect to measure the overall impact on demand.

The following derived formula can be used:

$$\frac{\dfrac{\text{the percentage change in quantity purchased}}{\text{initial amount purchased}}}{\dfrac{\text{the change in income per head}}{\text{initial income per head}}} = \text{income elasticity}$$

The following income elasticity is obtained:

$$\frac{\dfrac{75-50}{50}}{\dfrac{125-100}{100}} = \frac{\dfrac{25}{50}}{\dfrac{25}{100}} = \frac{0.50}{0.25} = 2.0$$

This means that every 1 per cent change in income per head results in a 2 per cent increase in the quantity of rice purchased. Since income per head increased from 100 to 125, which is a 25 per cent increase, the quantity of rice consumed will increase by 50 per cent (2 x 25). The income elasticity is, therefore, the increase or response of commodities purchased in the market as income per head rises. Income elasticity is a useful tool in estimating the future size of the market. Together with the predicted population growth rate, it is possible to make some accurate estimation of the future level of purchases.

Population growth factor on demand The impact of population growth could better be assessed if it were possible to disaggregate it further between urban and rural populations, and population structure by sexes and ages and socioeconomic groups. The same applies to income distribution, since the propensity to consume is different for different income levels. More disaggregated information (e.g. per caput rural and urban income) could help to achieve better sound estimates for projected demand. Population and income are those variables whose effect on total demand is more direct and of great magnitude. There are also other variables influencing demand, but at a lower extent, such as consumer tastes and nutritional goals set by the government.

For illustration purposes, let us say that the following income elasticities for the years 1, 2, 3, and 4 have been calculated as follows:

Years	Income elasticity
1–2	0.67
2–3	1.08
3–4	1.50

Each income elasticity refers to a period of one year and change from one year to the next. The following symbols can be used for income elasticity, population growth rates and the growth rates of markets:

n   = income elasticity;
P   = population growth rate;
m   = rate of growth of market consumption; and

y = growth rate of income per head.

All are for the same period of time. The following formula can be used:

$$(y.n) + p = m \tag{1}$$

For the three periods, and taking rate of growth of income per head of 6 per cent, we get the following results of calculations for the market growth rate:

Year	(y.n) + p	=	m		%
1–2	0.06 . 0.67 + 0.01	=	0.05	=	5
2–3	0.06 . 1.08 + 0.01	=	0.075	=	7.5
3–4	0.06 . 1.50 + 0.01	=	0.10	=	10.0

According to Figure 41, the quantity of rice purchased at the beginning of year 1 was 1,000,000 tonnes. During the year 1 to 2, the market increased by 5 per cent to 1,050,000 tonnes, while during year 2 to 3, it increased by 7.5 per cent to 1,128,750 tonnes and in the last period of 3 to 4 years, the market increased by 10 per cent to 1,241,625 tonnes.

Determinants of demand Elasticity, a measurement of the rate at which one variable responds to another (a percentage change in another), permits the estimation of future size of the market. There are as many elasticities of demand as its determinants (factors influencing demand), but the most important of these are: own-price elasticity, cross-price elasticity and income elasticity. These elasticities, responsiveness of the variables to another, is expressed in percentages to make comparison more meaningful rather than relative changes expressed in different units.

a) *Own-price elasticity of demand*

The own-price elasticity (E_p) is a measure of the responsiveness of demand to changes in the commodity own price. It is the percentage change in quantity demanded to a one per cent change in the price of the commodity. Computationally this may be expressed as:

$$E_p = \frac{dX}{X} \bigg/ \frac{dPx}{Px} \tag{2}$$

or

$$E_p = \frac{dX}{dPx} \frac{Px}{X} \tag{3}$$

where P and X are equilibrium price (Ep) and quantity of the commodity respectively. There are about five ranges of values of the own-price elasticity.

Elasticity of demand, therefore, also refers to the responsiveness of quantity demanded to a change responsive to prices (i.e. a small change in price leading to a relatively large change in quantity demanded). If the quantity demanded is unresponsive to price changes, demand is said to be inelastic. Elasticity, therefore, is a measure of the relationship between the proportionate change in price and the proportionate change in quantity demanded. Just as for income elasticity, we use the following formula:

Elasticity of demand = $\dfrac{\text{Percentage change in quantity demanded}}{\text{Percentage change in price}}$.

Where this ratio is greater than 1, demand is elastic; where it is less than 1, demand is inelastic and where it is equal to 1, demand has unit elasticity. Normally elasticity will be different at different prices, a demonstration that a demand curve does not have a constant elasticity (Figure 45).

In Figure 42, there has been a price change of 20 leones since the demand curve is a straight line, and the resulting changes in quantity are also equal amounting to 200 tons. However the elasticities of demand are not equal. When price changes from 200 leones to 180 leones, the elasticity of demand is as follows:

$$= \frac{\dfrac{\text{the percentage change in quantity demanded}}{\text{initial amount demanded}}}{\dfrac{\text{the change in price per ton}}{\text{initial price per ton}}}$$

$$= \frac{\dfrac{800 - 600}{600}}{\dfrac{200 - 180}{200}}$$

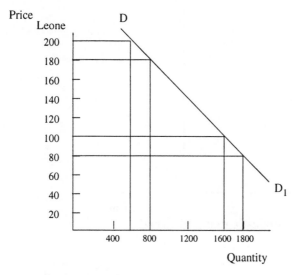

Figure 42 Demand function curve

$$= \frac{\dfrac{200}{600}}{\dfrac{20}{200}} = \frac{0.333}{0.100} = 3.33$$

When price changes from 100 leones to 80 leones, demand elasticity is:

$$\frac{\dfrac{1800 - 1600}{1600}}{\dfrac{100-80}{100}} = \frac{\dfrac{200}{1600}}{\dfrac{20}{100}} = \frac{0.125}{0.200} = 0.625$$

These examples demonstrate that elasticity of demand is a relationship between proportionate and not absolute changes in prices and quantity demanded. However, there are three exceptional cases where elasticity of demand is the same at all prices: i) a perfectly inelastic demand curve as illustrated in Figure 43 – in this example quantity demanded does not change as price changes, i.e. elasticity of demand is zero; ii) a perfectly elastic demand curve where the quantity demanded at the ruling price is infinite, i.e. elasticity of demand is ∞, as illustrated in Figure 44; iii) and demand curve with unit elasticity where the amount demanded always changes by exactly the same

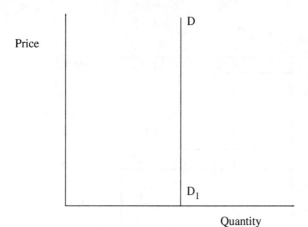

Figure 43 Perfectly inelastic demand curve

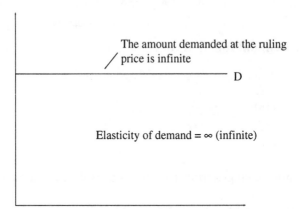

Figure 44 Perfectly elastic demand curve

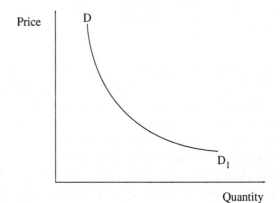

Figure 45 Demand curve with unit elasticity

percentage as price and, in this case, elasticity of demand, is unity and the demand curve (Figure 45) is a rectangular hyperbola.

Figure 41 illustrates the general behaviour of the market if price is increased or decreased. If the prices are higher than 250 leones for each kilogramme of rice, consumers of rice may buy less. This is because the consumer's income is limited for a given period of time. If price becomes greater than 250 leones, it means that the consumer must pay more of his income for the same quantity of the rice commodity. He responds by restricting purchases to some degree as price increases. Conversely, as price declines (less than 250 leones), the consumer may purchase a greater quantity of rice. However, it is difficult to predict the response of the consumer if the market price should change.

As is done with the estimation of market growth rate, we want to know the main forces likely to cause the changes in markets when contracts or similar arrangements for fixing prices do not exist. If the supply of rice increases, the price of rice declines. In Figure 41, when the price of rice was 300 leones per kg, the consumer was prepared to buy only 1,000 000 tonnes, but was prepared to increase purchases to 1,241,625 if price fell to 250 leones per kg, and was still prepared to increase purchases to 1,600,000 tonnes if price fell further to 200 leones per kg. Lower prices obviously were desired by consumers. However, if supply fell, the consumers were disappointed if they still wanted to buy the original amount of 1,241,625 tonnes because the market was able to supply only 1,000,000 tonnes. Those consumers who wanted to continue buying had to pay the somewhat higher price of 300 leones per kg in order to have the commodity.

The magnitude of the price elasticity of demand (Ep) is also determined to a large extent by: i) availability of substitutes (the demand of a commodity is more elastic if there are close substitutes); ii) the time period being considered (demand is more elastic in the long run when consumers can adjust fully); iii) the nature of the need that the commodity satisfies (in general, necessities such as salt are price inelastic, while luxury goods are price elastic); iv) the number of uses to which the commodity can be put (the more the possible uses of the good, the more price elastic it will be); and v) the proportion of income spent on the particular commodity. The concepts of price elasticity of demand can also be differentiated between *ordinary* and compensated demand elasticities. The *ordinary* price elasticity of demand measures the combined substitution and income effects (i.e. total effect) of a price change; while the *compensated* price elasticity of demand measures only the substitution effect of a price change. In most demand analyses it is the *ordinary* price elasticity of demand which is estimated.

b) *Cross-price elasticity of demand*

If a government imposes a tariff on an imported rice, the immediate effect on the market is an increase in the price for the commodity and a reduction in the volume purchased. If the tariff should fall, the amount purchased can be expected to rise. Both of these changes have to do with the availability of imported commodities which are related directly to import prices. Therefore, it is necessary to separate the supplies of commodities entering the market into domestically-produced and imported supplies. As prices of an imported commodity rise, less of the commodity is bought, consequently restricting demand to domestically-produced supplies. The increase in demand for domestically-produced supplies raises their prices. Meanwhile, if the prices of imported commodities fall, more of the supplies are purchased. The point is that commodities are usually substitutes of each other.

In the case of rice, maize can be a substitute. Prices of substitutes sold in competing markets can be expected to have additional effects on a market. If the price of maize declines during the same period, the quantity of rice that will be sold at 250 leones per kg will decline. This is because the consumer of rice has shifted his purchases to maize, whose price has fallen. This means that the quantity of rice of 1,241,625 tonnes cannot be expected to be sold at 250 leones per kg. This means that the effect of a price fall of maize is to cause the price of rice to fall for the existing supplies of 1,241,625 tonnes. Conversely, if the price of maize rises, the consumer would be expected to shift his purchases from maize to rice. The effect, therefore, is to increase the price of rice for the existing supplies of 1,241,625. When a commodity has no close substitutes it can be expected that the prices and volumes purchased of other commodities have correspondingly less influence on other commodity markets.

The cross-price elasticity of demand, therefore, relates a commodity X and another commodity Y, and is defined as the proportionate change in the quantity demanded of X resulting from a proportionate change in the price of Y (or a percentage change in the demand of X in response to a one per cent change in the price of Y). The cross-price elasticity, Exy, may be expressed as:

$$Exy = \frac{dx}{X} \bigg/ \frac{dPy}{Py} \tag{4}$$

or

$$Exy = \frac{dx}{dPy} \cdot \frac{Py}{X} \tag{5}$$

where

X   is the quantity demanded of commodity X; and
Py   is the price of the related commodity y.

The cross-elasticity of demand is a measure of the relationship between changes in the price of one commodity and the resulting changes in the quantity demanded of another commodity. It is a concept which is useful in measuring the extent to which goods are close substitutes or closely related complementary goods. This form of elasticity is measured as follows:

$$\text{Cross elasticity} = \frac{\text{Percentage change in quantity demanded of good X}}{\text{Percentage change in the price of Y}}$$

In the case of substitute goods, cross-elasticity of demand remains positive, meaning that an increase in the price of Y leads to an increase in the quantity demanded of X and vice versa. If the two goods are close substitutes, cross-elasticity of demand will have a high positive value. An increase of a 10 per cent increase in the price of Y, for instance, leads to a rise of 30 per cent in the quantity demanded of X. In this case the cross-elasticity of demand is +3. In the case of complementary goods, the cross-elasticity of demand will be negative because an increase in the price Y will lead to a fall in the quantity demanded of X and vice versa. When the goods are closely related complements, the cross-elasticity of demand will have a high negative value. This type of relationship arises because some goods are jointly demanded in the sense that the use of one implies the use of the other. It is for this reason that the change in the price of one will cause a change in the demand of the other. Technological advances could lead to a significant reduction in the cost of producing ox equipment and make them available at much lower prices. Such a development would, *ceteris paribus*, increase the demand for the labour-saving technology, ox equipment. On the other hand, goods which are close substitutes for one another are in competitive demand. A good is said to be in 'composite' demand when it is demanded for several different uses. The demands for such goods are the aggregates of the demands of the various users. Wool, produced in Lesotho, is demanded by many users (textile, carpet, blanket manufacturers). Accordingly the increase in the demand for wool by one industry will raise the price and consequently affect the prices of all the other commodities made from wool.

c) *Income elasticity of demand*

The income elasticity of demand is the proportionate change in the quantity demanded of a commodity X as a result of proportionate change in income (or a percentage change in the demand of X in response to a 1 per cent change in income). The income elasticity, Ey, can be expressed as

$$Ey = \frac{dx}{X} \bigg/ \frac{dy}{y} \tag{6}$$

$$or \ Ey = \frac{dx}{dy} \frac{Y}{X} \tag{7}$$

The main determinants of income elasticity include: i) the nature of the need that the commodity satisfies. This may be explained by Engel's Law, which states that the percentage of income spent on food declines as income rises. This principle can be used to classify goods into normal and inferior goods. If Ey remains positive then we have normal good, but if Ey is negative then the food is considered as being inferior. Normal goods may be further classified into necessities, inferior, and superior luxury goods; ii) the time period is also a factor because consumption patterns adjust, with a time-lag, to changes in income; and iii) the level of a country's development, indicated by the level of income per head. The poorest group in society, for example, consume more of their total expenditure (or income) for basic food while the richest groups consume a larger share of their income in luxuries.

The increase/decrease in the consumption of a given good when the total disposable income increases is measured by the income elasticity of the good. The income elasticity can range from negative to positive values and defines different categories of goods. As regards necessity goods, the elasticity is usually greater than 0 but lower than 1. In this case, the good consumption increases with the income but by a lower percentage. The marginal increase is lower the higher the disposable income and there tends to be a saturation point, after which consumption does not increase any more with income. As regards inferior goods, the elasticity is negative, as income increases correspond with a decrease in consumption. These are goods which have very close and better-quality substitutes. As income increases, consumers give up consumption of goods they consider inferior and shift their purchases to goods regarded as superior. Regarding superior/luxury goods, the elasticity is positive and greater than 1. The consumption of these goods increases by a percentage higher than the percentage increase in income. The demand curve of a given good can show different elasticities at different levels of income. A superior/luxury good, for instance, can become a necessity good when a certain income threshold is reached. A necessity good can turn into an inferior good at high income levels.

d) *Derived demand*

When discussing the structure of an economy, it was pointed out that some outputs from the three sectors are used for further production, an indication that any sector of the economy is interdependent with others. For instance, agricultural development requires an increasing economic demand for its products in domestic as well as international markets. For most parts, the demand for agricultural products depends on domestic industrial development that increases the number of gainful and productively employed non-agricultural and agricultural employees with purchasing power to buy farm products, and through domestic industries which utilize agricultural raw materials. A continuously-developing agriculture requires industrial products such as organic and inorganic fertilizers, pesticides, tools and implements, fuels and building materials for its future development. Consequently a production activity in one sector of the economy generates backward and forward linkages which have ramifications for the entire economy. These linkages are development inducement mechanisms within the productive sector of the economy, as given in the schematic illustration of possible backward and forward linkages. The input provision in non-primary economic activity, derived demand or backward linkage effect induces demand to supply through domestic production the required inputs, while output utilization or forward linkage effect induces attempts to utilize its outputs as inputs in some new activities. Some activities have multiple linkages (Hirschman, 1970, p. 100).

Animal industry is an example with multiple linkages. In Lesotho, for instance, before the arrival of the cotton and wool/mohair blanket, the Basotho used sheep skins and ox hides to make covers (*Karosses*). The skins and hides were not only utilitarian but also decorative. Following the discovery of diamonds in Kimberly in the 1860s, many Basotho went to work there, and at the end of their contracts they were either paid in guns or cash, the latter being used to buy blankets made of cotton. Meanwhile, a businessman, Douglas Fraser, having realized the huge potential for blankets, vigorously and successfully promoted the sales of imported blankets. Eventually the traditional skin or hide blanket was phased out and its place taken over by blankets woven of cotton and wool/mohair (substitute or competitive relationship). The advantages of the exotic blankets were that they were imported ready for wear and affordable, while the traditional skin blanket was cumbersome and labour-demanding to make. Meanwhile, the rinderpest disaster in late 1890s and the massive snowfall in the early 1900s significantly reduced the number of livestock in the country. These disasters helped to popularize and entrench the place of blankets made from cotton and wool/ mohair (Thabane, 1995, pp. 34–5).

The increase in demand for the blanket depended on the expansion of trade based on cotton. Since Lesotho did not enjoy a comparative advantage for the production of cotton, it had to import cotton raw materials from overseas. The British brought under their empire a number of developing countries, which became the suppliers of the raw cotton materials to Britain (backward linkage) while at the same time consumers of the British manufactures, mainly from Lancashire. Meanwhile the loss of animals due to the two disasters not only reduced sources of skins and hides but also made the Basotho reluctant to slaughter the few animals left, and with the introduction of exotic animals to supplement available animals, the Basotho were able not only to restitute their herd, but greatly expand the number of animals to supply wool/mohair (backward linkage). The skins and hides were instead used in the tannery industry in order to supply inputs into the manufacture of leather products (forward linkage), some of which were exported. Tannery requires tannin (an acid used in converting raw hide into leather), which is obtained from the bark of wattle trees. The increase in demand for leather goods raised demand for tannin (complementary relationship) which in turn raised demand for wattle and hence increased wattle production (complementary backward linkage) (see Figure 46).

Quantitative Demand Analyses

There are some seven functions used in estimating the demand parameters each of which depends on how the functions satisfy the criteria of: i) consistency to *a priori* relationship; ii) the level of significance of regression estimates; iii) validity of the model; iv) the magnitude of the coefficient of determination (R^2); and v) the standard error of the estimates.

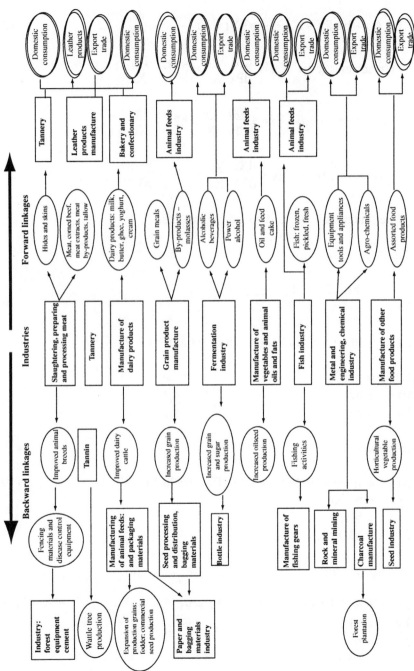

Figure 46 Intra- and inter-sectoral relationships between agricultural and industrial sectors

Linear Function

$$Xt = Ao + b1\ Px + b2\ Pr + b3\ Yt = Vt \tag{8}$$

own price elasticity, $Ep = \dfrac{dXt}{dPx} \dfrac{Px}{Xt} = b1 \smile \dfrac{Px}{Xt}$

cross-price elasticity, $Exr = \dfrac{dXt}{dPr} \dfrac{Pr}{X} = b2 \smile \dfrac{Pr}{Xt}$

income elasticity, $Ey = \dfrac{dXt}{dYt} \dfrac{Yt}{Xt} = b3 \smile \dfrac{Yt}{Xt}$

(Note that ao, b1, b2, and b3 are parameters.)

Double-log function

$$Xt \quad = ao\ Px^{b1}\ Pr^{b2}\ Yt^{b3}\ Vt \tag{9}$$

or $Xt \quad = In\ ao + b1\ In\ Px + b2\ In\ Pr + b3\ In\ Yt + Vt$

$Ep \quad = b1$
$Exr \quad = b2$
$Ey \quad = b3$

Semi-log function

$$Xt \quad = In\ ao + b1\ In\ Px + b2\ In\ Px = b3\ In\ Yt = Vt \tag{10}$$
$Ep \quad = b1/Xt$
$Exr \quad = b2/Xt$
$Ey \quad = b3/Xt$

Log-linear function

$$In\ Xt = ao + b1\ Px + b2\ Pr + b3\ Yt + Vt \tag{11}$$
$Ep \quad = b1\ Px$
$Exr \quad = b2\ Pr$
$Ey \quad = b3\ Yt$

Log-inverse function (log-reciprocal)

$$Xt = ao \, Px^{b1} \, Pr^{b2} \, e^{-b_3} \tag{12}$$
$$Ep = b1$$
$$Exr = b2$$
$$Ey = b3/Yt$$

Log-log inverse function

$$Xt = ao \, Px^{b1} \, Pr^{b2} \, e^{-b_3/Yt} \, Yt^{-b_4} \, Vt \tag{13}$$
$$Ep = b1$$
$$Exr = b2$$
$$Ey = b3/Yt - b4$$

Hyperbolic function

$$Xt = ao \, b1 \, Px + b2 \, Pr - b3 / Yt + Vt \tag{14}$$
$$Ep = \frac{b1 \, Px}{Xt}$$
$$Exr = \frac{b2 \, Pr}{Xt}$$
$$Ey = b3 / Xt \, Yt$$

To investigate the degree to which the determinants influence demand, we can apply simple regression to the quantity of demanded commodities, say of maize and rice, using data from Ghana (Tables 37 and 38) and the analysis considers three exogenous or independent variables as determinants of demand. This implies that other determinants of demand, such as consumer expectations, changes in tastes of the consumers, etc. are assumed to be constant over the period of analysis.

Linear Function

The general demand equation uses the linear function, which is the simplest form of demand analysis, and assumes the coefficient of elasticity to unity as income increases indefinitely.

Table 37   Data for demand analysis: maize

Year	Quantity demanded	Px	Pr	Income (million) ⌐	Population (million)	Xt	Yt
1977	391	11.9	19.7	4901.7	10.24	38.18	478.68
1978	402	7.8	15.5	5375.8	10.51	38.25	511.49
1979	410	6.7	11.4	5177.6	10.78	38.03	480.30
1980	426	11.4	20.6	5121.5	11.06	38.52	463.07
1981	438	9.7	13.7	4968.6	11.35	38.59	437.76
1982	449	8.2	20.8	4600.7	11.77	38.15	390.88
1983	461	18.4	28.1	4784.7	12.08	38.16	396.08
1984	468	7.8	22.0	4950.5	12.39	37.77	399.56
1985	490	6.1	15.4	5143.1	12.72	38.52	404.33
1986	502	7.7	15.9	5467.1	13.05	38.47	418.93
1987	510	8.8	17.9	5669.0	13.39	38.09	423.37
1988	521	8.5	16.7	5952.5	13.74	37.92	433.22

Table 38   Data for demand analysis: rice

Year	Quantity demanded	Px	Pr	Income (million) ⌐	Population (million)	Xt	Yt
1977	96.2	19.7	11.9	4901.7	10.24	9.39	478.68
1978	132.6	15.5	7.8	5375.8	10.51	12.62	425.97
1979	77.0	11.4	6.7	5177.6	10.78	7.14	480.30
1980	128.3	20.6	11.4	5121.5	11.06	11.60	463.07
1981	109.5	13.7	9.7	4968.6	11.35	9.65	437.76
1982	45.2	20.8	8.2	4600.7	11.77	3.84	390.88
1983	63.1	28.1	18.4	4784.7	12.08	5.22	396.08
1984	65.9	22.0	7.8	4950.5	12.39	5.32	399.56
1985	92.6	15.4	6.1	5143.1	12.72	7.28	404.33
1986	99.0	15.9	7.7	5467.1	13.05	7.59	418.93
1987	89.8	17.9	8.8	5669.0	13.39	6.71	423.38
1988	76.0	16.7	8.5	5952.5	13.74	5.53	433.22

Notes

1   Figures for income are computed at 1977 constant prices.
2   Xt is per capita quantity demanded, obtained by the ratio of total quantity demanded to population.
3   Yt is per capita income, obtained by deflating each year's income by the population.
4   Px and Pr are real price obtained by deflating the national retail price by the national consumer price Index (CPI).
5   The data for rice (Table 38) has been included as an exercise for the reader.
6   Per capita values are used to indicate a 'representative' consumer whose behaviour is supposed to reflect the average behaviour of the population. Also, per capita relationships have the additional advantage of being more meaningful and stable than relationship between aggregates.

$$Xt = f (Px\ Pr\ Yt)\ Vt \tag{15}$$

where

Xt	represents quantity demands;
Px	is the price of X;
Pr	is the price of related good;
Y_t	is the consumer income; and
V_t	is the error term.

The linear function would be:

$$Yt = Ao + b1\ Px + b2\ Pr + b3\ Yt + Vt$$

Using ordinary least squares (OLS) to estimate the parameters, one first computes the means of all the variables and the data transformed into the deviation form.

The mean values are:

$\bar{X}t = 38.22$ $\bar{P}x = 9.42$

$\bar{Y}t = 436.47$ $\bar{P}r = 18.14$

Data in deviation form

$Xt - \bar{X}t$ (y)	$Px - \bar{P}x$ (x1)	$Pr - \bar{P}r$ (x2)	$Yt - \bar{Y}t$ (x3)
-0.04	2.48	1.56	42.21
0.03	-1.62	-2.64	75.02
-0.19	-2.72	-6.74	43.83
0.30	1.98	2.46	26.60
0.37	0.28	-4.44	1.29
-0.07	1.22	2.66	45.59
-0.06	8.98	9.96	-40.39
-0.45	-1.62	3.86	-36.91
0.30	-3.32	-2.74	-32.14
0.25	-1.72	-2.24	-17.54
-0.13	-0.62	-0.24	-13.10
-0.30	-0.92	-1.44	- 3.25

The estimated linear equation is

$$Xt = 39 + 0.06 \, Px - 0.05 \, Pr - 0.001 \, Yt$$

Demand elasticities are then estimated as follows:

own price elasticity, $Ep = b1 \dfrac{Px}{Xt} = 0.06 \times \dfrac{9.42}{38.22} = 0.015$

cross-price elasticity, $Exr = b2 \dfrac{Pr}{Xt} = -0.05 \times \dfrac{18.14}{38.22} = 0.024$

income elasticity, $Ey = b2 \dfrac{Xt}{Xt} = -0.001 \times \dfrac{436.47}{38.22} = 0.011$

The usual statistics, such as the t-statistics, f-statistics, R^2, are computed in the usual way as part of the classical method to verify the validity and reliability of the model and estimates. In this example, the computer estimation of the linear function yielded the following results:

$$Xt = 38.5 + 0.041 \, Px - 0.03 \, Pr - 0.0003 \, Yt$$
$$\quad\quad\quad (1.247) \quad\quad (-1.668) \; (-0.141)$$

$$R^2 = 26.74 \quad\quad\quad\quad F = 97.34$$

Figures in parentheses are t-values.

The small differences observed between the parameter estimates between the two equations arose because the first one was manually calculated and the second was run on a computer. The differences are, therefore, due to rounding errors. Figure 47a provides a graphical presentation.

Double-log Function

The logarithmic function implies a constant elasticity throughout the period, i.e. the ratio between the percentage change in per caput consumption and income is constant. This is used only for food items that will remain well below the saturation level throughout the period. The linear function

$$Xt - ao + b1 \, Px + b2 \, Pr + b2 \, Yt + Vt$$

can be linearized by taking the natural logarithms.

In Xt = In ao + b1 In Px + b2 In Pr + b3 In Yt

By linearizing the function by taking its logarithms, the original data must also be transformed by taking the natural logarithms. Using the same notations we get the following transformed data:

In Xt	In Px	In Pr	In Yt
3.642	2.477	2.981	6.171
3.644	2.054	2.741	6.237
3.638	1.902	2.434	6.174
3.651	2.434	3.025	6.138
3.653	2.272	2.617	6.082
2.642	2.104	3.035	5.968
3.642	2.912	3.336	5.982
3.652	2.054	3.091	5.990
3.651	1.808	2.734	6.002
3.650	2.041	2.766	6.038
3.640	2.175	2.855	6.048
3.635	2.140	2.815	6.071
Means 3.643	2.198	2.872	6.075

The data are reduced to the deviation form.

In Xt - In $\bar{X}$t	In Px - In $\bar{P}$x	In Pr - In $\bar{P}$r	In Yt - In $\bar{Y}$t
(y)	(x1)	(x2)	(x3)
-0.001	0.279	0.109	0.096
0.001	-0.144	-0.131	0.162
-0.005	-0.296	-0.438	0.099
0.008	0.236	0.155	0.063
0.010	0.074	-0.255	0.007
-0.001	-0.094	0.165	-0.107
-0.001	-0.714	0.464	0.093
-0.011	-0.144	-0.219	-0.085
0.008	-0.390	-0.138	-0.073
0.007	-0.157	-0.106	-0.037
-0.003	-0.023	0.015	-0.027
-0.008	-0.058	-0.057	-0.004

Using the same procedures of regression analysis, the estimated double-log function yielded:

In Xt = 3.43 + 0.01 In Px - 0.02 In Pr - 0.03 In Yt

and the respective elasticities are:

own price elasticity, Ep = b1 = 0.01;
cross-price elasticity, Exr = b2 = 0.02; and
income elasticity, Ey = b3 = 0.03.

A computer estimation of the double-log function yielded:

In Xt = 3.83 + 0.012 In Px - 0.021 In Pr -) 0.025 In Yt
    (17.98) (1.064   (1.095)   )-0.782)

R^2 = 17.40 F 56.17

Figures in parenthesis are t-values. Figure 47b demonstrates graphically the relationships.

Semi-log Function

The semi-logarithmic function implies a decline in the absolute value of the income elasticity coefficient proportional to the changes in quantity consumed. It does not provide for a saturation level.

Yt = In a + b1 In Pr + b2 In Pr + b3 In Yt + Vt

The function implies taking the logarithms of the independent variables and regressing them on the actual values of the dependent variable Xt. In the same way as above the original data of the independent variables must be transformed followed by rewriting the data in the deviation form.

Xt	In Px	In Pr	In Yt
38.18	2.477	2.981	6.171
38.25	2.054	2.741	6.237
38.03	1.902	2.434	6.174
38.52	2.434	3.025	6.138

38.59	2.272	2.617	6.082
38.15	2.104	3.035	5.968
38.16	2.912	3.336	5.982
37.77	2.054	3.091	5.990
38.52	1.808	2.734	6.002
38.47	2.041	2.766	6.038
38.09	2.175	2.885	6.048
37.92	2.140	2.815	6.071
Means 38.22	2.198	2.872	6.075

$\bar{X}t - Xt$	In $\bar{P}x$ - In Px	In $\bar{P}r$ - In Pr	In $\bar{Y}t$ - In Yt
(y)	(x1)	(x2)	(x3)
-0.04	0.279	0.109	0.096
0.03	-0.144	-0.131	0.162
-0.19	-0.296	-0.438	0.099
0.30	0.236	0.153	0.063
0.37	0.074	-0.255	0.007
-0.07	-0.094	0.163	-0.107
-0.06	0.714	0.464	-0.093
-0.45	-0.144	0.219	-0.085
0.30	-0.390	-0.138	-0.073
0.25	-0.157	-0.106	-0.037
-0.13	-0.023	0.013	-0.027
-0.30	-0.058	-0.057	-0.004

The parameters computed in the usual way yielded

Yt = 42.85 + 0.46 In Px - 0.76 In Pr - 0.57 In Yt

Demand elasticities can now be computed as follows:

own price elasticity, $Ep = \dfrac{b1}{Xt} = \dfrac{0.46}{38.22} = 0.12$

cross-price elasticity, $Exr = \dfrac{b2}{Xt} = \dfrac{-0.76}{38.22} = -0.02$

income elasticity, $Ey = \dfrac{b3}{Xt} = \dfrac{-0.57}{38.22} = -0.015$

A computer estimation of the semi-log function yielded

Xt = 42.76 = 0.45 In Px - 0.75 In Pr - 0.556 In Yt
  (5.25)   (1.018)   (-1.201) (-0.456)

Figures in parenthesis are t-values. Figure 47c provides graphical presentation.

Log-linear Function

The functional form is

In Xt = ao + b1 Px + P2 Pr + b2 Yt +Vt

This functional form appears as a reverse of the semi-log function. In this case the actual value of the independent variables are regressed on the logarithm value of the dependent variable Xt. As usual the relevant data are transformed.

	In Xt	Px	Pr	Yt
	3.642	11.9	19.7	478.68
	3.644	7.8	15.5	511.49
	3.638	6.7	11.4	480.30
	3.651	11.4	20.6	463.07
	3.653	9.7	13.7	437.76
	3.642	8.2	20.8	390.88
	3.642	18.4	28.1	396.08
	3.632	7.8	22.0	399.56
	3.651	6.1	15.4	404.33
	3.650	7.7	15.9	418.93
	3.640	8.8	17.9	423.37
	3.635	8.5	16.7	433.22
Means	3.643	9.42	18.14	436.47

The deviation is then computed:

$X_t - \bar{X}_t$ (Y)	$\ln P_x - \ln \bar{P}_x$ (x1)	$\ln P_r - \ln \bar{P}_r$ (x2)	$\ln Y_t - \ln \bar{Y}_t$ (x3)
-0.001	2.48	1.56	42.21
0.001	-1.62	-2.64	75.02
-0.005	-2.72	-6.74	43.83
0.008	1.98	2.46	26.60
0.010	0.28	-4.44	1.29
-0.001	1.22	2.66	-45.59
-0.001	8.98	9.96	-40.39
-0.011	-1.62	3.86	-36.91
0.008	-3.32	-2.74	-32.14
0.007	-1.72	-2.24	-17.54
-0.003	-0.62	-0.24	-13.1
-0.008	-0.92	-0.144	-3.25

The parameters are computed in the usual way, yielding an estimated log-linear function expressed as:

$\ln X_t = 3.67 + 0.001\ Pr - 0.001\ Pr - 0.0004\ Yt$

The respective demand elasticities are as follows:

own price elasticity, $Ep = b1\ Px = 0.001 \times 9.42 = 0.01$;
cross-price elasticity, $Exr = b2\ Pr = 0.001 \times 18.14 = 0.02$; and
income elasticity, $Yr = b3\ Yt = 0.0004 \times 436.47 = -0.18$.

The computer estimation of the long-linear function yielded

$\ln X_t = 3.66 + 0.001\ x - 0.001\ Pr - 0.00003\ Yt$
     (155.8)   (1.24)   (-1.711) (-0.506)

$R^2 = 26.85$ $F = 97.00$

Figures in parenthesis are t-values.

Log-inverse Function

The log-inverse function implies a decline in the absolute value of the elasticity coefficient proportional to the increase in the per caput income. When income tends toward infinity, and the elasticity tends to zero, the consumption tends toward a saturation level. This function implies that a calorie intake increases rapidly when starting from a state of hunger but at high income levels it tends towards a limit determined by physiological criteria. It is expressed as:

$$Xt = aa + b1\ Px + b2\ Pr\ e^{-b3} / Yt$$

which can be linearized by taking the logarithms of both the dependent and independent variables as follows:

$$In\ Xt = In\ a + b2\ In\ Px + b2\ In\ Pr - b3 / Yt$$

The data is transformed in the usual way.

	In Xt	In Px	In Pr	Yt^{-1}
	3.642	2.477	2.981	0.00209
	3.644	2.054	2.741	0.00196
	3.638	1.902	2.434	0.00208
	3.651	2.434	3.025	0.00216
	3.653	2.272	2.617	0.00228
	3.642	2.104	3.035	0.00256
	3.642	2.912	3.336	0.00252
	3.632	2.054	3.091	0.00250
	3.651	1.808	2.734	0.00247
	3.650	2.041	2.766	0.00239
	3.640	2.175	2.885	0.00236
	3.635	2.140	2.815	0.00231
Means	3.643	2.198	2.872	0.00231

The transformed data in deviation form then becomes (using the usual x1, x2, x3 and y notations):

y	x1	x2	x3
-0.001	0.279	0.109	0.00022
0.001	-0.144	-0.131	-0.00035
-0.005	-0.296	-0.438	-0.00023
0.008	-0.236	0.153	-0.00015
0.010	0.074	-0.255	-0.00030
-0.001	-0.094	0.163	0.00025

-0.001	0.714	0.464	0.00021
-0.011	-0.144	0.219	0.00019
0.008	-0.390	-0.138	0.00016
0.007	-0.157	-0.106	0.00080
-0.003	-0.023	0.013	0.00050
-0.008	-0.058	-0.057	0.0

The computed parameters yielded the following results. In $Xt = 3.643 - 0.01 \ln Px + 0.02 \ln Pr - 15.19 Yt - 1$. Using the demand elasticities formulae for the log-inverse function, the estimated elasticities were:

own price elasticity, $Ep = b1 = -0.01$
cross-price elasticity, $Exr = b2 = 0.02$
income elasticity, $Ey = b3/Yt = \dfrac{-15.19}{436.47} = -0.035$

A computer estimation of the log-inverse function yielded

$$\ln Xt = 3.646 + 0.014 \ln Px - 0.024 \ln Pr - 14.85 Yt - 1$$
$$(119.38) \quad (1.219) \quad\quad (-1.462) \quad\quad (-1.014)$$
$$R^2 = 21.21 \quad\quad F\ 71.77$$

Figures in parenthesis are t-values.

Hyperbolic Function (or Inverse Function)

The estimation of hyperbolic functions expressed as $Xt = a + b1\ Px + b2\ Pr - b3\ Yt - 1$ is carried out as that of the linear function, the only difference being that the income variable (Yt) is transformed by taking its reciprocal. The estimated hyperbolic function yielded:

$$Xt = 38.05 + 0.058\ Px - 0.055\ Pr + 269.73\ Yt.$$

Computed demand elasticities yielded:

own price elasticity, $Ep = b1\ \dfrac{Px}{Xt} = 0.058 \times \dfrac{9.42}{38.22} = 0.0142$

cross-price elasticity, $Exr = b2 \dfrac{Pr}{Xt} = -0.055 \times \dfrac{18.14}{38.22} = -0.026$

income elasticity, $Ey = \dfrac{b3}{Xt\, Yt} = \dfrac{269.73}{38.22 \times 436.47} = 0.016$

A computer estimation of the hyperbolic function using the same data is as follows:

$Xt = 38.09 + 0.043\ Px - 0.035\ Pr + 142.16\ Yt\ -1$
      (38.70)   (12.85)   (-1.719)   (0.327)

$R^2 = 27.53$ $F = 101.29$

Figures in parenthesis are t-values. See Figure 47d for graphical illustration.

Log-log Inverse Function

The log-log inverse function provides for an increase in per caput consumption up to a maximum intake, followed later by a decline as income rises. It is expressed as $Xt = aa\ Px^{b1}\ Pr^{b2}\ e^{-b3}\ /Yt\ Yt^{-b4}$ which can be linearized as follows:

In $Xt =$ In $aa + b1$ In $Px + b2$ In $Pr - b3/_Yt - b4$ In Yt

The transformation of the data is done in the usual way:

In Xt	In Px	In Pr	In Yt	Yt $^{-1}$
3.642	2.477	2.981	6.171	0.00209
3.644	2.054	2.741	6.237	0.00196
3.638	1.902	2.434	6.174	0.00208
3.651	2.434	3.025	6.138	0.00216
3.653	2.272	2.617	6.082	0.00228
3.642	2.104	3.035	5.968	0.00256
3.642	2.912	3.336	5.990	0.00252
3.632	2.054	3.091	5.990	0.00250
3.651	1.808	2.734	6.002	0.00247
3.650	2.041	2.766	6.038	0.00239
3.640	2.175	2.885	6.048	0.00236

	3.635	2.140	2.815	6.071	0.00231
Means	3.643	2.198	2.872	6.075	0.00231

In deviation form, the data becomes:

y	x1	x2	x3	x4
-0.001	-0.279	0.109	0.096	-0.00022
0.001	-0.144	-0.131	0.162	-0.00035
-0.005	-0.296	-0.438	0.099	-0.00023
0.008	-0.236	0.153	0.063	-0.00015
0.010	0.074	-0.255	0.077	-0.00030
-0.001	-0.094	0.163	-0.017	-0.00025
-0.001	0.714	0.464	-0.093	0.00021
0.011	-0.144	0.219	0.085	0.00019
0.008	-0.390	-0.138	-0.073	0.00016
0.007	-0.157	-0.106	-0.037	0.00080
-0.003	-0.023	0.013	-0.027	0.00050
-0.008	-0.058	-0.057	-0.004	0.0

The computed parameters yielded the following results:

In X_t = In 3.85 + 0.02 In Px - 0.01 In Pr + 2.5 Y^{t-1} + 0.03 In Yt

and computer estimation of the log-log inverse function using the same data yielded.

In X_t = 2.91 + 0.07 In Px - 0.011 In Pr + 54.28 Yt^{-1} + 0.103 In Yt
        (4.619) (0.573)   (-0.544))   (1.488)   (1.175)

R^2 = 34.19   F = 90.9

Figures in parenthesis are t-values. See Figure 47e for graphical demonstration.

Selection of the Best Functional Form

After the computation one can proceed to evaluate the different functional forms to decide which one provides the best estimates. Some of these estimates can graphically be presented as in Figures 47a)–f). Engel curves express the expenditure on a commodity as a function of income only. An Engel curve is

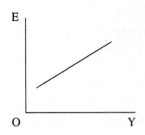

a) Linear
$$E - a + bY + U$$
$$\Sigma y = b\ Y/E$$

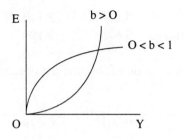

b) Double log
$$\ln E - \ln a + b\ln + U$$
$$\Sigma y = b$$

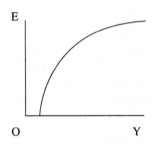

c) Semi-log
$$E = \ln a + b\ln Y + U$$
$$\Sigma y = b/E$$

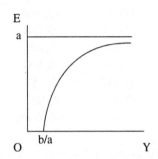

d) Hyperbolic (or inverse)
$$E = a - b/Y + U$$
$$\Sigma y = b/EY$$

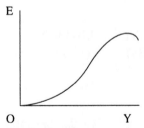

e) Log-log inverse
$$\ln E = \ln a - b/Y\ C\ \ln Y + U$$
$$\Sigma y = b/Y - C$$

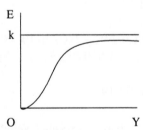

f) Log normal
$$E = k\Lambda\ (aY^b) + U$$
$$\Sigma y = \frac{aY\Lambda^1(aY)}{\Lambda\ (aY)}$$

Note: E = expenditure; Y = income; U = error term; Σy = income elasticity; a, b, c and k are parameters to be estimated; Λ (Z) denotes the standardized log normal distribution function at Z.

Figure 47 Graphical representation of Engel curves

a demand function derived by constrained utility maximization, and it is the locus of points of the quantity of a commodity that consumers will purchase at given levels of income per unit time, *ceteris paribus*.

In Engel curves studies, either the expenditure on a commodity or the quantity demanded can be used as the dependent variable. Under the assumption that consumers pay the same unit price for a particular commodity (which is usually the case when budget data is used), income elasticities obtained will be the same whether quantity or expenditure is used as the dependent variable. However, where households pay varying unit prices for the same commodity due to quality differences, income elasticities with respect to expenditure and quantity will be different (expenditure = quantity x price). The difference between the two is usually defined as quantity elasticity.

The analysis of Engel curves in Figures 47a)–f) may proceed with the use of different functional forms. Since economic theory provides only little information on the form of the functional relationship between expenditure and income, several researchers suggest that the use of any function should be assessed on its intuitive appeal and whether certain basic statistical or technical criteria are fulfilled. For example, it is expected that for most commodities there is some level of income below which the commodity is not purchased; and at some point a satiety level is reached. Also, since total expenditure must be equal the sum of individual expenditures, the functional form should satisfy the additivity criterion. Also, the type of function should be assessed for accuracy of fit, and the significance of the estimated parameters.

The regression outputs obtained from the various functional forms differ in magnitude in respect of the seven criteria indicated earlier. It is, therefore, necessary to compare the estimates of the different functional forms, choosing the best of the estimated functions that give the most reliable estimates. The main rationale for choosing any one of these functions is its ability to adequately explain the relationship being studied. Looking at the estimates, one can conclude that none of the functions satisfies the *a priori* relationship for the own price (Px) estimates. Since the quantity demanded of a commodity has an inverse relationship with its own price, one expects Px to be negative, but all the estimates for Px are positive. Similarly income is expected to be positively related to quantity demanded, but all the estimates for the income variable (Y) are negative except the hyperbolic and log-log inverse functions.

Also, for all the functions the estimated parameters are not significant at the 5 per cent level of significance, except the constant term, and Px in the case of the hyperbolic function. All the R^2 values are also low, ranging between 16.57 for the semi-log function to 34.19 for log-log inverse function.

The conclusion one can draw at this point is that none of the estimated functions could adequately explain the demand for maize in Ghana, using the data available. This may be because the time series (1977–88) was too short (it is always better to use a long time series for analysis). Another reason may be because of inconsistencies in the data (for example, a critical look at the data on quantity of maize demanded indicates that they are more likely to be estimated figures than real observations). On relative terms, however, the hyperbolic function may be chosen as the best among the seven functions that explain the demand for maize in Ghana. This is because the own price (Px) estimate is significant, the income (Y) variable has the correct sign, the R^2 value (27.53 per cent) has a higher value than all other functions (except the log-log inverse function), and the F-value is significant.

Interpretation of Estimated Parameters

For purposes of interpretation, one can use the estimates of the hyperbolic function which is considered the best among the seven functions:

$$Xt = 38.09^* + 0.043^* \quad Px \quad - 0.035\, Pr + 142.06 \quad Yt^{-1}$$
$$\quad (38.70) \quad (12.85) \qquad \quad (-1.719) \quad (0.327)$$

$$R^2 = 27.53 \qquad\qquad\qquad F = 101.29$$

* Significant at the 5 per cent level.

The demand elasticities are:

own price elasticity, $Ep = b1\dfrac{Px}{Xt} = \dfrac{.043 \times 9.42}{38.22} = 0.011$

cross-price elasticity, $Exr = b2\,\dfrac{Pr}{Xt} = \dfrac{0.035 \times 18.14}{38.22} = 0.017$

income elasticity, $Ey = \dfrac{b3}{Xt\ Yt} = \dfrac{142.06}{38.22 \times 436.47} = 0.009$

The R^2 of 27.53 means that the independent variables (price of maize, price of rice, and income variables) explain only 27.53 per cent of the variation in the demand for maize. This percentage is rather too low, and implies that other factors not included in the model account for the variation in the demand for maize. The own price elasticity (Ep) of 0.011 means that a 10 per cent increase in the price of maize elicits an increase in quantity demanded by 1 per cent, implying that the demand for maize is elastic since the change in price far outweighs the proportionate changes in quantity demands. The cross-price elasticity (Exr) of -0.017 implies that the demand for rice is complementary to the demand for maize in Ghana; and that a 10 per cent increase in the price of rice will result in a 1.7 per cent decrease in the quantity of maize demanded. It should be noted, however, that the estimate is not significant (implying that, in reality, the price of rice has no significant effect on the quantity of maize demanded). As a general rule, insignificant estimates cannot be used for forecasting purposes, even though forecasting is one of the basic aims of econometric analysis of this nature. Also, the income variable is not significant, implying that income has no significant effect on the demand for maize. But in terms of interpretation, the income elasticity of 0.009 implies that a 10 per cent rise in income level results in only a 0.9 per cent increase in the demand for maize (Asuming-Brimpong, 1992).

8 Analysis of Agricultural Supply Response

Introduction

Agricultural supply response in developing countries has been a subject for investigations for a long time. At one time it was argued that the farmers in developing countries had income targets and once that level had been met, they would make little effort to increase their production. It was also argued that the subsistence farmers were very risk averse and valued leisure highly. However, it was subsequently recognized that farmers respond positively to price signals, and the perverse reaction to the level of producer prices leading to backward-sloping supply curve for output was then accepted as being an obsolete assumption. A decade or so after political independence, a series of studies by individual scholars as well as bilateral and multilateral technical and financial agencies pointed out that inadequate government-administered prices were the principal reason for the poor performance of the agricultural sector in SSA countries. Supply response to price levels was then extensively studied. However, given the three distinct but interlinked levels of the economy, the analysis of the individual farm and aggregate agricultural supply response can best be systematically carried out at the three successive layers of the economy. The best starting point of analysis should be at the household and enterprise level, where the impacts of government policies are felt. The response at this level is then traced back to the meso-level where changes in economic/incentive determinants occur. Any change in these determinants is then traced back to the macro-level of the economy where policies are conceived and executed. It is the efficiency of policy management that will influence changes in incentive determinants.

In the analysis, the rural households are taken as the basic producing and consuming units which have outputs consisting of labour, capital agricultural as well as non-agricultural products, and service activities, of which marketing is a typical example. Some of these outputs are initially sold in local markets, while others are retained for household consumption. Sales of outputs provide cash income which the rural households use to purchase consumer goods and services, inputs and non-agricultural goods, and some cash may be saved for investment purposes. Some of the products are delivered to urban and industrial centres, with some being exported. The rural markets which facilitate these exchanges can, therefore, be categorized into product (output) markets, input markets, consumer goods markets, and financial markets. Changes in income and production levels will determine aggregate demand function because food demand, for instance, will be influenced by the real income, relative consumer prices, and agricultural and food supply will be influenced by relative product prices, input prices, the state of technology and institutional efficiency such as credit availability, marketing services, resource tenure, economic and institutional infrastructure, etc.

To gain a better understanding of the effects of national policy on smallholders, they should, therefore, be analysed within the marketing conceptual framework.

Concept of Elasticity

Equilibrium Price

In the analysis the elasticities are used to predict: i) the effects of government intervention, such as pricing policies, taxation, fiscal incentives; and ii) the impact of demand shifts, such as changes in export demand, income and population on prices and quantity of output. In demand and supply analysis, one has to recognize that equilibrium price varies according to the length of time in which market forces work themselves through. Usually it is also essential to make a distinction between the short period during which the reaction of producers to any change in their costs or in the demand of their products is limited to increasing and/or decreasing their production with a fixed quantity of factors of production, while in the long run there is sufficient time for producers to respond to a change in economic conditions by altering (increasing or improving through investment) the level of factors of production. The distinction between 'long' and 'short' period reaction is not only between the time that different sorts of decisions take to have effect, but also the nature of changes, whether temporary or longer-lasting, that the producer thinks have taken place. The producer may also attempt to foresee future changes based on his/her estimate of their permanence.

In demand and supply analysis, it is helpful to take it that the price of any product is determined by the interaction of its demand and supply curves. The demand curve is a graphical presentation of a demand schedule which indicates the quantities of the commodity bought at various prices, while the supply curve, also a graphical presentation, lists the quantities offered for sale at various prices. The demand curve indicates the relationship between prices and quantities demanded. In other words, the supply schedule and supply curve indicate the relationship between market prices and the quantities the suppliers are prepared to offer for sale. Hence the amount brought to the market is governed by the ruling market prices and is based on the law of supply, which states that more will be supplied at higher prices than at lower prices. The supply curve, therefore, slopes upward from left to right, as illustrated in Figure 48.

What the curve is trying to portray is that an increase in price of rice will make production of rice profitable, and will spur producers to expand outputs in response to increasing prices. In addition, the price increase will encourage new entrants into rice production, and the increase will result in the shift of the supply curve, as shown in the figure. The initial supply curve is represented by SS, but further increases will shift the curve to S_1, S_1. At price OP_1, suppliers are prepared to offer quantity OQ_c, whereas under the initial supply condition at that price (OP), the suppliers are prepared to supply OQ_d. At price OP_2 the quantity supplied increases from OQ_2 to OQ_3. The reverse can also happen if prices begin to fall, resulting in the curve shifting from $S_1 S_1$ to SS. The effect is to reduce the quantity supplied at all prices. These shifts in the supply curve are an indication of some basic changes in the condition governing supply. The producers are either motivated to supply more if they are experiencing some reduction in the costs of the factors of production or higher prices of their products. Conversely, a shift to lower levels of supply could be due to low prices of the products or an escalation of the cost of production.

For any economic good, there is a supply schedule as well as a demand schedule. If the two are brought together in a market (not necessarily in a geographic location), the quantity demanded will be equal at only one market price, OP, the equilibrium price, which is the only price at which the quantity supplied by willing sellers equals the amount cleared by willing buyers. At prices higher than the equilibrium price, the quantity supplied will exceed the quantity demanded, and the excess supply will oblige sellers to reduce prices in order to dispose of output, a situation often described as a buyers' market. Conversely, at lower prices the quantity demanded exceeds the amount supplied, giving rise to a shortage. Competition among buyers forces up prices, a condition termed a sellers' market. Thus market prices are determined by

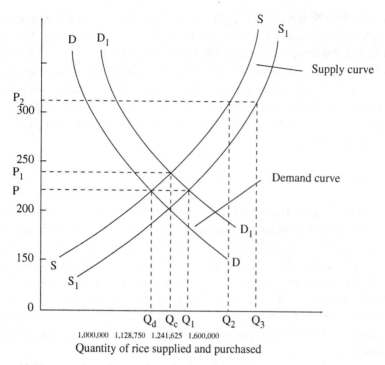

Figure 48 Demand and supply relationship (also used as Figure 34)

the interaction between demand and supply, and in competitive markets changes in market prices are due to changes in demand and supply. *Ceteris paribus*, an increase in demand raises the price and increases the quantity supplied. In the figure, DD is the original demand curve, the equilibrium price is OP and the quantity OQ_d is the amount demanded and supplied. If demand increases from DD to $D_1 D_1$, the immediate effect is to cause a shortage $Q_d Q_1$ at the ruling price OP. This shortage raises prices and the quantity supplied will increase until a new equilibrium price is established at OP_1 and the quantity demanded and supplied is OQc. This same figure can also be used to explain the effects of a fall in demand. If demand falls from $D_1 D_1$ to DD, there will be a surplus at price OP_1 equal to the horizontal distance between the demand curves. Suppliers will be obliged to lower prices in order to clear their excess stocks. The fall in price reduces the quantity supplied and increases the quantity demanded until a new and lower equilibrium price is established at OP.

The same figure can be used to demonstrate the effects of a change in supply. An increase in supply moves the supply curve to $S_1 S_1$. The immediate effect at price OP is a surplus $Q_d Q_1$. The surplus forces the price downwards, and quantity demanded increases until an equilibrium price OP_1 is re-established and the quantity demanded and supplied will be OQ_1. When supply falls from $S_1 S_1$ to SS there will be excess demand at price OP_1, represented by the horizontal distance between the supply curves. The excess demand will cause the price to rise, and the quantity that will be demanded will fall and the quantity supplied will increase until an equilibrium price is re-established at OP.

Elasticity of Supply

In the preceding section, it has been demonstrated that changes in demand and supply leads to changes in market prices as well as the quantity demanded and supplied. In analytical work, one would like to know the extent of changes which can be established by estimating elasticity of demand and supply. Estimating elasticity of demand had already been covered. In this chapter, elasticity of supply will be covered. Traditionally, when the elasticity of supply is not qualified, it is taken to mean price elasticity which measures the direction and extent of the sellers response to a change in price of his product which is expressed as:

$$\text{Supply elasticity} = \frac{\text{the percentage change in the quantity supplied}}{\text{the percentage change in price}}$$

It is the change in price that is the exclusive cause of the supply. As with demand elasticity, supply elasticity depends partly on the ease with which the producer can change from a given product to another (cross-elasticity) and partly on income effect of a change in price. We can illustrate these points by using the Sierra Leone rice supply used in demonstrating demand schedule. If the price of rice increases from 150 leones to 200 leones per kg, the quantity of rice supplied increases from 1,000,000 to 1,050,000 tons. In this case elasticity of supply is

$$\frac{\dfrac{50,000}{100,000}}{\dfrac{50}{150}} = \frac{0.05}{0.33} = 0.15$$

When the price increases from 200 to 250 leones per kg, the quantity of rice supplied increases from 1,050,000 to 1,128,750. Elasticity of supply equals

$$\frac{\dfrac{78,750}{1,050,000}}{\dfrac{50}{200}} = \frac{0.075}{0.250} = 0.300$$

When the price of rice increases to 250 to 300 the quantity of rice supplied increased to 1,241,625

$$\frac{\dfrac{1,12875}{1,128,750}}{\dfrac{50}{300}} = \frac{0.10}{0.17} = 0.588$$

As with demand elasticity, a supply is called inelastic when the fraction is less than one, and elastic if it is greater than one. Also as with demand curve, the supply curve varies in elasticity throughout its length, frequently being more elastic to the left, in the region of low prices, than to the right of the supply curve. This arises because of the typical condition of decreasing return in the short run. As output is expanded, the production needs a greater quantity of factors of production to produce a given increment of output. This is the principle of the law of diminishing return or the law of increasing cost. Supply reactions are also dependent on the time period. Within each production period, one can expect a small supply response, as shown by the above calculations. At the extreme limit, in the very short period, the so-called market period, the supply curve will be completely inelastic, represented by a vertical line, indicating that the quantity supplied will be cleared whatever the price. The longer the period that elapses, the greater will be a supply response due to either greater investments or general improvement as explained earlier.

Cross-elasticity of Supply

In chapter 2, competitive crop relationships were illustrated. It was shown that cotton has a number of effective competitors, particularly food crops, especially for both land and labour. In analytical work, cross-elasticity of supply measures the economic relationships between products on the supply side. It is measured, for two competing crops x and y, by where the change in the price of y is the exclusive

the percentage change in supply of x

the percentage change in the price of y

cause of the change in the supply of x. If the elasticity is positive, it means that the fall of the price y and a rise in the price of x induces an increase of x and vice versa. If elasticity is positive, a rise of price y, inducing an increased supply of x, or a fall in the price of y, inducing a decreased supply of x, means x and y are joint products. An example is mutton and wool, which was explained using the example of Lesotho sheep and goat production. If the elasticity is negative, a rise in the price of y inducing a fall in the supply of x, then x and y are competing products, and the higher the value of elasticity, the closer the competition.

Recent Studies of Supply Response

The issue of peasant farmer behaviour has been a subject for discussion for a long time, usually centred around his/her responsiveness to prices, for which various hypotheses had been advanced. These hypotheses can be grouped into three categories:

- that peasant farmers respond quickly, normally and efficiently to relative price changes;
- that the marketed output of subsistence farmers is inversely related to prices; and
- that institutional constraints are so limiting that any price response is insignificant.

Schultz (1964), for instance, argued that the rate at which a peasant accepts a factor of production depends on its revenue and/or profit, due allowance being given to risk and uncertainty. The second hypothesis, which contends that marketed production of peasant farmers is inversely related to prices, is based on the concept of target income whereby it is argued that peasant farmers may have fixed or relatively fixed monetary obligations. Once the limited objectives have been attained he makes no further effort to earn more money. This hypothesis has been disputed and is now regarded professionally as being obsolete, since empirical evidence has demonstrated that farmers do respond to price signals (effort-incentive). Bond (1983), for instance, summarized the results of many agricultural price response studies, and indicated the respective short-run and long-run elasticities for cocoa in Ghana 0.39, 0.77; coffee in Africa 0.12, 0.44; cotton in Uganda 0.25; groundnuts in Nigeria 0.24, 0.24; palm kernels in Nigeria 0.22, 0.22; palm oil in Nigeria 0.29; rubber in Liberia 0.14, 0.22; sisal in Tanzania 0.06, 0.48; and tobacco in Malawi 0.48, 0.48. Scandizo and Bruce's (1980) study of individual cash crops indicated that elasticities ranged from 0.1 to 0.8 in the short run to 0.2 to 1.2 in the long run. Cleaver studied the level of price discrimination in 31 SSA countries by working out nominal protection coefficient. Using these data, the countries were categorized into those with low levels of discrimination (15 per cent below import or export parity level), medium level (between 15 and 40 per cent below import or export parity level) and high level (more than 40 per cent below import or export parity level). The review indicated that farmers were responsive to changes in input and output prices. It further indicated that countries with low or no farm price discrimination recorded an average annual growth rate of agricultural production between 1970–80 of 2.9 per cent per annum, while countries with medium farm price discrimination recorded 1.8 per cent a year, with countries having high farm price discrimination achieving only 0.8 per cent annual growth rate (Cleaver, 1985).

In Ghana, Asante et al. (1988) showed that the greatest influence of supply response of maize was found to be a rainfall factor, giving a high elasticity of 2.29. This finding is in line with FAO studies which indicated that improvement in agricultural production has also been impeded by adverse climatic and ecological conditions. In Lesotho also it had been confirmed that it is normal rainfall amount that is the most significant factor in supply response. Since the late 1970s until the mid-1990s, Lesotho's agricultural policies had been dictated by political expedience, to reduce heavy dependence on food imports from South Africa and to protect domestic producers from some perceived unfair competition from the then-subsidized, large-scale South Africa producers. With assistance from a number of financial and technical agencies, the government of Lesotho promoted food self-sufficiency with a primary focus on increasing output of the dominant cereal, maize initiated in 1980/81 involving, amongst other things: i) setting fixed producer prices for maize grain well above world prices and substantially higher than South African producer prices; ii) subsidizing heavily government-provided tractor services; iii) supplying improved seed and subsidized fertilizer to participating farmers; and iv) providing loans at subsidized interest rates. The output of regression analysis, based on rainfall and real producer prices of maize for the period 1984–94, indicated that elasticity of supply of 2.3 was due to rainfall and accounted for 56 per cent of the variation in maize production and was significant at the 95 per cent confidence limit. The price factor was negatively correlated to maize output. Nearly 60 per cent of Lesotho's cultivated land is devoted to maize, 20 per cent to sorghum and 10 per cent to wheat. All, except a small percentage, is rain-fed, making national output vulnerable to drought and highly unstable. The national average rainfall, therefore, had an important impact on domestic production of the three staple cereals, while price and fiscal stimuli had practically no impact on supply response, at least for maize.

Cleaver, in studying the impact of supply response to relative changes in economic determinants, extended his previous study to include the impact of currency exchange rate adjustment on agricultural production. He demonstrated that countries with a positive rate of real currency depreciation recorded agricultural growth rate, on average, of 2.6 per cent a year, while those countries for which currency appreciated (negative real depreciation), achieved only 1.5 per cent agricultural growth rate a year between 1970–81 (Cleaver, 1988). Following the implementation of macroeconomic policy reforms, Cleaver analysed whether the elimination of indirect discrimination improved overall agricultural growth performance in general and not only of tradeables. He compared the agricultural growth rates of Sub-Saharan Africa countries under adjustment with those not under adjustment. He confirmed that in the 1970s, before adjustment began, there was no difference in agricultural growth between the two groups. Difference began to emerge in the early 1980s when adjustment programmes were initiated (Table 39) (Cleaver, 1988). Agricultural production growth rate more than doubled

Table 39   Recent agricultural performance of countries in Sub-Saharan Africa

Agricultural production

| | Growth % per annum | | |
	Countries under adjustment	Countries not under adjustment	Difference in growth rates
1970–80	1.1	0.9	0.2
1980–85	2.7	1.8	0.9
1986	5.8	4.3	1.5
1987	1.5	-1.1	2.6
Index of food production per capita			
1979–81 = 100	97	97	0

between 1980–85 and 1985–87 in countries that adopted wide-ranging strong reform measures while countries without such reforms have seen their agricultural growth rates stagnate at the low levels that prevailed in the early 1980s.

Jaeger investigated the effects of government distortionary intervention on the agricultural supply response, especially the direct control of producer price for principal export crops and the indirect effect of exchange rate policies. His investigation showed that the share of export crops' values retained by the producers (as measured by the real protection coefficient) dropped from about 90 per cent to 50 per cent on average between 1971 to 1983. His econometric analysis combining cross-section and time-series data confirmed other research results which indicated that, in the short-run, export supply with respect to the real exchange rate varied from 0.1 to 0.3 for tree crops exporters and 0.6 for annual crop exporters. Jaeger (1992), therefore, demonstrated that the tree crops exports are moderately responsive to changes in price incentives but stronger in respect of real exchange rate.

Meanwhile Balassa undertook regression analysis (the ratio of agricultural exports to output for changes in the real exchange rate and foreign income) to test the responsiveness of agricultural exports to changes in incentive level. As illustrated in Table 40, he was able to demonstrate that agricultural export elasticities were higher than elasticities of all exports of all goods and services and almost as high as those for merchandise exports (Balassa, 1986).

Table 40   Elasticity of ratio of exports to output, 1965–82

| | **Elasticity of exports with respect to real exchange rate** | |
Exports/output	*Developing countries*	*Sub-Saharan Africa*
Exports and services/total output	0.48	0.88
Merchandise exports/total output	0.77	1.01
Agricultural exports/total output	0.68	1.35
Net agricultural exports/agricultural output	4.96	11.47

Source: Balassa, 1986, op cit.

The elasticities of net agricultural exports were found to be higher than elasticities of agricultural imports because as the exchange rate rose, agricultural exports rose and agricultural imports became more expensive and, therefore, fell. It was, therefore, concluded that the short-run response of export crops, and especially net agricultural exports to exchange rate changes was large. For Sub-Saharan Africa, the high response could be explained by the fact that most countries are small and heavily dependent on foreign trade. Diakosavvas and Kirkpatrick, in a separate study, regressed the ratio of agricultural exports to agricultural production (X/Q) on real exchange rate movements lagged one year and changes in foreign income (FY), taking GDP of industrial countries as a proxy. The purpose of FY was to capture the factor of foreign demand for agricultural exports. For Ghana, for instance, the result of the analysis indicated that a 1 per cent increase (depreciation) in the real exchange rate was associated with 0.15 per cent increase in the ratio of agricultural exports to agricultural production. The explanatory power (R^2) was only 0.13. Apart from the weak demand for agricultural products in industrial countries, there had been a persistent deterioration in the international terms of trade for these products. While export prices have been falling, those of imports have been rising.

Successive Tiers of Analysis of Supply Response

The vigour of agricultural supply response depends to a large extent on peasant farmers' behaviour in production and the way they are likely to form expectations about price. In his production activities, a peasant farmer has several alternatives: i) producing food crops and other goods for his own consumption; ii) producing cash crops; iii) making his labour available for wage employment (or participating in artisanal employment to supplement income); and iv) taking time for recreation. Changes in the prices of any of these consumption or production activities affect production decision. The way in which each crop enterprise is affected by a change of these prices depends on the relative weights of substitution and income effects in the consumption process and upon whether or not subsistence goods are considered as being inferior in consumption. It follows, therefore, that the effect of producer prices in cash crop production cannot be considered in isolation from other variables. As was discussed earlier, changes in money wages can generate resource shifts out agricultural production to wage employment in the industrial and service sectors.

Analysis at the Micro-level

The main interest in analysis at the micro-level is on agricultural supply response, taken to mean output changes on individual farms (endogenous variables) resulting from the combination of different levels of factors of production. The levels of the different inputs are influenced by economic determinants (the exogenous factors). In this context, therefore, a supply function represents the level of outputs on farms as a result of the use of alternative combinations of explanatory variables. Usually the analysis is extended to cover the level of marketed output (marketed surplus, i.e. the residual amount after allowing for family consumption from the individual farms). On the basis of this definition, it is obvious that the effect of government intervention manifests itself through the vigour of supply response, either in the form of total farm output or marketed surplus. These outputs are a result of a deliberate production and marketing decisions of households, due allowance being given to the effects of exogenous shocks such as an unpredictable non-price factor like unfavourable weather conditions, outbreaks of diseases and pests, or inhospitable external economic environment.

In any economy there is an array of prices, and a change in any one price in principle leads to a change in agricultural production. Producer responses vary depending upon which price is changed. In the analysis, the elasticity estimates are used to predict: i) the effects of intervention, such as pricing policies, taxation, subsidies, etc.; and ii) the impact of demand (the external economic environment factor), income and population on prices and quantity of output. Firstly, there is a need to make a distinction between the elasticity of response to the change in the relative price of the agricultural product and the elasticity of response to changes in the relative price of factor inputs. Secondly, there is also the need to make a distinction between the elasticity of response of an individual crop to a change in the relative producer price and the elasticity of aggregate agricultural production to the change in the general level of agricultural prices. Thirdly, there is a difference between the response to price changes of marketed surplus and of the production of cash crops (crops for which there is little family consumption).

Agricultural supply response to prices Most of the estimates of price responsiveness are obtained from production functional form, which is a mathematical relationship describing the way in which the quantity of a particular product depends upon the quantities of particular inputs used in the production process. It provides information concerning the quantity of output that may be expected when particular inputs are combined in a specific manner. The approaches used in supply response analysis are usually divided into two broad categories: i) the positivistic approaches, which are based on econometric/statistical models; ii) normative approaches, which are based on programming models. The positivistic approaches cover direct and duality approaches, the latter covering the profit and cost parameters. The direct approach involves obtaining estimates of behavioural parameters directly from econometric/statistical analysis of historical time series data. Given the knowledge of the peasant farmers' present state of farming, their production function in crop production may be stated as follows:

$$Q = f (A, L, K, T) \tag{1}$$

where

Q	is quantity produced;
A	is actual acreage under cultivation;
L	is labour;
K	represents capital; and
T	denotes technology.

It is usually assumed that the farmer growing a particular cash crop, say cotton, is a profit maximizer and is also operating within a perfectly competitive condition, and whose production process involves the variable productive services of land, labour, capital and technology as presented in the equation. The technological package usually consists of seeds, technical production inputs and advisory services.

Conceptually, the short run can be defined as the period in which productive capacity cannot be changed but output can be varied by using the fixed capacity with different amounts of variable factors. For annual crops like cotton, whose growing season is less than a year, output in the short run can be altered by varying either the acreage under cultivation or the intensity of farming or both. These technological packages can be taken not to vary significantly and can be taken to be constant. Thus the production function in equation (1) becomes

$$Q = f (A, L, K) \tag{2}$$

and the total cost function can be written as

$$C = C (A, L, K) = mA, wL \text{ and } rK \tag{3}$$

where

m, w, and r are the given prices of land, labour and capital inputs.

Since perfect competition is assumed and perfectly competitive producers face a given price (P>O) from their agricultural products, total revenue function is given by the equation

$$R = PQ = Pf (A, L, K) \tag{4}$$

Equations (3) and (4) can now permit the profit function to be expressed as follows:

$$L = R\text{-}C = Pf (A, L, K) - (mA + wL + rK) \tag{5}$$

Equation (5) can be rewritten (Seini, undated, p. 23):

$$L = PQ - (mA + wL + rK) \tag{6}$$

Assuming that in equilibrium, profit is maximized when desired output Q^d is produced, then solution of equation (6) yields

$$Q^d = g (P, m, w, r) \tag{7}$$

In the case of cotton, whose sowing-to-sowing cycle is one year or less, $Q^d = Q$, which means that only acreage under cultivation in the current year is important. However, for perennial crops, the stock of trees corresponds to fixed factor, so that in the short run, output can be changed only by varying the intensity of farming and in the long run, capacity can be changed by varying the acreage under planting. For annual crops, there is likely to be a high correlation between elasticity of acreage and elasticity of output with respect to price, whereas for a perennial crop, there is likely to be little relationship between elasticity of acreage and the elasticity of output. This is because it takes many years for a tree to mature and to reach peak output.

Equation (7), therefore, expresses desired output as a function of the prices of inputs in the production function. The use of these inputs on one crop represents a loss in their use in the production of substitute crops. In other words, their use in one crop production involves an opportunity cost which is measured by the output forgone in their use in the next best alternative. If it is assumed that the price of the next best alternative is a measure of its value, then Q^d can be expressed as a function of relative prices as follows:

$$Q^d = g\left(P_c / P_I\right) \tag{8}$$

where

P$_c$ is the price of a crop, say cotton; and
P$_I$ is the price of substitute crop, say groundnut.

In this case, therefore, the desired output becomes a function of the price of cotton relative to the price of substitute crop (groundnuts). As stated earlier, the quantity of cotton produced is determined principally by yield and area brought under cultivation. Land area can, therefore, be used as a proxy for desired output and equation (8) becomes

$$A^d = g\left(P_c / P_I\right) \tag{9}$$

This equation expresses the area brought under cotton production as a function of the price of the crop own-price relative to the price of (cross-price) its best competitor in production process.

Before peasant farmers respond to price incentive, they must have formed some expectations about prices. Several models have been developed to explain *price expectation formation*. The most widely-used model is the work of Marc Nerlove (1958), which postulates that farm output and investment decisions are made on the basis of expectation of high profitability, and that price changes are permanent and not seriously affected by violent fluctuation. Price expectations have, therefore, become an integral part in economic models of agricultural production decision-making processes. Supply response is greatly influenced by price expectations which include such theories as *naive* expectation, *adaptive* expectation, *extrapolative* expectations and *rational* expectation. In analysis, the expected price for period it is defined as $_{t-1}P^e_t$, with the expectation being formed in period t-1. As regards *naive expectations*, the model used is a simple modification of the existing static concepts because it postulates expectations to equal prices at the time the expectations are formed. It is for this reason that the expectations are assumed to be naive. It is expressed as

$$P^e_t = a_o + b_1 P_{t-1} \tag{10}$$

It is taken that farmers will fully adjust to desired output in each period according to the price level in the preceding period. This is often known as the *cobweb* model. The cobweb model assumes that producers are influenced solely by the most recent season's prices, with the expectation that the prices will prevail during the next season. It is a way of explaining the possible dynamic relationships inherent in adjustment process. In analysing market behaviour, the cobweb model regards the supply of a commodity as a function of its past price, demand as a function of its current prices and the production decisions based on expected prices.

The cobweb model usually does not take into account the 'learning' process in adjustment. A better alternative model is the *adaptive expectations* model, which assumes that producers revise their expectations according to their most recent experience. Nerlove (1958), using the adaptive expectation model, advanced the idea of an expected normal price. According to Nerlove, production decisions are based on the long-run average price. According to the adaptive expectation model, current expectations are derived by modifying previous expectations in light of the current experience (error learning model). Notationally it is expressed as:

$$P^e_t - P^e_{t-1} = b \ (P_{t-1} - P^e_{t-1}) \tag{11}$$

This model represents the general interpretation that price expectation in the coming period is revised in proportion to the error made in predicting price in the preceding period. In analysis, the expected normal price P^e_t is represented as geometrically distributed lag of all past prices as follows (Seini, undated, p. 26):

$$P^e_t = \sum_{r=0}^{\infty} b \ (1 - b)^r P_t - r - 1 \tag{12}$$

The *extrapolative expectation* model attempts to explain price expectations in markets with price cycles. These are expectations based on the assumption that current price or price trend will continue. In this model, the expected price is defined as (Seini, p. 27):

$$P^e_t = a_o + b_1 P_{t-1} + b_2 (P_{t-1} - P_{t-2}) \tag{13}$$

where

P^e_t is the expected price for period (t) at (t-1); and

P_{t-1} is the actual price in period (t-1).

The use of this model is to take into account the effect of the most recent trend in prices on future prices. The extrapolative property of the model depends on the value b_2, the 'coefficient of expectation'. If it is greater than zero, then the forecaster is extrapolating the past trend, expecting it to continue; if it is less than zero, the reversal of the trend is expected.

Rational expectations are conditioned expectations of the forecast variable. Decision-makers take into account both demand and supply conditions when forming price expectations. This implies that the relevant set on which expectations are formulated include data on both parameters of demand and supply in the system, and knowledge of exogenous variables. Expectations can be taken to be rational if

$$P^e_t = E\,(P_t\,/O_{t-1}) \tag{14}$$

where

O_{t-1} is the available information set; and
E   exogenous variables.

The other issue in agricultural supply analysis is that of *adjustment constraint*. Some of the above models were used in a static fashion. Under the assumption of perfect competition, profit maximization and the absence of fixed factors of production, supply function is similar to the marginal cost curve (chapter 2). In agricultural supply analysis, a static model is inadequate because: i) the production process, apart from involving fixed factors of production, cannot be adjusted instantaneously because of its biological nature; ii) the production process takes place under risks and uncertainty (chapter 3). This means that delays exist in adjusting from current production to the desired level. Because of these limitations, dynamic elements are introduced to explain how output adjustments over time and/or price expectations are formed. Lags in economic relationships are caused by technical, institutional and psychological reasons. For these reasons, the reaction to a change in causal variables is spread over a number of time periods. Adjustment lags, therefore, occur and can be expressed as:

$$A_{t-1} = V\,(A^d_t - A_{t-1})\; 0 < v < 1 \qquad \text{'V' is constant} \tag{15}$$

where

A^d_t is the desired crop area;
A_{t-1} is the present area lagged one period; and
v   is the coefficient of adjustment.

In this model an attempt is made to bring the actual area cultivated to its desired level and that the adjustment is only partially successful during any one period. A broader implication is that farmers continue consciously to adjust to the long-run desired acreage to be cultivated. Time is required for producers to adapt to and to be able to operate their farms with a different enterprise mix.

The usual model specification takes the general model of

$$A^d_t = a + bx_t + et \tag{16}$$

where

A^d_t denotes desired area under a crop, say cotton;
X_t represents the expected value of the economic variable; and
et   is a random error term.

To allow for the possibility of adjustment lags, a Nerlovian partial adjustment model is specified as in model (15). The Nerlovian coefficient 'v' of adjustment lies between 0 and 1. Usually it is assumed that a producer is able to change the area under the crop in any one year only to the extent of a fraction of 'v' of the difference between the area they would like to plant and the area already planted in the preceding year. 'v', therefore, is a condition of how fast the farmers are adjusting to their expectations. A value of 'v' close to 0 means that farmers are adjusting slowly to the changing relative prices, while a value of 'v' close to 1 means that the farmers are quickly adjusting to changing levels of prices. Substituting equation (16) into (15) and readjusting gives an estimable model:

$$A_t = av + bv\, X_t + (1-v)\, A_{t-1} + vet \tag{17}$$
$$A_t = bo + b1\, X_t + b_3\, A_{t-1} + ut$$

The economic decision variable Xt taking V=1 in equation (17) is specified as the expected return from the crop (cotton) relative to its competitor. Hence the economic decision variable is to reflect the use of relative prices in terms of the crop and its competitor. Notationally it can be expressed as

$$X_t = P_{ct-1}/P_{gt-1} \tag{18}$$

where

P_{ct-1} is the lagged price of the crop (cotton); and
P_{gt-1} being the lagged price of its competitor (groundnut).

The model specification in equation (17) becomes

$$A_t = b_0 + b_1 (P_{ct-1}/P_{gt-1}) b_3 A_{t-1} + ut \tag{19}$$
$$A_t = b_0 + b_1 P_{ct-1} - b_1 P_{gt-1} + ut$$

Equation (18) is the estimating equation and, using ordinary least squares method, estimates of the parameters can be obtained either in its linear form or in logarithmic form. The quantification of the impact of policies required to achieve higher long-term agricultural growth is usually complicated because some of the factors such as the adoption of new improved technologies are partially dependent on the price structure which farmers face. Higher farm prices spur greater effort to increase production. However, there are also many constraining factors like inadequate infrastructure, research to generate improved technologies, institutional constraints such as credit needed to acquire improved technologies, etc. These factors fall under the category of public goods and their provision depends on government willingness to devote sufficient budgetary resources to agriculture. The other complication regards isolating statistically the price effect from the non-price factors.

The combination of these constraining factors holds back adjustment to full potential of supply response. These points can be illustrated with the help of Figure 49. Let DD be the demand function for agricultural products and SS corresponding to the short-run supply function, and that the amount demanded and supplied is OQ at the equilibrium price OP. If demand increases to its full potential level $D_\pi D_\pi$, the effect would be a shortage QQ_1 at the equilibrium price OP. The shortage would raise prices and the quantity supplied increases until a new equilibrium price at OP_1. However, given the effects of constraining factors, the quantity supplied does not reach its potential level $S_\pi S_\pi$ but increases to $S_v S_v$ and demand of net $D_v D_v$ at a new equilibrium price Op_v. The quantity supplied at this price (Op_v) would be OQ_v. This leaves a shortage

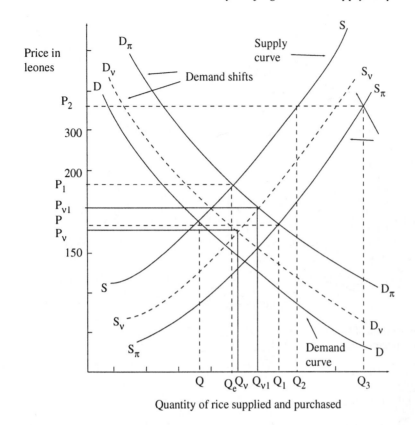

Quantity of rice supplied and purchased

Figure 49 Price-induced and non-price shifts

$Q_v Q_{v1}$ of quantity supplied. The shortage raises prices and the quantity supplied would increase until an equilibrium is re-established at OP_{v1}, and the quantity supplied would increase to OQ_{v1}. In this example, the Nerlovian coefficient equals to $OQ_1 - OQ_{v1}$ divided by OQ_1. If the value is large it means that farmers are adjusting fast, and vice versa.

Non-price aspect of supply response Agricultural supply response does not adjust instantaneously because of its biological nature which can be affected by non-price factors such as weather conditions, external shocks, shortages of factors of production, inappropriate technology etc. In SSA countries, for instance, the current major problem facing them is the escalation of the narrowing of the basic life-resource base. Sub-Saharan Africa generally has a narrow agricultural land base (see Map 2).

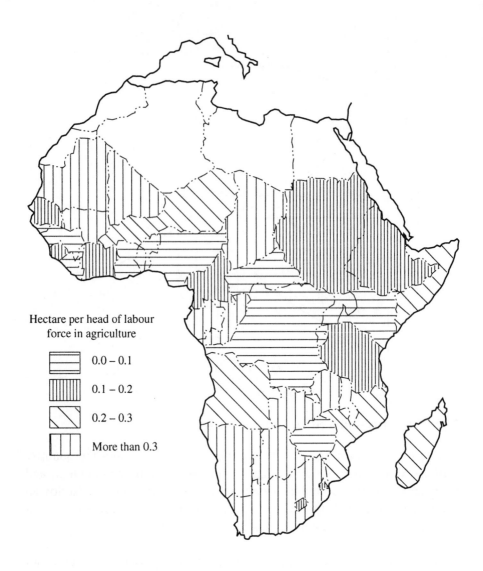

Hectare per head of labour
force in agriculture

	0.0 – 0.1
	0.1 – 0.2
	0.2 – 0.3
	More than 0.3

Note: A total of 17 countries covering 606,507,000 ha (or about 30 per cent of land area of SSA) have each labour force in agriculture having less than 0.1 ha. Zaire and CAR belong to this group becuase about 80% of land is under humid tropical forest.

Source: Computed from FAO country tables, op. cit.

Map 2   Availability of agricultural land (ha) per head of labour force in agriculture in Sub-Saharan Africa – 1989

Analysis at the Meso-level

The preceding section was concerned with supply response of individual crops. At the national level, the main concern is with regard to aggregate agricultural supply response, which can change in response to: i) a change in the relative prices of export versus food crops; and ii) a change in the aggregate agricultural price index. How aggregate production responds to change in the aggregate agricultural price index depends on such factors as resource mobility out of or into the agricultural sector, investment levels, and availability of productive resources and their efficient use. At the micro-level agricultural supply response is traditionally influenced by changes in economic determinants (relative prices) and the domestic terms of trade operating at the meso-level of the economy. These shifts of incentives at the meso-level are conditioned by macroeconomic policy instruments – typically brought about by the execution of monetary, fiscal, trade and exchange rate, credit, interest rate and pricing policies. At this level, the main concern is with the analysis of the impact of terms of trade, economic efficiency and exchange rate changes on supply response.

Terms of trade In most African countries the agricultural sector is still prominent in several areas of the macroeconomy: i) in internal balance (employment, food supply, supply of raw materials to industry, major source of fiscal resources, and GDP); and ii) in the external balance (exports and imports). The agricultural sector, therefore, still remains a major sector for broader economic growth. It is generally argued that the removal of distortions in the economy would improve the aggregate changes in the internal terms of trade in favour of the agricultural sector. Consequently, in analytical work, the terms of trade between the agricultural and non-agricultural sectors is often the focus of analysis in arriving at a decision on producer prices and on the magnitude of exchange rate adjustment. The other critical issue is that of efficiency in agriculture which is of importance in the context of public as well as private investment programmes. Often the style by which an economy is managed results in adverse terms of trade for the agricultural sector. If the economy is in its long-run equilibrium, when resources are actually at their desired levels, and returns to any given resource are the same in every use in the economy at any moment of time, then there would be no need to transfer a resource from one sector to another. However, the equilibrium can be distorted by changes in price structure.

The terms of trade, from the analytical point of view, is based on the hypothesis that if all prices were freely determined in open markets and if effective rates of taxation were the same for all commodities, then the value-added (Va_a) in agriculture as a ratio of GDP (Y) would have become higher. Instead, in SSA countries, for many years, vis-à-vis the non-agricultural sector, there has been negative effective protection (NEP) as compared with almost zero effective protection (ZEP) for the non-agricultural sector. Government-administered controlled prices kept real price lower for the agricultural sector than would have been obtained under open markets and equitable taxation. The burden of lower agricultural price was not adequately compensated by subsidies. In a controlled market, NEP implies:

$$\left[\frac{\bar{P^a}_c - P^a t}{P} - \frac{s.\, Ca}{P} \right] < 0 \tag{20}$$

where

P_a^c is the controlled price of agriculture;
P_a^f is the corresponding free market price; and
p   is the general price level; and
s   is effective rate of subsidies.

In this case the internal terms of trade for the agricultural sector can be improved by raising administered prices in real terms either by freeing all markets in order to eliminate disparity between P_a^c and P_a^f or increasing the effective rate of subsidies. However, subsidies are not always the best way of utilizing budgetary resources. The best option for improving the terms of trade for the agricultural sector is by raising P_a^c/P by freeing the markets.

In SSA the agricultural sector remains one of the major sources of government revenue through taxation of international trade, direct and indirect taxes. Consequently it has to be taken into account when analysing changes in terms of trade. If Va represents the quantity of agricultural output, Gr total government revenue, Gra government revenue derived from agriculture, Grn government revenue obtained from non-agricultural sources, and e is the currency exchange rate, then an increase (currency appreciation) or a decrease (currency depreciation) in 'e' will alter the internal terms of trade either in favour of or against the agricultural sector. Notationally, if other policies remain unchanged, the above relationships can be expressed as:

$$dVa = \frac{dVa}{de}\ e + \frac{dVa}{dPc_a} \cdot P^c_a \tag{21}$$

and

$$dGr = \frac{dGrn}{de} \cdot e + \frac{dGrn}{dP^c_a} - P^c_a + \frac{dGra}{dP^c_a} - P^c_a + \frac{dGra}{de} \cdot e \tag{22}$$

In analytical work the crucial issue is the determination of the magnitude required to raise the producer price to attain a given Va if the exchange rate ê is depreciated. Conversely, it is also necessary to determine to what extent the exchange rate should be lowered in order to attain a given change in government revenue if the producer price is raised by a given magnitude. Usually currency depreciation lowers the terms of trade for the agricultural sector because the aggregate price level (P) rises, while it tends to raise government revenue through the inflationary effect on nominal income and the substantial dependency of government revenue on international trade. Conversely, increases in producer prices raise the internal terms of trade for the agricultural sector but lower government revenue. To measure these changes the analyst has to take into consideration the elasticity of supply of Va (i.e. vs). If the elasticity is greater than unity, then government revenue need not fall because of the increase in the producer price. The basic equation used in analytical work is based largely on equations 21 and 22 which can be rewritten as:

$$\hat{P}^c_a = \frac{\hat{V}}{\eta pc - Vs} - \hat{e} \cdot \frac{\eta e}{\eta pc} \tag{23}$$

where

η is the elasticity of the terms of trade (P^c_a/p);
vs   is elasticity of supply with respect to P^c_a/P; and
$(^\wedge)$ circumflex over a variable indicates a rate of change.

In answering the question regarding the magnitude of raising the P^c_a to attain a given Va, the aim is to increase the producer price large enough to neutralize the adverse effects on the agricultural terms of trade due to currency depreciation while at the same time inducing the desired quantity increase. As regards the magnitude of lowering the exchange rate (ê) to attain a given change in government revenue (Gr) if the producer price is raised, determination is based on the following equation:

$$\frac{\hat{Gr}}{Sn\,(Yn + Yt) + Sa\,(\eta e + vs + ße)} - \frac{Sn(Ynpc + Ytpc) + Sa(\eta pc - vs + Bpc) - P^c{}_a}{Sa(Yn + Yt) + Sa\,(\eta e.vs + ße)} \quad (24)$$

where

    Sn, Sa   the shares of non-agriculture and agriculture in total tax income;
    Yn   is the elasticity of real non-agricultural income;
    Yt   is the elasticity of the tax rate of non-agricultural income;
    ηe is the elasticity of terms of trade = $e.P^c{}_a$; and
    ß   is elasticity of the tax rate on agriculture.

The exchange rate change must be large enough to neutralize any negative impacts on government revenue of the exogenously-determined producer price increases.

Supply response Most studies of response in agriculture have been presented in terms of the quantity response to real producer price changes. The basic model used has been essentially the Nerlovian framework, which postulates that farm output and investment decisions are made on the basis of expectation of high profitability, and that price changes are permanent and not seriously affected by violent fluctuation. In the basic model of supply response, output depends on changes in the basic equation. Thus the aggregate production growth function can be expressed as

$$Vt = f\,(Aa, La, Ka, Ta, S, Pr, Z, \quad\quad\quad\quad\quad\quad (25)$$

where

    Vt   is the growth rate of the volume of agricultural production in time t;
    La   is the rate of change in labour employed in agricultural production;
    Aa   is the rate of change in arable and permanent crop area;
    T   is technology used in production represented by the level of the technical production and productive inputs, and structural change;
    S   is the quality of arable land or soil;
    Pr   is real producer price or government policy; and
    Z   represents weather conditions and other variables whose effects are not captured through producer price variables.

The variables with subscripts 'a' are flow variables which measure growth rates. The others, S, Z, are seen as stock variables and the average values are used. The model incorporates the fact that it takes time to adjust acreage to its desired level, as explained earlier. Divergencies, therefore, occur between potential and actual yield.

Using a more complete model of aggregate supply response in the agricultural sector, based on the work of Johnson, is viewed as comprising of a group of households that consume part of their outputs and allocate time in agricultural work, non-agricultural pursuits, and recreation. In this respect, it is the marketed output that should be the focus of analysis. Agricultural credit (production and marketing) also play a crucial role in production and as crop finance. Domestic marketing, including transportation costs, is reflected in the price structure. A more detailed equation can be expressed as (Johnson, 1989, pp. 19–34):

$$Vt = (\frac{Pn}{Pa} \cdot Hh + \frac{Wa}{Pa} \cdot (La - N + X_1 + Lna) + \frac{Pz}{Pa} \cdot Z) -$$
$$(\frac{Lnf}{Pa} + C_n + \frac{Ds}{Pa}) - (\frac{Wn}{Pa} \cdot L_{na} + \frac{Rt}{Pa} \cdot K_{lc}) \tag{26}$$

where

Pn	is the price of non-agricultural commodity;
Pa	is the price of agricultural commodity or
P^c_a	is the controlled price of agricultural commodity;
Z is	the non-labour inputs such as fertilizer;
Wa	is nominal wage rate in agriculture;
Pz	is price of other variables inputs like fertilizer;
Ds	is savings of agricultural households in financial institutions or in valued resources like livestock;
Lna	is labour supplied to non-agricultural sector by farmers;
Lnf	is non-farm, non-labour income of farmers;
La	is total labour used in producing V;
N	is total agricultural household time available;
X_1	is recreation taken by agricultural households;
C_h	is agricultural households' consumption of V;
H_h	is agricultural households' consumption of the non-agricultural commodity;
Klc	are physical assets of land and capital; and

Rlc   is rental on physical assets.

These variables are partially indicated in the illustration which represents a typical household and factors influencing his decisions. As illustrated (Figure 50) the total produce of the agricultural households together with income obtained from artisanal employment is used up in purchases of non-agricultural commodities (H_h), non-family labour ($La - N + Y_1 + Lna$), physical variable inputs (Pz) and physical assets (Klc) plus the consumption of savings either in the form of savings in the banking system or valued resources (Ds). The total production process can then be defined as the sum of marketed surplus (Vm) and subsistence or own consumption (Ch) expressed as:

$$V = V_m + C_n \tag{27}$$

It is also necessary to include value added, defined as the difference between total output (V) and the real cost of purchased inputs expressed as:

$$\frac{VAa}{Pa} = V - \frac{Pv}{Pa} \cdot Lnf - \frac{Wa}{Pa} \cdot (La - N + Y_1 + L_{na}) \tag{28}$$

where

VAa   is value-added in agriculture.

Since output is a function of A, La, Klc, real value of value added can be expressed as a function of output and factor prices.

$V = V (A, La, Klc)$ and

$$\frac{VAa}{Pa} = P \frac{(Pv}{Pa} - \frac{Wa}{Pa)} \cdot V) \text{ which can be rewritten as} \tag{29}$$

$$\frac{VAa}{PaV} = \frac{(Pv}{Pa} \cdot \frac{Wa)}{Pa} \tag{30}$$

From equations 29 and 30 the ratio of real value added (VAa) to output (V) decreases as the prices of inputs increase relative to Pa in a way that depends on the input coefficient in the production process and the elasticity of substitution among inputs marginal rate of substitution. Equation 26 is, therefore, quite general. The basic hypothesis of the expanded model is that

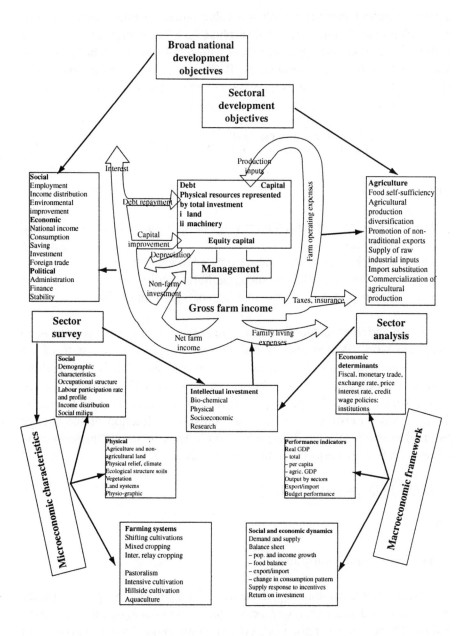

Figure 50 Schematic illustration of factors influencing smallholder behavioural characteristics

marketed output increases with the value added to total output and the accumulation of savings. Marketed surplus (V_m), however, tends to diminish with real wage outside agriculture and with non-farm, non-labour incomes available to agricultural households. If the marketing costs are taken into account and that saving ratios increase with real interest rates (Dsr) or value of valued resources, then Vm can be expressed as:

$$Vm = Vm \left(\frac{Pv}{Pa}, \frac{Wa}{Pn}, \frac{Ra}{Pa}, \frac{Pn}{Pa}, Dsr, \frac{Lnf}{Pa}, \frac{Wn}{Pa}, Ds, i_a, m_a \right) \qquad (31)$$

where

Dsr   is real interest earned on savings in financial institutions or valued resources;

Ds   is stock of domestic credit extended to agriculture;

ia   is interest rate charged on agricultural credit; and

ma   is transport and other marketing costs per unit of Vm.

Not all variables included in the above general equation can be used in all analytical work. Which ones to consider will depend on the state of the country's economy and what variables are to be influenced. In her study, Bond developed an equation based on Nerlove methodology (Nerlove, 1958). She took it that the actual changes in per capita total agricultural output (Q_t) from the previously existing level (Q_{t-1}) are only some fraction of the change required to achieve the equilibrium level ($\bar{Q}_t$). Thus, assuming the proportion achieved is β 'k' the equation can be written as

$$\ln Q_t - \ln Q_{t-1} = \beta \, (\ln \bar{Q}_t - \ln Q_{t-1}) \qquad (32)$$

where

In   is natural logarithm.

The equilibrium output ($\bar{Q}_t$) depends on the aggregate real producer price (PR_t), measured as the average producer prices of major agricultural products deflated by the consumer price index (CPI), a time trend (t) to take into account the effect of long-run structural changes on equilibrium output, and a dummy variable to capture the influences of unpredictable weather patterns:

$$\text{In}\bar{Q}_t = a_o + a_1 \text{ In } Pr_t + a_2 t + a_3 Z_t \tag{33}$$

$$\text{In } Q_t = b_o + b_1 \text{ In } PR_t + b_2 \text{ In } Q_{t-1} + b_3 t + b_4 Z_t \tag{34}$$

$b_o = \beta a_o; b_1 = \beta a_1; b_2 = 1-\beta; b_3 = \beta a_2;$
$b_4 = \beta a_3; B = 1-b_2 a_1 = b_1/(1-b_2);$ and
$a_2 = b_3 (1-b_2).$

Large values of β imply relatively fast adjustment so that the lower the estimate of b_2, the faster equilibrium output adjusts (Bond, 1983, p. 720).

The results of her studies are partially presented in Table 41.

Table 41   Three SSA countries: elasticity coefficients for aggregate agricultural supply responses, 1963–81

Country	bo	b1	b2	b3	b4	D - W	R2	SEE	Years
Ghana	1.74	0.20	0.42	-0.01		2.11	0.824	0.06	1963–81
	(2.27)	(3.16)	(2.55)	(1.70)					
Kenya	2.52	0.10	0.36	-0.003	0.04	2.24	0.676	0.02	1966–80
	(2.93)	(3.06)	(1.91)	(1.86)	(2.61)				
Tanzania	4.66	0.03	–	0.02	–	2.28	0.961	0.01	1972–81
	(21.27)	(0.69)	(8.98)						

Note: Numbers in parenthesis are t-statistics significant at 95 per cent confidence level.

Source: Bond, 1983, p. 721, Table 4.

The regression outputs presented in the table indicated that the constant (bo) was interpreted as subsistence output, or the level of output that had to be produced regardless of the producer price. This coefficient was highest in Tanzania. The regression outputs indicated that, the relative price, the coefficient of which was positive, was an important determinant of overall agricultural output particularly for Ghana and Kenya. For Ghana, the size of the coefficient (b2) showed a rise of 10 per cent in the real overall aggregate producer price resulting in an increase of 2 per cent in the overall agricultural output after one year. For the nine countries studied, the average of the estimated price elasticities was 0.12, which was lower than the estimates obtained for individual crops which was, for short-run own-price elasticity, about 0.5. Although the long-run own-price elasticity for individual crops was expected to be large, it also averaged about 0.5. In most countries studied, agricultural output exhibited a negative time trend, possibly reflecting the unfavourable investment in agriculture, the deterioration of the infrastructure and support services in rural areas. The dummy variable for weather conditions was the most significant factor in a number of countries reflecting that weather was a more important determinant of total agricultural output than any other variable.

Exchange rate One method often used to assess the overall supply response is to study the impact of currency adjustment on a country's volume and value of export, since SSA countries' exports come predominantly from the agricultural sector (Diakosavvas and Kirkpatrick, 1990). The impact of exchange rate was extensively covered in chapter 5 under 'Determinants of Exchange Rates'. However, there is a need to revisit the Salter-Swan model in respect of the analysis of the relationship between prices, expenditure, and the external balance as they relate to supply response. This model, the 'dependent economy' two sector framework, distinguishes between traded (T) and non-traded (NT) sectors. Exportable goods in this model are taken to include those commodities having surplus over home consumption which is exported, while importables include those commodities which have deficit between consumption and domestic production. The deficit is met through imports. Also the exportables and importables are treated as a single class of goods because any quantity of exportables can be exchanged for importables at their ruling prices. The critical issue is the need to maintain the balance of payment viability either by increasing the production of exportables or by means of greater domestic production of importables (import substitution).

These relationships can be illustrated with the help of a modified Salter-Swan graphic presentation (Figure 51). The horizontal axis represents tradeables while the vertical axis represents non-tradeable goods. The production of traded and non-traded goods is bound by the frontier NT obtained at least cost combination given domestic resources and technologies. All the points inside the curve represent combinations of production which are obtained by not utilizing national resources fully (underemployment) or in excess but used inefficiently (overemployment). In the short run it can be shifted to the right or left by changes in the quality and quantity of the technical base for agricultural production.

In the figure, the line EE_1 represents the combination of tradeable and non-tradeable goods which can be produced by a given amount of expenditure (E). Given the prices of tradeables (P_t) and non-tradeables (P_{nt}) respectively,

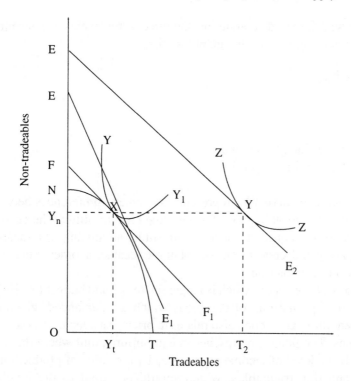

Figure 51 The impact of money supply and exchange rate adjustment on agricultural supply response

OT is the quantity of tradeables which can be purchased by total expenditure E if it were spent fully on tradeable goods, or ON if E were spent on non-tradeable goods. The EE_1 slope represents the relative prices between tradeables and non-tradeable goods expressed notationally as

$$P_t + T + P_{nt} \times NT = E \text{ (total expenditure)} \qquad (35)$$

$$NT = \frac{E}{Pnt} - \frac{Pt}{Pnt} \times T \text{ budget line} \qquad (36)$$

where

$-\dfrac{Pt}{Pnt}$ is the slope.

In a country with free trade conditions, the price of tradeables is determined by the world price and the exchange rate so that

Pt = ER x Pw;

where

ER   is the exchange rate; and
Pw   is the world market price.

The indifference curve YY_1 represents consumers' preferences between tradeable and non-tradeable goods for the same level of utility. The curve is concave because the consumer needs to substitute an amount of tradeables with an increasing or decreasing amount of non-tradeables in order to maintain the same level of satisfaction.

The point x of the curve, which is tangential to NT and budget line FF_1 at x, indicates the optimal mix of the goods which are demanded, given the level of expenditure, and which also relates to prices between tradeables and non-tradeables. The point x represents an equilibrium point where the level of FF_1 equals the level of income represented by the value of production of tradeables and non-tradeables. which should be equal to the level of consumption.

However this condition holds only if:

- expenditure coincides with production and full employment of domestic resources;
- the demanded traded goods equal to production; imports equal to exports and perfect balance in the foreign trade;
- the exchange rate is in equilibrium; and
- the demand for non-traded goods equals to domestic production; and point x represents the most profitable proportion for producing each types of good given marginal costs being proportional to relative prices; the marginal rate of production substitution (tangent to NT curve) is equal to the marginal rate of consumers' substitution (the tangent to YY_1 curve).

This equilibrium, however, is too idealistic to maintain in the real world because many factors interact differentially to throw the economy into disequilibrium. With the help of the figure, the FF_1 can shift to EE_2 curve. In this case the consumption or demand is in excess of the income curve NT. In other words, what is spent by consumers is more than what is available from domestic production of tradeable and non-tradeable goods. Consumers' demand of tradeables is OT_2, while domestic production is OT; the demand for non-tradeable is ON, but domestic production is only OY_n., the transformation curve which traces the combination of traded and non-traded goods which are produced given the domestic factor supply, technical knowledge, combination and adaptation of resources, and social conditions. This curve is known as the efficiency frontier because all its points represent the maximum combination production of the tradeable and non-tradeable goods. If the deficit cannot be supplied by external trade, disequilibrium will be resolved through inflationary price increases. This situation results in a current account deficit (xy) because the demand for tradeables is greater than OT, the quantity which the country can produce. If the demand for tradeables is less than OT_2 (supply being in excess of demand), it implies a surplus in the current account balance. Similarly if the demand for non-tradeables is greater than ON (supply), there is over-employment of domestic resources, and alternatively if the demand for non-tradeables is less than ON, then there is underemployment of domestic resources. There are, therefore, four combinations, each characterized by a specific current account and employment situation. Such positions are either *exante* situations (before the consumer spends all the money in excess), during which the economy is under the process of movement when current account is either increasing or decreasing; the domestic prices are rising or falling; or *ex post* situation (after consumers have spent their income) when expenditure equals income plus current account deficit (at time of disequilibrium), and the production of non-tradeables equals demand.

Excess demand can be generated by an increase in the money supply often induced by the necessity of financing budget deficits or by excess expansion of credit through the banking system or non-banking institutions for government and private sector borrowing. If the demand for non-tradeable goods cannot be met through domestic supply, in an open economy, the internal excess demand raises prices resulting in the increase of prices of non-tradeables in respect of tradeables. In response to the change in relative prices, the production of non-tradeable goods will increase because resources will be diverted from the production of tradeables. Meanwhile, the demand for non-tradeables will tend to decrease following increases in their prices and consumption will be shifted to tradeables. The supply of tradeable goods will fall because of lower prices and the associated shift of resources to the production of non-tradeables. The demand for tradeables will increase on account of their lower prices and the associated substitution effect with non-tradeable goods.

In a situation like this, the gap between tradeable production and tradeable supply will be the trade balance deficit. A permanent trade balance deficit leads to a deficit in the balance of payments and unsustainable external debt burden, in the absence of substantial capital inflows either through foreign aid and/or large remittances from emigrants. In the past the government response to balance of payment stress was to curb imports, ration foreign currency, fix exchange rate, control prices, keep active very unproductive parastatals – all of which provoked strong disequilibrium in the economy. To revive growth impulses of the productive sectors it became inevitable to implement sustained structural adjustment programmes. The adjustment programmes contributed in varying degree to improving supply response.

Efficiency One other concern in improving supply response is the exact mix of policies for enhancing economic efficiency and increasing productivity of resources in agriculture, thereby causing farmers' response to price changes or reducing their costs of production. In this respect there are two broad elements to consider: inter- and intra-sectoral efficiency. The guiding principles in taking a specific approach have been discussed in chapters 2, 3, 4 and 5. As regards inter- sectoral efficiency, the key issue is to maintain optimal structure of relative prices. Under normal conditions, for any two commodities, say i and j, it is considered optimal to equalize the ratios of prices to marginal costs so that

$$P_i/MC_i = P_j/Mc_j$$

where

P_i, P_j are the respective prices of the commodities; and
MC_i, MC_j are the respective marginal costs of the commodities.

For internationally-traded commodities, and with administered prices and controlled markets, the efficiency is arrived at by equating the relative domestic prices so that

$$\frac{Pdi}{Pw_i} = \frac{Pdi}{Pw_j} \tag{37}$$

$$\frac{Pdi}{Mc_i} = \frac{Pdj}{Mc_j} \tag{38}$$

where

Pw   is world market price in domestic currency equivalence

The intersectoral efficiency is, therefore, concerned with the internal and international terms of trade and supply response. The basic paradigm here is to ensure that resources are allocated to sectors where they are most productive and the choices equate commodity i as the agricultural sector and j for non-agricultural sector. The intra-sectoral efficiency, on the other hand, is concerned with those aspects pertaining to pricing policies for factors of production, products, interest rates, marketing costs and margins, market integration or fragmentation, delivery services, etc.

Analysis at the Macroeconomic Level

The macroeconomic policy reforms were expected to eliminate distortions in the economies in order to regain price and financial stability to lay the foundation for self-sustaining growth. It was also believed that the elimination of distortions in the economy would improve incentives. As a result of macroeconomic policy reforms, real producer prices of export crops were substantially improved. During adjustment, the domestic terms of trade in favour of export crops also improved. In most African countries market price data are unavailable. Official prices which are usually reported do not reflect actual market prices because, during adjustment, the producer prices of producers of food crops had always been determined by the interplay of supply and demand within the context of the parallel market and greatly depreciated exchange rate conditions in that market. Consequently, trade liberalization and exchange rate adjustment had very little influence on the food sub-sector. To ascertain the validity of these assumptions dynamic analyses (see appendix for regression equations) were carried out to assess the sources of domestic structural inflation. Regression equations are presented in the appendix and outputs in Table 42.

Monetary variables Excessive monetary creation especially to finance budget deficits has traditionally been blamed for being a major source of domestic inflation. The result of this study does support this contention. In equation

Table 42   Results of regression analyses of the sources of inflation in Sub-Saharan Africa

	R^2	R	SE	F	Sign. F	Sig. T
A Monetary variables 1980/87						
1 $P^c t = 10.64 - 1.37Y^c t + 0.92M^c t\text{-}1 - 0.47M^c t1$	0.92	0.96	1.26	25.48	0.005	0.016
(0.0003) (0.006) (0.097)						
2 $P^c t = 16.77 - 1.39Y^c t + 1.22M^c t \quad - 0.86M^c t - 0.24A^c t$	0.95	.97	.08	49.74	0.005	0.010
(0.002) (0.005) (0.024) (0.007)						
B Structural variables 1980/87						
i Agricultural supply bottleneck						
3 $P^c t = 8.29 - 0.56F^c t$	0.74	.86	2.19	20.71	0.004	0.004
(0.004)						
4 $P^c t = 10.29 - 0.38Y^c t - 0.46F^c t$	0.74	.86	2.19	10.86	0.015	0.013
ii The export instability index						
5 $P^c t = 8.44 - 0.56F^c t - 0.04X^c t$	0.73	.35	2.24	10.28	0.17	0.007
(0.007) (0.428)						
6 $P^c t = 32.76 - 0.58F^c t + 0.06X^c t - 26.421^c t$	0.86	.93	1.59	15.55	0.011	0.023
(0.94) (0.164) (0.054)						
iii The foreign exchange bottleneck						
7 $P^c t = 8.77 - 0.54F^c t - 0.08X^c t + 0.14T^c t$	9.73	.85	2.21	7.42	0.941	0.101
(0.013) (0.253) (0.347)						
8 $P^c t = 12.48 - 0.75Y^c t - 0.34F^c t \ 0.16T^c t$	0.77	.88	2.07	8.95	0.030	0.014
(0.170) (0.123) (0.253)						
9 $P^c t = 10.89 - 0.43F^c t - 0.51Y^c t + 0.02X^c t$	0.67	.82	2.45	5.81	0.061	0.141
(0.261) (0.683) (0.911)						
iv The public sector constraint						
10 $P^c t = 24.22 - 0.62F^c t - 17.571^c t$	0.81	.90	1.87	15.85	0.007	0.043
(0.002) (0.132)						
11 $P^c t = 23.28 - 0.56F^c t - 0.19Y^c t - 15.46^c t$	0.78	.88	2.03	9.04	0.030	0.079
(0.027) (0.649) (0.248)						
13 $P^c t = $ not enough data						
14 $P^c t = 11.20 - 0.50Y^c t - 0.39F^c t + 0.03X^c t$	0.71	.84	2.32	6.58	0.050	0.025
(0.320) (0.118) (0.54)						
15 $P^c t = 8.37 - 0.55F^c t - 0.01X^c t$	0.69	.83	2.39	8.73	0.023	0.009
(0.013) (0.858)						

Note: R^2 is coefficient of determination adjusted for degree of freedom; R is correlation coefficient ; F(stat) is F statistics at 5 per cent level; Sig T is test of significance in parentheses.

Sources: UNDP/World Bank, *African Economic and Financial Data*, Washington, 1989; IBRD, *World Tables, 1989–90*, World Bank, Washington DC; IMF, *International Financial Statistics Yearbook*, 1989.

(1), 92 per cent of the variation in the general price level is explained by the variation in money supply, and there is a strong positive correlation (R) of 0.96. When the expectation factor $(A^o)t$ was included in the regression analysis, the R^2 increased from 0.92 to 0.95, and the elasticity of $(M^o)t$ increased from 0.92 to 1.22, meaning that the monetary variable has a strong influence on the development of domestic prices, and the least influence was exerted by the expectation factor which has an elasticity of 0.24.

Structural variables

i) Agricultural supply variable The regression analyses also confirmed that it was not the monetary factor which was a major determinant of domestic inflation but also structural variables which made substantial contribution to inflationary pressure. The result of the analyses indicated that there was a significant relationship between changes in food prices and per capita growth in food output. Accordingly, the agricultural supply bottleneck index $(F^o)t$ yielded R^2 ranging from 0.56 when $(F^o)t$ was the only independent regressor to 0.46 when other variables were included. The result also indicated that for every 1 per cent increase in the food output, there was a 0.46 to 0.56 per cent decrease in the general price index. The results were consistent with the 50 per cent share of food in the general price index. The regression output indicated that 74 per cent (explanatory power R^2 being 0.74) of the variation in food price movement was accounted for by the variation in real per capita agricultural GDP, and that a unit increase in the GDP output $(Y^{oa})t$ resulted in 0.38 unit decline in food price. The analyses confirmed that the agricultural factor had influence on the domestic price development.

ii) The export and import variables The regression results of analysis (see appendix for equations) and (6) indicated that the export instability has a very feeble relationship with the domestic price development (elasticity of only 0.04). When the $(F^o)t$ and $(I^o)t$ were included, the explanatory power (R^2) improved from 0.73 to 0.76 but when the $(T^o)t$ variable is added (equation 7), declined substantially from 0.86 to 0.73. Since the elasticity of 0.14 is low but positive, it meant that the $(T^o)t$ has a weak influence on the domestic price movement. The weak influence on domestic prices of the export factor could be explained by the fact the agricultural exports in general had domestically low price supply response as well as low income elasticity of demand in the major consuming industrial countries.

It is for this reason that the $(1^o)t$ factor (equation 10) with R^2 being 0.81

and elasticity of 17.57 (i.e. a 1 per cent increase in import prices results in 17.57 per cent increase in domestic prices) has a strong influence on the domestic market, largely as a result of cost-push inflation, because of the inclusion of some key imports in the production process, and the inability for the domestic industry to substitute for these inputs. Although the share of imports in the GDP is only about 15 to 20 per cent, prices of imported commodities exert considerable influence on domestic prices through: i) imported inflation; ii) impact on related commodities (cross-elasticity); and iii) the level of domestic currency depreciation.

Factors Influencing the Vigour of Supply Response

Policy Conflicts

Technological change and economic growth require increases in capital formation. This is unlikely to occur in a situation where agricultural prices are depressed either as a result of direct government control or indirectly because the intersectoral terms of trade remaining against agriculture. In such a situation capital could move out of agriculture, thereby retarding the necessary technological improvement in the sector. The objective of macroeconomic stability under policy reforms was to bring about improvement in the policy environment which was expected to restore investment confidence, a necessary condition for the expansion of the productive base of the economy and the resuscitation of self-sustaining economic growth processes. Despite the moderate improvement in the performance of the productive sectors of the economy, and the maintenance of fiscal austerity, domestic inflation has not been contained.

Allocative response to changes in policy variables – unfounded assumptions
Recent policy reforms, the major thrust of which had been the elimination of overvalued exchange rates, reduction in industrial protection and fiscal austerity, took for granted that there was flexibility in the economies, opportunities for income maximization (or cost reduction) and the potential for expansion of the productive capacity, the combination of which would ultimately lead to faster economic growth. They further presupposed easy product transformation within the agricultural sector given price changes and sectoral adaptation, rapid factor mobility in response to relative price changes, a per cent shift of factors from one commodity to another in response to a per

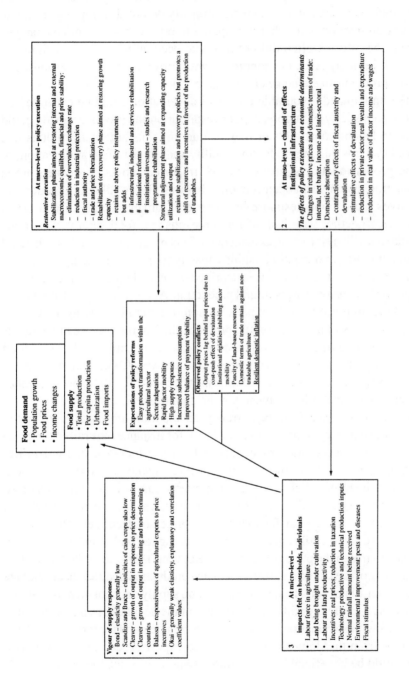

Figure 52 Schematic illustration of successive tiers of agricultural supply response analysis

cent change in relative prices. Subsistence farming systems have been developed over years and farmers traditionally do not shift rapidly from one mode of production to another in response to relative product price changes. Further, the reforms often did not take into account the structural rigidities that exist in many African economies, with different levels of responses to relative product price changes (see Figure 52).

The anticipated favourable effects of devaluation could be frustrated by low price elasticity of supply. A poor response on the production side could be due to labour constraints or may be due to: i) institutional rigidities like tenurial systems that inhibit factor mobility and efficient factor allocation; or ii) the proportionate rise in the cost of imported inputs consequent upon devaluation which, in an open economy, has the effect of blunting production incentives. Low supply response can also stem from the paucity of land-based resources. Together with lack of foreign exchange, food supply constraints become mutually reinforcing as inadequate food production intensifies demand for food imports, and the diminishing capacity to import, agriculture, as well as other sectors of the economy, is deprived of needed inputs, thus effectively hampering expansion in agricultural production. And yet currency depreciation by making imported foods expensive could generate a swing to greater subsistence consumption, and could provide relief for the balance of payments by reducing food imports. This potential is not being exploited because food supply is not keeping pace with population growth. Continued shortage of food leads to secular domestic inflation as it accounts for about 50 per cent of the consumer price index in most African countries.

The stimulative effects of currency devaluation are usually frustrated because the currency depreciation in Ghana, for instance, has raised the price of tradeable commodities much faster than the increase in food prices effectively turning the domestic terms of trade against the food sub-sector. Following the removal of subsidies on imported inputs including subsidized interest on agricultural credit, there was a sharp decline in the relative profitability of the use of fertilizers. The prices of fertilizers sharply and suddenly escalated while the prices of cereals, lagged far behind and were not expected to match the prices of fertilizers. Between 1980 and 1988, the relative profitability of the use of fertilizers on maize production declined at an average rate of about 14 per cent. Hence domestic food supply may not increase rapidly in response to currency adjustment because of the decline in real income often associated with devaluation, effectively reducing demand for food and shifting resources from the domestic food sector to export production. Lower food prices could be beneficial in containing inflation but since the terms of trade remain against the food sector, not much private investment will take place in the sector, and as food output lags behind population increase, it will ultimately lead to a rise in domestic inflation.

Usually domestic inflation is reflected in government expenditure but not necessarily in revenue, because of under-declaration of tax returns. Reducing fiscal deficit becomes very difficult, and inflationary deficit financing through the banking and non-banking systems is frequently used. Financing deficits reduces financial resources which should be available to the private sector for investment. As investment is reduced, the expansion in the productive base of the economy is adversely affected as a result of the lack of domestic savings for investment purposes. Heavy reliance on foreign savings increases the debt burden, and debt repayment reduces the availability of investable funds. Thus the expected self-sustaining economic growth objective cannot be realized. Breaking the existence of the circular relationship between macroeconomic parameters is, therefore, proving a daunting task and the high inflation can be expected to persist.

Circular relationship between macroeconomic parameters The resilience of inflation has continued to exacerbate the structural weakness of the African economies, especially its impact on the value of domestic currency. The causes of the resilience of the high secular inflation, in the light of fiscal and monetary restraints, has been a subject of debate among scholars, some of whom contend that the tight credit controls within the framework of fiscal austerity may be proving counterproductive in that they restrain the expansion in production for the domestic market needed to mop up excess liquidity. This in turn results in the bank's reluctance to accept deposits when prospects for on-lending are so limited, and also to a build-up of increased inflow of private remittances and official transfers. Also, the persistence of high domestic inflation means that interest rates charged by commercial banks remain generally high. With relatively high interest rates, the government's declared objective of increased private investment in agriculture through financial intermediation cannot be met. And yet the most significant way to increase the access of smallholders to productive assets is to make institutional credit available to them. Improving the availability and terms of credit are important means of increasing the access of smallholders to the capital assets essential for increasing their output.

The other problem relates to the dual effects of policy instruments used in adjustment, some of which yield conflicting results. A typical example is exchange rate adjustments, which have dual effects. Apart from ensuring payment of remunerative prices for export products, a switch in expenditure from imported goods to domestically produced goods, exchange rate adjustments have also produced effects which are in conflict with their role as stimuli for increased agricultural output. The currency devaluation increased the burden of foreign debt repayment as more domestic capital is required to meet the same amount of foreign debt, thus causing disequilibrium in liquidity and capital ratios for most banks. The result has been an inadequacy of domestic investment funds within the economy, leading to a low utilization capacity and associated infrastructural problems. And yet merely adjusting prices is not enough. More often than not the rural agricultural population lives in areas badly served by transport networks and other forms of communication, agricultural services, marketing facilities, etc. The policy issues of most importance for a successful adjustment are to deal with these constraints such as the provision of road and transport infrastructure, improvement in crop storage, services such as extension, credit and research, and marketing.

As already discussed, the structure of farming systems involving different methods of soil management and fertility maintenance (fallow) can no longer be sustained, and there are now physical indicators of accelerating environmental deterioration resulting in low yields of crops and livestock. What is required is to expand fertility-restoring farming practices which include the use of agro-chemicals. And yet successive devaluations and the removal of subsidies on inputs have led to an increase in domestic costs of agro-chemicals (FAO, 1992) far beyond the reach of most small-scale farmers, an effect in direct conflict with the government's declared objective of increasing smallholder productivity through the use of improved technological packages, most of which require imported technical production inputs. This has assumed significance because the increasing population pressure on land has been progressively undermining the ecological balance. Thus in Sub-Saharan Africa, poor supply response can also be explained by the inability to expand export production because of the paucity of the land-resource base, which is progressively being degraded. Poor export response to devaluation, if coupled with low price elasticity for imports can, at least, in the short term, lead to a deterioration in the balance of payments. Depending on the extent of devaluation and the degree of openness of the economy, the inflationary effects of the high cost of imports can quickly be transmitted domestically (cross-elasticity effect) thus paving the way for wage-price spiral upwards.

The resilience of inflation can also be explained by a self-perpetuating inflationary pressure which can distort resource allocation. Usually, high inflation encourages investment in sectors with quick returns, especially speculative trade. The rapid erosion of the value of the domestic currency by high domestic inflation, and the consequent over-valuation of the currency in the absence of regular exchange rate adjustment, usually combine to make imported goods relatively cheaper than their domestic substitute.

The macroeconomic policy reforms also incorporated adjustment of the pricing of public utilities (energy, water, etc.) at their real economic values. In the case of energy, increases in electricity prices forced the low income segment of the population to shift to the use of charcoal to satisfy their domestic energy requirements. Accordingly, the need for fuel and shelter (poles) leads to loss of forest cover. To neutralize the destructive effects of this policy, the design of macroeconomic policies should take into account key biological aspects of the use of domestic human waste and animal droppings in producing biogas for replacing fuelwood as a major source of domestic energy, while at the same time using the residue of biogas production to fertilize soil and also improving vegetation cover through sustained effort in implementing afforestation, reforestation and agro-forestry programmes.

Data Limitations and the Need for their Systematic Generation

The traditional agricultural production systems which were known to be stable and biologically efficient could only be sustained under land-abundant situations that allowed a resting phase long enough to restore soil fertility. As there is now empirical evidence of land degradation and soil erosion, it was expected that this phenomenon would be reflected in changes in the levels of factor productivity – either a decline or an increase as farmers respond by investing in land-productivity improvement (Boserup hypothesis). The analysis of changes in internal factor productivity was an attempt to measure the sustainability of resource use under changing farming systems (agricultural production intensification). The measure was based on the concept of inter-temporal total factor productivity (TFP) which was expected to indicate changes in productivity over time, i.e. changes in productive capacity of a system between two or more periods. It was also expected that as land per head of labour force in agriculture declined, farmers could innovate by investing in or adopting regenerative technologies to sustain productivity and increase output per unit area of production. Incremental output was expected to compensate for the decline in land per head of labour force.

Regression outputs of the micro-level econometric analyses (Okai, 1988, 1994) did not confirm the above expectations. The outputs did not indicate whether there was a decline or increase in factor productivity. There are many explanatory factors. One limitation was the paucity of data used in the analyses, which obliterated the regression outputs. Using growth rates, which could only be more meaningful for a single-country study, was probably not a suitable analytical procedure for SSA countries unless they could be reduced to a comparative common denominator. The 38 countries faced different vagaries of weather conditions at different times. The use of a common base year to compute growth rates could exaggerate performance for countries starting from a low base while it could underrate growth for countries whose performance was above long-term average. Under the circumstances the choice of a base year was most likely to affect all coefficients. Also, the incentive structures under an array of economic regimes in the countries studied were not uniform and so there were differences in behavioural response to economic opportunities. The other limitation was the differences in the level of factor productivity in different micro-ecological environments (physio-graphic units). Thus the analyses would have yielded better results had this factor been included in the investigation of productivity of different production systems based on the concept of interspatial total factor productivity. It would have incorporated and valued differences in quantity and quality of resource stock. It is a measure of the productive capacity of one system over another. A farming system could be more economically viable than another if the interspatial TFP (ITFP) is higher than the reflective ITFP index associated with the other.

The incorporation of ITFP index was difficult because usually national statistics are too aggregative and not disaggregated to geographical areas. The limitation is made difficult because in SSA resource statistics are almost totally absent. Traditionally, other than climatic data, resource statistics had not been regularly collected by national statistics offices. Resource data available had been based on field surveys by individuals, especially on land degradation and soil erosion. Since there had not been an established method of estimating soil degradation and erosion, results of field surveys indicated different levels of soil loss for the same ecological zone (Blaikie, 1989). In addition, the interactions between different farming systems and their forces have different erosion hazards through their effects on soil erodability and physical protection from splash erosion.

Another data limitation was in respect of lack of adequate information on farmers' adaptations and recommendations of resources under increasing environmental stress. It had been observed that in response to increasing ecological degradation, farmers have either shifted to growing crops that are drought resistant, tolerant to low soil fertility, or nitrogen-fixing plants (Okai, 1992, pp. 63–4) or engaging in wage labour to supplement income from agriculture. However, not many field investigations had been undertaken into the link between non-farm activities and on-farm investments. The link is usually influenced by many factors. The primary concern of any household is with utility maximization on goods consumed, leisure, income stability, risk management and coping, and food security. The physical environment, such as climate, that makes agriculture particularly risky in certain geographical areas, could discourage investment of on-farm and non-farm income in agriculture. In some countries in West and East Africa, however, several civil servants and businessmen had been investing non-farm income on land for the production of rice, horticultural and floricultural crops, and beef ranching because the economic returns on the investment have been profitable. Spatial differences in the quality of social, economic, commercial and institutional infrastructure could make it difficult for farmers in marginalized zones to export or sell their surplus outputs at competitive prices and this aspect discourages investment in agriculture in order to increase outputs beyond household requirements. Farmers also have to respond in different patterns to deficiencies in labour, financial and product markets. All these issues require systematic investigation to generate the required data for purposes of analysis.

Appendix: Regression Formulae for Computing Sources of Structural Inflation

1   Monetarist Approach

$$(\frac{P^0}{P}) t = a^0 + b^0 (\frac{Y^0}{Y}) t + c^0 (\frac{M^0}{M}) t - 1 = (\frac{M^0}{M}) t + u^0 \quad (14)$$

where

$(\frac{P^0}{P}) t$ = the annual percentage change in the general price level in time t;

$(\frac{Y^0}{Y})$ = the annual percentage change in nomnal GDP;

$(\frac{M^0}{M}) t$ = the annual percentage change in the money supply (defined as currency with the public and demand deposits);

$(\frac{M^0}{M}) t - 1 = (\frac{M^0}{M}) t$ lagged by one year

$$(\frac{P^0}{P}) t = a^1 + b^1 (\frac{Y^0}{Y}) t + c^1 (\frac{M^0}{M}) t + d^1 (\frac{M^0}{M}) t - 1 + e^1 (\frac{A^0}{A}) + u^1 \quad (15)$$

where

$\frac{A^0}{A}$ = a proxy for the cost of holding money, where A^0 the cost of holding money is not the market rate of interest realized from investment in non-monetary assets, but rather a proxy for the expected rate of inflation. In this study, the annual percentage change of the GDP deflator is used as a rough proxy.

2   Structuralist Approach

a) The agricultural supply bottleneck For this analysis, the annual percentage rate of change in domestic food prices minus the annual percentage change in the general cost of living index, i.e.

$(\frac{F^0}{F}) t$ was used as the independent regressor.

The regression equations are defined as

$$(\frac{P^0}{P})t = a^2 + f^0 (\frac{F^0}{F})t + u^2 \ (16)$$

$$(\frac{P^0}{P})t = a^3 + b^2 (\frac{Y^0}{Y})t + f^1 (\frac{F^0}{F})t + u^3 \ (17)$$

where

$(\frac{Y^0}{Y})t$ = the annual percentage change in the nominal GDP.

b) The export-instability index For this analysis, the export instability index is measured by the annual percentage change in dollar-export receipts lagged by one year, i.e.

$$(\frac{X^0}{X})t$$

The regression equations are defined as

$$(\frac{P^0}{P})t = a^4 + f^2 (\frac{F^0}{F})t + g^0 (\frac{X^0}{X})t + u^4 \ (18)$$

$$(\frac{P^0}{P})t = a^5 + f^3 (\frac{F^0}{F})t + h^1 (\frac{X^0}{X})t - 1 + i^0 (\frac{I^0}{I})t + u^5 \ (19)$$

where

$(\frac{X^0}{X})t - 1 = (\frac{X^0}{X})t$ lagged by one year

$(\frac{I^0}{I})t$ is the annual change in the import/GDP ratio, i.e. imports divided by GDP divided by the same the previous year.

c) The foreign exchange bottleneck For this analysis, i) the average annual percentage rate of change in the terms of trade and ii) the average import ratio, were used as independent regressors. The regression equations are defined as

$$\left(\frac{P^0}{P}\right) t = a^6 + f^4 \left(\frac{F^0}{F}\right) t + g^1 \left(\frac{X^0}{X}\right) t + j^0 \left(\frac{T^0}{T}\right) t + u^6 \ (20)$$

$$\left(\frac{P^0}{P}\right) t = a^7 + b^3 \left(\frac{Y^0}{Y}\right) t + f^5 \left(\frac{F^0}{F}\right) t + j^1 \left(\frac{T^0}{T}\right) t + u^7 \ (21)$$

where

$$\left(\frac{T^0}{T}\right) t \quad = \quad \text{the anual percentage rate of change in the unit cost terms of trade.}$$

$$\left(\frac{\overset{.}{P^0}}{P}\right) t = a^8 + b^4 \left(\frac{Y^0}{Y}\right) t + f^6 \left(\frac{F^0}{F}\right) t + g^2 \left(\frac{X^0}{X}\right) t + u^8 \ (22)$$

d) The 'public sector' constraint The public sector balance (i.e. largely public sector deficit) as a percentage of GDP as independent regressor, i.e.

$$\left(\frac{D^0}{D}\right) t \quad = \quad \text{the annual percentage rate of change in the public sector defined as a percentage of GDP.}$$

The regression equations are defined as

$$\left(\frac{P^0}{P}\right) t = a^9 + k^0 \left(\frac{D^0}{D}\right) t + u^9 \ (23)$$

$$\left(\frac{P^0}{P}\right) t = a^{10} + f^7 \left(\frac{F^0}{F}\right) t + i^1 \left(\frac{I^0}{I}\right) t + u^{10} \ (24)$$

$$\left(\frac{P^0}{P}\right) t = a^{11} + f^8 \left(\frac{F^0}{F}\right) t + b^5 \left(\frac{Y^0}{Y}\right) t + i^2 \left(\frac{I^0}{I}\right) t + u^{11} \ (25)$$

$$\left(\frac{P^0}{P}\right) t = a^{12} + f^9 \left(\frac{F^0}{F}\right) t + g^3 \left(\frac{X^0}{X}\right) t + i^3 \left(\frac{I^0}{I}\right) t + u^{12} \ (26)$$

$$\left(\frac{P^0}{P}\right) t = a^{13} + b^6 \left(\frac{Y^0}{Y}\right) t + f^{10} \left(\frac{F^0}{F}\right) t + h^1 \left(\frac{X^0}{X}\right) t - 1 + u^{13} \ (26) \quad \left(\frac{P^0}{P}\right) t = a^{14} + f^1$$

References

Chapter 1

Alderman, I. and Morris, C.T., 'A Factor Analysis of the Interrelationship between Social and Political Variables and Per Capita Gross National Product', *Quarterly Journal of Economics*, 79, pp. 555–78, 1965.

Alderman, I. and Morris, C.T., *Society Politics and Economic Development: a Quantitative Approach*, Johns Hopkins University Press, Baltimore, 1967a.

Alderman, I. and Morris, C.T., *Economic Growth and Social Equity in Developing Countries*, Stanford University Press, Stanford, California, 1967b.

Bauer, P.T., 'Remembrance of Studies Past: Retracing First Steps' in G.M. Meier and D. Seers (eds), *Pioneers in Development*, Oxford University Press, New York, 1984.

Boserup, E., *The Conditions of Agricultural Growth: the Economics of Agrarian Change Under Population Pressure*, Aldine Publishing Co., Chicago, 1965.

Denison, E.F., *The Sources of Economic Growth in the United States*, Committee of Economic Development, New York, 1962.

Gittinger, J.P., *Economic Analysis of Agricultural Projects*, Johns Hopkins University Press, 2nd edn, 1982.

Hayami, Y. and Ruttan, V.W., *Agricultural Development: an International Perspective*, Johns Hopkins University Press, Baltimore, 1971, reprint 1985.

Hoselitz, B.F., 'Non-economic Barriers to Economic Development', *Economic Development and Cultural Change*, 1, pp. 8–21, 1952.

Hoselitz, B.F., *Sociological Aspects of Economic Growth*, Free Press, Glencoe, Illinois, 1960.

IBRD, *Accelerated Development in Sub-Saharan Africa: Agenda for Action*, World Bank, Washington DC, 1981.

IBRD, *Towards Sustainable Development in Sub-Saharan Africa: a Joint Programme of Action*, World Bank, Washington DC, 1984.

IBRD, *Sub-Saharan Africa: From Crisis to Sustainable Growth*, World Bank, Washington DC, 1989.

IBRD, *Adjustment in Africa: Reforms, Results and the Road Ahead*, Oxford University Press, 1994.

Kendrid, J.W., *Productivity Trends in the United States*, National Bureau of Economic Research, New York, 1961.

Killick, T., *Policy Economics: a Textbook on Applied Economics of Developing Countries*, Heinemann, London, 1981.

Lewis, W.A., 'Economic Development with Unlimited Supplies of Labour', *Manchester School of Economics and Social Studies*, Vol. 22, 1954.

Lewis, W.A., *Theory of Economic Growth*, George Allen and Unwin Ltd., London, 1972.

Little, L.M.D. and Mirrlees, J.A., *Project Appraisal and Planning for Developing Countries*, Basic Books, New York, 1974, 1982.

415

M¨aler, K.G. and Munasinghe, M., 'Macro-economic Policies, Second-best Theory and the Environment', *Environment and Development Economics*, Part 2, Cambridge University Press, 1996.

McNamara, R.S. *The Challenges for Sub-Saharan Africa*, Sir John Crowford Memorial Lecture, World Bank, Washington, DC, 1985

Myrdal, G., *Asian Drama: An Inquiry into the Poverty of Nations*, Pantheon, New York, 1964.

Norgaard, R.B., 'Coevolutionary Agricultural Development', *Economic Development and Cultural Change*, University of Chicago Press, pp. 525–46, 1984.

Okai, M., 'Agricultural Development of Lango District of Northern Uganda with Particular Reference io Labour Productivity', unpublished MSc (Agric.) thesis, University of East Africa, Makerere University, Kampala, Uganda, 1968.

Okai, M., 'The Condition of Rural Women in Sub-Saharan Africa', *Development Journal of the Society for International Development*, 1, p. 48, 1995.

Ruttan, V.W., 'Cultural Endowments and Economic Development: What Can We Learn from Anthropology', *Economic Development and Cultural Change*, University of Chicago Press, pp. S 247–71, 1988.

Santiago, C.E., 'The Dynamics of Minimum Wage Policy in Economic Development: a Multiple Time-Series Approach', *Economic Development and Cultural Change*, Vol. 38, No. 1, 1989.

Scandizzo P.L., 'Methodologies for Measuring Agricultural Price Intervention', *World Bank Staff Paper*, No. 394, 1980.

Schultz T.W., 'The Declining Economic Importance of Agricultural Land', *Economic Journal*, 61, pp. 72–140, 1951.

Schultz, T.W., *Transforming Traditional Agriculture*, Yale University Press, New Haven, Connecticutt, 1964.

Squire, L. and Van der Tak, H.G., *Economic Analysis of Projects*, Johns Hopkins University Press, Baltimore, for World Bank, 1975.

UNDP, *Agroecology: Creating the Synergism for Sustainable Agriculture*, UNDP Guidebook series, New York, 1995.

Ward, W.A., Deren, B.J. and D'Silva, E.H., *The Economics of Project Analysis a Practitioner's Guide*, EDI Technical Materials, World Bank, Washington DC, 1995.

Chapter 2

Acharya, S.N., 'Perspective and Problems of Development in Low Income Sub-Saharan Africa', *World Bank Working Paper*, No. 300, 1978.

Allan, W., *The African Husbandman*, Oliver and Boyd, Edinburgh, 1967.

Baker, P.R., 'Nomadism in Africa', undated reprint, School of Development Studies, University of East Anglia, Norwich, UK.

Behnke, R., 'Natural Resource Management in Pastoral Areas', *Development Policy Review*, Vol. 12, pp. 5–27, 1994.

Belshaw, D.G.R., 'Taking Indigenous Knowledge Seriously: the Case of Inter-cropping Techniques in East Africa' in D. Brokensha, D. Warren and O. Werner (eds), *Indigenous Knowledge Systems and Development*, University Press of America, Lanham, Maryland, pp. 197–204, 1980.

Belshaw, D.G.R. and Hall, M., 'The Analysis and Use of Agricultural Experimental Data', *East African Conference of Agricultural Economists*, Makerere University, Kampala, Uganda, 1965.

Berry, S.S., 'The Food Crisis and Agrarian Change in Africa: a Review Essay', *African Study Review*, 2 (2), pp. 9–112, 1984.

Blaikie, P., 'Class, Land-use and Soil Erosion', reprint, *Overseas Development Institute*, No. 21, 1981.

Blaikie, P., 'Environment and Access to Resources in Africa', *Africa*, 59 (1), 1989.

Brown, B.H., 'The Ecology of Man and Domestic Stock' in D.J. Pratt and M.J. Gwyne (eds), *Rangeland Management and Ecology in East Africa*, Hodder and Stoughton, London, 1977.

Brown, G.J., 'Land as a Factor in Poverty Alleviation in Namibia Environmental Consideration' in *Land as a Factor in Poverty Alleviation in Namibia*, Ministry of Land, Resettlement and Rehabilitation, Windhoek, Namibia, 1993.

Carter, M.R., 'Environment, Technology and the Social Articulation of Risk in West African Agriculture', *Economic Development and Cultural Change*, University of Chicago Press, Chicago, pp. 557–90, 1997.

Cleave, J.H., *African Farmers: Labour Use in the Development of Smallholder Agriculture*, Praeger Publishers, New York, 1974.

Dahl, G. and Hjort, A., 'Having Herds', *Studies in Social Anthropology*, 2, Stockholm, Sweden, 1976.

Ehui, S.K. and Spencer, D.S.C., 'Measuring the Sustainability and Economic Viability of Tropical Farming Systems: a Model for Sub-Saharan Africa', *IITA Research*, No. 9, Ibadan, Nigeria, 1994.

Fafchamps, M., 'Solidarity Networks in Preindustrial Societies: Rational Peasants with a Moral Economy', *Economic Development and Cultural Change*, University of Chicago Press, Chicago, pp. 147–73, 1992.

FAO, 'Common Land Resources in Africa', regional workshop on *Communal Property in Africa: Policies and Prospects in Accra, Ghana*, FAO, Rome, Italy, 1991.

Fielder, R.J., 'The Role of Cattle in the Economy', *African Social Reviews*, pp. 327–61, 1973.

Fumagalli, C.T., 'An Evaluation of Development Projects among East African Pastoralists', *Social Sciences and African Development Planning*, State University of New York, Buffalo, 1979.

Karsheans, M., 'Environment Technology and Employment: Towards a New Definition of Sustainable Development', *Development and Change*, Vol. 24, pp. 723–56, 1994.

Livingstone, I., 'The Socio-economics of Ranching in Kenya', *Research in Economic Anthropology*, Vol. 2, 1977.

Livingstone, I., 'Economic Irrationality among Pastoral People: Myth or Reality?', *Development and Change*, 8, pp. 209–230, 1977.

MacMaster, D.N., 'A Subsistence Crop Geography of Uganda' in D. Stamp (ed.), *The World Land Use Survey*, London, 1965.

Niemeijer, D., 'The Dynamics of African Agricultural History: is it Time for a New Development Paradigm?', *Development and Change*, Vol. 27, No. 1, pp. 87–110, 1996.

Okai, M., 'Agricultural Development of Lango District of Northern Uganda with Particular Reference to Labour Productivity', unpublished MSc (Agric.) thesis, University of East Africa, Makerere University, Kampala, Uganda, 1968.

Okai, M., 'Choice of Strategies for Agricultural Development Under Increasing Population Pressure: The Uganda Case', unpublished MPhil thesis, University of London, 1974.

Okai, M., 'Agricultural Price Policies and Delivery Systems in Africa', *First Government Consultation on the Follow-up to the WCARRD*, FAO, Rome, Italy, 1983.

Okai, M., 'The Consequences of Market Intervention; Pricing Policies and Population Trends for Agriculture in Sub-Saharan Africa', unpublished PhD thesis, 1988.

Okai, M., 'Atheoretic Viewpoint on Socio-Cultural Aspects of the Spread of Human Immune Virus and Acquired Immune-Deficiency Syndrome in Sub-Saharan Africa: a New Agenda for Agricultural Supply Response', paper presented at *World Health Day Symposium*, Maseru, Lesotho, 1997.

Okigbo, B.N., 'Broadening the Food Base in Africa: the Potential of Traditional Food Plants', *Food And Nutrition*, Vol. 12, No. 1, 1986.

Pearce, D., Barbier, E. and Markandya, A., 'Sustainable Development and Cost-Benefit Analysis', Canadian Environment Assessment Workshop, 1988.

Phillipe-Plateau, J., 'Land Tenure System in Sub-Saharan Africa', an internal discussion paper, FAO, Rome, Italy, 1990.

Picardi, A.C. and Seifert, W.W., 'A Tragedy of the Commons in the Sahel', *Ekistics*, 258, pp. 297–304, 1977.

Piesse, J., Thirtle, C. and van Zyl, J., 'Effects of the 1992 Drought on Productivity in the South African Homelands: an Application of the Malmquist Index', *Journal of Agricultural Economics*, Vol. 47, No. 2, 1996.

Pomela, M.E., *Adoption of New Maize Technologies on Small Farmers in Lesotho*, Agricultural Research Division, Maseru, Lesotho.

Robertson, A.F., *The Dynamics of Productive Relationships – African Share Contracts in Comparative Perspective*, Cambridge University Press, Cambridge, 1987.

Rweyemamu, J., *Under Development and Industrialisation in Tanzania: a Study of Perverse Capitalist Industrial Development*, Oxford University Press, Nairobi, Kenya, 1973.

Safilios-Rothschild, C., 'The Persistance of Women's Invisibility in Agriculture: Theoretical and Policy Lessons from Lesotho and Sierra Leone', *Economic Development and Cultural Change*, 1985.

Schneider, H., 'Economic Development and Economic Change: the Case of East Africa Cattle', *Current Anthropology*, 15, 3, pp. 259–76, 1974.

Stocking, M.A., 'Relationship of Agricultural History and Settlement to Severe Soil Erosion in Rhodesia', *Zambezia*, VI (ii), 1978.

Stoorvogel, J.J. and Smaling, E.M.A., 'Assessment of Soil Nutrient Depletion in Sub-Saharan Africa: 1983–2000', Winard Staring Centre, Wageningen, The Netherlands, 1990.

Chapter 3

Abercrombie, F.D., 'A Sectoral Approach to the Cattle in West Africa', *Development Digest*, 13, 2, pp. 70–81, 1975.

Arecchi, A., 'Rural Settlement Experiences in Post-Colonial Africa', *Ekistics*, 304, pp. 47–56, 1995.

Ashby, J.A. and Sperling, L., 'Institutionalizing Participatory, Client-Driven Research and Technology Development in Agriculture', *Development and Change*, Vol. 26, pp, 754–70, 1995.

Baldus, R.D., 'The Introduction of Cooperative Livestock Husbandry in Tanzania', *Land Reform*, pp. 37–47, 1978.

Barrows, R., and Roth, M., 'Land Tenure and Investment in African Agriculture: Theory and Evidence', *The Journal of Modern African Studies*, 28, 2, pp. 265–97, 1990.

Behnke, R., 'Natural Resource Management in Pastoral Areas', *Development Policy Review*, Vol. 12, pp. 527, 1994.

Eicher, C.K. and Baker, D.C., 'Research on Agricultural Development in Sub-Saharan Africa: a Critical Survey', *MSU International Development Papers*, No. 1, 1982.

Feder, G. and Noronha, 'Land rights Systems and Agricultural Development in Sub-Saharan Africa', *Research Observer*, No. 2, World Bank, 1987.

Fielder, R.J., 'The Role of the Cattle in the Economy', *African Social Reviews*, pp. 327–61, 1973.

Fumagalli, C.T., 'An Evaluation of Development Projects among East African Pastoralists', *Social Sciences and African Development*, Planning State University of New York, Buffalo, 1979.

Green, J.K., 'Evaluating the Impact of Consolidation of Holdings Individualisation of Tenure, and Registration of Title: Lessons from Kenya', LTC Paper No. 129, Land Tenure Centre, University of Wisconsin, Madison, 1987.

Haugerund, A., 'The Consequences of Land Tenure Reform among Smallholders in the Kenya Highlands', *Rural African*, 15/16, Winter–Spring, pp. 65–89, 1983.

Hill, P., 'The Myth of the Amorphous Peasantry: a Northern Nigeria Case Study', *Nigerian Journal of Economic and Social Studies*, 1968.

Johnson, O.E., 'Economic Analysis: the Legal Framework and Land Tenure Systems', *Journal of Law and Economics*, XV, pp. 259–76, 1972.

Koehn, P., 'State Land Allocation and Class Formation in Nigeria', *Journal of Modern African Studies*, 21, No. 3, pp. 461–81, 1993.

Lawry, S.W., 'Transactions in Cropland Held Under Customery Tenure in Lesotho' in Bassett, T.J. and Crummey, D.E. (eds), *Land in African Agrarian Systems*, University of Wisconsin Press, Madison, pp. 57–74, 1993.

Lunning, H.A., 'The Impact of Socio-Economic Factors on the Land Tenure Pattern in Northern Nigeria', *Journal of Administration Overseas*, 4, No. 3, pp. 173–82, 1965.

Mukwaya, A.B., *Land Tenure in Baganda: Present-Day Tendencies*, East Africa Studies No. 5, Makerere Institute of Social Research, Kampala, Uganda, 1961.

Netting, R.M.C.C., 'Household Organization and Intensive Agriculture: the Kofyar Case', *Africa*, 35, No. 4, pp. 422–29, 1985.

Okai, M., 'Cultivation Practices in Lango District with Particular Reference to Ox-Cultivation', unpublished special project for the degree of BSc (Agric.), University of London (Makerere), Kampala, Uganda, 1964.

Okai, M., 'Agricultural Development of Lango District of Northern Uganda with Particular Reference io Labour Productivity', unpublished MSc (Agric.) thesis, University of East Africa (Makerere), Kampala, Uganda, 1968.

Okoth-Ogendo, H.W.O., 'African Land Tenure Reform' in Heyer, J. et al. (eds), *Agricultural Development in Kenya: an Economic Assessment*, Oxford University Press, Nairobi, Kenya, 1975.

Ole Parkipuny, M.S., 'Some Crucial Aspects of Masai Predicament', unpublished PhD manuscript, University of Dar-es-Salaam, Tanzania, 1977.

Phillipe-Plateau, J., 'Land Tenure System in Sub-Saharan Africa', an internal discussion paper, FAO, Rome, Italy, 1990.

Phillipe-Plateau, J., 'The Evolutionary Theory of Land Rights as applied to Sub-Saharan Africa: a Critical Assessment', *Development and Change*, Vol. 27, pp. 29–86, 1996.

Picardi, A.C. and Seifert, W.W., 'A Tragedy for the Commons in the Sahel', *Ekistics*, 258, pp. 297–304, 1977.

Pomela M.E., *Adoption of New Maize Technologies on Small Farmers in Lesotho,* Agricultural Research Division, Maseru, Lesotho.

Robertson, A.F., *The Dynamics of Productive Relationships – African Share Contracts in Comparative Perspective*, Cambridge University Press, Cambridge, 1987.

Shepherd, A., 'Agrarian Change in Northern Ghana: Public Investment, Capitalistic Farming And Famine' in J. Heyer et al. (eds), *Rural Development in Africa*, New York, St Martins Press, pp. 168–92, 1981.

Chapter 4

Alan, C.G. et al., *African Survey*, John Wiley and Sons, New York, 1973.

Anderson, D., 'The Economics of Afforestation: a Case Study in Africa', *Occasional Paper No. 1*, New Series, World Bank, 1988.

Ashby, J.A. and Sperling, L., 'Institutionalizing Participatory, Client-Driven Research and Technology Development in Agriculture', *Development and Change*, Vol. 26, pp. 754–70, 1995.

Baldwin, K.D.S., *Demography for Agricultural Planners*, FAO Policy Analysis Division, 1975.

Block, S.A., 'A New View of Agricultural Productivity in Sub-Saharan Africa', *American Journal of Agricultural Economics*, pp. 619–24, 1994.

Caldwell, J.C., *African Rural-Urban Migration: The Movement of Ghana's Town*, Columbia University Press, New York, 1969.

CGIAR, 'Sustainable Agricultural Production: Implications for International Agricultural Research', Consultative Group on International Agricultural Research, *FAO Research and Technology Paper 4*, FAO, Rome, Italy, 1989.

Conway, G.R., 'Agro-ecosystem Analysis', *Agricultural Administration*, 20, pp. 31–55, 1985.

Dumar, E., 'Women and Development in Ghana', *Rural Africa*, 1983.

Eicher, C.K., Zall, T., Kocher, J. and Winch, F., 'Employment Generation in African Agriculture', *Research Report No. 9*, Michigan State University, 1970.

Harris, J.R. and Todaro, M.P., 'Migration, Unemployment and Development: a Two-Sector Analysis', *American Economic Review*, 60, 1970.

Hicks, J.R., *Value and Capital*, 2nd edn, Oxford University Press, Oxford, 1946.

Knight, J. and Sabot, 'From Migrants to Proletarians: Employment Experience, Mobility and Wages in Tanzania', *Oxford Bulletin of Economics and Statistics*, London, 1982.

Lynam, J.K. and Herdt, R.W., 'Sense and Sustainability: Sustainability as an Objective in International Agricultural Research', *Agricultural Economics*, 3, pp. 381–98, 1989.

MPED, Ministry of Planning and Economic Development, Entebbe, Uganda, 1971.

Nobe, G.K. and Seckler, D.W., 'An Economic Analysis of Soil-Water Problems and Conservation Programme in the Kingdom of Lesotho', *LASA Research Report No.3*, Maseru, Lesotho, Ministry of Agriculture, 1979.

Okai, M., 'Choice of Strategies for Agricultural Development Under Increasing Population Pressure: The Uganda Case', unpublished MPhil thesis, University of London, 1974.

Okai, M., 'The Development of Ox-Cultivation in Uganda', *East African Journal of Rural Development*, Vol. 6, No. 2, 1975.

Okai, M., 'The Consequences of Increasing Population Pressure for Land-Carrying Capacity in Sub-Saharan Africa', *Proceedings of the Union for African Population Studies on Population and Environment*, Gaborone, Botswana, 1992.

Okai, M., 'Choice of Strategies for Agricultural Development Under Increasing Population Pressure: The Uganda Case', unpublished MPhil thesis, University of London, 1994.

Okigbo, B.N., 'Broadening the Food Base in Africa: The Potential of Traditional Food Plants', *Food and Nutrition*, Vol. 12, No. 1, FAO, Rome, 1986.

Osunsade, F.L. and Gleason, P., *IMF-Assistance to Sub-Saharan Africa*, IMF, 1992.

Roder, W., *'Environmental Assessment of the rural Development Program, Swaziland*, Cincinnati, University of Cincinnati Press, 1977.

USAID, 'Draft Environmental-Profile of Ruanda', Arid Information Centre, Tucson, Arizona, 1981.

Wen, G.J., 'Total Factor Productivity Change in China's Farming Sector: 1952–1989', *Economic Development and Cultural Change*, 1993.

World Commission on Environment and Development, *Our Common Future*, Oxford University Press, 1987.

Zacharia, K. et al., 'Demographic Aspects of Migration in West Africa', Vol. 2, *World Bank Staff Working Paper*, No. 415, 1980.

Chapter 5

Belshaw, D.G.R., 'The Utility of Social Accounting Prices and other Indicators in Formulating Agricultural Pricing Policy: an Assessment in the Context of Kenya and Tanzania', a paper presented at a regional workshop on *Experiences in Agricultural Sector Planning in Africa in the Context TCDC*, FAO Regional Office for Africa, Accra, Ghana, 1985.

Brett, E.A., *Colonialism and Under-Development in East Africa: the Politics of Economic Change 1919–1939*, Heinemann, London, 1973.

Brett, E.A., 'State Power and Economic Inefficiency: Explaining Political Failure in Africa', *IDS Bulletin*, Vol. 17, No. 1, Institute of Development Studies, University of Sussex, UK, 1986.

Creupelandt -FAO Internal Communication, 1987.

Economic Commission for Africa, 'Review of Food and Agricultural Policies in Selected African Countries: A Basis for Improving Government Policy Planning Capacities', conference paper for the 17th meeting and 21st session of the Commission and 12th meeting of the Conference of Ministers.

FAO, *Regional Food Plan for Africa*, FAO, Rome, Italy, 1978.

FAO, *Agricultural Price Policy in Africa*, 13th FAO Regional Conference for Africa, conference document, Rome, Italy, 1984.

FAO, *Agricultural Price Policy Experience in the ECOWAS Region*, Report No. TCP/RAF/4406, Rome, Italy, 1986.

FAO, 'Structural Adjustment, Food Production and Rural Poverty', *Proceeding of the International Conference on the Human Dimension of Africa's Economic Recovery and Development*, Khartòum, Sudan, 1987.

Hesp, P. and Van der Laan, L., 'Marketing Boards in Tropical Africa: A Survey', seminar on marketing boards in tropical Africa, 1981.

Hopcraft, P., 'Grain Marketing Policies and Institutions in Africa', *Finance and Development*, Vol. 24, No. 4, 1987.

Low, P., 'Export Subsidies and Trade Policy: the Experience of Kenya', *World Development*, Vol. 10, No. 4, 1982.

Gilles, M. and Michel, N., 'Short-Terms Responses to Trade and Incentive Policies in the Ivory Coast: Comparative Static Simulation in a Computable General Equilibrium Model', *World Bank Staff Working Paper*, No. 647, 1984.

Okai, M., 'Agricultural Price Policies and Delivery Systems in Africa', *First Government Consultation on the Follow-up to the WCARRD*, FAO, Rome, Italy, 1983.

Okai, M., 'The Consequences of Market Intervention; Pricing Policies and Population Trends for Agriculture in Sub-Saharan Africa', unpublished PhD thesis, 1988.

Seidman, A.W., *Ghana's Development Experience 1951–65*, East Africa Publishing House, Nairobi, 1978.

Tshibaka, B., 'The Effects of Trade and Exchange Rate Policies on Agriculture in Zaire', *Research Report 56*, International Food Policy Research Institute, Washington DC, 1986.

World Bank, *Towards Sustainable Development in Sub-Saharan Africa: A Joint Programme of Action*, World Bank, Washington DC, 1985.

Chapter 6

Bhagwati, J.N., 'Directly Unproductive, Profit-Seeking DUP Activities', *Journal of Political Economy*, 90, pp. 988–1002, 1982.

Cleaver, K.M., 'The Impact of Price and Exchange Rate Policies and Agriculture in Sub-Saharan Africa', *World Bank Staff Working Paper*, No. 728, 1985.

Cleaver, K.M., 'Agricultural Policy Reform and Structural Adjustment in Sub-Saharan Africa: Results to Date', internal paper, World Bank, Washington DC, 1988.

Economic Commission for Africa, 'Review of Food and Agricultural Policies in Selected African Countries: A Basis for Improving Government Policy Planning Capacities', conference paper for the 17th meeting and 21st session of the Commission and 12th meeting of the Conference of Ministers.

Ellis, F., 'Agricultural Price Policy in Tanzania Revisited', mimeo, School of Development Studies, University of East Anglia, Norwich, UK, 1985.

IBRD, *Sub-Saharan Africa: From Crisis to Sustainable Growth*, World Bank, Washington DC, 1990.

IBRD, 'Analytical Approaches to Stabilisation and Adjustment Programmes', *EDI Seminar Paper No. 44*, 1993.

IMF, *Macro-economic Adjustment: Policy Instruments and Issues*, IM Institute, 1992.

Jansen, D., *Trade Exchange Rate and Agricultural Pricing Policies in Zambia*, World Bank, The Political Economy of Agricultural Pricing Policy: Comparative Studies, 1988.

Kruger, A.O., 'The Political Economy of Rent-Seeking Society', *American Economic Review*, 64, pp. 291–303, 1974.

Nweke, F.I., 'Direct Governmental Production in Agriculture in Ghana', *IPCC Business Press*, 1978.

Okai, M., 'Agricultural Marketing Subsidies in West Africa', *Economic Development Institute*, World Bank training course on agricultural marketing policy issues, Abidjan, Côte D'Ivoire, 1988.

Okai, M., 'Sub-Saharan Africa Experience with Macro-Economic Disequilibria and Structural Adjustment with Particular Reference to the Agricultural Sector', *Proceedings of the Conference of the Ghana Economics Teachers' Association*, Adisadel College, Cape Coast, Ghana, 1991.

Salter, W.E.G., 'Internal and External Balance: the Role of Price and Expenditure Effects', *The Economic Record*, 35, pp. 226–38, 1959.

Struthers, J., 'Inflation in Ghana 1966 –78: Perspective on Monetarist vs Structuralist Debate', *Development and Change*, Vol. 2, Sage, London, 1981.

Tabatabia, H., 'Economic Stabilisation and Structural Adjustment in Ghana 1983–86', *Labour and Society*, Vol. 11, No. 3, 1986.

UNDP/World Bank, *African Development Indicators*, World Bank, Washington DC and UNDP, New York, 1992.

Watts, M.J. and Basset, T.J., 'Crisis and Change in African Agriculture: a Comparative Study of the IvoryCoast and Nigeria', *African Studies Review*, 28 (4), 1985.

Chapter 7

Asuming-Brempong, S., 'Guidelines for the Analysis of Demand for Agricultural Products', FAO Regional Officer for Africa, 1991.

King, G., *Natural and Political Observations and Conclusion, Upon the State and Condition of England*, reprint, Johns Hopkins University Press, Baltimore, 1936.

Thabane, M., 'Some Economic and Technological Factors behind the Adoption of the Blanket as Basotho Dress', *Review of Southern African Studies*, Vol. 1, No. 1, 1995.

Chapter 8

Asante, E.O., Asuming-Brempong, S. and Bruce, P.A., 'Ghana Grain Marketing Study', Ministry of Food and Agriculture, Accra, Ghana, 1989.

Balassa, B., 'Economic Incentives and Agricultural Exports in Developing Countries', *Proceedings Of the Eighth Congress of the International Economic Association*, New Delhi, India, 1986.

Balassa, B., ' Incentive Policies and Agricultural Performance in Sub-Saharan Africa', *World Bank Policy, Planning and Research Working Paper* 77, Washington DC, 1988.

Binswanger, H., 'The Policy Response of Agriculture', *Proceedings of the World Bank Annual Conference on Development Economics*, World Bank, Washington DC, pp. 231–69, 1989.

Bond, M., 'Agricultural Responses to Prices in Sub-Saharan African Countries', *IMF Staff Papers*, Vol. 30, 1983.

Cleaver, K.M., 'The Impact of Price and Exchange Rate Policies and Agriculture in Sub-Saharan Africa', *World Bank Staff Working Paper*, No. 728, 1985.

Cleaver, K.M., 'Agricultural Policy Reform and Structural Adjustment in Sub-Saharan Africa: Results to Date', internal paper, World Bank, Washington DC, 1988.

De Wilde, J., *Experience with Agricultural Development in Tropical Africa*, Johns Hopkins University Press, Baltimore, Maryland, 1967.

Diakosavvas, D. and Kirkpatrick, C., 'Exchange Rate Policy and Agricultural Export Performance in Sub-Saharan Africa', *Development Policy Review*, Sage, London, 1990.

Ehui, S.K. and Spencer, D.S.C., 'Measuring the Sustainability and Economic Viability of Tropical Farming Systems: a Model for Sub-Saharan Africa', *IITA Research*, No. 9, Ibadan, Nigeria, 1994.

FAO, *African Surveys*, FAO, Rome, 1961.

FAO, *Regional Food Plan for Africa*, FAO, Rome, 1986,

FAO, *Country Tables: Babis Data on the Agricultural Sector*, FAO, Rome, Italy, various papers.

FAO, 'The Impact of Structural Adjustment on the Use of Agricultural Inputs in Africa: the Case of Fertilizer', FAO/FIAC seminar on fertilizer strategies for Sub-Saharan Africa, Accra, Ghana, 1992.

IBRD, *World Tables*, Vol. 1, *Social Data*, 2nd edn, World Bank, Washington DC, 1984.

IBRD, *Accelerated Development in Sub-Saharan Africa: An Agenda for Action*, World Bank, Washington DC, 1981.

IBRD, *Towards Sustained Development in Sub-Saharan Africa: A Joint Programme of Action*, World Bank, Washington DC, 1994.

IBRD, *Adjustment in Africa: Reforms, Results and the Road Ahead*, World Bank, Washington DC, 1994.

IFAD, *The State of World Rural Poverty: A Profile of Africa*, International Fund for Agricultural Development, Rome, Italy, 1994.

Jaeger, W., 'The Effects of Economic Policies on African Agriculture', *World Bank Discussion Paper, Policy Planning Research*, WBD 147, World Bank, Washington DC, 1992.

Jaeger, W. and Humphreys, C., 'The Effect of Policy Reforms on Agricultural Incentives in Sub-Saharan Africa', *Proceedings of Conference of American Agricultural Economies Association*, 1988.

Johnson, O.E.G., 'The Agricultural Sector in IMF Stand-by-Arrangements' in S. Commander (ed.), *Structural Adjustment and Agriculture Theory and Practice in Africa and Latin America*, ODA, James Currey, London, 1989.

Khan, M. and Knight, N. 'Theoretical Aspect of the Design of Fund Supported, Adjustment Programs', *Occasional Paper 55*, IMF, Washington DC, 1985.

Nerlove, M., *The Dynamics of Supply: Estimates of Farmers Response to Price*, Johns Hopkins University Press, Baltimore, 1958.

Okai, M., 'The Consequences of Market Intervention; Pricing Policies and Population Trends for Agriculture in Sub-Saharan Africa', unpublished PhD thesis, 1988.

Okai, M., 'The Consequences of Increasing Population Pressure for Land-Carrying Capacity in Sub-Saharan Africa', *Proceedings of the Union for African Population Studies on Population and Environment*, Gaborone, Botswana, 1992.

Osunsade, F.L and Gleason, P., *IMF Assistance to Sub-Saharan Africa*, IMF, Washington DC, 1992.

Piesse, J., Thirtle, C. and van Zyl, J.,'Effects of the 1992 Drought on Productivity in the South African Homelands: an Application of the Malmquist Index', *Journal of Agricultural Economics*, Vol. 47, No. 2, 1996.

Scandizzo, P. and Bruce, C., 'Methodologies for Measuring Agricultural Price Intervention Effects', *Journal of Agricultural Economics*, Vol. 47, No. 2, 1996.

Schulz, T.W., *Transforming Traditional Agriculture*, Yale University Press, New Haven, 1964.

Seini, W., 'The Economic Analysis of the Responsiveness of Peasant Cotton Farmers to the Price Incentives in Ghana', *Technical Publication Series No. 51*, Institute of Statistical, Social and Economic Research (ISSER), University of Ghana, Legon, undated.